JUDAISM OF THE
SECOND TEMPLE PERIOD

JUDAISM OF THE
SECOND TEMPLE PERIOD

VOLUME 2

The Jewish Sages and Their Literature

David Flusser

Translated by
Azzan Yadin

William B. Eerdmans Publishing Company
Grand Rapids, Michigan / Cambridge, U.K.

The Hebrew University Magnes Press • Jerusalem, Israel

Jerusalem Perspective • Jerusalem, Israel

Originally published in Hebrew under the title
Yahadut Bayit Sheni: Hakhameiah ve-Sifrutah
(Jerusalem: Hebrew University Magnes Press and Yad Izhak Ben-Zvi Press, 2002).

Published 2009 by
Wm. B. Eerdmans Publishing Co.
2140 Oak Industrial Drive N.E., Grand Rapids, Michigan 49505 /
P.O. Box 163, Cambridge CB3 9PU U.K.
The Hebrew University Magnes Press, P.O. Box 39099, Jerusalem, Israel
Jerusalem Perspective, Jerusalem, Israel *http://www.jerusalemperspective.com*

Printed in the United States of America
www.eerdmans.com

14 13 12 11 10 09   7 6 5 4 3 2 1

Library of Congress Cataloging-in-Publication Data

Flusser, David, 1917-2000.
 [Yahadut Bayit sheni, hakhameiah ve-sifrutah. English]
 Judaism of the Second Temple period, the Jewish sages and their literature /
 David Flusser; translated by Azzan Yadin.
    p.   cm.
 ISBN 978-0-8028-2458-5 (cloth: alk. paper)
 1. Judaism — History — Post-exilic period, 586 B.C.–210 A.D.
 2. Jews — History — 586 B.C.–70 A.D.   I. Title.

BM176.F5413   2009
296.09′014 — dc22

                                        2009019372

Contents

Foreword

Those who do not know Hebrew may finally read the English versions of David Flusser's collected essays. The present volume, *Judaism of the Second Temple Period: The Jewish Sages and Their Literature,* is the culmination of a remarkable effort and collaboration on the part of translator Azzan Yadin and three publishers: Magnes Press, Jerusalem Perspective, and Eerdmans. It is with great satisfaction that the publishers bring Flusser's insights to a wider audience.

Flusser conversed fluently in nine languages and read scholarly literature in an additional seventeen. His first language was German. His second, learned fluently only after his immigration to Israel, was Hebrew. Consequently, most of Flusser's published writings are in German or Hebrew. Only a small percentage of Flusser's articles were authored in English. The scope and importance of Flusser's research are so great that it is unthinkable that his Hebrew and German writings should for long remain untranslated to English. Flusser's contributions to the study of Jewish Literature of the Second Temple Period, including Jewish-Hellenistic literature, apocryphal works, rabbinic literature and the New Testament, is inestimable. Jerusalem Perspective is pleased to have had a hand in this publishing endeavor.

Though Flusser wrote less often in the English language, he did succeed in producing two volumes in English: with the help of his student R. Steven Notley, he wrote *Jesus: The Sage from Galilee* (4th ed.; Eerdmans, 2007); and with the help of his student Brad H. Young, he collected most of his English articles into *Judaism and the Origins of Christianity* (Jerusalem: Magnes Press, 1988, 725 pp.).

My relationship with Flusser was one of a pupil to his mentor. Enrolled as a student in the department of Jewish History at the Hebrew University, I began to study New Testament and Early Christianity with Flusser in 1964. At that time, he was only 46 years old. He continued to enlighten me until the final days of his life, even from his hospital bed at the Hadassah University Medical Center in Jerusalem. Professor Flusser died on September 15, 2000, his 83rd birthday.

Flusser was one of the world's leading Jewish authorities on the New Testament and Early Christianity. His pioneering research on Jesus and Christianity's relationship to Judaism won him international recognition. Flusser's collaboration with Robert L. Lindsey, beginning in 1961, resulted in a new approach to the Synoptic Gospels, the approach espoused by The Jerusalem School of Synoptic Research (www.js.org), which is an association of Jewish and Christian scholars. This unique cooperation was capped recently by the twelve essays (including one by Flusser, published posthumously) of *Jesus' Last Week: Jerusalem Studies in the Synoptic Gospels* (ed. R. S. Notley, M. Turnage and B. Becker; Leiden: E. J. Brill, 2005).

In my judgment, disciples should assure that all the unpublished material of a prominent teacher is published before they publish their own research. The teacher's work takes precedence over the disciple's. With this in mind, I approached Hai Tsabar, director of Magnes Press, the publishing arm of the Hebrew University, about the possibility of translating into English the two-volume collection of Flusser's Hebrew articles that Magnes Press recently had published. To my delight, Hai was as enthusiastic about the project as I was. It is my pleasure here to thank him publicly for facilitating this difficult and lengthy project.

Even before the project was envisioned, Jerusalem Perspective had made an effort to expand Flusser's English bibliography. Since 1989, we have published most of Flusser's English output; note these examples: ". . . To Bury Caiaphas, Not to Praise Him" (*Jerusalem Perspective* 33 & 34 [July-Oct. 1991], 23-28), and "New Portrait of Salome" (*Jerusalem Perspective* 55 [April-June 1999], 18-23). These and Flusser's other recent articles also have been published electronically at http://www.jerusalemperspective.com/.

The publishers wish to express their appreciation to Serge Ruzer. In consultation with Flusser, Ruzer collected, arranged, and brought to press the two volumes of Flusser's published Hebrew articles. (The present volume is the translation of the second volume of that collection.) The publishers are greatly indebted to the volume's translator, Azzan Yadin, Associate Professor of Jewish Studies at Rutgers University. My thanks are extended to the editors and graphic artists of Wm. B. Eerdmans Publishing Company, who have given us a product worthy of Flusser's genius.

Finally, I would like to sincerely thank the members of the Branch family, the donors who made this volume possible (see p. x).

DAVID BIVIN
Jerusalem Perspective
http://www.jerusalemperspective.com/

Acknowledgments

The publishers are deeply grateful to the following donors. Their generosity made the publication of this volume possible.

Stephen and Jean Branch
(in memory of Buddy and Iris Branch)

Patricia West Branch

Steven Czarsty, Jr., and Judith Czarsty
(in memory of Mr. and Mrs. Alexander Branch)

S. P. Branch
(in memory of Bible translators William and Betty Sedat, Guatemala)

1. Daniel and the Book of Daniel

The present study seeks to address the following question: why was the Book of Daniel the only apocalyptic work incorporated into the biblical canon? Moreover, Daniel is the only apocalyptic book that was composed before the destruction of the Second Temple but describes events subsequent to the revelation at Sinai. As I will show, these issues are related.[1]

It appears that most scholars are indeed correct to assume that the purely apocalyptic chapters of Daniel, i.e., chapters seven through twelve, were composed at the time of the decrees of Antiochus IV (Epiphanes), decrees to which these chapters allude. In contrast, the first part of the Book of Daniel, chapters one through six, do not contain any reference to Antiochus IV, and outside of chapter two, no apocalyptic visions either. Chapter two tells of Nebuchadnezzar's dream, in which the king saw a statue made up of four distinct materials, alluding to the four kingdoms.[2] The king

---

1. For a discussion of the Book of Daniel see Hayim Arieh Ginsburg in the *Biblical Encyclopedia* (Hebrew) (Jerusalem, 1964), volume 2, columns 680-697. The Qumran fragments that refer to Daniel were published in *DJD* XXII, 95-184, the same volume that contains the prayer of Nabonidus (83-93). As for fragments of the Book of Daniel itself, they are found in 1Q71-72 and 4Q112-116, as well as 6Q7. On Nebuchadnezzar and Nabonidus see I. Efal, *Biblical Encyclopedia*, volume 5, columns 737-738, and H. Tadmor, "The Rise of Cyrus and the Historical Backdrop of His Declaration" (Hebrew), in *A History of the Jewish People* (Tel Aviv, 1983), 5-36, 253-255. See also two of my articles, "The Four Empires in the Fourth Sibyl and the Book of Daniel," and "The Hubris of the Antichrist in a Fragment from Qumran," both in *Judaism and the Origins of Christianity* (Jerusalem, 1988), pages 317-344 and 207-213, respectively.

2. See the discussion in Flusser, "The Four Empires."

demanded that his magicians tell him the content of his dream, but they replied that there is no one on earth who can do so, and that no king has ever made such a request of his magicians. Ultimately, Daniel arrives and not only tells the king the content of his dream; he interprets the dream as well. Now, the response of the Babylonian magicians to the king's request is inaccurate. According to Herodotus, Croesus king of Lydia tested the Greek oracular institutions by asking, "What is the king doing today?" and the Delphic oracle was able to provide the supplicants' questions before they communicated them.[3] According to the ancient source of chapter two of Daniel, the king's request was no doubt reasonable. It is likely, then, that the source of chapter two preceded the narrative of chapters one through six, and most certainly existed before the decrees of Antiochus. One scholar dates the composition of the chapter before 193 B.C.E.[4]

It is difficult to ascertain whether the extant version of chapter two was composed with the first part of the book, or was inserted after the first part was already written. In either case, it is an unusual chapter, for while other chapters in the first part portray Daniel as a seer, there he does not deal with apocalypticism. Rather, they preserve legends surrounding the beloved figure of Daniel and his three companions toward the end of the Babylonian Empire and the dawn of the Persian. These may be traditions that formed around a person who once existed, and, due to this person's ability to foretell the future, the second, apocalyptic part of the book (from chapter seven on) was later added. It is also possible that the same is true of chapter two, which contains legends that predate the cessation of prophecy. As a rule, books composed during the days of the prophets were candidates for canonization. It is likely, then, that the legends surrounding the figure of Daniel caused it to be included in the biblical canon. Indeed, the canonization process of the Book of Daniel may have begun even prior to the addition of the second, apocalyptic part, in the days of Antiochus IV.

As noted,[5] it can be demonstrated that Daniel chapter two is based on an earlier version of the story of Nebuchadnezzar's dream. I believe the same is true for chapter five, at least as far as the famous writing on the wall is concerned (Daniel 5:25-28).[6] The writing states: *mene mene tekel upharsin,* which Daniel interprets as follows: *mene,* God has numbered (Aramaic *mena*) the days of your kingdom and brought it to an end; *tekel,* you have been weighed

---

3. On Croesus, see Herodotus, *History,* 2.47; on the Delphic oracle, see my "The Four Empires," 326, n. 36, and Plutarch, *De Garrulitate,* 20.

4. A. Bentzen, *Daniel* (Tübingen, 1952), 31.

5. See above, n. 3.

6. See *Biblical Encyclopedia,* volume 2, column 692.

(Aramaic *tekilta*) and found wanting; *peres*, your kingdom has been divided (Aramaic *perisat*) and given to the Medes and the Persians. Note that these words refer to three units of weight: *mena*, which is fifty shekels but in Babylon sixty; *tekel*, the Aramaic form of the shekel itself; and *peras*, one half of a *mena*.

To my mind, the correct interpretation of the writing on the wall is found within the Book of Daniel itself. That is, I believe we are faced with a well-attested phenomenon both from the history of prophecy and from the psychology of dream symbolism. Namely, in dreams and visions words become concrete objects whose names express the underlying word. To arrive at the correct interpretation it is first necessary to uncover the word symbolized by each object. The classic example of this technique is found in Jeremiah 1:11-12. The prophet is shown the branch of an almond tree *(shaqed)*, which God then interprets: "For I am diligent *(shoqed)* to bring my Word to pass." Another famous dream is Alexander the Great's, who while laying siege to Tyre, dreamt of a dancing satyr.[7] His dream interpreter explained the dream as a sign that he would conquer Tyre, for the satyr *(satyros)* means that "Tyre is yours" *(sa Tyros)*. The Greek words, then, took on the concrete form of the satyr. Freud cites Alexander's dream in *The Interpretation of Dreams*, as well as many other relevant examples.[8]

In light of all this, I see no reason not to count the writing on the wall as another indication that the first part of the Book of Daniel is based on earlier sources. As for the writing itself, we have seen that it lists three measures of weight. We have also shown that there are many examples in which words are symbolically represented as concrete objects, and that it is the objects that appear in the vision (for example, the almond branch) rather than the word. Moreover, we have seen — and will demonstrate this further in what follows — that the first part of Daniel is a late version of an earlier collection of stories. If so, perhaps we may assume that in the earlier version of the writing on the wall there appeared three weights rather than the names of the three weights.

Belshazzar was Nabonidus's son and the last king of Babylonia.[9] Nabonidus is not mentioned in the Book of Daniel, but there are allusions to his royal acts in the Nebuchadnezzar legends and it is well known that a legendary portrait of Nabonidus is preserved in chapter four. There Nebuchadnez-

7. See R. A. Pack (ed.), *Artemidori Daldiani, Onirocriticon libri* (Leipzig, 1964), volume 4, §24, page 260.

8. S. Freud, *The Interpretation of Dreams*, trans. Joyce Crick (Oxford, 1999).

9. See Tadmor, *A History of the Jewish People*. A new inscription of Nabonidus was discovered in Sela, Jordan.

zar is depicted as an insane king who is punished by God, sent out of the city to a desert exile, lives among the wild animals and eventually repents, thanks to Daniel. The way station between history and this legend is the basis for the prayer of Nabonidus preserved in the Qumran texts. There a Jewish man causes Nabonidus to turn away from his idolatry and accept the God of Israel, and this man may have been Daniel.

Nabonidus was a religious reformer. He preferred Sin, the moon god, over the other traditional Babylonian gods. In the last years of his reign he went too far, and his deeds were perceived as an attack on the status of the city of Babylon, its gods and its priests. When he finally returned from Teima, he completed what he began. The temple was restored and the statue of Sin returned to its plinth in a stunning procession, with the king himself serving in the temple.[10] In the Book of Daniel, chapter three, we are told that the king erected a great gold statue in the plain of Dura, which is part of the province of Babylon, and commanded all his subjects to bow down to the statue. Whoever refused would be thrown into a fiery furnace. Three young Jewish men (Daniel is not mentioned in this chapter), refusing to bow down to the idol, are thrown into the furnace, but miraculously survive.[11] It seems to me there is a clear connection between the worship of the statue of Sin in the days of Nabonidus and the story of the golden statue in Daniel, chapter three. All the more so in light of the scholarly view that the tales of Nebuchadnezzar in chapter four of Daniel contain echoes of Nabonidus and his royal actions.

As for the Nabonidus period itself, while it is theoretically possible for an idolatrous religion to respect Judaism, despite its opposition to idolatry, it is more likely that the pagan reformer, who demands of all full recognition of his gods, demands this of the Jews as well. It is therefore not impossible that the Jews did indeed suffer under Nabonidus's religious reforms.[12] Incidentally, the story of Daniel in the lions' den (in chapter six, the final chapter of the first part of the book) is nothing more than a pale parallel to the story of the three young men in the fiery furnace. Moreover, Darius, the Mede emperor, was a peace-loving ruler caught up in a web of intrigue. Regarding one matter there is no doubt: the first part of the Book of Daniel was composed before the second, and contains not even a hint of the decrees of Anti-

10. See H. Tadmor's section in H. H. Ben Sasson (ed.), *A History of the Jewish People* (Cambridge, MA, 1976), 164-165.

11. Tractate Semahot (8.15), one of the minor tractates of the Talmud, explains why other Jews willing to martyr themselves are not saved. The same issue appears in the commentary to Daniel by the church father Hippolytus.

12. Might the Book of Judith also contain distant echoes of these events?

ochus IV. It follows that the martyrological stories preserved in these chapters are the earliest extant tales of Jewish martyrs.[13]

This survey seeks to provide an explanation for the canonization of the apocalyptic Book of Daniel, and its inclusion in the third section of the Hebrew Scriptures, the *ketuvim* or "writings." Ultimately this came about because of the first part of the book, chapters one through six, which contain legends about Daniel as a man, a seer and healer from the end of the Babylonian era and the beginning of the Persian. While chapter two does contain apocalyptic material, it predates Antiochus IV, during whose reign the second part was composed, and may indeed be a secondary addition. As for the tales in the first part of the book, they were dear to the hearts of the Jews of the day because they contain the two earliest accounts of Jewish martyrs.

---

13. I do not consider the Scroll of Esther as a story that ultimately deals with martyrology. In 1 Maccabees 2:59-60, Mattathias, on his deathbed, recalls a series of biblical exemplars to his sons, ending with the three young men in the furnace and Daniel. See also above, note 11.

2. Judaism in the Second Temple Period

I. The Sources

One of the main obstacles to understanding the religious and spiritual life of Second Temple Judaism is the varied nature of the historical sources. The different cultural background of the sources makes it difficult for the individual scholar to deeply investigate the different genres, especially since the differences in the sources often reflect the different social context of their authors.

The most important source, the writings of Josephus Flavius, is, in this regard, itself a composite source.[1] First, because Josephus preserves the views of foreign authors who write about the Jews from without. Second, he made use of Hellenistic-Jewish sources and even came to accept some of their positions. Third, he reflects the ideas and beliefs of his Jewish environment, that is, of the sages; and fourth, his audience is non-Jewish and he presented his material in a way that they could understand. The situation is similar with the Greek and Roman scholars who discussed the Jews: even if they were not influenced by anti-Semitism, they certainly could not acquire a deep understanding of Jewish thought.[2]

The Jewish-Hellenistic corpus, whose main (but not sole) representatives are Philo and the author of the Wisdom of Solomon, represents an ad-

---

1. Josephus, of course, wrote his works in Greek, but he was well versed in the Jewish sources and had a strong rabbinic background with regard to Scripture, Jewish law, and homiletic writings.

2. See the sources collected in M. Stern (ed.), *Greek and Latin Authors on Jews and Judaism: From Herodotus to Plutarch* (Jerusalem, 1974).

mixture of authentic Jewish content and selected Greek ideas. In this regard, the Jewish-Hellenistic writings are peripheral to the issues at hand.

The same can almost be said of the apocryphal books, those that were not included in the Jewish canon. Most of this literature is rooted in apocalyptic circles that do not reflect the views of mainstream Judaism. Some of the apocryphal texts — Jubilees, 1 Enoch, the Testaments of the Patriarchs — emerged out of the same spiritual and religious movement as the Qumran community. Most scholars identify the Qumran sect with the Essenes, a group attested in the writings of Josephus and Philo. The Qumran writings, the Dead Sea Scrolls, are, then, sectarian in nature and reveal only certain aspects of Second Temple Judaism.

Similar considerations hold for the New Testament. Though the texts collected in the New Testament are a valuable source for understanding the religious life of the day, they are, after all, the religious expression of a Jewish sect that would eventually break away from Judaism.[3]

An important source for the study of the religious ideas of the Second Temple period is the Wisdom of Ben Sira (or Sirach), which was composed around the year 180 B.C.E. But even this book, which is in no way sectarian, represents the views of a single, tentative man, who belonged to clearly-defined social circles.[4]

The Talmudic and midrashic literature is a very important repository of the opinions and beliefs of those who represent mainstream Second Temple Judaism, namely, the rabbinic sages. Unfortunately, there are relatively few historical statements from the Second Temple sages preserved in this corpus, and less still from the sages of the Hellenistic period. Talmudic literature also contains few historical references to the period in question. Nonetheless, internal evidence and comparative analysis with texts composed during the time of the Second Temple indicate that the rabbinic corpus contains some valuable material, dating back to the days of the Second Temple and the Hellenistic period. One must bear in mind, however, that both the content and the form of this material may have been reworked over the course of its transmission, sometimes more than once.

In sum, we find that the extant historical sources for the study of Second Temple Judaism reveal different and distinct aspects of the period. So much so that one scholar, specializing in one set of sources, may arrive at different conclusions than a colleague investigating another set of sources. The

---

3. With the exception of Luke, all the authors of the New Testament were Jews.

4. Ben Sira was a priest and affiliated with the circles from which the Sadducees later emerged.

present study will aim to represent the different genres of Second Temple literature as expressions of a single religious worldview. This worldview, which differs from that of the biblical period, cannot overlook the marked differences that existed between the different religious and social groups that eventually caused a schism within the Judaism of the day.

II. Purification and the Emergence of Different Religious Movements

One of the core beliefs of Second Temple Judaism was to view the totality of the Jewish people as an organic whole, almost like a single body that was chosen by God. This view would eventually give rise to the term *Knesset Israel*,[5] and likewise to the conceptually loaded term *ekklesia* in the early Church. The individual religious communities that proliferated during this period emerged from this overarching view of Israel's sanctity, even though each group established its own ways to live a life of sanctity and saw itself as *verus Israel*. Other groups, correspondingly, were seen as having strayed from the straight path or, at the very least, failed to live up to the highest aspirations of Jewish sanctity. If so, it was the concept of inclusive Jewish sanctity that engendered the religious splits within the Jewish people. These splits led to increased tension between the warring factions and occasionally to political schisms within the broader populace, and eventually to persecutions and civil war. Ironically, an ideology of Jewish unity set the stage for separatist tendencies, whose most extreme form is visible in the Qumran sect. This group saw itself as the true Israel, while the rest of the Jewish world was "futility, for futile are those who do not know the covenant. And all those who scorn his word he shall cause to vanish from the world" (1QS 5.19-20). Small wonder, then, that another Second Temple Jewish sect could see itself as the true Israel, *verus Israel*, even when it broke off from Judaism itself. The sect in question is, of course, Christianity, whose idea of *ekklesia*, "church," was influenced by the Qumran community.

The rallying flag for most of these religious communities during the Hellenistic period was ritual purity. Indeed, the entire Second Temple period was characterized by the later rabbis as the period when "purity burst out in Israel" (b. Shabbat 13a; p. Shabbat 1.5, 3b). The attention to matters of ritual purity was so extreme that "the impurity of the knife's blade was more difficult for them than loss of life" (t. Yoma 1.12).[6] Nor were ritual matters restricted to

---

5. As far as I know, the term is attested in rabbinic literature from the days of Rabbi Aqiva, that is, the second century C.E.

6. See also W. Bacher, *Die Aggada des Tannaiten* (Strasbourg, 1903), 1.44, n. 2.

the area of the Temple. Purity strictures spread throughout Jewish society, playing the same role in everyday religious observance that would later be allotted to dietary restrictions, *kashrut*. There is, however, an important difference between purity and dietary laws, as the latter apply equally to all Jews, while the adoption of the former — at least outside the area of the Temple — was a matter of personal choice. As a result, there emerged different levels of purity: "For Pharisees the clothes of a non-scholar count as *midras* [transmitting impurity when one steps or leans on them]; for them that eat the *terumah* offering the clothes of Pharisees count as *midras;* for them that eat the *qedushah* offering the clothes of them that eat the *terumah* count as *midras;* for them that eat the sin offering the clothes of them that eat the *qedushah* count as *midras.* Yose ben Yoʿezer was the most pious in the priesthood, yet for them that ate the *qedushah* his apron counted as *midras*" (m. Hagigah 2.7).

The Pharisees, whose legal doctrines were preserved in the rabbinic corpus, set themselves apart from the impurities of the lay folk and maintained strict rules of purity, including the consumption of non-Temple foodstuff. From a halakhic perspective, the Pharisees were nothing more than a group that maintained a certain level of purity. "Anyone who accepts four things is accepted as a companion *(haver):* that he not give offerings and tithes to the ʿ*am ha-*ʾ*aretz,* that he not undergo purification with the ʿ*am ha-*ʾ*aretz,* and that he eat non-sacrificial meat in a state of purity, and that he commit to being faithful" (t. Demai 2.2).

According to the Mishnah we just cited, the Pharisees maintained the lowest level of purity in their daily life. The same mishnah goes on to mention the case of Yose ben Yoʿezer, one of the "pairs" cited in the opening chapter of m. Avot, whose apron counted as *midras* for them that ate the *qedushah.* Yose ben Yoʿezer is referred to as "the most pious in the priesthood," or, more literally, as "the pious within the priesthood" *(hasid she-ba-kehunah).* The question is whether the term *hasid* refers here to his personal piety, or was he perhaps part of the *Hasidim,* the religious community that joined the Hasmoneans in the early days of the rebellion against the Seleucid empire? A later Midrash records that Yose ben Yoʿezer was executed by "Eliyaqim" (or "Yaqim"), that is, by Alcimus, the Antiochean high priest who served at the outbreak of the Hasmonean revolt.[7] Interestingly, 1 Maccabees 7.16 recounts that Alcimus executed sixty of the *Hasidim.* All this suggests that Yose ben Yoʿezer, who was executed by Alcimus, was one of the sixty *Hasidim,* and that Mishnah Hagigah 2.7 is reporting that this man was a *hasid* — a member of the *Hasidim* — who served in the priesthood. If the fact that "his apron

---

7. See G. Alon, *Studies in Jewish History* (Hebrew) (Tel Aviv, 1957), 1.148-176.

counted as *midras*" for them that ate the *qedushah* alludes to his strict level of purity observance, we may assume that the rest of the *Hasidim* likewise observed laws of purity. It appears, then, that from a halakhic perspective, the purity observance of the *Hasidim* was stricter than that of the Pharisees. We know the *Hasidim* primarily as a military group that joined Mattithias the Hasmonean when he decided to allow battle for the sake of self-defense on the Sabbath (1 Macc 2.40-42). But it appears the group was also defined in terms of their commitment to a certain level of ritual purity.

Another group that defined itself in terms of its rules of ritual purity is the Qumran sect, which most scholars identify as Essene. The centrality of purity is evident throughout the Dead Sea Scrolls.[8] The Qumranites were very strict in matters of purity and impurity, and believed that ritual impurity is acquired not only through contact with an impure substance, but through sin itself. Thus they state: "he should not go into the waters to share in the pure food of the men of holiness, for one is not cleansed unless one turns away from one's wickedness, for he is unclean among all the transgressors of his word" (1QS 5.13-14). Prior to immersion, then, members of the community had to turn away from their wrongdoing, to repent before God, thus removing from their own being the impurity that attends sin. "And by the compliance of his soul with all the laws of God his flesh is cleansed by being sprinkled with cleansing waters and being made holy with the waters of repentance" (1QS 3.8-9). John the Baptist too adopted this special conception of immersion (Josephus *AJ* 18.117), and it is here that we find the origins of the Christian baptism, though the church rejected the idea of physical purity.[9]

The Sadducees are the only Second Temple group whose identity was not founded on matters of purity, and they even appear to have needled the Pharisees for their strictures (p. Hagigah 3.5, 79d). We know relatively little about the Sadducees, largely because we learn about them primarily from the polemics of their opponents: rabbinic texts, Josephus, the Dead Sea Scrolls,[10] and the New Testament. It is probably imprecise to define their worldview simply as conservative; theirs is an almost atrophied conservatism. They rejected the legitimacy of the Oral Torah — whose authority was not widely established in their day, rejected the ideas of physical resurrection and the immortality of the soul, as well as the Holy Spirit (Acts 23:8) and the existence of angels. They likely considered these harmful folk beliefs; however it is not

8. J. Licht, *Megillat ha-Serachim* (Jerusalem, 1971), 294-303.

9. See D. Flusser, "The Baptism of John and the Dead Sea Sect," *Essays on the Dead Sea Scrolls: In Memory of E. L. Sukenik,* C. Rabin, Y. Yadin and J. Licht (eds.) (Jerusalem, 1961), 209-239.

10. See D. Flusser, "Pharisees, Sadducees, and Essenes in Pesher Nahum," *Judaism of the Second Temple Period: Qumran and Apocalypticism,* 214-257.

clear how they could anchor their position in the Hebrew Bible, which contains clear endorsements of some of the rejected views. They most likely had to employ creative exegesis to harmonize their beliefs with the biblical text.

The various sects — Pharisees, Essenes, Sadducees — came into existence during the Hasmonean period, and are first mentioned by Josephus in his discussion of John Hyrcanus.[11] Josephus mentions the Pharisees and the Sadducees in the days of John Hyrcanus, and the Essenes in the chapters dealing with Aristobulus the First. And yet, the worldviews of these three movements preceded their emergence as distinct social groups.

III. Belief in Divine Providence

The greatness of the Second Temple period lies in the fact that it produced the first Jewish theology. To be sure, the Hebrew Bible is a religious document par excellence. But in a sense its teachings are like the light of the first day of creation that was still diffuse and not limited to its various centers. The Hebrew Bible is a sublime religious text; however it lacks the systematic discussions of faith necessary for theology proper. It was during the Second Temple period that a theology emerged, one that deals with the attributes of God, and with the role of mankind — and of Israel — in the divine plan. Clearly the crystallization of the different religious groups served as a catalyst for the demarcation of various theological positions, as each community developed its own views that served to demarcate it from the others.

One of the questions that occupied the thinkers of the period involved divine providence and human free will. According to Josephus, this question divided the three Jewish groups.[12] The Sadducees denied divine providence altogether and asserted that everything depended on the human will. They held that the belief in divine providence was tantamount to blaspheming God. Not only did God not create evil, He does not even foresee it; if divine providence did exist, God would have to be the cause of evil too. The Sadducee position is best understood as a response to two theological issues: the question of divine providence proper and the belief in life after death. If there

11. *AJ* 13.171.

12. See my "Josephus on the Pharisees and the Stoa," pp. 221-231 the present volume. An important corrective to my argument is provided by S. Pines, "A Platonic Paradigm for One of the Reports of Josephus Flavius concerning the Pharisee Doctrine of Providence and Free Will" (Hebrew), *Iyyun* 24 (1973-1974), 227-232. It stands to reason that Josephus similarly adopted a Platonic model in describing the Pharisee view concerning the interaction of fate and human freedom.

is no life after death one might conclude that life in this world is the result of man's free will and that reward and punishment are the result of man's own wisdom or folly. It appears that the Sadducees believed that God gave Israel the written Torah as a guide for one's free-will decisions.

According to the Qumran scrolls and the account of Josephus, the Essenes consistently espoused predestination: "Before they existed He established their entire design. And when they have come into being, at their appointed time, they will execute all their works according to his glorious design, without altering anything" (1QS 3.15-16). For the Essenes, this was the logical conclusion of their monotheistic faith. Indeed, they believed in a double predestination *(praedestinatio duplex),* which divides mankind into the sons of light and the sons of darkness. Addressing God, they say: "For you created the just and the wicked" (1QH^a 12.38), and believed that "you, you alone have [created] the just man, and from the womb you determined him for the period of approval, to keep your covenant, and to walk on all (your paths). . . . But the wicked you have created for [the time] of your wrath, from the womb you have predestined them for the day of slaughter. For they walk on a path that is not good, they reject your covenant, their soul loathes your [. . .], and they take no pleasure in what you command, but choose what you hate" (1QH^a 7.17-21). The belief in predestination was linked, for the Essenes, to an ethical dualism. They saw themselves as the elect of God, the sons of light, a view that strengthened their sectarian tendencies.

The Pharisees believed in divine providence, and recognized an element of providence in each and every action (Josephus *BJ* 2.162-163). That said, some actions are wholly the result of divine providence, while others — most notably righteous or wicked behavior — are dependent on human agency (*AJ* 13.172). So whereas the Sadducees rejected divine providence altogether, the Pharisees attributed to it all actions except human moral behavior. Indeed, the Pharisees believed that providence plays a role even in moral actions, which are the result of both divine and human will. This view stood in obvious contrast to the predestination of the Essenes, according to which human behavior cannot alter in any way the already fixed decrees of God.

From the discussion thus far it is evident that the different views staked out by the Sadducees, the Pharisees and the Essenes regarding free will and divine providence are different permutations of a monotheistic worldview. Each represents the conclusion that flows from a certain set of assumptions regarding human free will and the question of good and evil. It seems to me that the Pharisee position is closest to that of the biblical corpus, e.g., the Book of Jonah with its description of the repentance of the people of Nineveh which overcame God's decree. The Pharisee view was preserved in great detail in the writings of Josephus, but not so much in the rabbinic corpus. Nonetheless, there is no reason to doubt the veracity of his reports, as they preserve a worldview that is both complete and fascinating.

As noted, there were speculations regarding divine providence prior to the formation of the three Jewish "schools." These theological motifs are already attested in the Wisdom of Ben Sira (composed circa 180 B.C.E.), as in the following verses, that allude to a doctrine of divine predestination (16.26-27):

> When the Lord created his works from the beginning,
> and, in making them, determined their boundaries,
> he arranged his works in an eternal order,
> and their dominion for all generations.

Another passage may even contain hints of a doctrine of double predestination (33.10-15):

> All human beings come from the ground,
> and humankind was created out of the dust.
> In the fullness of his knowledge the Lord distinguished them
> and appointed their different ways.
> Some he blessed and exalted,
> and some he made holy and brought near to himself;
> but some he cursed and brought low,
> and turned them out of their place.
> Like clay in the hand of the potter,
> to be moulded as he pleases,
> so all are in the hand of their Maker,
> to be given whatever he decides.
>
> Good is the opposite of evil,
> and life the opposite of death;
> so the sinner is the opposite of the godly.
> Look at all the works of the Most High;
> they come in pairs, one the opposite of the other.

Still, Ben Sira rejects the idea that God is the source of evil, and so emphasizes man's free will (15.11-17):

> Do not say, "It was the Lord's doing that I fell away";
> for he does not do what he hates.
> Do not say, "It was he who led me astray";

for he has no need of the sinful.
The Lord hates all abominations;
such things are not loved by those who fear him.
It was he who created humankind in the beginning,
and he left them in the power of their own free choice.
If you choose, you can keep the commandments,
and to act faithfully is a matter of your own choice.
He has placed before you fire and water;
stretch out your hand for whichever you choose.
Before each person are life and death,
and whichever one chooses will be given.

Clearly, then, the question of divine providence, and even its explicit thematization, predates the three schools, each of which chose the position best-suited to its general worldview and developed it into a fully-formed ideology. These ideologies then served each group in its own spiritual life, as well as in its inter-group polemics.

IV. The Oral Torah

As we have seen, the Second Temple period was fecund for Jewish religious thought. But this fecundity was not limited to intellectual advances, rather it found expression in Jewish life and religious law as well. The Oral Torah, broadly understood, contains both legal doctrine *(halakhah)* and non-legal teachings *(aggadah),* and its roots reach back to the period prior to the Second Temple. Though it is true that the sages upheld the Oral Torah, it does not follow that they created it, only that they assiduously developed it. The polemic position of the Pharisees was not aimed at creating the Oral Torah, but rather at making it authoritative for everyday Jewish life and the basis for Jewish law. The Sadducees, on the other hand, rejected the authority of the Oral Law and apparently sought to base all legal decisions on the Written Torah. We know nothing of the theoretical position of the Essenes regarding the Oral Law, but the Qumran texts indicate they observed its rulings — sometimes more stringently than the sages themselves — and often developed it so as to fit their sectarian views. Here too we find the rabbinic sages representing the mainstream Jewish position. No wonder, then, that the representatives of the sage-Pharisees would become national leaders; as with other matters, they did not set forth a novel position regarding the Oral Law, but sought to fortify an accepted national principle.

There are typological similarities between Second Temple Judaism and other religions that believe in an ancient oral tradition that must not be committed to writing. Consider the religious beliefs of ancient Gaul, as described in Caesar's *Gallic War* (6.14.1-4). The Gallic priests, druids, are not obligated to pay taxes or serve in the army, and generally are relieved of civic obligations. As a result, many families send representatives to join the druids. Caesar reports that they commit to memory whole books, some devoting more than twenty years to these pursuits.[13] It is thought that they are prohibited from recording such matters in writing, though in other affairs, both private and public, they write using Greek letters. Caesar provides two reasons for the Gallic teachers' refusal to write. First, they did not want their teachings to be widely disseminated. Second, they believed that people who trust the written word dull their faculty of memory and eventually forget everything. Similar ideologies are known from India as well.

Clearly, then, the notion of oral study is not unique to the Jews, a fact that suggests that the principles and methods of the Oral Torah greatly precede the Second Temple period. According to the sages, there exists a chain of tradition that stretches from their own time back to Moses, and this appears to be fundamentally correct. To be sure, it is difficult to assess the halakhic and aggadic achievements of the sages during the Persian and early Hellenistic periods, but it appears that this is when they fixed the rules of purity and impurity, as well as the foundations of prayer. Indeed, analysis of Second Temple sources suggests that many of the halakhic and aggadic issues are much earlier than had previously been assumed. In appears, then, that the foundations of the Oral Torah were already set in the early Second Temple period. Second Century C.E. sources, for example, reveal a fully developed halakhic framework, alongside a fairly elaborate worldview. The question that arises, then, is when precisely the Oral Torah ideology first appeared, and in what circles. The identification of the Oral and the Written Torahs is evident in the formula that is spoken during the Jewish wedding ceremony. In the Book of Tobit, which was apparently composed during the Persian period, we find the first mention of the ketubah, the Jewish wedding contract. Sarah's father takes her in his hands and gives her to Tobias as a wife, saying: "Behold, pray take her according to the Law of Moses (κατὰ τὸν νόμον Μωυσέως)" (7.13). This formula is reminiscent of the phrase "according to the law of Moses and Israel" that is used in Jewish weddings to this very day. The Mishnah contains a similar state-

---

13. For a comparative analysis of mnemonic devices used in committing sacred writings to memory, see J. C. Greenfield, "*ratin magosha* (The Sorcerer Whispers)," *Joshua Finkel Festschrift* (New York, 1974), 63-69.

ment, "according to the Law of Moses and Jewish custom *(dat moshe ve-yehudit)*" (m. Ketubot 7.6).[14] The expansion of the Tobias formula to "the Law of Moses and Jewish custom" may be the result of a desire to distinguish the Jewish rite from its Samaritan counterpart. The word *yehudit* which appears alongside "Moses" refers to the Jewish religion *(ha-dat ha-yehudit)*. Later, however, this phrase was no longer understood as referring to the Oral Torah, but rather to decrees instituted by the sages themselves. With time, the phrase *dat yehudit* gave way to the current formulation, *dat Israel,* since the word *yehudi* was not the common Hebrew term for Jews.[15]

Jewish life in the Second Temple period revolved around *halakhah,* Jewish law, and there is no reason to think it was particularly onerous. The *halakhah* was at that time a natural component of Jewish life in the Land of Israel, though apparently not so much in the Jewish Diaspora. Philo, for one, reports that some of the Jews of Alexandria interpret the laws of the Torah as mere allegory,[16] with some Jews ignoring all the commandments save Yom Kippur.[17] This does not seem to have been the case in the Land of Israel, where, *pace* a number of Christian scholars, we do not find any tension between religious faith and the commandments. Indeed, it was the seamless unity between halakhic behavior and spiritual ideals that allowed the leaders of different movements to develop their sublime religious ideas. The halakhic framework was a self-evident reality and the yoke of Torah and commandments was unquestioned and light. In other words, *halakhah* was not a divorced autonomous realm; it was part of the very fabric of the daily spiritual life of the Jewish people. Its self-evidence allowed the sages to channel their energies in other directions, freeing them up to develop their religious worldviews and to attain their intellectual and practical achievements, their theology and ethics. Today it is difficult for us to comprehend the spiritual freedom of men like Simon the Righteous, Yose ben Yoezer, and Hillel the Elder — a freedom that manifests itself within a normative halakhic framework. The Mishnah tractate Avot ("Wisdom of the Fathers") contains fewer halakhic discussions than do the synoptic gospels, but its authors were nonetheless key figures in the establishment of the halakhic system.

14. The Palestinian Talmud (Yebamot 15.1, 14d; Ketubot 4.8, 29a) contains a somewhat different phrase: "According to the *dat* (religion) of Moses and the Jews *(yudai)*." Clearly, the use of the word *dat,* along with the term *yudai,* suggests a Persian context: *dat* is a Persian word, and the Jews were called *yehudim* in the Persian period.

15. However, the earlier formula is found in Aramaic.

16. Philo, *De Migratione Abrahami* 89f.; I. Heinemann, *Philos griechische und jüdische Bildung* (Breslau, 1932), 454-455.

17. Philo, *De Specialibus Legibus* 1.186.

V. Peshat and Derash

We cannot survey the full range of interpretive approaches from the Second Temple period. What should be emphasized is that it was during this era that there emerged the idea that the biblical text contains a deeper, non-literal sense. Such interpretive approaches are well-known from other nations. The Greeks, for example, interpreted Homer's poems allegorically and found in them the most sublime religious truths. Jewish non-literal interpretation is rooted in the conviction that Scripture in general and the Pentateuch in particular contain a broader sense than can be conveyed in actual language. It is a mistake, then, to claim that Jewish interpretation seeks to accommodate Scripture to the needs of the day.

Jewish interpretation takes as its object both the biblical stories and the language of the Bible. The deeds of the forefathers are a sign for future generations, and already the Book of Deuteronomy interprets the manna that fell from heaven as God's attempt "to make you understand that one does not live by bread alone, but by every word that comes from the mouth of the Lord" (Deut 8.3). In other words, the manna is interpreted as referring to the words of God. As for the interpretation of words, the sages even went as far as interpreting Hebrew words in light of the Greek. Thus, the *hadar* (citrus) tree mentioned in Leviticus 23:40 is interpreted as a "watered" tree, the Hebrew *hadar* playing on the Greek ὕδωρ, water.[18]

Another type of interpretation is found among eschatological readers, who understand the words of the biblical prophets as alluding to their present reality. Thus we find the Qumran authors interpreting Habakkuk's proclamations regarding the Chaldeans as if aimed at the Romans of Pompeii's day. On their interpretation, the "Teacher of Righteousness" knew the mysteries hidden within the words of the prophets, mysteries even the prophets themselves did not understand: "Then the Lord answered me and said: 'Write the vision; make it plain on tablets so that a runner may read it.' And God told Habakkuk to write what was going to happen to the last generation, but he did not let him know the consummation of the era. And as for what he says 'so that a runner may read it,' its interpretation concerns the Teacher of Righteousness, to whom God has made known all the mysteries of the words of his servants, the prophets" (1QpHab 6.14–7.5). According to the Qumran texts, the prophet prophesied without knowing the meaning of his own words. Indeed, he even alludes to the eventual appearance of his

---

18. P. Sukkah 3.5, 53d; b. Sukkah 53a. It should be noted that the rabbis never used the Greek meaning of Hebrew roots in determining Jewish law.

true interpreter — the "Teacher of Righteousness" who is also the founder of the Qumran sect.

One of the earliest extant midrashim is preserved in the Book of Tobit: "So you will be laying up a good treasure for yourself against the day of necessity. For almsgiving delivers from death and keeps you from going into darkness" (4.9-10, and see also 12.9).[19] This passage is a midrash to Proverbs 10:2, "treasures gained by wickedness do not profit, but righteousness *(tzedaqah)* delivers from death." The phrase "treasures gained by wickedness" is understood as monies that are not given to the poor, and therefore one who does give to the poor is providing himself with good treasures, set aside for a day of tribulation. The interpretation understands the word *tzedaqah* in its regular meaning of charity, even though this is not the meaning in Proverbs. A similar midrash is found in Ben Sira 29.11-12:

> Let your treasure be in the precepts of the Most High, and it will
>   benefit you more than gold.
> Store your alms *(tzedaqah)* in the hearts of the poor, and it will obtain
>   help for you against all evil.

Similarly, in the Psalms of Solomon (9.5): "The one who does what is right *(tzedaqah)* saves up life for himself with the Lord, and the one who does what is wrong causes his own life to be destroyed" and in 2 Enoch (13.84). As a rule, the sages use the word *tzedaqah* without knowing its origins or how it came to mean "a charitable gift to the poor." Still, we find both in rabbinic sources (t. Pe'ah 4.18-19) and in the Gospel of Matthew (6:19-21) the phrase "treasures in heaven" without citing the verse from Proverbs. It appears, then, that toward the end of the Second Temple period the interpretation of the verse was forgotten, though its conclusions lived on.

Jewish interpretation is not always as simple as the previous example suggests. One example of a more complex hermeneutic is found in the Damascus Document (6.2-10):

> But God remembered the covenant of the forefathers. And he raised from
> Aaron men of knowledge and from Israel wise men, and made them lis-
> ten. And they dug the well, "A well that the princes dug, the well that the
> princes dug, that the nobles of the people delved, with the staff
> *(mehoqeq)*" (Num 21:18). The well is the law. And those who dug it are the
> converts of Israel, who left the land of Judah and lived in the land of Da-

---

19. The entire midrash is found in the short version of the Book of Tobit, which most scholars consider to be the later of the two versions.

mascus, all of whom God called princes, for they sought him, and their renown has not been repudiated in anyone's mouth. And the staff is the interpreter of the law, of whom Isaiah said, "he produces a tool fit for its purpose" (Isa 54:16). And the nobles of the people are those who came to dig the well with the staffs that the scepter decreed, to walk in them throughout the whole age of wickedness.

The Qumran author interprets the words of the Bible as referring to the history of the sect. It is widely accepted that the waters symbolize the Torah itself, and so the digging of the well is the active search for the meaning of Scripture. The princes mentioned in the verse are members of the Qumran community, while staff — a word that comes from the same root as law and legislation — is the leader of the sect, who is referred to as *doresh ha-torah*. The Qumranites, then, are the diggers of the well, while their leader, the "staff" known as *doresh ha-torah,* informs them of the true meaning of Scripture. He is also the instrument mentioned in Isaiah, which God "fit for its purpose." But Numbers 21:18 speaks of "the well that the princes dug, that the nobles of the people delved, with staff, from the wilderness to Mattanah." The staff, then, is not only the man who properly interprets the laws of the Torah, he is the instrument by which the well is dug. Phrased differently, *doresh ha-torah* establishes the interpretive canons, which explains why "the nobles of the people are those who came to dig the well with the staffs that the scepter decreed, to walk in them throughout the whole age of wickedness."

The Aramaic targumim contain a similar interpretation of the song of the well: first it was the princes that dug the well of Torah, that is, the patriarchs, Abraham, Isaac, and Jacob. The nobles of the people continued the enterprise, these being Moses and Aaron, while the *mehoqeq* refers to the Jewish scribes, who used the "scepters" mentioned later in the verse. Clearly, then, the sages like the Qumran authors seek to interpret every word separately, assigning each a unique meaning. The Qumran authors read the song of the well as a symbol of the history of their sect, while the sages understand it as a symbol of Jewish history as such.

The choice of this passage from the Dead Sea Scrolls was not motivated by the desire to demarcate the interpretive practices of Qumran from those of other Second Temple groups. To the contrary, my aim is to show how similar sectarian midrash is to that of the sages. If we compare these sources to the interpretation of Philo, who was deeply influenced by Greek interpretive practices, we find that his interpretation of Numbers 21:18 is similar to that found in the Damascus Document. According to Philo, the well was dug by the nobles of the people because it is the task of prominent men and leaders to seek after Wisdom. But the prominent men in question are not political or military rulers, but rather those who possess outstanding spiritual and intellectual faculties (*On Drunkenness* 113). The well, for Philo, symbolizes the deep primordial knowledge, knowledge that must be uncovered so that it may irrigate the fields of our intellect (*On Dreams* 2.271). Needless to say, no one is suggesting that Philo was influenced by the Qumran interpretation, but rather that they share a number of precepts: first, the belief that the true religious message is to be found beneath the literal meaning of Scripture. Second, that Torah is symbolized by water. We can see, then, that non-literal midrash — and occasionally the interpretations themselves — was shared by all aspects of Second Temple Judaism.

VI. The Temple

Simon the Righteous would say: "The world rests on three things — Torah, the Temple cult, and deeds of lovingkindness" (m. Avot 1.2). It appears the great innovation in the words of this high priest was in placing Torah and deeds of lovingkindness on the same level as the Temple cult. Many scholars assume that there was great tension between the Temple cult and the spiritual world of the sages. But despite some inevitable tension with the democratizing impetus to spread the study of Torah throughout all social strata of Israel, the temple maintained its central place in the national life of the nation throughout the Second Temple period.[20] Indeed, many of the sages and the political leaders of the period were of priestly descent, and in this regard there was no difference between the Sadducees and the Pharisees. Similarly, the high status of the priesthood among the Pharisees is attested in both Josephus and the Dead Sea Scrolls. The standing of the priests, which cut across sectarian lines, is, *eo ipso,* an indication of the centrality of the temple in everyday life. In the early Second Temple period, when Judea was not yet an independent state, the temple was the center of Jewish life, and it remained the destination of pilgrimage throughout the period.[21] The Jewish yearning for the First Temple, and the nostalgic recollection of its glory, also strongly influenced the eschatological thinking of the day.[22] An indication of the deep admiration the Pharisee sages felt for the temple is their decision to leave its ad-

20. On the centrality of the temple and the temple ritual see S. Safrai's article in H. H. Ben Sasson (ed.), *A History of the Jewish People* (Cambridge, MA, 1976), 307-384.

21. S. Safrai, *Second Temple Pilgrimage* (Hebrew) (Tel Aviv, 1965).

22. On Jerusalem and the temple in Second Temple Jewish thought see my "Jerusalem in Second Temple Literature," pp. 44-75 in the present volume.

ministration under the authority of the Sadducee families of Aaronite descent. As a result, the temple became a Sadducee center, a fact that undoubtedly did not find favor in the eyes of the people, who were mostly aligned with the Pharisees. The temple remained the spiritual center of Judaism in theory as well as practice. In a later period the sages speak of two unities: the unity of God and the unity of Israel. But this is merely a weak echo of the earlier view that is reflected in the words of Josephus (*AJ* 4.201), who argues that one can worship God only in Jerusalem: "In no other city let there be either altar or temple; for God is one and the Hebrew race is one."

The Jewish holidays were celebrated both in the temple and in synagogues, which all faced the Jerusalem temple. The only holidays recognized in those days were those mentioned in the Bible. Other celebrations were relegated to the status of memorial days. To be sure, from the time of the Maccabees on there was a proliferation of these memorial days, as evidenced by the books of the Maccabees and the Fast Scroll *(megillat ta'anit)* alike. But of these, only Hanukkah has survived, a memorial day in honor of the dedication of the temple by the Hasmoneans. In the temple, Hanukkah was celebrated with the recitation of the *hallel*, the Psalm-based liturgy recited on major holidays, but we have no information regarding other rituals associated with the eight days of the holiday, though it stands to reason that there was a temple equivalent to the lighting of the Hanukkah candles. The eight-day duration of the holiday was patterned after Sukkot: "They celebrated it for eight days with rejoicing, in the manner of the festival of booths, remembering how not long before, during the festival of booths, they had been wandering in the mountains and caves like wild animals. Therefore, carrying ivy-wreathed wands and beautiful branches and also fronds of palm, they offered hymns of thanksgiving to him who had given success to the purifying of his own holy place" (2 Macc 10.6-7). Another Hasmonean holiday that apparently enjoyed widespread support was Nikanor Day, a commemoration of Judah Maccabee's victory over the Seleucid general. According to 2 Maccabees (15.36), this holiday was celebrated one day before Mordecai Day, this being the first known mention of Purim. This means that Nikanor Day coincided with the Fast of Esther, though this is in fact not an issue since the Fast of Esther is first mentioned in the post-Talmudic literature of the Geonim, and even then it is performed only by the most righteous. Nor does the proximity between Nikanor Day and Purim suggest the latter was not valued. Clearly, the notion that the Scroll of Esther was composed in the Hellenistic period is fundamentally flawed — the Persian nature of the scroll is evident both in its literary form and in its content. Since the story of Esther contains the commandment to observe Purim, there can be no doubt that by the late Second

Temple period Jews had been celebrating the holiday for generations. Purim was apparently a popular holiday — both pre- and post-70 — and any doubts regarding the holiday and the Scroll of Esther came from the sages, not from the common folk.

It is worth noting that neither Hanukkah nor Purim managed to attain the elevated status that the temple-centered biblical holidays did. Here, then, is another indication of the importance of the temple during the period under consideration. One might even say that the Second Temple played a more important role than the first, even though it was during this period that new institutions arose alongside temple worship: Torah study and the halakhic framework. Perhaps the most striking indication of the temple's status is the aforementioned fact that questions of purity and impurity — an area originally confined to the temple space — burst into the everyday life of different Jewish communities. Ironically, it was the light that shone forth from the Jerusalem temple and illuminated Jewish life throughout Israel; it was this light that paved the way for Jewish existence after the destruction of the temple.

VII. Prayer

Though scholars are not able to determine the precise time when the language of individual prayers was fixed, it is widely held that the origins of Jewish prayer are to be found as far back as the Persian period.[23] Recent scholarship is increasingly aware of the connection between temple and synagogue prayer. Indeed, the idea that prayers emerged as a substitute for temple worship is implausible.[24] Prayer is tied not only to the cycle of the day (e.g., the recitation of the *shema'*); the main prayer, the *'amidah,* also called the Eighteen Benedictions, is tied to the sacrificial cycle of the temple. To this day, Jews face the temple in Jerusalem when they stand in prayer.

Little is known about the origins of the synagogue, but it is clear that during the Second Temple period they were everywhere. The synagogue served as a meeting place where Jews gathered to study and pray. The studying and praying community forms a microcosm of the Jewish people as a whole. The ten-person quorum, the *minyan,* is alluded to in 2 Maccabees

23. J. Heinemann, *Prayer in the Tannaitic and Amoraic Period* (Hebrew) (Jerusalem, 1964); I. Elbogen, *Jewish Liturgy: A Comprehensive History,* trans. Raymond P. Scheindlin (New York and Philadelphia, 1993).

24. On prayer and its role in the synagogue see S. Safrai, "The Synagogue and Synagogue Worship" (Hebrew), in *Society and Religion in the Second Temple Period: Jewish History* (Tel Aviv, 1982), 52-55.

(5.27), a work composed during the reign of John Hyrcanus. There we find that Judah Maccabee joined nine other companions and lived a life of holiness in the desert with them. Similarly, the Dead Sea Scrolls speak of the place "where there are ten men of the Community council" (1QS 6.3), suggesting that the Qumran community too considered the ten-person group an important organizational unit.

The praying congregation represented the Jewish community as a whole, but at the same time was linked to the temple. The core of the Eighteen Benedictions was the Benediction of the Temple Worship *(birkat ha-ʿavodah)*, and fragments of that Second Temple prayer are still extant: "Show favor toward your people Israel . . . and may you accept the offerings of Israel and their prayers with love and favor, and may the worship of your people Israel always be pleasing to you." As this formula makes clear, Jews would pray the Eighteen Benedictions at the time that sacrifices were being offered in the temple, the prayer serving as a collective wish that the temple offerings be accepted favorably by God. Already at an early time, then, the Eighteen Benedictions accompanied the temple sacrifices and, at the same time, served as a vehicle for petitioning for God's grace and mercy.

Jewish prayer in general, and the Eighteen Benedictions in particular, served, then, to petition and praise God. These were almost always collective addresses to God spoken in the first person plural. There were cases of first person singular prayers, and some of the sages taught their disciples individual prayers, but most of these eventually were transformed into the plural, and the overall impression is that the prayers were understood as expressing the voice of the entire synagogue congregation. Different liturgies circulated, and in some cases the same formula served different functions. These differences are evident to this day in the prayer customs of different Jewish communities, and at times even within the same community. But, as noted, the liturgical framework appears to have been established already in the Persian, or perhaps the early Hellenistic period.

The following are a few issues surrounding the Eighteen Benedictions.[25] The opening phrase of the individual benedictions, "Blessed art thou, O Lord," is a product of the Second Temple period and is attested in various forms in apocryphal literature as well as the Dead Sea Scrolls. The Eighteen Benedictions is a series of blessings that today numbers nineteen. It is now customary to omit the central blessings on holidays, substituting a blessing for the sanctity of the day. The first three benedictions and the last three benedictions are recited every day of the year. This change is due to the gener-

---

25. See my "Jerusalem in Second Temple Literature," in the present volume.

ally held view that the central benedictions (numbers 4-16) are petitionary, but that petition is not required on holidays, only thanksgiving.

Analysis of the benedictions suggests that they were primarily aimed at asking for worldly success rather than deep and sublime religious ideas. Originally only two benedictions dealt with the end of days, both of them based on Psalm 147:2 ("The LORD builds up Jerusalem; he gathers the outcasts of Israel"). From this verse two benedictions emerged: one asking for the rebuilding of the eschatological Jerusalem, another for the ingathering of the Jewish exiles. It further appears that these were the two main tenets of eschatological belief in Jewish literature prior to the Hasmonean period. Today the benedictions end with the phrases "who gathers the dispersed of his people Israel" and "the builder of Jerusalem," respectively, but originally they were apparently related. To clarify the eschatological dimension of the Eighteen Benedictions, I cite a passage from Ben Sira (51.21-35), which consists of a prayer in which each stich is followed by the phrase "for his steadfast love endures forever."

> Give thanks to the LORD, for he is good,
>   for his steadfast love endures forever.
> Give thanks to the God of praises,
>   for his steadfast love endures forever.
> Give thanks to the guardian of Israel,
>   for his steadfast love endures forever.
> Give thanks to him who formed all things,
>   for his steadfast love endures forever.
> Give thanks to the redeemer of Israel,
>   for his steadfast love endures forever.
> Give thanks to him who gathers the dispersed of his people Israel,
>   for his steadfast love endures forever.
> Give thanks to him who builds his city and his sanctuary,
>   for his steadfast love endures forever.
> Give thanks to him who makes a horn to sprout for the house of David,
>   for his steadfast love endures forever.
> Give thanks to him who has chosen the sons of Zadok to be priests,
>   for his steadfast love endures forever.
> Give thanks to the shield of Abraham,
>   for his steadfast love endures forever.
> Give thanks to the rock of Isaac,
>   for his steadfast love endures forever.
> Give thanks to the mighty one of Jacob,
>   for his steadfast love endures forever.

Give thanks to him who has chosen Zion,
    for his steadfast love endures forever.
Give thanks to the King of the kings of kings,
    for his steadfast love endures forever.
He has raised up a horn for his people, praise for all his loyal ones,
For the children of Israel, the people close to him. Praise the LORD.

It should be noted that this prayer was not translated into Greek by Ben Sira's grandson, so it most probably was not part of the original composition. The prayer is very similar to the Eighteen Benedictions, but for the time we will limit our observations to the question of eschatology. Alongside the allusion to the rebuilding of Jerusalem ("Give thanks to him who builds his city and his sanctuary"), there is also the reference to the ingathering of exiles ("Give thanks to him who gathers the dispersed of his people Israel"). In addition, the author gives thanks to "him who makes a horn to sprout for the house of David" and to "him who has chosen the sons of Zadok to be priests." It appears, then, that the prayer in Ben Sira is alluding to a version of the Eighteen Benedictions, one that included blessings not only for the ingathering of exiles and rebuilding of Jerusalem, but also for the coming of the Messiah from the House of David.[26] Such a blessing is, in fact, extant in the present version of Eighteen Benedictions, namely, the benediction that opens with the words: "Cause the shoot of David to grow quickly, in these days." This special messianic blessing was adopted in Babylonia and from there spread to the Jewish world. The Palestinian liturgy, in contrast, mentioned the Messiah in the concluding formula of the Jerusalem benediction: "Blessed are you, Lord, the God of David, the builder of Jerusalem." However, the formula of Ben Sira suggests that originally two Palestinian customs coexisted. In one the Messiah was mentioned in the Jerusalem benediction, while in the other, whose echoes are heard in Ben Sira and which eventually took root in Babylonia, Jerusalem received one blessing and the Davidic Messiah another. In the latter too the Eighteen Benedictions liturgy is based on the Palestinian enumeration which did not include a separate blessing for the Messiah. As a result, the "Eighteen" Benedictions in fact refer to a series of nineteen blessings, since all the Jewish communities have adopted the Babylonian custom and dedicate a separate blessing to the Davidic Messiah.

Additional evidence for the existence of a Palestinian benediction for the Messiah comes from Luke 1:68-69: "Blessed be the Lord God of Israel, for

---

26. Y. Liver, *The History of the House of David* (Hebrew) (Jerusalem, 1959), especially 107-112.

he has looked favorably on his people and redeemed them. He has raised up a mighty savior for us in the house of his servant David." The language is similar, on the one hand, to Ben Sira's "who makes a horn to sprout for the house of David," and, on the other, to the Eighteen Benedictions' "Cause the shoot of David to grow quickly, in these days, and raise his horn with your salvations. . . . Blessed are you, Lord, who causes the horn of salvation to grow." With regard to the eschatological expectations, then, there appear to have existed differing versions in the Palestinian liturgy already at a fairly early period.

As for Ben Sira's phrase, "who has chosen the sons of Zadok to be priests," we do not have any clear parallel in the existing Eighteen Benedictions. It is possible, however, that the blessing concluding "blessed are you, Lord, support and haven for the righteous [*tzaddiqim*]," once referred to the priestly sons of Zadok.[27]

The analysis thus far indicates that the number of eschatological benedictions grew over the centuries, and blessings that were originally concerned with other matters took on an eschatological flavor. Thus, for example, Ben Sira's exhortation to "give thanks to the redeemer of Israel" corresponds to the following benediction from today's liturgy: "Behold our poverty and support us in our quarrels and provide full salvations for us soon, for the sake of your name, for you are a mighty redeemer. Blessed are you, Lord, who redeem Israel." The blessing originally referred to redemption from worldly difficulties rather than hopes for the distant future. Thus Rashi, in his commentary to the Babylonian Talmud (Megillah 17b): "This does not refer to the redemption from exile, rather that He redeem us from the difficulties that always plague us."

Today, two benedictions stand between those for the ingathering of exiles and "support and haven for the righteous." One of these, "return our judges as before," is rather obscure and it may well be that it was originally understood as a way of emphasizing the kingdom of heaven. The current formulation is apparently subsequent to the destruction of the Second Temple.[28] Following it, is the benediction of the *minim* (heretics) that originally opened with the words "May the informants and the *minim* have no hope," though the word *minim* (which can refer specifically to Christians or Jewish-Christians) was omitted as a result of Christian censorship. The Talmud

27. On the importance of this benediction see Flusser, "Jerusalem in Second Temple Literature," pp. 44-75 in the present volume.

28. On the original meaning of this benediction, apparently an anti-Sadducee polemic, see my "Jerusalem in Second Temple Literature," pp. 44-75 in the present volume.

teaches that this benediction was fixed by Shmuel the Lesser during the Jamnia (Yavne) period, and it referred not only to Christians but to other heretics as well. However, from the second century on, Jews directed the blessing particularly at the Christians, as a number of the Church Fathers testify. Nonetheless, the benediction itself precedes the emergence of Christianity, for we find in the Tosefta (Berakhot 3.5): "One may include the benediction of the *minim* in that of the separatists, and the benediction of the gentiles in that of the elders, and the benediction of David in that of Jerusalem. And if one said each as a blessing unto itself, he has fulfilled his legal obligation." The benediction, then, preceded Christianity and stood as a warning against those who separated themselves from Israel, for whatever reason. Shmuel the Lesser established a special prayer against the *minim* in order to emphasize the need to maintain one's distance from those who broke with mainstream Judaism as a result of their religious separatism. However, as the Tosefta indicates, the *minim* could have been included in a benediction against separatists as such rather than being allotted their own benediction. In its present form, the benediction against the *minim* does not include the word *perushim,* "separatists," but it maintains a variety of derogatory terms: *minim,* informants, evil doers, and hypocrites. It appears that such concatenations were common in Jewish circles, as the following passage from the Tosefta suggests (Sanhedrin 13.5): "the *minim,* informers, hypocrites and heretics, as well as those who cause terror in the Land of the Living, those who deny the resurrection to the dead . . . will be locked in hell and they will be judged in it for all eternity, forevermore." The upshot of all this is that the benediction against the *minim,* at least in its primitive form, predates Christianity, and served as a protection of sorts against those who threatened the Jewish collective.

This was not the only blessing aimed at excluding from Judaism the perceived enemies of Israel. Another such blessing is today found at the conclusion of the Torah service:[29] "Blessed are you, Lord, who gave us the Torah of truth, and planted eternal life in our midst." However the original version of this blessing is preserved in a prayer called *qedusha de-sidra,* which states: "Blessed are you, God, who created us for His glory, and separated us from those who err and gave us the Torah of truth, and planted eternal life in our midst." Now, who are "those who err"? Apparently those who do not believe in the Torah of truth and eternal life, where the former seems to refer to the Oral Torah, following the words of the prophet Malachi (2:6): "True instruction was in his mouth, and no wrong was found on his lips. He walked with me in in-

---

29. On this benediction see my discussion in "Sanktus und Gloria," *Abraham unser Vater, Festschrift Otto Michel* (Leiden and Cologne, 1963), 141-143.

tegrity and uprightness, and he turned many from iniquity." If so, those who err are none other than the Sadducees, who do not accept the Oral Torah and do not believe in the resurrection of the dead, i.e., eternal life. This blessing, too, particularly in the more primitive form preserved in the *qedusha de-sidra*, was a Pharisaic attempt to warn the people against Sadducean beliefs. Finally, there appears to be one more benediction that was originally aimed against a particular group, in this case the eschatological authors who composed their own prophetic works, much to the dismay of the sages. I refer here to the blessing recited after the *haftarah*, the reading from the prophets that follows the Torah reading, "Blessed are You, LORD, who chose good prophets and showed favor toward their pronouncements, spoken in truth." The addressees, once again, are the false prophets whose books were rejected by the sages.

In its original form in the *qedusha de-sidra*,[30] the anti-Sadducee benediction is followed by the following statement: "He will open our heart with his torah and guide our heart toward fear of God, and place in our heart the love and the fear of God, so that we do his will with a whole heart and a willing spirit, lest we labor for naught and produce alarm." Note that in the letter sent by the Jews of Jerusalem to their Egyptian brethren in 143 B.C.E., we find: "May he give you all a heart to worship him and to do his will with a strong heart and a willing spirit. May he open your heart to his law and his commandments, and may he bring peace . . . and may he not forsake you in time of evil" (2 Macc 1.3-5). Clearly, the prayer preserved in the *qedusha de-sidra* existed in a more primitive form already in the days of the Maccabees. If so, the *qedusha de-sidra*, a relatively minor prayer in today's liturgy, preserves two very early passages, one the product of the Pharisee-Sadducee polemics, the other dating back to the middle of the second century B.C.E. In light of this, it would be a mistake to propose a late date for any Jewish prayer without proof, as even prayers whose present form was established post-70 may contain early historical material that can be retrieved through careful textual and historical analysis. This principle applies to all the short benedictions that appear in different parts of the daily Jewish liturgy, which might be the reformulation of an ancient benediction or a late creation that preserves early material. An example of the latter is the blessing for beverages and food grown outside of Israel: "Blessed are You, Lord our God, king of the universe, through whose word all things came into being." Embedded in this benediction is the formula found in the opening of the Gospel of John (1:1-3): "In the beginning was the word. . . . All things came into being through it, and without it not one thing came into

---

30. On this benediction see my "Jerusalem in Second Temple Literature," in the present volume, 59, n. 31.

being." Apparently the phrase "all things came into being through His word" was an ancient Jewish formula that was used for foods that do not fit into existing categories, a formula that predates the language of the benediction.

VIII. Jewish Messianism

Judaism, as a historically-rooted faith in a chosen people, contains an inherent need for eschatological belief. The God of all chose Israel as a nation, but the people cannot observe the entirety of Jewish teaching in the present, and so the full realization of the covenant between God and His people is deferred to the future. The God of Israel is the maker of heaven and earth, the creator of the world and of mankind. Judaism believes that a day will come when mankind, or at least part of mankind, will recognize its maker. Naturally, the belief in a future time in which all promises will be fulfilled grows stronger and more urgent the further the actual condition of Israel and of humanity falls from the ideal state.

Of course, Jewish eschatology precedes the Second Temple period and is attested throughout the Hebrew Bible. The facts that the Jews were dispersed among the nations during the Second Temple period, Israel was often under foreign occupation, and the temple fell short of the glory of its predecessor — all these heightened the messianic tension within Judaism. Israel was not the only people to embrace eschatological hopes, as similar beliefs spread among the nations of the east in the wake of Alexander's conquests. The establishment of the Hellenistic empire, and the ensuing political and spiritual crises, influenced the "messianic" hopes of these people.[31] These hopes found their expression in various messianic prophecies concerning a great conqueror who would arise from the east, defeat the Greeks, and return things to their previous state.

These hopes were particularly fierce in Egypt and Persia. In Egypt, the idea of a divine king was already well established in the popular imagination, paving the way for a restorative ideology that appealed to all who hated the Macedonian occupiers. The Persian religion was also inherently focused on the end of days in which truth triumphs and deceit will be forever vanquished. Here too, then, was a religious framework hospitable to the "messianic" view that the destruction of evil will include the annihilation of the foreign invaders.[32] Judaism contained *both* the belief in a messianic king and

31. S. K. Eddy, *The King Is Dead* (Lincoln, 1961).

32. D. Flusser, "The Four Empires in the Fourth Sibyl and in the Book of Daniel," *Israel Oriental Studies* 2 (1972), 148-175.

the eschatological hope — fertile ground for a messianic hope for political redemption.

Most of the messianic prophecies of the nations prior to the Roman conquest have been lost. They reach us only as faint echoes from the time following the Roman victory, when the conquering Greeks became allies of the conquered eastern nations. As a result, most of the messianic prophecies against the Romans were preserved in Greek.

The alliance between the natives and the Greeks gave rise to a series of new political messianic prophecies.[33] Thus, Mithridates, King of Pontus, could harness the political messianism that emerged after the defeat of Antiochus III at the hands of the Romans. It is not coincidence that while messianic beliefs were driving the Jews in their war against Rome, a rebellion broke out in Gaul, under the encouragement of the local priests.[34] There is a connection between the messianic stirrings within Second Temple Judaism, and parallel developments among other nations of the day.[35]

As noted, the primary font of Jewish eschatology was the particular structure of the Torah, but we cannot overlook the specific atmosphere that gave rise to the messianic tension of the Second Temple period. For while Judaism, and the Hebrew Bible, contain a belief in the end of days, this time was not always understood as imminent. Moreover, it cannot be argued that the individuals who did not believe they were living in the last generation weakened the belief in an imminent eschatological reality. The messianic Jewish movements were the result of a mainstream Jewish belief in the end of days, not vice versa.

To repeat, it appears the Eighteen Benedictions once contained only two eschatological blessings: "builder of Jerusalem" and "who gathers the exiles." These hopes were expressed in this form in the Book of Tobit, which was likely composed in the Persian period: "After this they all will return from their exile and will rebuild Jerusalem in splendor; and in it the temple of God will be rebuilt, just as the prophets of Israel have said concerning it. Then the nations in the whole world will all be converted and worship God in truth. They will abandon their idols, which deceitfully have led them into their er-

---

33. See H. Fuchs, *Der geistige Widerstand gegen Rom* (Berlin, 1964).

34. The inciting priests recited a poem according to which after the burning of the temples in Rome in the days of Nero, the gods went into exile and relocated to Gaul. See Fuchs, *Der geistige Widerstand,* who cites Tacitus, *Annals,* 4.54.

35. There also is a contemporary parallel, namely, the liberation movements — some with a clear eschatological component — that arose in response to European colonialism. These movements, many of them associated with cargo cults, looked forward to a time when white rule would be overturned, and a new world order established.

ror; and in righteousness they will praise the eternal God" (Tobit 14.5-7). The same two hopes find expression in the prayer of Tobias (chapter 13), which further contains a wonderful description of the eschatological Jerusalem: "The gates of Jerusalem will be built with sapphire and emerald, and all your walls with precious stones. The towers of Jerusalem will be built with gold, and their battlements pure gold" (Tobit 13.16). The eschatological prayer of Ben Sira similarly touches on the same two motifs (36.1-17):

> Have mercy upon us, O God of all,
>> and put all the nations in fear of you.
> Lift up your hand against foreign nations
>> and let them see your might.
> As you have used us to show your holiness to them,
>> so use them to show your glory to us.
> Then they will know, as we have known,
>> that there is no God but you, O Lord.
> Give new signs, and work other wonders;
>> make your hand and right arm glorious.
> Rouse your anger and pour out your wrath;
>> destroy the adversary and wipe out the enemy.
> Hasten the day, and remember the appointed time,
>> and let your people recount your mighty deeds.
> Let survivors be consumed in the fiery wrath,
>> and may those who harm your people meet destruction.
> Crush the heads of hostile rulers,
>> who say "There is no one but ourselves."
> Gather all the tribes of Jacob
>> and give them their inheritance, as at the beginning.
> Have mercy, O LORD, on the people called by your name,
>> on Israel, whom you have named your firstborn.
> Have pity on the city of your sanctuary,
>> Jerusalem, the place of your dwellings.
> Fill Zion with majesty,
>> and your temple with your glory.
> Bear witness to those whom you created in the beginning,
>> and fulfill the prophecies spoken in your name.
> Reward those who wait for you
>> and let your prophets be found trustworthy.
> Hear, O LORD, the prayer of your servants,
>> according to your goodwill toward your people.

The prayer of Ben Sira is especially important since it reflects the eschatological beliefs current near the Hasmonean period. Ben Sira's views are, of course, linked to those of the biblical prophets, but he offers an original and interesting development of his own. For example, he states that the final redemption will be like the first redemption, i.e., the exodus from Egypt. He also speaks of the destruction of the nations that are hostile to Israel, and of his hope that the ingathering of exiles will include the Israelite tribes settling in their ancestral territories. He mentions Jerusalem and the Jerusalem temple, and finally he recalls the words of the prophets and prays for their fulfillment. For Ben Sira, then, the prophets are understood as seers and eschatological visionaries, a widespread view in this period.

We also saw that Ben Sira and the Book of Tobit speak of the eschatological Jerusalem and the eschatological temple. The hope for a renewed Jerusalem at the end of days is already attested in the writings of the prophets, beginning with Ezekiel, where it is undoubtedly tied to the destruction of the First Temple at the hand of the Babylonians. However, the return to Zion and rebuilding of the temple did not extinguish this hope, since in the early Second Temple period Jerusalem did not enjoy the glory and prestige bestowed on it during the time of the First Temple. Some of the most sacred objects had disappeared, among them the tent of meeting and the tablets of the law, and part of the restorative hopes involved the return of these objects. Similarly, it was widely held that in the eschaton the temple would be returned to a state befitting its status as the locus of Jewish messianic expectations. Already in the Book of Tobit (14.5) we are told that the temple of that day was not like the First Temple.

Another text composed in the early days of the Hasmonean dynasty, 1 Enoch 90.28-29, foresees an eschatological shift in which the present temple is uprooted and relocated to "the South," and a new, more glorious temple, created by God, is placed in the now vacant site. The author of this passage is quite supportive of the early Hasmonean rulers, but nonetheless speaks of a grander temple built by God — a discrepancy that may be attributed to the fact that late in the Hasmonean period many considered the temple to be a place of sin. It is no surprise, then, that the Dead Sea Scrolls contain a passage that is openly hostile to the present temple but speaks of a future temple that will not be built by human hands.[36] The tension between the present and future temple is further apparent in Jesus' saying that he will destroy this temple

---

36. The text was published by J. M. Allegro, *Discoveries in the Judean Desert: Qumran Cave 4* (Oxford, 1968), 1.53. See also D. Flusser, "Two Notes on the Midrash on II Sam. 7," *IEJ* 9 (1959), 99-104.

that is made with hands and build another, not made with hands.[37] However, after the destruction of the Second Temple, the expectation of a new, eschatological temple was radically transformed. The tension toward the temple, now destroyed by the Romans, dissipated, and the hope for a new temple became a national hope for restoration of a now temple-less nation. Nonetheless, the hope for a speedy building of the temple has its roots in a relatively early time in the Second Temple period.

Interestingly, neither Ben Sira nor the Book of Tobit refers to the messiah, even though the belief in the eschatological renewal of the Davidic dynasty is attested in the time of the First Temple. The Book of Daniel, too, does not allude to a messianic figure, though it is an eschatological text from the early Hasmonean period. It appears the belief in a personal messiah grew stronger during the Hasmonean rule, a result of the political intrigues of the day. It is attested in a highly developed form in the Sibylline Oracles (Book 3), but the first book to discuss this theme at length is the Psalms of Solomon, which was composed during Pompey's reign. The simplistic view that the Hasmonean rise to power caused their opponents to emphasize the Davidic nature of the messiah is without merit, since the early Hasmoneans ruled first as high priests and only later as kings. And even when the Maccabees did assume the crown, this would not necessarily have caused their opponents to deny the legitimacy of Hasmonean rule since, halakhically, the kings of Israel do not have to be from the House of David.[38] Even so, it appears that the rise to kingship of Aristobulus I and his heirs did strengthen the biblically-rooted belief in a Davidic messiah. This may explain the absence of any reference to a Davidic messiah in pre-Hasmonean literature. Clearly, the loss of political independence also played an important role in the promulgation of the messianic-kingship idea, as this figure symbolized the hope for liberation from foreign rule.

The Qumran community believed in two messiahs, "the messiahs of Aaron and of Israel."[39] The eschatological priest is also called משיח, messiah, the Hebrew term that literally means "anointed," which he was. The belief in two messiahs is already evident in the prophecies of Zechariah (4:14), who refers to "the two anointed ones," meaning the high priest and the Davidic king. Later, this view spread beyond the confines of the Qumran community and took hold among the wider Jewish populace. In the Talmud we hear of an eschatological "righteous priest." The Qumran literature is unique in that it as-

---

37. Mark 14:58; Matt 26:61; John 2:19; and see also Mark 15:29; Matt 27:40; Acts 6:14.

38. On this question see Liver, *The History of the House of David*, 112-117.

39. On this view see Liver, *The History of the House of David*, 117-140, and cf. J. Liver, "The Doctrine of the Two Messiahs in the Sectarian Literature in the Time of the Second Commonwealth," *HTR* 52 (1959), 149-185.

signs the high priest a more important role than the Davidic messiah, no doubt a reflection of the prominence of priests — Zadokite priests in particular — at Qumran. The members of the sect hoped to conquer Jerusalem in the end of days and install one of its priests as high priest in the temple. Thus the importance they assigned the Aaronite messiah; in all probability the community did not include descendents of the House of David.

The Qumranites also believed that prophecy would be renewed in the end of days, and hoped for the advent of a prophet alongside the two messiahs. It is hard to grasp the full significance of the cessation of prophecy in the early Second Temple period. Those who lived during that time realized that the channels of divine inspiration ceased to flow; without a prophet to provide divine sanction for earthly events there could be no fixed and trusted mundane reality.[40] The first evidence of hope for an eschatological renewal of prophecy is found at the end of Malachi. The anonymous author appends to the book a poetic hope for prophetic renewal: "Remember the teaching of my servant Moses. . . . Lo, I will send you the prophet Elijah before the great and terrible day of the LORD comes. He will turn the hearts of parents to their children and the hearts of children to their parents, so that I will not come and strike the land with a curse" (Mal 4:4-6). Here the prophet marks the end of prophecy and voices the hope for a future renewal in the form of Elijah, the prophet who did not die but ascended to heaven in a whirlwind. Incidentally, the eschatological role of Elijah is already noted in Ben Sira (48.9-11).

But the eschatological prophet was not always identified with Elijah. In the Dead Sea Scrolls[41] and 1 Maccabees ("Simon should be their leader . . . until a trustworthy prophet should arise" [14.41 and see also 4.46 and 9.27]) we find references to anonymous prophets. The scrolls suggest that textual warrant for this belief is found in Deuteronomy 18:15: "The LORD your God will raise up for you a prophet like me from among your own people; you shall heed such a prophet." This connection is also found in Philo's *The Special Laws* 1.65. It seems the Jews of the Second Temple period saw themselves as having no access to divine inspiration, yet remembered that they are the sons of prophets. The Book of Tobit states that "we are the descendents of prophets" (4.12), while Hillel the Elder states: "Let Israel be, for if they are not

---

40. E. E. Urbach, "Halakhah and Prophecy" (Hebrew), *Tarbiz* 18 (1947), 1-27; idem, "When Did Prophecy Cease?" (Hebrew), *Tarbiz* 17 (1956), 1-11.

41. 1QS 9.11 speaks of the future advent of "the messiahs of Aaron and Israel." All told, then, we have three messianic figures: the prophet, the priestly messiah, and the royal messiah. Allusions to all three are found in the collection of biblical verses known as the Testimonia (4QTest), and see J. M. Allegro, "Further Messianic References in Qumran Literature," *JBL* 75 (1956), 174-187.

prophets, they are indeed the sons of prophets" (b. Pesahim 66a). The same designation is found in Acts 3:25. These sources suggest that the phrase "descendents of prophets" *(bnei nevi'im)* was used to refer to the fact that Jewish prophecy has ceased, yet Israel is commanded to preserve the embers of prophecy and still possess an inspired, intuitive understanding of Jewish law and of the words of the biblical prophets.

IX. Eschatological Seers

Eventually, the Jewish world accepted that prophecy had indeed ceased and came to see the sages, with their oral tradition, as heirs to the prophets. The sages themselves state that "after the destruction of the temple prophecy was taken from the prophets and given to the sages" and "the sage is greater than the prophet" (b. Bava Batra 12a). But there is another view attested in that same discussion that holds that "after the destruction of the temple prophecy was taken from the prophets and given to fools and children." This statement indicates the sages' resistance to the new prophecy that emerged during the Second Temple period, prophecy that modern scholars refer to with the term apocalypticism. But it seems the broader populace did not share the sages' views and considered the new seers to be full-fledged prophets. It is hard to know today whether these seers hoped for an eschatological renewal of prophecy or considered themselves to be prophets. In either case, it is clear that the apocalyptic Qumran community did expect a renewal of prophecy,[42] while the extant apocalyptic texts composed outside of Qumran are attributed to authors who lived in the time of the biblical prophets. It appears that the true authors chose pseudepigraphic attribution in order to endow their works with the authority of hoary antiquity. The need to situate these books in the prophetic period suggests a broad consensus regarding their own period as no longer prophetic. Thus we find, on the one hand, eschatological seers whom many Jews viewed as prophets even while most recognized that prophecy had ceased, and, on the other hand, the sages who opposed this novel form of prophecy. There was even a special blessing said before the *haftarah* reading that was apparently aimed against these prophetic books. The phrase "trustworthy prophet" in 1 Maccabees (14.41) indicates that already in the Hasmonean period there were those who objected to the apocalyptic seers. Neither the "trustworthy prophet" nor its counterpart, "false prophet," is biblical — a clear indication that the terms were coined for polemic purposes.

---

42. See Allegro, "Further Messianic References."

Many scholars classify Second Temple doctrines regarding the end of days under the heading of apocalyptic literature. But the truth is that the apocalyptic texts express views that were part of mainstream Judaism of the day, though much of this was due to the influence of these very texts. Be that as it may, the beliefs in an ultimate redemption, a messiah, the kingdom of heaven, etc. are all part of the biblical heritage and largely determined by the structure of Jewish doctrine, so that they could have emerged as a result of the political and economic difficulties that beset Israel and the ancient near east and provided fertile ground for the despair and the hope that nourish eschatological visions. It is worth noting that the sacred history of the Hebrew Bible points toward the end of days. During the return of the Babylonian exiles there arose prophets, among them Second Isaiah, Haggai and Zechariah, who believed that the ingathering of exiles and reconstruction of the razed temple were proof that the end of days was upon them. But this was not so, and so the eschatological writers turned to offering contemporary interpretations of ancient prophecies. This is the origin of, among others, the pesher texts of Qumran, which interpret the words of biblical prophets as statements about the Dead Sea community itself. The underlying assumption of this genre is that "all the ages of God will come at the right time, as he established for them in the mystery of his cunning" (1QpHab 7.14), and "the final age will be extended and go beyond all that the prophets say, because the mysteries of God are wonderful" (1QpHab 7.7-8). Within this scheme, God's command that Habakkuk "Write the vision; make it plain on tablets, so that a runner may read it" refers to the Teacher of Righteousness who will interpret the words of the prophets. So God "told Habakkuk to write what was going to happen to the last generation, but he did not let him know the consummation of the era" (1QpHab 7.1-2); it was rather to the Teacher of Righteousness that "God has made known all the mysteries of the words of his servants, the prophets" (1QpHab 7.4-5). The Teacher of Righteousness received mysteries denied prophets themselves. Contemporary interpretations of the prophets are widespread among apocalyptic authors.

A core tenet of Second Temple apocalypticism was that theirs was the last generation before the end of days, an imminent messianic expectation. However, it would be a mistake to try to reduce apocalypticism to this view. A more accurate statement would be that the apocalyptic worldview holds that the forces driving history toward the end of days are already in effect. Indeed, there could be thinkers for whom it is enough that we have passed the halfway point. And if a seer fixed a date for the eschaton that passed without incident, he could always claim that he erred in interpreting the signs. As the history of non-Jewish messianic movements clearly indicates, the disappointment of an unfulfilled prediction often does not mark the end of the movement. Sometimes the opposite is the case — the failure gives rise to a new round of eschatological calculations or to a decision to desist from calculating, but the movement can go on, internal tensions notwithstanding.[43] It stands to reason that this would be the case for the messianic movement of Second Temple Judaism; eschatological hope, not specific calculations, lies at the heart of the matter.

There are important differences between biblical prophecy, on the one hand, and apocalypticism, on the other. The biblical prophet, for one, prophesies as the result of being overpowered — possessed, even — by a heavenly power, while the apocalyptic seer seeks out the vision and may even prepare himself for it through fasting and prayer. There is no doubt that the visions of Second Temple seers were authentic, but the apocalyptic literature of the period is more literary, more fictive, than biblical prophecy. To be sure, the biblical prophets spoke of the end of days, but this was not their primary function; the apocalyptic authors considered eschatological visions their main calling. Another difference involves the function of repentance. Classical prophecy believed in the efficacy of repentance for reversing a heavenly decree, while apocalyptic authors did not think decrees could be altered but that those who repent will be spared the inevitable punishment. The same eschatological logic dictates that not only the events of the end of days are inevitable; the entire course of human history has been predestined. Thus the parallel periodization of world history and Jewish history, and the schematic approach to history itself. Eschatological determinism is clearly evident in the predestination ideology of the Qumran community. But apocalyptic authors did not confine themselves to the end of time — the pseudepigraphic attribution to early prophets required that some chronicle history at least from biblical times. It is usually possible to date these compositions according to the events they foresee, which are accurate up to a point and suddenly diverge from historic reality. One interesting example is the Book of Daniel, which was composed in the early Hasmonean period. The prophetic passages in the book may be some of the most accurate information concerning the period, that is, up to that point when the author no longer "prophesies" concerning his own period and begins speaking of the future. The break occurs with the words "in the time of the end" (Dan 11:40). The Qumran community knew that the events prophesied prior to "in the time of the end" had already occurred during the reign of Antiochus Epiphanes. This is the reason they used

43. See D. Flusser, "Salvation Present and Future," *Types of Redemption* (Leiden, 1970), 46-61.

only a small fraction of the Book of Daniel, from 11:40 on, as "historical background" for the eschatological vision recorded in the War Scroll.

The Book of Daniel is the only apocalyptic book to be included in the biblical canon.[44] It was held in great esteem by the eschatological authors of the Second Temple period, who alluded to it often and proposed new interpretations of the book. Daniel himself states that he examined the Book of Jeremiah (the reference is to Jeremiah 25:11) and sought of God understanding of the prophet's words. The author of 4 Ezra draws from Daniel on this point, while serving, in turn, as an inspiration for Revelation, though 4 Ezra is not mentioned there. We find, then, a chain of transmission from early biblical prophecy to Christian authors.

In a sense, the Book of Daniel stands apart from the apocalyptic compositions, due to its proximity to the new apocalyptic genre familiar from Qumran. This literature develops ideas found in the Book of Daniel, but in many ways breaks with the book and introduces new motifs. The discovery of the Dead Sea Scrolls has allowed scholars to situate historically a number of Second Temple books whose social and spiritual context was heretofore unknown; among them: 1 Enoch, Jubilees, and the Testament of the Twelve Patriarchs. In its present form, 1 Enoch (preserved fully in Ethiopic) is a collection of texts attributed to Enoch. The Qumran library contains Enoch fragments in Aramaic, though in and of itself this would not constitute definite proof for an affiliation between Enoch and the sectarian Qumran writings.[45] However, the ideas expressed in 1 Enoch are often very close to the social and religious worldview of the Qumran community. 1 Enoch is mentioned in Jubilees, a survey of Israel's history from the Genesis account to the days of Moses. Not only its general worldview, but the content of the eschatological chapters indicates that this work too belonged to the same apocalyptic stream as the Dead Sea texts. Jubilees was written in Hebrew, as the fragments discovered at Qumran prove, and appears to have served as a model for the Damascus Document from Qumran.[46] As for the Testament of the Twelve Patriarchs, its current form is based on a Greek composition, but one of its sources is the Testament of Levi, Aramaic fragments of which were discovered among the scrolls.[47] Like the Qumran texts, the Testament of Levi considers the messiah from the House of Aaron to be more important than his Davidic counterpart,

44. See "Daniel and the Book of Daniel," pp. 1-5 in the present volume.

45. See *Biblical Encyclopedia* (Hebrew) (Jerusalem, 1954), 6.689-692, s.v. חנוך; J. T. Milik and M. Black (eds.), *The Books of Enoch: Aramaic Fragments of Qumran Cave 4* (Oxford, 1976).

46. CD 15.3-4.

47. The book is quoted in CD 4.15. And see D. Flusser, "Testaments of the Twelve Patriarchs," *EJ* 13.184-186.

and the work is cited, moreover, in the Damascus Document. The Testament of the Twelve Patriarchs contains explicitly Christian passages, but its theology is particularly close to Qumran's; it was apparently composed in circles affiliated with Qumran, and contains early material including passages from the Aramaic Testament of Levi and the Testament of Naphtali (in Hebrew), both of which were preserved at Qumran. Taken together, the evidence points to 1 Enoch, Jubilees, and the Testament of the Twelve Patriarchs all being composed in the circles from which the Dead Sea community emerged.

Analysis of these compositions, alongside the Qumran writings, indicates that alongside the political aspects of the end of days, these authors were concerned with the divine mysteries of the cosmos — man's place in the world, man's relation to God, and mysteries of the divinity itself. Within these Essene circles we find an admixture of eschatology and mystical motifs that will find fuller expression in later Jewish mysticism such as *ma'aseh merkavah* (the mysteries of the Godhead) and *ma'aseh bereshit* (cosmological and cosmogenic mysteries). These mystical tendencies separate the Essene authors from the Book of Daniel, which is primarily concerned with the vision of the end time, though there too we find some mystical passages. It appears that during the first century B.C.E. a split occurred between apocalyptic mysticism and eschatological visions. Thus, the Psalms of Solomon, whose Hebrew original did not survive and is extant only in its Greek translation, is concerned only with eschatological visions, and the same is true of Revelation (composed in the days of Emperor Domitian), 4 Ezra, and the Apocalypse of Baruch, which were composed circa 100 C.E. In 4 Ezra, an angel sent to the seer says:

> And he said to me, "If I had asked you, 'How many dwellings are in the heart of the sea, or how many streams are at the source of the deep, or how many streams are above the firmament, or which are the exits of Hades, or which are the entrances to Paradise?' perhaps you would have said to me, 'I never went down into the deep, nor as yet into heaven.'"
> (4 Ezra 4.7-8)

That is, the author does not believe that one can attain knowledge of the matters discussed in 1 Enoch and later Jewish mysticism. Nonetheless, 4 Ezra itself contains many allusions to such mystical thinking. So while the first century B.C.E. witnessed a split into political eschatology, on the one hand, and a more mystical approach emphasizing mysteries of God, the world, and the fate of the soul, on the other, the division is not absolute. So while 2 Enoch (Slavonic Enoch), for example, clearly belongs to the mystical group, it is not disinterested in the end of days.

X. Heavenly Beings

The Bible recognizes a heavenly entourage that surrounds God, as well as celestial messengers, the angels, sent to mankind. The divine congregation or pantheon is an inheritance from pre-biblical beliefs, or perhaps the influence of Canaanite beliefs. The angels, who function as a line of communication between God and man, are mentioned frequently in the Bible. Sometimes the angel serves as God's mouthpiece, a stand-in for God, and is even referred to in place of God. Nonetheless, ancient Judaism was forged in the fires of an anti-pagan revolution, and heavenly beings are only a tolerated vestige of an earlier era, or perhaps even an element that arouses a modicum of suspicion. But the Second Temple period witnessed a fundamental change in this regard: the importance of angels grows, and for the first time they are mentioned by name (we have already seen that the Book of Tobit speaks of the angel Raphael). There also emerges an angelic hierarchy, involving seven or, in some sources, four archangels. Many angels besides are mentioned by name, and they will take on an increasingly important role in later mystical literature. It was commonly held that every nation is affiliated with its own demigod, an idea linked exegetically to Deuteronomy 32:8-9: "When the Most High apportioned the nations, when he divided humankind, he fixed the boundaries of the peoples according to the number of the Israelites *(bnei yisrael);* the LORD's own portion was his people, Jacob his allotted share." This, in any case, is the Masoretic reading. But the Septuagint and a Qumran fragment read, "he fixed the boundaries of the peoples according to the number of the gods" *(bnei el),* and this appears to be the original version. If so, Deuteronomy holds that God apportioned the nations to his demigods, but kept Israel as his own lot. This verse, then, appears to be the origin of the belief in angels as demigods assigned to particular nations, though there may also be a secondary Persian influence. According to Jubilees (15.31) and Ben Sira (17.17), the nations are given over to their heavenly ministers, but Israel belongs to God alone — in accordance with Deuteronomy. But the more dominant Second Temple view, one that is attested in both Daniel (10:21) and the Qumran scrolls, identifies Israel's heavenly minister as the angel Michael.

An exegetical motif that typifies Second Temple Judaism's belief in angels — a belief shared by all Jewish groups except the Sadducees[48] — is found in 1 Enoch. There the author interprets Isaiah 6:3, "Holy, holy, holy is the LORD of hosts; the whole earth is full of his glory," as follows: "Holy, holy, holy, Lord of the Spirits; the spirits fill the earth" (39.12). The author of

---

48. See Acts 23:8.

1 Enoch understands the word "hosts" as referring to spirits, while the "glory" that fills the earth is also spirits. On this reading, the whole world is full of spirits.

But not all the spirits are good; there are some bad spirits, i.e., spirits of Belial, in the terminology of the Qumran community — a sign of the dualistic thinking prevalent in those days. The difference between good and evil, between light and darkness, between the righteous and the wicked, enjoyed pride of place in the religious thought of the time. And there were those who, in keeping with this dualistic view, divided the angels into good and evil, angels of light and angels of darkness, a prominent motif in the Qumran literature. This is also the context in which we usually encounter the story of the fallen angels. Though there are several extant versions of this story, all can be traced to the enigmatic passage in Genesis 6:1-4, which tells of the sons of God (or of the gods) who took for themselves human women. The passage ends with the statement that the "Nefilim" roamed the earth at this time, a word that was later interpreted as a reference to angels that had fallen (from the Hebrew verb *nafal*), which was in turn explained as the result of their rebellion against God. The story is alluded to in Ben Sira (16.7), according to whom God "did not forgive the ancient giants who revolted in their might." The story of the fallen angels, which would become central to Christian art and literature, was driven not only by the mythological drive of the period, but by an attempt to explain the presence of evil in the world. Over time, however, the futility of this answer was recognized, since the revolt was suppressed and the rebellious angels imprisoned. To work around this difficulty, Jubilees (10.10) has the head of the evil angel delegation request that a tenth of them be released to serve Satan on earth. Here, then, it is Satan who heads the forces of evil, a figure known from Job and Zechariah. In other sources, this office is held by Belial, or "the prince of depravity." Second Temple Judaism also refers to (plural) Satans, though in later Christian thought there is only one.

The story of the fallen angels is not inherently tied to that of original sin. The angelic descent to earth and seduction of the human women occurred, after all, before the flood. But already in 1 Enoch we find (69.1) that one of these angels, Adriel (or Gaderel), had tempted Eve. In 2 Enoch (7.5) this motif is developed further, and Eve is tempted by Satan-El, the leader of the evil angels. According to the Book of Adam and Eve (17.4) Satan himself speaks to Eve through the serpent, the first identification of the two.

In Genesis Rabbah (48.9) we find a tradition that the Israelites brought the names of the angels with them from the Babylonian exile. It is unclear, however, whether this is a historically accurate report or perhaps a reflection of the fact that the belief in good and evil heavenly forces was prevalent in Babylonia since very early on. Even if the latter is the case, it is certainly possible that Second Temple Judaism was influenced by Persian religious thought with regard to angels (as well as other matters). The narrative of the Book of Tobit,[49] for example, which takes place in Persia and was apparently composed during the Persian period, recounts the story of the angel Raphael helping Tobias rescue his wife from the clutches of the demon Ashmodai. There is broad scholarly consensus that Ashmodai is a Persian name meaning "demon of fury." Perhaps we may discern here a trace of Persian dualism, the conflict between the angelic forces of light and the forces of darkness that include this "demon of fury." If so, the Book of Tobit bears witness to the Persian influence on Second Temple Jewish views concerning demons and angels. We should also mention that the idea of seven archangels parallels the seven immortal saints of Persian religion. Angels and evil spirits occupy an important place in the Qumran worldview as well, as does an overarching dualism that divides angels, spirits, and humanity into sons of light and sons of darkness — a division reminiscent of the Persian light-darkness dualism. That said, no proof has been uncovered for direct Persian influence on the Qumran community, and one might argue that the distinction between the righteous and the wicked is both typical and crucial to Judaism as a whole. Nonetheless, the similarity between the Qumran worldview and Persian religious thought is so great, that it is difficult to discount the possibility that such influence indeed existed. We know that there is some Persian influence on Jewish beliefs regarding the afterlife — it appears that the various beliefs in a "river of fire," including the idea that the dead are tested in such a river, has its roots in Persia. Persian religious texts speak explicitly of a river of fire that purifies the righteous but burns the wicked.[50] The Persians also believed in a resurrection of the dead, and there are scholars who argue that in this too Persia exercised its influence over Israel. For even if we admit that the belief in resurrection has biblical roots, it did not develop into a Jewish dogma until the Second Temple period, so that even if it was not lifted wholesale from the Persians it nonetheless developed under their influence. After all, Persian messengers and sages traveled throughout the ancient Near East and beyond it — especially during the Hellenistic period — spreading Persian teachings where they went. It is quite possible, then, that this was the only religious tradition to exercise a meaningful influence over Jewish doctrine.

49. See *Biblical Encyclopedia* (Hebrew), 3.367-375, s.v. ספר טוביה.

50. See C. M. Edsman, "Le Baptême de feu," *Acta Seminarii Neotestamentici Upsaliensis* 9 (Uppsala, 1940), as well as my "Baptism of John and the Dead Sea Sect."

All in all, we have seen that Judaism was re-mythologized, so to speak, during the Second Temple period, and that this dynamic may not have been due exclusively to internal forces. Rather, the transformation may have occurred as the result of an encounter with a religious tradition that is, on the one hand, very similar to Judaism, and, on the other, contains within it a spiritual mythology of sorts.

3. Jerusalem in Second Temple Literature

Our discussion of those aspects of Second Temple literature that express the Jewish hopes for the city's future, will not focus on the supernatural depiction of Jerusalem in the eschatological works of that period, nor on the idea of a heavenly Jerusalem, nor again on expressions of love for the city. Instead, we turn our gaze toward a group of texts that are, to my mind, of great interest but remain relatively unknown.

When Josephus discusses the Jewish constitutions (*AJ* 4.200-201 and see also *Contra Apion* 2.193 and Philo, *On the Special Laws* 1.67), he states that there will be one city in Canaan chosen by God as the site of a temple and an altar: "In no other city let there be either altar or temple; for God is one and the Hebrew race is one." This statement recalls the tripartite rallying cry of France under Louis XIV: "une foi, une loi, un roi." But it is more important to recall the sages' statement that the one God corresponds to His one people, Israel. This idea is expressed in the sublime words of the Sabbath afternoon prayer: "You are one and Your name is one and who is like Your nation Israel, a single nation upon the land." This was the view of Jews after the destruction of the temple and of Jerusalem. But while the temple and the city still stood, there were three singular entities: one God, one city, and one people. It is worth noting that according to the prevalent Jewish view of the time, there is no real distinction between the temple and Jerusalem. A vision composed in the days of Judah Maccabee and preserved in 1 Enoch (89.50-73)[1] provides a symbolic narrative of Jewish history in

1. See my essay, "Vision of Seventy Shepherds."

which Jerusalem is described as the "house" and the temple is described as the tower of the house.[2]

In Jewish circles, then, holiness is not limited to the temple proper,[3] but encompasses all of Jerusalem. At the same time, Jerusalem functions as a concrete realization of sorts of the Jewish people itself. The place of Torah, which is identified in what follows with wisdom, is, according to Ben Sira, Jerusalem (Ben Sira 24.1-12):

> Wisdom praises herself,
>   and tells of her glory in the midst of her people.
> In the assembly of the Most High she opens her mouth,
>   and in the presence of his hosts she tells of her glory:
> I came forth from the mouth of the Most High,
>   and covered the earth like a mist.
> I dwelt in the highest heavens,
>   and my throne was in a pillar of cloud.
> Alone I compassed the vault of heaven
>   and traversed the depths of the abyss.
> Over waves of the sea, over all the earth,
>   and over every people and nation I have held sway.
> Among all these places I sought a dwelling place;
>   in whose territory should I abide?
> Then the Creator of all things gave me a command,
>   and my Creator chose the place for my tent.
> He said, "Make your dwelling in Jacob,
>   and in Israel receive your inheritance."
> Before the ages, in the beginning he created me,
>   and for all the ages I shall not cease to be.

2. It is true that in 89.36 the temple itself is referred to as the "house." The statement in 90.28-29 and 35-36 most likely refers to the eschatological temple, rather than eschatological Jerusalem. The author was apparently inconsistent in his terminology. As a rule, the "house" symbolizes either the temple (or tabernacle) or Jerusalem, while the tower always refers to the temple. Therein lies the significance of the description of Enoch's ascent in the same passage (87.3): "Those [angels] which had come out last seized me by my hand and took me from the generations of the earth, lifted me up into a high place, and showed me a high tower above the earth, and all the hills stood beneath it." Thus, already in the days of Judah Maccabee there were those who believed in the existence of a heavenly temple. See also below, n. 63.

3. At the end of chapter nine of the minor tractate Derekh 'Eretz we find: "Abba Isi b. Yohanan in the name of Samuel the Small: The world is likened to a person's eyeball: the white of the eye [corresponds to] the ocean which surrounds the whole world; the iris to the inhabited world; the pupil of the eye to Jerusalem; the face in the pupil is the Temple, may it be rebuilt speedily in our days" (*The Minor Tractates of the Talmud*, 2.591-592).

In the holy tent I ministered to him,
    and so I was established in Zion.
Thus in the beloved city he gave me a dwelling place,
    and in Jerusalem was my domain.
I took root in an honored people,
    in the portion of the Lord, his heritage.

Ben Sira is the first witness to the view that Torah is identical to wisdom. The Ben Sira passage is also important because it alludes to the famous midrash according to which the Torah was first offered to all the nations. For the present argument, however, the key issue is that Ben Sira considers the Jerusalem temple to be the natural site of Torah, i.e., wisdom.

Another relevant passage is Ben Sira's eschatological prayer (36.11-14):

Gather all the tribes of Jacob
    and give them their inheritance, as at the beginning.
Have mercy, O LORD, on the people called by your name,
    on Israel, whom you have named your firstborn.
Have pity on the city of your sanctuary,
    Jerusalem, the place of your dwellings.
Fill Zion with majesty,
    and your temple with your glory.

We should note the two-fold nature of the main eschatological expectation: the renewal of Jerusalem and the ingathering of the exiles. The last verse of the Ben Sira passage draws on the prophecy of Haggai, who early in the Second Temple period heard the LORD say: ". . . and I will fill this house with glory, says the Lord of hosts. . . . The latter glory of this house shall be greater than the former, says the LORD of hosts" (Hag 2:7-9). It is important to emphasize that the expectation that Jerusalem would be rebuilt did not emerge following the destruction of the Second Temple, but the First. This expectation finds its fullest expression in the words of the consoling prophet known as Second Isaiah. We find there a brilliant supernatural description: "O afflicted one, storm-tossed, and not comforted, I am about to set your stones in antimony, and lay your foundations with sapphires. I will make your pinnacles of rubies, your gates of jewels, and all your wall of precious stones" (Isa 54:11-12). The rebuilding of the city and the temple during the return to Zion did not satisfy this hope. For the eschatological flames had been fanned following the first destruction, and, more importantly, the reality of Second Temple Jerusalem — city and edifice alike — did not match the glory of the

First Temple period. The eschatological fervor surrounding Jerusalem is already evident following the Hasmonean rededication of the temple; for example, in an apocalyptic work written in the days of Judah Maccabee and preserved in 1 Enoch, according to which, in the end of days, the temple will be transferred to the south, and God will lower from heaven a larger and more glorious temple in its place (1 Enoch 90.28-29). It is possible that the term "house" *(bayit)* refers here to the eschatological temple rather than Jerusalem as a whole.[4] For our purposes, the key element here is that the idea of the replacement of the temple — and of Jerusalem — did not come about as a result of the destruction of 70 c.e., or even out of a pre-70 fear for its destruction. The motif is early, and born of a messianic hope and expectation, for according to 1 Enoch, the current temple will not be destroyed at all, but moved to the south.[5]

It follows that the hope for an eschatological temple and city could not have subsided after Herod greatly expanded and glorified the temple. First, because the expectation had already taken root and, more importantly, because Herod himself, the great builder, was not considered worthy in the eyes of the people to be associated with the fulfillment of eschatological hopes.[6] And when, under the Roman yoke, the fates of Jerusalem and the temple were in doubt, the hope for the city's reconstruction grew that much stronger. The prophets of destruction, Jesus of Nazareth among them,[7] prophesied that the

---

4. See n. 2, above.

5. See D. Flusser, "Two Notes on the Midrash on 2 Sam, VII," *IEJ* 9 (1959), 99-104.

6. It is possible, of course, that pro-Herod ideologues sought to convince the public that Herod's construction was the fulfillment of these messianic hopes. It is worth noting the language that Herod uses, according to Josephus, before beginning the construction (*AJ* 15.385-387): "This was the temple which our fathers built to the Most Great God after their return from Babylon, but it lacks sixty cubits in height . . . but no one should condemn our fathers . . . for it was Cyrus and Darius, the son of Hystaspes, who prescribed these dimensions for the building, and since our fathers were subject to them and their descendants and after them to the Macedonians, they had no opportunity to restore this first archetype of piety to its former size. But since, by the will of God, I am now ruler and there continues to be a long period of peace and an abundance of wealth and great revenues, and — what is most important — the Romans, who are, so to speak, the masters of the world, are my loyal friends, I will try to remedy the oversight caused by the necessity and subjection of that earlier time, and by this act of piety make full return to God for the gift of this kingdom." If so, Herod alludes to the four kingdoms — Babylon, Persia, Greece and Rome — and links the construction of the glorious temple with the last of these. It is possible that Josephus is using a source that was more explicitly pro-Herodian. See in this regard, D. Flusser, "The Four Empires in the Fourth Sibyl and in the Book of Daniel," *Israel Oriental Studies* 5 (1972), 158-159.

7. See my "Two Notes on the Midrash on 2 Sam, VII." Jesus is the only pre-70 source to explicitly speak of the temple's destruction and rebuilding by non-human hands. As this view is

city and the temple would be rebuilt by God himself. This became a widely held view after the Romans destroyed the temple. So while the expectation that Jerusalem would be rebuilt underwent a number of transformations, its origins reach back to the destruction of the First Temple.

Ben Sira's oration concerning Jerusalem opens with the entreaty "have mercy" (Ben Sira 36.12), and this is no coincidence — this is the opening of the benediction for Jerusalem recited on the 9th of Av, the traditional date of the destruction of both temples. Thus we find in the Jerusalem Talmud (Berakhot 4.3, 8a): "Have mercy, O LORD our God, with your abundant mercies and faithful grace, on us and on your people Israel, and on your city Jerusalem and on Zion, the dwelling place of your glory. . . ."[8] Though the benediction goes on to speak of the city as "grieving, devastated, razed and destroyed," it is clear that the opening of the benediction preserved in the Jerusalem Talmud is a version of the Jerusalem blessings recited while the temple still stood.[9]

Here is the prayer for Jerusalem in the Eighteen Benedictions found in Rav Saadia Gaon's prayer book: "Have mercy, O LORD our God, on your people Israel, and on your city Jerusalem and on your sanctuary and on Zion, the dwelling place of your glory, and build up Jerusalem in your mercies. Blessed are You LORD, builder of Jerusalem." A somewhat different version of this blessing is famously found in the Jewish grace after meals: "Have mercy, O LORD our God, on your people Israel, and on your city Jerusalem and on Zion, the dwelling place of your glory, and on the kingship of the house of David, your anointed one, and on the great and holy house that bears your name . . . build up Jerusalem, the holy city, hastily in the present day. Blessed are you, Lord, builder of Jerusalem."[10] The phrase "build up Jerusalem, the holy city, hastily in the present day" has a parallel in the present liturgy of the Eighteen Benedictions: "Build it up soon, in the present day, as an eternal edifice." Today's accepted version opens with the words "and you shall return to your city, Jerusalem, with mercy, and shall dwell in it as you have spoken." If so, the blessing was altered to better fit the

---

widely attested after 70, we may infer that it was shared by other pre-70 seers of Jerusalem's downfall. Late Second Temple prophecies of destruction, prophecies that make no mention of a future rebuilding, are both numerous and well-attested.

8. On the different versions of the 9th of Av benediction for Jerusalem see I. Elbogen, *Jewish Liturgy: A Comprehensive History,* trans. Raymond P. Scheindlin (New York and Philadelphia, 1993), 48.

9. See Elbogen, *Der jüdische Gottesdienst* (Olms, 1962), 53.

10. On the benediction for Jerusalem according to Rav Saadia Gaon, see *Siddur Rav Saadia Gaon* (Jerusalem, 1963), 102, and see also 105.

post-70 reality than the "have mercy" benediction in the 9th of Av liturgy of the Palestinian Talmud.[11]

The ancient Jerusalem benediction, naturally, does not contain any reference to the destruction of the temple, but rather expresses a hope for a glorious future for both the temple and the city of Jerusalem. It is not concerned primarily with the present time, but with a messianic future. Though rarely noted, even the Jerusalem blessing in the Jewish grace after meals reflects a Second Temple reality. The same is true of the parallel in Ben Sira 36.11-12, which speaks of a future reality and is, moreover, part of a broader eschatological prayer. More evidence can be adduced. At the end of Ben Sira (51.21-35) we find a *hallel*, a psalm of praise, where God is called "he who builds his city and his temple." This section is part of the material appended after chapter 50, which was the original end of the book and is, indeed, not found in the Greek translation. We do not know when these addenda were composed, but it was undoubtedly pre-70, as the following verses clearly indicate (51.26-29, 33):

> Give thanks to him who gathers the dispersed of his people Israel,
> for his steadfast love endures forever.
> Give thanks to him who builds his city and his sanctuary,
> for his steadfast love endures forever.

---

11. The *nahem* ("console") blessing of the Ashkenazi 9th of Av liturgy shows no trace of the original Jerusalem benediction. The Jerusalem benedictions in the *Shemoneh Esreh* may be divided into four types: (A) The first is discussed in the body of the present essay, namely, a pre-70 blessing that opens with the words "have mercy." This type is attested in the Rav Saadia Gaon prayer book, in an ancient Palestinian liturgical passage preserved in the Cairo Genizah, and in the liturgy of the Jews of Persia, where we find the following: "Have mercy on us, O LORD our God, on us and on Israel your people and on Jerusalem your city and on Zion, the dwelling place of your glory, and build up Jerusalem as an eternal edifice as you have spoken. Blessed are you, LORD, builder of Jerusalem." (B) A second type that includes an additional phrase immediately before the mention of the future rebuilding of Jerusalem: "You shall reside within your city Jerusalem, as you have spoken." This benediction is found in the liturgy of the Jewish communities of Yemen, Spain, and in Maimonides' prayer book and reflects the language of Zechariah 8:3, "Thus says the Lord: I will return to Zion, and will dwell in the midst of Jerusalem." Though Zechariah refers to the future return to Jerusalem, the liturgy itself does not in any way suggest that it was composed after the destruction of the temple, and may indeed be a Second Temple text. (C) In other benedictions, before the mention of the future rebuilding of Jerusalem, we find: "Return in your mercies to your city, Jerusalem." This is attested in the liturgy of the Aleppo community, as well as Romania and Italy, and in the prayer book of Rav Amram Gaon, and expresses the post-destruction yearning of the Jewish people. (D) The Ashkenazi liturgy is a secondary composite of these earlier versions: "Return in your mercies to your city, Jerusalem, and you will reside in it as you have spoken."

> Give thanks to him who makes a horn to sprout for the house of David,
>   for his steadfast love endures forever.
> Give thanks to him who has chosen the sons of Zadok to be priests,
>   for his steadfast love endures forever. . . .
> Give thanks to him who has chosen Zion,[12]
>   for his steadfast love endures forever.

Both the hope for the building of Jerusalem and the conclusion "builder of Jerusalem" date from the Second Temple period. Moreover, the conclusion of the Jerusalem benediction is taken from Psalm 147:2, "The LORD builds up Jerusalem; he gathers the outcasts of Israel."

In today's liturgy, the Jerusalem benediction is followed by the benediction for the house of David, which opens with the words "cause the shoot of David. . . ."[13] This benediction is a later addition to the original liturgy, the nineteenth of the Eighteen Benedictions, which makes explicit reference to the messianic hope. But it is not a late addition: it is clear that it was recited in Second Temple Israel, as the opening of the prayer preserved in the first chapter of Luke indicates: "Blessed be the Lord God of Israel, for he has looked favorably on his people and redeemed them. He has raised up a mighty savior for us in the house of his servant David" (Luke 1:68-69). A comparison of this prayer with the benediction for the house of David supports the scholars that argue the latter is an ancient Palestinian composition. To this we must add the words of Ben Sira, cited above, "Give thanks to him who makes a horn to sprout for the house of David"! Ben Sira's language approximates Psalm 132:17, but, scholars have noted, there is also an affinity between Ben Sira's *hallel* and the Eighteen Benedictions.

A detailed justification of assumptions regarding the nature of the early Eighteen Benedictions lies beyond the purview of the present study. Suffice it to say that the changes in the liturgy of the *Shemoneh Esreh* came about as the result of the variation and the proliferation of benedictions, and that it is unlikely that the core of the liturgy underwent meaningful change after the Hasmonean period. The variation in question — potentially encompassing

---

12. Compare the Palestinian Talmud, Yoma 44b concerning the conclusions of the four blessings spoken by the high priest on Yom Kippur. In Ben Sira's *hallel* God is called "guardian of Israel" and "redeemer of Israel," while the high priest speaks of God "Who elects Israel." The conclusions of the high priest's benedictions, which parallel Ben Sira's *hallel*, are: "On the temple, Who elects the temple, and Rav Idi says, Who dwells in Zion . . . on the priests, who elects the priests."

13. The important witnesses of the Jerusalem Benediction can be found in J. Heinemann, *Prayer in the Tannaitic and Amoraic Period* (Hebrew) (Jerusalem, 1964), 48-51.

every local custom and every individual reciter — stems from the possibility of breaking down each liturgical unit into two or more discrete benedictions. Thus, the Tosefta states (t. Berakhot 3.25): "One may include the benediction of the *minim* in that of the separatists, and the benediction of the gentiles in that of the elders, and the benediction of David in that of Jerusalem. And if one said each as a blessing unto itself, he has fulfilled his legal obligation." Indeed, the early Palestinian liturgy, attested in the piyyutim and the Genizah, contains no free-standing "shoot of David" *(tzemah david)* benediction, as the Jerusalem benediction concludes, "Blessed are you, Lord, God of David, builder of Jerusalem." As noted, it appears the tradition of reciting the "builder of Jerusalem" and "shoot of David" benedictions was already in place pre-70. If so, the phrase "God of David, builder of Jerusalem" is a secondary composite; the Jerusalem benediction originally referred only to the building of Jerusalem, making no mention of the belief in the coming of the Messiah. The growing/yearning for messianic redemption was channeled into the Eighteen Benedictions in two ways: the phrase "God of David" was incorporated into the conclusion of the Jerusalem benediction, and a new benediction, "shoot of David," was then added (as noted, a phrase already attested in Luke's gospel). But this is not the end of the process. Though in today's liturgy the benedictions for Jerusalem and "shoot of David" are separate, the Ashkenazi and Sephardi versions of the former refer to the Messiah: "Establish with haste the throne of David within it [= Jerusalem]." The increased yearning for the coming of the Messiah is further evident in comparing the *Shemoneh Esreh* of Rav Saadia Gaon with the Jerusalem benediction in the grace after meals. The former makes no mention of the Messiah, since the subsequent blessing is devoted to precisely this topic. But the Jerusalem benediction in the grace speaks of "the reign of the house of David, your messiah."[14] The upshot of all this is that the ancient liturgy gave voice to the Jewish hope that Jerusalem be built (or rebuilt), but was silent regarding Jewish messianic expectations. There are, famously, Second Temple eschatological works that make no mention of the coming of the Messiah. I will argue below that certain passages in the Book of Tobit indicate there were pre-70 texts that discussed the building of Jerusalem but not the Messiah. If so, it is no wonder that the *Shemoneh Esreh* once referred to the building of Jerusalem while maintaining its silence with regard to the Messiah.

It remains for us to discuss the Eighteen Benedictions liturgy. We have

---

14. The "have mercy" blessing that concludes the grace does express messianic yearnings. But the version in Saadia Gaon's grace contains the phrase "May you reestablish the kingdom of the House of David in our days" (p. 102).

already cited Tosefta Berakhot 3.25 and cannot here unpack the full meaning of this passage. Saul Lieberman, in his commentary on the Tosefta, writes: "thus we learn that this blessing was originally aimed against the *perushim*, the separatists . . . individuals who sought to break away from the community . . . in times of trouble and turbulence. . . . This execration was aimed at the sects and the individuals who threatened the nation's solidarity. The benediction against the separatists existed long before Shmuel the Lesser, but he *fixed* its liturgy so as to explicitly refer to the *minim* since they began to pose just such a threat."[15] Incidentally, the Tosefta passage suggests that the opponents of the sages early on referred to them as *perushim*, separatists (but also as "Pharisees"), no doubt to portray them as a sectarian splinter group. But it seems to me that Lieberman has not adequately defined the groups against which Birkat ha-Minim was aimed. For we find in Tractate Semahot 2.8: "Regarding those who separate from the community, and fashion themselves free of commandments, and respect for holy days, and attendance at synagogue and houses of study, and the *minim* and the apostates and the informants, not only do we not mourn them, but rather (upon their death) their relatives will rejoice and wear white clothing, and hold a feast, since one who hates the Lord has died. As it is written: 'Do I not hate those who hate you, O Lord? And do I not loathe those who rise up against you? I hate them with perfect hatred; I count them my enemies.'" The same verse is cited in Avot de Rabbi Natan (version A, §16): "But hate the sectarians, apostates, and informers . . . if he acts as your people do, thou shalt love him; but if not, thou shalt not love him."[16] Of particular interest for the history of this benediction is the list of the wicked found in Tosefta Sanhedrin 13.5: "the *minim*, the apostates, the informers, and the heretics, as well as those who deny the Torah and separate themselves from the community and deny the resurrection of the dead. . . ."[17] All this suggests that the terms *minim*, informants, and "those who separate from the community" (in the Tosefta: *perushim*, separatists) populate lists of those worthy of hatred, that is, those who do not merit the commandment "Thou shalt love thy neighbor as thyself." Note also the contrast between the separatists and one who "acts as your people do." Taken together, this pair al-

---

15. See Lieberman in his commentary *ad loc.*, 54.

16. *The Fathers According to Rabbi Nathan*, translated by Judah Goldin (New Haven, 1955), 87. See also b. Shabbat 116a; A. Büchler, *Studies in Sin and Atonement*, 31-32, n. 1.

17. Note too the Yemenite version of Birkat ha-Minim, which begins "May the apostates have no hope, and all the *minim* and the informants instantly perish." The term "informants" (*moserim*) is also found in the liturgy of the Jewish communities of Romania and Aleppo. On this topic see Flusser, "4QMMT and the Benediction Against the *Minim*," in *Judaism of the Second Temple Period: Qumran and Apocalypticism*, 70-118.

ludes to Isaiah 8:11: "For the Lord spoke thus to me while his hand was strong upon me, and removed me *(ve-yassireni)* from walking in the way of this people." To be sure, the MT reads *ve-yissreni*, that is, 'he warned me,' but the reading "removed me" is reflected in the Greek translations, and is the reading attested in the complete Isaiah scroll discovered at Qumran. We see, then, that the Qumran community considered this verse — in its non-Masoretic form — as a biblical justification for their break with mainstream Judaism. The community defined itself as "the sons of Zadok, the priests, and the men of their covenant who have turned away from the path of the nation" (1Q28a [= 1QRule of the Congregation] 1.2-3) or as "the congregation of all the sons of justice, those who establish the covenant, those who avoid walking on the path of the people" (11Q13 [= 11QMelchizedek] 2.24).[18] The Essenes, then, were proud of having broken with the way of the Jewish people. Translated from biblical to Second Temple idiom, they were proud to have separated themselves from the community — just like the separatists who are contrasted with those who "act as your people do." Both phrases, it seems, can be traced to a sectarian interpretation of Isaiah 8:11, adopted by the Essenes and perhaps by other separatist groups. The phrase "those who separate themselves from the community," the *perushim*, took on an extremely negative meaning for the anti-separatists, and was eventually incorporated into a benediction against separatists, *minim*, and informants. Ironically, the benediction was ushered into the liturgy by the very group known as *perushim*, the Pharisees!

If Birkat ha-Minim is linked to the Essenes, the benediction that precedes it is aimed against the Sadducees.[19] According to Rav Saadia Gaon, just prior to the prayer's conclusion there appeared the phrase "Return our judges as before and our advisors as in earlier days" (based on Isaiah 1:26), to which the Palestinian liturgy appends "and rule over us, You alone."[20] Now, another brief prayer, "Instruct us" (הבינינו) refers to "those who err."[21] Even if "Instruct us" is not a witness to an earlier version of the benediction, it indicates how the benediction was once understood. Historically, "those who err" can only be the Sadducees. They, after all, refused to judge according to the Oral Torah, and this appears to be the core issue for the benediction.

If so, "Return our judges" and Birkat ha-Minim were aimed at two Jewish groups, casting both in a negative light. A third benediction, "The Bene-

18. See Flusser, "Pharisees, Sadducees, and Essenes in Pesher Nahum," *Judaism of the Second Temple Period: Qumran and Apocalypticism*, 225-226.

19. My thanks to Prof. Shmuel Safrai for this insight.

20. See the discussion in Elbogen, *Jewish Liturgy*, 45.

21. "Instruct us" is found in b. Berakhot 29a.

diction of the Righteous,"[22] reads: "For your righteous and your holy, and for the converts who put their trust in You. Give us and give them a good reward with those who do your will in the Land of Israel, a support and safe haven for the righteous." Aside from the general terms "righteous" and "proselytes,"[23] the benediction deals with prominent groups within Pharisaic Judaism: the *Hasidim*, the elders, and the scribes, i.e., the sages. If so, these three benedictions proceed as follows: "Return" originally addressed the Sadducees, expressing the hope that they will judge according to the correct halakhah; Birkat ha-Minim attacks the separatists and was once aimed against the Essenes, whose separatist ideology is now well attested in the Dead Sea Scrolls; the third benediction petitions for God's mercy for the Pharisees and mentions the most prominent Pharisee groups. The three benedictions, then, are tied to the three groups Josephus repeatedly mentions: the Sadducees, the Essenes, and the Pharisees. Elsewhere,[24] I have shown that this tripartite division is attested in the Dead Sea Scrolls as well. The three benedictions were incorporated into the Eighteen Benedictions in the late Hasmonean period. This is evident from the fact that the benediction preceding them concludes with "who gathers the dispersed of his people Israel" while the benediction that follows concludes with "the builder of Jerusalem"; both are based on Psalm 147:2: "The LORD builds up Jerusalem; he gathers the outcasts of Israel."

However, the primary goal of the preceding analysis is not to establish

---

22. On which, see Elbogen, *Jewish Liturgy,* 45-46. It seems to me that the sources Elbogen cites indicate that the conclusion of the benediction is a composite of later versions and, moreover, that some of these versions shortened the list of figures enumerated. The scribes, for example, referred to in the phrase "the remnant of their scribes," are omitted in many versions, even though the phrase is attested in Megillat Ta'anit: "On the seventeenth (of Adar) the nations rose against the remnant of the scribes in the land of Chalcis in the house of Zabdi, and there was salvation," and see also the comments that follow in Megillat Ta'anit. The event in question took place in the days of Alexander Jannaeus.

23. It may be that proselytes were not mentioned in the original version. Recall the language of t. Berakhot 3.25: "One may include the benediction of the *minim* in that of the separatists, and the benediction of the gentiles in that of the elders, and the benediction of David in that of Jerusalem. And if one said each as a blessing unto itself, he has fulfilled his legal obligation." We saw above that Birkat ha-Minim was originally aimed against the separatists, and that Shmuel the Lesser fixed its current format. We further saw that the Eighteen Benedictions did not originally make any reference to the Messiah. These were only later included in the benediction for Jerusalem or in a separate blessing. A similar dynamic may be at play with regard to the proselytes in Birkat ha-Tzaddiqim. Moreover, unlike the *Hasidim,* the elders, and the scribes, the proselytes are not an institution of Pharisaic Judaism. It was only when the status of proselytes became prominent in mainstream Jewish thought that they were incorporated into Birkat ha-Tzaddiqim, or became the subject of a separate benediction.

24. Flusser, "Pharisees, Sadducees, and Essenes in Pesher Nahum."

the time and sense of the three benedictions that appear between "who gathers the dispersed" and "the builder of Jerusalem." We have managed to show that before the late Hasmonean period, these two benedictions were consecutive, and that the early *Shemoneh Esreh* did not mention the Messiah. Proceeding with this line of argument, we may state that the yearnings for the building of Jerusalem and the ingathering of exiles are the only eschatological petitions in the original Eighteen Benedictions. "Shoot of David" did not exist, and the remaining benedictions have no eschatological force. It is true that the yearning for redemption caused eschatological motifs to be incorporated in other benedictions — a complicated process that we cannot fully address here. Suffice it to say that the *gevurot*, the second section of the Eighteen Benedictions, once concluded with a statement about "the mighty God," or "master of mighty deeds." If the benediction spoke of God as "mighty," "who resurrects the dead," and "who is great in redemption," it appears that the resurrection of the dead here refers to salvation from a disease or danger. It would appear, then, that the conclusion "who resurrects the dead" was introduced by the Pharisees as an eschatological polemic against the Sadducees, who denied the resurrection of the dead.[25] Similarly, the benediction of redemption *(birkat ha-ge'ulah)*, the seventh of the Eighteen Benedictions, originally referred to redemption from trials and tribulations, not to an eschatological event.[26]

Indeed, from the destruction of the First Temple, when Jerusalem was razed and the majority of the Jewish people went into exile (a condition that still holds today), the main hopes of the people revolved around the building of Jerusalem and the ingathering of exiles. These twin hopes are maintained in Ben Sira's *hallel* ("Give thanks to him who gathers the dispersed of his people Israel. . . . Give thanks to him who builds his city and his sanctuary"), a composition whose exact date is not established and may be tied to the Eighteen Benedictions, and to the text of Ben Sira 36.11-14. There too the author asks for the ingathering of exiles and immediately turns to petition for mercy on Israel and the Jerusalem temple. A clear example of the link between these two motifs is found in 4 Ezra 4.36–5.9:

> Look about thee, O Jerusalem, towards the east, and behold the joy that cometh to thee from God. For behold thy children come, whom thou sentest away scattered, they come gathered together from the east even to

25. See Elbogen, *Jewish Liturgy*, 45-46.

26. See Elbogen, *Jewish Liturgy*, 46. Even the current version of this benediction contains only one word with clear eschatological meaning, "immediately," that is absent from the Palestinian liturgy.

the west, at the word of the Holy One rejoicing for the honour of God. Put off, O Jerusalem, the garment of thy mourning, and affliction: and put on the beauty, and honour of that everlasting glory which thou hast from God. . . . Arise, O Jerusalem, and stand on high: and look about towards the east, and behold thy children gathered together from the rising to the setting sun, by the word of the Holy One rejoicing in the remembrance of God. For they went out from thee on foot, led by the enemies: but the Lord will bring them to thee exalted with honour as children of the kingdom.

Some scholars point to the affinity between the late sections of the Book of Baruch, which include the passage just cited, and the Psalms of Solomon, a work composed in response to Pompey's conquest of Jerusalem in 63 B.C.E. And here too we find the conjunction of the two motifs — building the city and ingathering of exiles — most prominently in Psalm 11: "Sound in Zion the signal trumpet of the sanctuary; announce in Jerusalem the voice of one bringing good news, for God has been merciful to Israel in watching over them. Stand on a high place, Jerusalem, and look at your children, from the east and the west assembled together by the Lord" (Psalm 11.1-2). The good news of the psalm is summarized in verses 8 and 9: "May the Lord do what he has spoken in the name of his glory. May the mercy of the Lord be upon Israel forevermore."[27] According to Psalm 17 (vv. 28-35), both events are performed by the Messiah. The author of the Psalms of Solomon introduces a third eschatological motif which, while already well-established as an independent motif, comes to be linked in Second Temple literature with the two events under discussion. Namely, that the nations of the world will recognize the God of Israel and come to Jerusalem: "And he (the Messiah) will have gentile nations serving him under his yoke, and he will glorify the Lord in (a place) prominent (above) the whole earth. And he will purge Jerusalem and make it holy as it was even from the beginning, for nations to come from the ends of the earth to see his glory, to bring as gifts her children who had been driven out, and to see the glory of the Lord with which God has glorified her" (Psalms of Solomon 17.30-31).

The same three motifs are also intertwined in the Book of Tobit, one of the earliest post-biblical Jewish books (excluding Daniel, which is biblical but later). It appears the Book of Tobit was composed as early as the Persian period.[28] The book contains two eschatological passages. The first is the

---

27. The ingathering of exiles is further discussed at 8.34.

28. See s.v. ספר טוביה in the *Biblical Encyclopedia;* Y. M. Grintz, *Studies in the Second Temple Period* (Hebrew) (Jerusalem, 1969), 49-66; J. Lebram, "Die Weltreiche in der jüdischen

thanksgiving prayer of Tobit, the father of Tobias, in chapter 13 where he sees the exile as a divine punishment but one that leads to redemption:

> He will afflict you for your iniquities, but he will again show mercy on all of you. He will gather you from all the nations among whom you have been scattered. If you turn to him with all your heart and with all your soul, to do what is true before him. Then he will turn to you and will no longer hide his face from you . . . and his tabernacle will be rebuilt in you in joy. . . .[29] A bright light will shine to all the ends of the earth; many nations will come to you from far away, the inhabitants of the remotest parts of the earth to your holy name, bearing gifts in their hands for the King of heaven. Generation after generation will give joyful praise in you, the name of the chosen city will endure forever. . . . Go, then, and rejoice over the children of the righteous for they will be gathered together and will praise the Lord of the ages. . . . For Jerusalem will be built as his house for all ages. How happy I will be if a remnant of my descendants should survive to see your glory and acknowledge the King of heaven. The gates of Jerusalem will be built with sapphire and emerald, and all your walls with precious stones. The towers of Jerusalem will be built with gold and their battlements with pure gold. The streets of Jerusalem will be paved with ruby and the stones of Ophir. The gates of Jerusalem will sing hymns of joy, and all her houses will cry, Hallelujah!

In Tobit's prayer, which the narrative sets before the destruction of the First Temple, there is no clear distinction between the return to Zion and the eschatological events. This despite the fact that Tobit does allude to such a difference when he states, "How happy I will be if a remnant of my descendants should survive to see your glory and acknowledge the King of heaven." This conceptual blurring is not unexpected in a chapter that is mostly poetry. Not so in his concluding words in chapter 14, which constitute a clearly enunciated and methodic historical survey that includes the end of days.

The second eschatological passage is the concluding words of Tobit in chapter 14.4-7. Tobit knows that . . .

> All of our kindred, inhabitants of the land of Israel, will be scattered and taken as captives from the good land; and the whole land of Israel will be desolate, even Samaria and Jerusalem will be desolate. And the temple of

Apokalyptik: Bemerkungen zu Tobit 14.4-7," *ZAW* 76 (1964), 328-331; and Albright's comments in *Bibliotheca Orientalis* 17 (1960), 42.

29. This passage exhibits a literary affinity to Jubilees 1.13-18.

God in it will be burned to the ground, and it will be desolate for a while. But God will again have mercy on them, and God will bring them back into the land of Israel; and they will rebuild the temple of God, but not like the first one, until the period when the times of fulfillment shall come. After this they all will return from their exile and will rebuild Jerusalem in splendor; and in it the temple of God will be rebuilt, just as the prophets of Israel have said concerning it. Then the nations in the whole world will all be converted and worship God in truth. They will all abandon their idols, which deceitfully have led them into their error; and in righteousness they will praise the eternal God. All the Israelites who are saved in those days and are truly mindful of God will be gathered together; they will go to Jerusalem and live in safety forever in the land of Abraham, and it will be given over to them. Those who sincerely love God will rejoice, but those who commit sin and injustice will vanish from the earth.

The portrait that emerges is unambiguous. After the destruction of Jerusalem and the temple, there will be a return to Zion that culminates in the construction of a new temple that will be unlike its predecessor. At this point the author breaks with the familiar historical developments and proceeds to describe the eschatological future. The Second Temple will be unlike the First until the very end of days. Only then, in the end of days, will the temple be erected in its full glory. Then also will all the Jewish exiles return to Jerusalem, the city and temple be rebuilt in accordance with the words of the prophets, and nations of the world will abandon their idolatrous customs and recognize the true God of Israel. Though the author mentioned the coming of the nations to Jerusalem in chapter 13, he does not do so here. Israel will inhabit its land forever; those who love God will prosper, while the wicked will be wiped out.

Chapter 14 of the Book of Tobit is the most important eschatological text outside the biblical canon from the period preceding the Maccabees. The discussion of the incoming of exiles and the building up of the temple and Jerusalem is reminiscent of the Book of Baruch, Ben Sira, and early versions of the *Shemoneh Esreh* liturgy, none of which mention the advent of the Messiah (or Messiahs). The earliest work to do so — and here it is two Messiahs, apparently one of the house of David, the other of the house of Joseph — is from the time of Judah the Maccabee (1 Enoch 90.37-38).[30] The work in question discusses the eschatological battles (90.19); God sitting in final judgment

---

30. See my article "Seventy Shepherds, Visions," in the *Encyclopaedia Judaica*.

(90.20-27); the construction of the eschatological temple (90.28-29); the ingathering of exiles and global acceptance of the kingship of God (90.30-33); the ultimate redemption (90.36-37); and, at the very end, the two Messiahs. The events unfold in a most unusual order. All three motifs — Jerusalem is built up, the exiled communities return to Israel, and the nations accept the kingship of God — are present, but the two Messiahs appear only at the end of the process and have no defined role.

The second document presents a different picture, as the messianic ideal plays a significant role in it. I am referring to the early stratum of the third book of the Sibylline Oracles, composed in Egypt in roughly 140 B.C.E. Here too we find a discussion of the return to Zion, with all of Israel securely established around the temple of the great God, and the nations of the world abandoning their idolatry and believing in the Lord.

It appears, then, that there are no extant documents from the period following Haggai and Zechariah and prior to the Maccabees that mention the Messiah, but only the two pillars of eschatological national redemption — the rebuilding of Jerusalem and the ingathering of exiles. This absence may be due to the frustrated messianic hopes associated with the figure of Zerubavel. But whatever the reason, it is clear that the ideals of a built-up Jerusalem and ingathered exiles play a much more important role than that of an individual messianic figure.

The most important document that links Jerusalem and the ingathering of exiles was composed by Judah Maccabee himself a few days before the rededication of the temple. I am referring to the letter preserved in 2 Maccabees 1.10–2.18, sent by "the people of Jerusalem and of Judea and the senate and Judas, to Aristobulus, who is of the family of the anointed priests, teacher of King Ptolemy, and to the Jews in Egypt" (2 Macc 1.10), requesting that the Jews of Egypt join in celebrating the dedication of the temple. This letter met with a strange fate. In 1933, an important scholar devoted half a page to this document and determined that it is a forgery,[31] a view accepted by other scholars. On what grounds did he make this assertion? The opening saluta-

---

31. E. Bickermann, "Ein jüdischer Festbrief vom Jahre 124 v. Chr (II Macc. 1,1-9)," *ZNW* 32 (1933), 233-254. The document in question is discussed in part of page 234. As for the letter to which he devoted this study, Bickermann proposes a historical and theological reading of its opening (2 Macc. 1.2-6), without realizing that this passage was not composed in any fixed historical situation, but rather is liturgical, part of the prayer that begins with the words "And a redeemer shall come to Zion" (*qedusha de-sidra*). This was already recognized by D. M. M. Sluys, *De Maccabaeorum libris I-II quaestiones* (Amsterdam, 1904), 62. See also, F. M. Abel, *Les livres des Maccabées* (Paris, 1949); D. Flusser, "Sanktus und Gloria," *Abraham unser Vater. Festschrift für Otto Michel* (Leiden, 1963), 289.

tion is a Greek phrase *(chairein kai hygiainein)* meaning "greetings and good health" and parallels the Hebrew *shalom u-verakhah*. Now, according to Bickermann, this salutation is not attested until roughly the year 60 B.C.E., and remained current until the last quarter of the first century C.E. It is methodologically questionable to date a document — and in this case a copy, not the original — by the fact that it opens with *shalom u-verakhah* rather than *shalom*. In this case, however, even the facts are wrong: the same Greek phrase is already attested in an epistle from the fourth century B.C.E.![32]

A more substantive argument against the authenticity of Judah's letter might be that in it he discusses the death of Antiochus IV (2 Macc. 2.13-17), while 1 Maccabees places his death only after the rededication of the temple. But this simply means that we have conflicting accounts of Antiochus IV's death, and it is for scholars to determine which is historically true. As it happens, there are historical reasons to prefer the chronology of 2 Maccabees: "Some argued against this book that it wrongly placed the death of Antiochus IV (chapter 9) prior to the purification of the temple (10.1-8), whereas in 1 Maccabees the order is reversed . . . but now we have discovered that news of the death of Antiochus reached Babylonia no later than December of 164 B.C.E., meaning that he died some time before that date. Since the temple was purified in *Kislev* [which corresponds to December] of that year, it now appears the account of 2 Maccabees is historically plausible."[33] If news of the death of Antiochus reached Babylonia no later than December of 164, it is no wonder that Judah learned of the fact shortly before the dedication — he and his colleagues were very interested in the fate of Antiochus. In short, the claim that the letter is a forgery is odd; 2 Maccabees' claim that Antiochus died before the rededication of the temple is reasonable, and there is no reason to doubt that the letter was authored by Judah Maccabee. Having established that, we may now turn to the actual words of Judah Maccabee concerning the purification of the temple and the future ingathering of exiles (2 Macc 2.16-18):

> Since, therefore, we are about to celebrate the purification, we write to you. Will you therefore please keep the days? It is God who has saved all

32. See the references in H. G. Liddell, R. Scott, *A Greek-English Lexicon* (Oxford, 1842).

33. Menahem Stern, *Documents concerning the Maccabean Revolt* [Hebrew] (Tel Aviv, 1965), 21-22, and see also 57. Stern continues: "It is also possible that the news [of Antiochus's death] reached Israel only after the dedication was complete, thus explaining the chronological order of 1 Maccabees." This suggestion must, however, be rejected since Judah knew of Antiochus's death before the dedication of the temple. Stern adopted this position because he was misled by Bickermann's essay, stating (p. 19) that the letter is a "fiction."

his people, and has returned the inheritance to all, and the kingship and the priesthood and the consecration, as he promised through the law. We have hope in God that he will soon have mercy on us and will gather us from everywhere under heaven into his holy place, for he has rescued us from great evils and has purified the place.[34]

This, then, is the true miracle of Hanukkah: God saved his people from great harm, and purified the temple. We find here the "double causality" so typical of Jewish religious thought: God redeemed his nation and purified the temple, but these acts were, all the same, performed by Judah Maccabee and his cohorts. The passage further clarifies the ultimate goal for the dedication of the temple: Judah hoped it would usher in a new era in the history of the Jewish people. Up to that point, the Jews of Israel and of the Diaspora lived under foreign rule, the Jerusalem priesthood was corrupt, and the temple defiled. Now God's promises to Israel had been fulfilled. Our author emphasizes that the dedication of the temple constitutes divine redemption for Israel as a whole; the redemption is not limited to the Jews of Jerusalem and Judah, but to the entire nation, including the Jews of Egypt — the letter's addressees — who share in the divine patrimony.[35] In other words, Judah suggests that the rededication of the temple represents partial independence for all Jews.

The rededication of the Second Temple brought about important gains in other areas too: the Hellenized priesthood were driven out and the authentic priesthood reinstated, and, now cleansed of impurity, the temple was once again a sanctified site for the nation as a whole — a symbol of national unity as well as the resting place of God's presence and a site of pilgrimage. But Judah Maccabee went one step further, asserting that the dedication of the temple was a preliminary step toward the fulfillment of the biblical promise of the ingathering of exiles: "for [God] has rescued us from great evils and has purified the place." In addition to the fulfillment of the divine promise concerning the national inheritance, the kingship, and the priesthood, the rededication of the temple began the fulfillment of the ingathering of exiles. It seems to me that Judah is not calling on his Egyptian brethren to immigrate to Israel, primarily because of the challenges such a move would present to the immigrants, and the additional difficulties the Egyptian authorities might

34. An excellent Hebrew commentary on this passage is found in A. Hartum, *The Apocryphal Books: 2 Maccabees* (Tel Aviv, 1959), 13-14.

35. The author here refers to kingship, though he employs (perhaps knowingly) an imprecise Greek term, *basileion* (something that pertains to kingship) and not *basileia*. *Basileion* can also mean "capital city," though that does not fit the context. The letter was likely written in Greek as it is addressed, *inter alios,* to Aristobulus, a Jewish scribe who wrote in Greek.

impose. Judah, like all Jews, understood the ingathering of exiles as a future event, like the other divine promises — some of which were fulfilled with the rededication of the temple. As such, it is safe to say that Judah Maccabee understood the latter event as, in some sense, eschatological or at least as a harbinger of redemption.

The importance of the passage under discussion, then, lies in the light it sheds on Judah Maccabee's actions. Some scholars have characterized them as purely religious or cultic, but Judah Maccabee did not distinguish between abstract religious matters and the political-national enterprise (a position that guided his actions throughout his life). For the purposes of the present discussion, note that, like other sources, Judah Maccabee's epistle closely links the Jerusalem temple and the ingathering of exiles.

There is no need to recount the yearning for Jerusalem's redemption that awakened within the Jewish nation after the city came under the rule of the Romans. The hope for redemption finds its expression in, among others, the Gospel of Luke. There we are told that Jesus' parents brought the infant to the temple, where two elderly people, inspired by the Holy Spirit, recognized that the baby was the future redeemer of Israel: "Now there was a man in Jerusalem whose name was Simeon; this man was righteous and devout, looking forward to the consolation of Israel, and the Holy Spirit rested on him. It had been revealed to him by the Holy Spirit that he would not see death before he had seen the Lord's Messiah" (Luke 2:25-26). Here "the consolation of Israel" clearly refers to the hope for a future redemption.[36] Luke goes on to tell of "a prophet, Anna the daughter of Phanuel, of the tribe of Asher" who, as Simeon was praising the child, "began to praise God and to speak about the child to all who were looking for the redemption of Jerusalem" (Luke 2:38). According to Luke, then, Simeon was one of those "looking forward to the consolation of Israel," while Anna was "looking for the redemption of Jerusalem" — phrases that are essentially identical. The "redemption of Jerusalem" is reminiscent of the language on the coinage of the two revolts: "the liberty of Zion" and "for the redemption of Zion" from the revolt of 70 C.E., and "for the liberty of Jerusalem" from the Bar Kosiba revolt. Luke provides indirect evidence for the existence of pious groups who sat in Jerusalem awaiting consolation, i.e., awaiting the redemption of Jerusalem. Another witness to this phenomenon is found in the Psalm Scroll of Qumran (11QPsalms 22.2-8):

36. This is also the meaning of *nehamah*, "consolation," in rabbinic Hebrew, e.g., in the phrase "let me see the consolation" attributed to Rabbi Shimon ben Shetah and Yehudah ben Tabbai (b. Makkot 5b; b. Sanhedrin 37b), and to Rabbi Elazar ben Zadok, who lived during the destruction of the temple.

Great is your hope, O Zion;
    Peace will come and the expectation of your salvation.
Generation after generation shall dwell in you,
    and generations of the devout shall be your splendor.
Those hungering for the day of your salvation
    and who rejoice in the abundance of your glory. . . .
How they have waited for your salvation;
    how your perfect ones have mourned for you!

We now turn to hopes of a different kind, hopes spurred on by fear for the continued existence of the Jews in the Land of Israel and in Jerusalem, their capital. Many Jews interpreted the words of the biblical prophets to mean that the eschatological battles would be fought in Israel. Still, there were those who believed that Jerusalem itself would not be harmed.

In 1 Enoch, chapters 37–71, we find a composition attributed to the biblical Enoch — a composition not attested in the Qumran library — that deals, *inter alia,* with a messianic figure known as "the Son of Man" *(bar enash).* Some scholars have suggested that the absence of this part of Enoch from the Dead Sea Scrolls fragments, along with the New Testament identification of the Son of Man with Jesus, indicates that the composition is Christian.[37] However, the Son of Man appears in Jewish texts, such as the Book of Daniel. Moreover, the Enoch composition has no Christian traits. And its absence from the Dead Sea Scrolls may be due to its adoption of the lunar calendar, while the Qumran community was opposed to the lunar calendar, preferring its own solar calendar that is alluded to in other parts of 1 Enoch. Consider, by way of example, 1 Enoch 41.8: "Surely the many changes of the sun have (both) a blessing and a curse, and the course of the moon's path is light to the righteous but darkness to the sinners, in the name of the Lord of the Spirits, who created the distinction between light and darkness and separated the spirits of the people, and strengthened the spirits of the righteous in the name of his righteousness." If so, the dualism of light and darkness, righteous and wicked, is common to this part of 1 Enoch and to the Qumran writings, but the lunar calendar is here accepted, whereas the Qumranites reject it outright. Also, 1 Enoch 51.1 speaks of resurrection, while the Essenes apparently believed in the eternity of the soul, but not in resurrection.[38]

One scholar has suggested, rightly, that the passage concerning the

---

37. See J. T. Milik, *Dix ans des découvertes dans le desert de Juda* (Paris, 1957), 31.

38. See Y. Grintz, *Studies in the Second Temple Period* (Hebrew) (Jerusalem, 1969), 120-121 and 130-132. I differ slightly from Grintz.

Parthian and Mede invasion of Israel (see below) is reminiscent of the Herodian period (40-38 B.C.E.), and he suggests the composition dates to the days of Herod, or Herod's successor, Archelaus, or the Roman consuls.[39] This hypothesis may be further strengthened. In one of the passages (67.8-10), the author speaks of hot water springs:

> Those waters shall become in those days a poisonous drug of the body and a punishment of the spirit unto the kings, rulers, and exalted ones, and those who dwell on the earth; lust shall fill their souls so that their bodies shall be punished, for they have denied the Lord of the Spirits; they shall see their own punishment every day but cannot believe in his name. In proportion to the great degree of the burning of their bodies will be the transmutation of their spirits forever and ever and ever, for there is no one that can speak a nonsensical word before the Lord of the Spirits. So the judgment shall come upon them, because they believe in the debauchery of their bodies and deny the spirit of the Lord.

The insistent language of this passage indicates that the author here alludes to a specific event, most likely Herod's trip to the hot springs of Callirhoe at the time of his final illness.[40] If so, the work in question was written toward the end of Herod's life, or some time after his death. Its author was sympathetic to the Qumran community, but not one of its members.

As noted, the subsequent passage (1 Enoch 56.5-8) may well reflect the Parthian invasion of Israel in the early days of Herod, though here the battle is situated in the eschatological future:

> In those days, the angels will assemble and thrust themselves to the east at the Parthians and Medes. They will shake up the kings (so that) a spirit of unrest shall come upon them, and stir them up from their thrones; and they will break forth from their beds like lions and like hungry hyenas among their own flocks. And they will go up and trample upon the land of my elect ones, and the land of my elect ones will be before them like a threshing floor or a highway. But the city of my righteous ones will become an obstacle to their horses. And they shall begin to fight among themselves; and (by) their own right hands they shall prevail against themselves. A man shall not recognize his brother, nor a son his mother,

---

39. E. Sjöberg, *Der Menschensohn im Äthiopischen Henochbuch* (Lund, 1946), 39. See also I. C. Hindley, "Towards a Date for the Similitudes of Enoch," *NTS* 14 (1967), 551-565. The latter dates the work to Trajan's war against the Parthians, but fails to convince.

40. Already suggested by R. H. Charles, *The Apocrypha and Pseudepigrapha* (Oxford, 1923), 2.232.

until there shall be a (significant) number of corpses among them. Their punishment is (indeed) not in vain. In those days, Sheol shall open her mouth, and they shall be swallowed up into it and perish. (Thus) Sheol shall swallow up the sinners in the presence of the elect ones.

From this description it follows that in the end of days the Parthians and Medes will invade Israel and overrun it, but they will not conquer Jerusalem. The city will stand as an obstacle for their horses, and the enemy armies will destroy each other as a result of infighting:

And it happened afterward that I had another vision of a whole array of chariots loaded with people; and they were advancing upon the air from the east and from the west until midday. And the sound of their chariots (was clamorous); and when this commotion took place, the holy ones in heaven took notice of it and the pillars of the earth were shaken from their foundations; and the sound (of the noise) could be heard from the extreme end of the sky unto the extreme end of the earth in one hour. Then all shall fall down and worship the Lord of the Spirits. Here ends the second parable. (1 Enoch 5.1-3)

This vision refers to the eschatological return of the ten tribes. Clearly, then, the Parthian and Mede invasion, and their inability to conquer Jerusalem — which pave the way for the return of the tribes — are likewise eschatological events. The fact that this is the end of the second parable of 1 Enoch is also not without eschatological significance.

We find, then, that during the late Second Temple period there were those who believed that when the foreign armies invade and Israel is vanquished, Jerusalem itself will not be conquered. Naturally, once this questionable view was promulgated, it came to serve as an ideology to guide present action.[41] Even after the Romans conquered Antonia, the fortress Herod had built to the north of Jerusalem, and the daily sacrifices were halted, Yohanan of Gush Halav cried out to Josephus not to fear conquest since Jerusalem is God's city (*BJ* 6.98). To the (misplaced) confidence of Yohanan, Josephus replied: "Who knows not the records of the ancient prophets and the oracle which threatens this poor city and is even now coming true?" (*BJ* 6.109).[42] On one hand, then, we find absolute confidence that the city of God cannot be

---

41. See the sources cited in M. Hengel, *Die Zeloten* (Leiden, 1961), 227-228. Hengel does not distinguish between the belief that Jerusalem will not be conquered, and the belief that the temple will not be destroyed.

42. It is not clear which verses Josephus has in mind.

defeated, and, on the other, the view — derived from the prophets — that the city is destined to fall.[43]

The same view — that Israel would be conquered but not Jerusalem — is evident in the 1 Enoch section discussed above. Others believed that the enemies would indeed conquer Jerusalem, but God's temple would be spared, most famously the Zealots during the siege. This is apparently the reason they refused to leave the temple even though the Romans allowed them to do so. Particularly instructive are the cries of the besieged Jews (*BJ* 5.458-459): they scoff at death and prefer it to enslavement; so long as they live and breathe, they will fight the Romans with no regard for their city, since Titus states that it will be destroyed regardless; and should the temple be destroyed, God has a greater residence, namely the world. But that will not happen, since God is Israel's ally and will save the temple. Thus, the Jewish fighters laugh at the Roman threats — empty threats, after all, since everything depends on God's will.

Josephus's words express many of the feelings that animated the rebels: they fought their desperate battle because they preferred freedom over slavery; if the city was to fall in any case, surrendering to the Romans would be a meaningless act; and if the temple were destroyed, God has a better abode in any case. Josephus understood this last statement as a reference to the world, but the rebels undoubtedly had in mind the heavenly temple.[44] All the same, the rebels did not believe the temple would be destroyed since it was the home of the Almighty. This last notion is of interest to the present discussion. However, before returning to the main topic at hand, it is worth discussing, if briefly, the rebels' claim that God has a better abode than the temple.

I suggested that the rebels were referring, in fact, to the heavenly temple (part of the heavenly city of Jerusalem), while Josephus understands them to be speaking of the world. Here we find one of the many places where

43. According to Hengel (*Die Zeloten,* 227 n. 2), the view that Jerusalem cannot fall found adherents even among the Roman warriors. According to Dio Cassius (*Roman History* 66.5), over the course of the siege on Jerusalem, some of the Roman soldiers lost heart and, having heard the city was invulnerable, deserted to the Jewish side. Hengel's interpretation of Dio Cassius is not the only possible one. Rather, the Roman historian may have meant that the military difficulties encountered thus far had led some in the Roman camp to believe that Jerusalem could not be conquered. All the same, the soldiers did cross over to the Jewish camp. Moreover, in the next passage Dio Cassius tells of Roman soldiers who were afraid to enter the temple compound, doing so only when forced to by Titus. So there may, after all, be a connection between the Roman desertions and the Jewish belief that the city cannot be conquered.

44. See Shmuel Safrai, "The Heavenly Jerusalem," *Ariel* 23 (1969), 11-16. On the heavenly Jerusalem see also the learned comments of H. Bietenhard, *Die Himmlische Welt im Urchristentum und Spätjudentum* (Tübingen, 1951), 192-204.

Josephus provides erroneous commentary to his own material. These glosses, the motivation for which is not always clear, sometimes are little more than a stylistic reworking. But here, when he suggests that the divine abode that is greater than the temple is the world, it is no doubt because the notion of a heavenly temple would strike his readers as foreign and quite odd. That said, Josephus did have some support for his interpretation. Philo, for one, states that the highest and most real temple is the world itself (*De Specialibus Legibus* 1.12.66), so Josephus may well have been influenced by the views of Hellenistic Jews. But the rebels themselves undoubtedly had the heavenly temple in mind, a view that finds a fascinating parallel in the Apocalypse of Baruch (2 Baruch), a work composed some thirty years after the destruction of the temple. There God speaks to Baruch, saying:

> This city will be delivered up for a time, and the people will be chastened for a time, and the world will not be forgotten. Or do you think that this is the city of which I said: "On the palms of my hands I have carved you"?[45] It is not the building that is in your midst now; it is that which will be revealed, with me, that was already prepared from the moment that I decided to create Paradise. And I showed it to Adam before he sinned. But when he transgressed the commandment, it was taken away from him — as also Paradise. After these things I showed it to my servant Abraham in the night between the portions of the victims. And again I showed it also to Moses on Mount Sinai when I showed him the likeness of the tabernacle and all its vessels. Behold, now it is preserved with me — as also Paradise. (2 Baruch 4.1-6).[46]

Clearly, 2 Baruch mentions the heavenly temple as a consolation for the loss of Jerusalem and the earthly temple. Like 2 Baruch, the Jewish rebels imply that there is a better abode for God than the terrestrial temple, should the latter be destroyed. If, then, these views are fundamentally aligned, the question presents itself as to whether the rebels too expected a heavenly temple to descend in place of its razed earthly counterpart? The answer appears to be no, since 2 Baruch states that in the end of days Jerusalem will be *rebuilt* (32.1-6), rather than descend from the heavens. As noted, this was a widespread Jewish belief from the destruction of the first temple on, and in its supernatural version meant that God (or perhaps angels) would miraculously rebuild the city. As noted, already in the days of Judah Maccabee we find the view that God

---

45. Cf. Isaiah 49:16.
46. On the eschatological temple and Jerusalem more generally, see Pierre Bogaert, *Apocalypse de Baruch* (Paris, 1969), 421-425.

will provide a new temple and place it in on the Temple Mount (1 Enoch 90.29). Moreover, according to Isaiah (54:11-12) and later the Book of Tobit, eschatological Jerusalem is described as a miraculous event. Moreover, the Isaiah scroll from Qumran, reflecting the reading that underlies the Septuagint, reads:[47] "Your builders outdo your destroyers, and those who laid you waste go away from you" (Isa 49:17). If so, Jerusalem will be built faster than it is destroyed. Evidently, the belief that Jerusalem and the temple would be rebuilt in the future by God is, if one may speak thus, natural. The belief in a heavenly Jerusalem, which includes a temple, is not fundamentally eschatological: the heavenly temple and the surrounding city are simply the supernal counterpart to the terrestrial.[48] As a result, there was no compelling reason for the heavenly Jerusalem to take the place of the now-razed earthly city, though such a view did circulate as a marginal folk belief already in the first century C.E., and may date back to temple times, when the prophecies of destruction began to appear. From all this we can understand why this was originally a marginal belief, while the main hope lay in the eschatological rebuilding of Jerusalem by either divine or human hands. Indeed, it was only in the medieval midrashic works that the descent of heavenly Jerusalem, along with its temple, became a central motif. As an interesting side note, in modern Hebrew, "supernal Jerusalem" (or "heavenly Jerusalem") is generally understood as an eschatological phrase.

The only ancient source to explicitly state that the heavenly Jerusalem will descend to earth is Revelation, which was composed during the reign of Domitian. There John of Patmos speaks of "the new Jerusalem that comes down from my God out of heaven" (Rev 3:12; 21:2, 10). Other ancient sources are ambiguous. According to 1 Enoch (90.29), God will provide the new temple; 4 Ezra states that the eschatological Jerusalem will be revealed: "For behold, the time will come, when the signs which I have foretold to you will come to pass, that the city which now is not seen shall appear, and the land which now is hidden shall be disclosed" (4 Ezra 7.26). If this passage refers to the eschatological Jerusalem,[49] it does not mention a descent from heaven, only that it is "now hidden," i.e., exists but is invisible to us. So even though the rebels' statement about the better divine abode can be interpreted as a reference to a heavenly temple descending to earth (Revelation testifies that such

47. This may be the original reading, on which see D. Flusser, "The Text of Isaiah XLIX,17 in the DSS," *Textus* 2 (1962), 140-142.

48. See the discussion in Safrai, "The Heavenly Jerusalem," 11-12.

49. According to J. Licht, *The Apocalypse of Ezra* (Jerusalem, 1968), 42: "The city symbolizes the world. The world that exists among us and appears as the only reality will be replaced in the world to come by another, hidden reality." I find Licht's interpretation very unconvincing.

hopes existed at the time), 2 Baruch maintains a similar belief, but elsewhere speaks of rebuilding Jerusalem in the eschaton. Rabbinic literature records the notion of Jerusalem's heavenly descent only from the middle ages.[50] It stands to reason, then, that were we to ask an ancient Jewish sage about Jerusalem and the temple, he would respond that they were to be built by human hands; were we to ask one of the *Hasidim,* he would respond that God would build them; and one of the simple folk with mystical and apocalyptic tendencies would reply that they would descend from heaven, though without ruling out the other two possibilities.

As noted, Josephus contrasts the rebels' apocalyptic outlook with other, opposite views, such as that of Yohanan of Gush Halav who did not fear the conquest of Jerusalem since it was God's city (*BJ* 6.98). Josephus responds to these words with an oration that concludes as follows: "God it is then, God Himself, who with the Romans is bringing the fire to purge His temple and exterminating a city so laden with pollutions" (*BJ* 6.110, and see also 4.323). The Romans, then, are mere tools in the hands of God, who uses their flames to purify the city — a *prima facie* expression of Josephus's cynical defense of the Romans. But in fact this is not the case. In the eschatological apocalypses of the time we find references to a purifying fire that will consume that which is to be consumed and purify that which is to be purified, and Josephus adapts this view to the Romans' setting Jerusalem and the temple ablaze. It is worth noting, in this context, the following phrase from the Ninth of Av blessing for Jerusalem: "For you, Lord, lighted it with fire, and with fire will you build it, in future days." It is hard to know what Josephus was thinking when he wrote about Jerusalem in the End of Days, or if he even was thinking along the apocalyptic lines suggested by this motif. For the logical conclusion is that Jerusalem is purified by fire in order to make room for the pure and perfect Jerusalem of the future. It may be that Josephus had something like this in mind, but decided, for obvious reasons, not to elaborate on the matter. Moreover, it is clear that Josephus, like all Jews, believed that the Roman Empire would eventually fall (see *AJ* 10.276-277, 209-210), but expressed this view cautiously. Thus, it is possible —

---

50. Safrai ("The Heavenly Jerusalem," 16 n. 48) suggests that the Jerusalem blessing for the Ninth of Av (the day commemorating the destruction of the temple), which was undoubtedly composed shortly after the destruction, assumes that the eschatological Jerusalem will be of heavenly origin. Thus, in the "console" *(Nahem)* blessing we find: "For you, Lord, lighted it with fire, and with fire will you build it, in future days." In the *Jewish War* 6.285, Josephus tells of a false prophet who tempted the masses to the burning temple so that they might see the signs of redemption. That prophet undoubtedly thought that just as the temple burned to the ground a new one would take its place.

though far from certain — that when Josephus states that the Romans are purifying Jerusalem of its abominations, he is alluding to the future establishment of the city.

Having discussed one part of the rebels' statement — that there exists a better divine abode than the earthly temple — we turn now to the other, namely, their faith that the temple would not be destroyed because it is God's resting place in the world. According to Dio Cassius, after the temple gates opened before the Roman troops, they did not rush in on account of a "superstition," and had to be forced to enter by Titus.[51] Now, it is unlikely that the Roman soldiers accepted the Jewish rebels' belief that the temple was impregnable; they simply feared the wrath of the Jewish God who was seated in his temple and might very well punish the conquering forces.

As noted, there was a pre-70 belief that Jerusalem would not be conquered (1 Enoch 56.5-7; BJ 6.98). Others thought that the city might fall, but the temple itself would not be destroyed — a view that likely gained currency when Jerusalem was conquered but the temple remained in the hands of the Jewish rebels. This position finds expression in Revelation 11:1-2: "Then I was given a measuring rod like a staff, and I was told, 'Come and measure the temple of God and the altar and those who worship there, but do not measure the court outside the temple; leave that out, for it is given over to the nations, and they will trample over the holy city for forty-two months." Scholars have rightly noted, that while Revelation was composed after the destruction of the temple, this passage represents an earlier stratum composed while the temple still stood.[52] According to this prophecy, the temple proper would stand even though the temple court was destined to be trampled by the nations. Since this was precisely the situation after the fall of the city but before the destruction of the temple, some scholars have argued that the Revelation passage originates in a call to arms of the Zealots.[53] But even if the dating of the passage is correct, it is unlikely that the besieged rebels formulated an *ad hoc* ideology that accepts the conquest of Jerusalem but maintains that the temple will remain standing — and that this view found its way out of the city and, somehow, to the author of Revelation. Indeed, if its origins *were* in Jerusalem, this view would not have lasted beyond the events of 70, and particularly the

51. Dio Cassius, *Roman History,* 66.6. See also G. Alon, *Studies in Jewish History* (Tel Aviv, 1957), 208.

52. See my discussion in "The Baptism of John and the Dead Sea Sect," *Essays on the Dead Sea Scrolls: In Memory of E. L. Sukenik,* ed. C. Rabin, Y. Yadin, and J. Licht (Jerusalem, 1961), 209-239.

53. Thus Hengel, *Die Zeloten,* 249, n. 45. The first to propose this hypothesis was Wellhausen.

razing of the temple, which so clearly contravened it. Moreover, I have been able to identify a Jewish source for Revelation (which I hope to discuss elsewhere),[54] which includes details not mentioned in Revelation 11. The source in question was widely available and, naturally, could not have been written during the short time that the temple was besieged and the city taken. In short, the belief that Jerusalem might fall but the temple remain standing existed before Titus's conquest of the city. Indeed, according to Josephus (*BJ* 1.347), this view circulated during the siege of Jerusalem in 37 B.C.E. At that time, the weak gathered around the temple and, struck by religious mania, prophesied about the present days. The parallel in *Jewish Antiquities* (14.470) indicates that these prophecies involved the temple and the redemption of Israel.[55] If so, prophecies like the one found in Revelation, according to which Jerusalem will be trampled by the nations but the temple will not fall, are attested as early as 37 B.C.E.

We further established that among those who expected a hostile invasion whose target was Jerusalem, some believed that Israel would be conquered but the city itself would withstand the attack, while others thought the city would fall, but the temple remain standing. But there was a third group that believed the temple would fall, including, most famously, Jesus, who came to Jerusalem as a prophet of destruction.[56] The most important passage in this context is the prophecy of Jerusalem's destruction and future liberation, the most original version of which is found in Luke, chapter 21. Even this version, however, consists of two sources and shows traces of the editors' hands.[57] The primary source speaks of a future destruction of the temple

54. The source in question is preserved in the seventh book of Lactantius, *Divinarum Institutionum,* where it is attributed to the Persian Hystaspes. Though cited in abbreviated form, the passage alludes to the events described in Revelation 11:1-2, particularly in the statement that the evil king will "try to destroy the temple of God" in the end of days (*Div. Inst.* 7.17.6).

55. The *Antiquities* passage is a free adaptation that blurs many of the details.

56. See D. Flusser, "A New Testament Prophecy concerning the Liberation of Jerusalem," *Eretz Israel* 10 (1971), 226-236.

57. As recently noted by my friend R. Lindsey, who has reconstructed the two sources and published them as hectographs. Lindsey suggests that the second source, which refers to the end of days, was preserved by Luke in its original form and structure. Luke 21:12-19, however, derives from a different source, one preserved independently in Matthew 10:17-23, with light editing. The passage deals with the future persecution of Jesus' disciples. For a recent study on the significance of the fall of Jerusalem for the three synoptic gospels, employing current scholarly tools, see L. Gaston, *No Stone on Another* (Leiden, 1970), who cites (363-364) 2 Baruch 1.4; 5.1; 6.9; 13.9, sources relevant to the present discussion. Gaston discusses the downfall prophecy in Luke (355-365), arguing that it was composed *before* the destruction of the temple, following the important article of C. H. Dodd, "The Fall of Jerusalem," *Journal of Roman Studies* 37 (1947), 47-54.

(Luke 21:5-7, 20-24, 28-33), with interpolations from an eschatological "Son of Man" prophecy (Luke 21:8-11, 25-27, 34-36). The fall of Jerusalem and the coming of the Son of Man are described as follows (Luke 21:20-28):

> When you see Jerusalem surrounded by armies, then know that its desolation has come near. Then those in Judea must flee to the mountains, and those inside the city must leave it, and those out in the country must not enter it; for these are days of vengeance, as a fulfillment of all that is written. Woe to those who are pregnant and to those who are nursing infants in those days! For there will be great distress on the earth and wrath against this people; they will fall by the edge of the sword and be taken away as captives among all nations; and Jerusalem will be trampled on by the Gentiles, until the times of the Gentiles are fulfilled. . . .[58] Now when these things begin to take place, stand up and raise your heads, because your redemption is drawing near.

Elsewhere,[59] I have shown that the Lukan version of the prophecy is reworked in Mark, and Matthew tends to follow this revised version. This is significant because it indicates that Luke's is the more primitive version and thus a more reliable witness to Jesus' original prophecy of destruction. Here, then, is another argument for a pre-70 dating of the prophecy. Moreover, the prophecy accords with what we know of Jesus' political worldview. Even a cursory examination of his teachings reveals that, to the extent that he was an apocalyptic prophet, he opposed the zealous visionaries who fanned the flames of anti-Roman rebellion. We saw that the rebels hoped that Jerusalem — or at least the temple — would not fall, whereas Jesus urges his disciples to flee: "So when you see the desolating sacrilege standing in the holy place, as was spoken of by the prophet Daniel (let the reader understand), then those in Judea must flee to the mountains; someone on the housetop must not go down to take what is in the house; someone in the field must not turn back to get a coat. Woe to those who are pregnant and to those who are nursing infants in those days!" (Matt 24:15-19), adding "Pray that your flight may not be

---

58. Verses 25-27 have been deleted. They are from the second source and speak of the end of days rather than the fall of Jerusalem. The interpolation may have slightly damaged the original text, which may have alluded to the end of days, though this allusion was lost in the reworking. As a result, the beginning of verse 28 ("Now when these things begin to take place") may have been formulated to fit the interpolated eschatological prophecy. But based on the extant evidence, it is best to interpret the phrase "when these things begin to take place" as referring to the fulfillment of "the times of the Gentiles" — an encouraging sign.

59. Flusser, "A New Testament Prophecy Concerning the Liberation of Jerusalem," *Eretz Israel* 10 (1971), 226-236.

in winter or on a Sabbath!" (Matt 24:20).[60] This defeatist advice was undoubtedly unpopular among the zealot rebels. And indeed, the Christian community left Jerusalem before the war, following a prophetic revelation.[61]

The overall structure of the prophecy is clear enough: the destruction of Jerusalem at the hands of the enemy represents "days of vengeance, as a fulfillment of all that is written," a time when "there will be great distress on the earth and wrath against this people." Along with the death and destruction comes exile, though Jerusalem will not remain trampled by her enemies forever, for when the times of the Gentiles will be fulfilled, she will be released from their yoke. This is the standard scheme of destruction, exile, and redemption, so familiar from Leviticus and Deuteronomy, but here applied to Jerusalem. A fascinating comparison can be made between Jesus' prophecy and the historical survey in chapter fourteen of the Book of Tobit, discussed above. There the author speaks of the exile following the fall of Judah and Israel: "even Samaria and Jerusalem will be desolate." This will be followed by a return of the exiles: "and they will rebuild the temple of God, but not like the first one, until the period when the times of fulfillment shall come." Then all the exiled Jews will return and "rebuild Jerusalem in splendor; and in it the temple of God will be rebuilt, just as the prophets of Israel have said concerning it." The similarities and differences to Jesus' teaching are evident. Tobias applies the ancient paradigm to the First Temple: destruction and exile, the return to Zion and the rebuilding of Jerusalem. However, the full redemption, the final building of Jerusalem, will come only after the end of the time we live in, after "the times of fulfillment have come." The Book of Tobit, like Jesus, clearly assumes historic periodization, such that the final redemption will come only when the preceding times have been fulfilled. However, in the Book of Tobit this historical fulfillment is not linked with any catastrophic event, apparently because the author, who lived in the Persian period, had no reason to believe that the temple would again be destroyed. In contrast, Jesus lived in a time when the temple was under clear and, as it turned out, imminent threat, allowing him to speak openly about the destruction of Jerusalem and the subsequent exile. Indeed, Jesus frames these events as the fulfillment of Scripture, evidence that already in his day there were those who interpreted some biblical passages as alluding

60. For a discussion of this verse see Flusser, "A New Testament Prophecy," n. 11. Mark 13:18 states only, "Pray that it not be in winter." Mark has clearly omitted mention of the Sabbath. It is also possible that Matthew added the phrase "your flight," whereas the statement originally referred to the siege.

61. See Eusebius, *Historia Ecclesiastica* 3.5.3. Eusebius states that this was a special revelation, and, therefore, unrelated to Jesus' teaching in the gospels.

to the destruction of the Second Temple.[62] Jesus too states that the city will be built after the fulfillment of the times, but these are no longer times as such, but the "times of the Gentiles," the end of the period in which Jerusalem is trampled by the Gentiles. Here, then, we find a paradoxical shift: the Lukan prophecy is the first witness to the renewal of the biblical schema, attested in the teachings of the prophets and the writings of the Second Temple scribes: Jerusalem will be destroyed but then redeemed. Here, however, it is not the First Temple that is in question, but the Second. This cyclical view of Jewish history as moving from exile to redemption remained in place up to the Six-Day War, at which point a different paradigm reasserted itself unnoticed, namely, that of Ben Sira and the Book of Tobit: Jerusalem is destroyed, the exiles return, the Jews and Jerusalem are redeemed. Here, of course, it is the Second Temple, not the first, that is intended.

To reiterate: the point of departure of the Jewish ideological engagement with Jerusalem is the destruction of the First Temple, not the second. Already then, Jerusalem was the focus of Jewish hopes and, later, of Jewish fears. Since the expectations of the returning exiles concerning the glory of Jerusalem were not met, they were deferred and took on an eschatological character, a belief in the future Jerusalem. This hope was linked with another deferred hope, namely, for the ingathering of exiles: "The LORD builds up Jerusalem; he gathers the outcasts of Israel" (Ps 147:2). These two hopes found expression in the liturgy of the Eighteen Benedictions well before any messianic hopes. The yearning for the rebuilding of Jerusalem and the ingathering of exiles was tied in Second Temple literature with the prophetic vision of the nations of the world recognizing God's kingship. The Book of Tobit clearly voices these hopes, while the most concrete manifestation of the hope for Jerusalem and the exiles was the dedication of the Temple by Judah Maccabee. This is evident from his letter to the Jewish community in Alexandria, which ties the purification of the temple to the ingathering of exiles. Already in the days of Judah Maccabee we find evidence of a belief that the current temple would be divinely transported and God would set in its place an eschatological temple. This belief was transformed post-70; redemption would not be preceded by the dislocation of the temple and the city of Jerusalem, but by their destruction.

Beginning in the late Second Temple period, when Rome casts its pall over Israel, the hopes for a glorious future for Jerusalem are intertwined with fear for the city's existence. Biblical prophets nowhere foresee a second de-

---

62. The Book of Tobit refers only to past catastrophes, which are understood as the fulfillment of the words of the prophets, and to the future building of Jerusalem.

struction, only visions of Jerusalem's future glory and splendor. In a time of distress, under the domination of Rome, the belief that Jerusalem would not fall again fueled the belligerent ideology of the anti-Roman rebels. There were those who believed the city would not fall, while others held that, even if Jerusalem were overrun, God would protect his earthly abode. But the mere threat to the city opened in many hearts the wound caused by the destruction of the First Temple. And those who thought a second destruction inevitable turned to Scripture and found verses to bolster their position (see Luke 21:22; *BJ* 6.109). Thus we find that both the desperate hope of the rebels and the fear of their opponents sought justification in the same book, sacred to both sides. The turning point was the destruction of the temple. The position enunciated in Luke 21 would dominate for many generations. The Second Temple was destroyed, followed by a long period of exile, while the Jewish people hoped for a return to Zion and the rebuilding of Jerusalem.[63]

63. As noted, during the Second Temple period the sanctity of the temple was extended to Jerusalem as a whole. On the halakhic ramifications of this development see S. Safrai, *Second Temple Pilgrimage* (Hebrew) (Tel Aviv, 1965), 151-155.

4. The Image of the Masada Martyrs in Their Own Eyes and in the Eyes of Their Contemporaries

Dedicated to my friend, Shmuel Safrai

Was the memory of the Masada martyrs effaced from the rabbinic sources? Shmuel Safrai, to whom this essay is dedicated, believes he has found mention of them in a midrash to Deuteronomy 32:23: "'I will heap disasters upon them' — the Holy One Blessed Be He said: I bring them into a fortress and bring them upon them one at a time."[1] But even if this passage does allude to the Masada martyrs, it does not state whether their deeds are judged favorably or not. According to the oration Josephus attributes to Elazar ben Yair, the defenders of Masada took their lives primarily because of their love of liberty,[2] lest they be enslaved by their captors. However, the main motivation

---

1. *Midrash Hagadol* to Deuteronomy 32:23 (page 718 in the S. Fisch edition [Jerusalem, 1973]), whence it was copied to *Midrash Tannaim*. For a discussion of the topic at hand see M. Stern, "The Suicide of Elazar ben Yair and His Men at Masada, and the 'Fourth Philosophy,'" *Zion* 47 (1982), 367-397 (reprinted in M. Stern, *Studies in Second Temple History* [Jerusalem, 1991], 313-343). See also V. L. Trimble, "Masada, Suicide, and Halakhah," *Conservative Judaism* 31 (1977), 45-55.

2. Tacitus writes (*Histories* 5.3.5) that the Jews believe the souls of those who die in battle or by the hands of the court to be immortal, and thus their desire to beget many children and their tendency to scorn death. Josephus (*BJ* 1.650-653; *AJ* 17.149) recounts that in the final days of Herod, two sages convinced their disciples to remove the golden eagle that hung over the temple gate, arguing that even if they failed they would die a martyr's death and thus gain eternal blessedness. The disciples were, in fact, caught, and greeted their fate with open arms. See O. Michel and O. Bauernfeind (eds.), *Flavius Josephus: De Bello Judaico* 1.2 (Munich, 1969), 172. Yohanan Levy ("Tacitus on the Antiquity and Customs of the Jews," *Jews and Judaism through Hellenistic Eyes* [Hebrew] [Jerusalem, 1974], 109-162 and especially 116, n. 55) rightly claims that the belief that warriors are rewarded with eternal life is regularly attributed by Greek and Ro-

must have been the clear knowledge that they would be killed by their Roman captors. Josephus too notes that the certainty of death influenced Elazar ben Yair's terrible decision, including this very argument in the two orations he places in the mouth of his protagonist.[3] Our focus, however, is not on the psychological motivation of the suicide, but rather two other issues that strike me as critical. Using the reports of Josephus, I will examine how the Masada warriors' contemporaries understood their actions, paying close attention to the psychological link between Second Temple zeal and the suicide of these zealots.[4] But before turning to these two topics, we will deal briefly with the Second Temple concept of liberty.[5]

I

The concept of liberty, in its various historical manifestations, is a core element in the heritage of European culture. Its roots reach back to antiquity, both in Greek and Israelite thought. Liberty as a political rallying cry and ideal played an important role in Greco-Roman culture. "In the period that the polis played a central political role, its citizens understood themselves as free men by virtue of their association with the polis — Athens, Sparta, or

---

man authors to barbarian nations. See also M. Stern, *Greek and Latin Authors on Jews and Judaism* (Jerusalem, 1980), 2.19 §§41-42.

3. Josephus, *BJ* 7.321 and 324.

4. The term "zealot" refers throughout to all the Jewish rebels of the period, not to a defined group. On the rebel groups and individuals of the day see M. Stern, "Zealots," *Encyclopaedia Judaica Year Book* (Jerusalem, 1973), 135-152. See also Stern, "The Suicide of Elazar ben Yair," 389, n. 120; M. Hengel, *Die Zeloten* (Leiden, 1961); C. T. R. Hayward, "The Fourth Philosophy: Sicarii and Zealots," in E. Schürer, *The History of the Jewish People in the Time of Jesus Christ* (Edinburgh, 1979), 598-606. Stern ("The Suicide of Elazar ben Yair," 396-397) admits that the Sicarii and the Zealots shared an ideological base. See also H. Cotton and Y. Preiss, "Who Conquered Masada in 66 C.E. and Who Occupied It until It Fell?" (Hebrew), *Zion* 55 (1990), 449-454. Stern's essays on the Zealots and the Sicarii are now available in his *Studies*, 277-343. On the link between zealotry and the Masada suicide see Stern, "The Suicide of Elazar ben Yair," 139, 150-151, and his notes therein. We should also mention here the suicide of the defenders of Yodfat.

5. On liberty in antiquity see Hengel, *Die Zeloten;* S. Pines, "Jewish Thought and Its Influence on the Surrounding World" (Hebrew), *Studies in the History of Jewish Thought* (Hebrew) (Jerusalem, 1986), 126-129. A fuller version of this article appeared as "The Transformation of the Concept of Liberty," *Between Analysis and Action: Studies in Honor of Nathan Rotenstreich (Iyyun)* (Hebrew) (Jerusalem, 1984), 244-259. See also F. S. Jones, *'Freiheit' in den Briefen des Apostels Paulus* (Göttingen, 1987); L. I. Rabinowitz, "Freedom," *Encyclopaedia Judaica* 8.117-119; Michel and Bauernfeind, *De Bello Judaico*, 267-268.

other Greek and Roman cities."[6] Among the ancient Greek partisans of liberty, pride of place goes to the tragedian Euripides (5th century B.C.E.), who links the idea of self-sacrifice with liberty.[7] Most impressive are the dramatic descriptions of Euripidean protagonists who freely give their life for the sake of liberty. It is no coincidence, then, that the slogan "to die a free man," which Josephus places at the opening of Elazar's Masada speech, originates in Euripides' tragedy *The Children of Heracles* (line 559), and a similar statement is found in his *Orestes* (lines 1170-1171) — there in the context of suicide.

There is, then, a Greek literary influence on the liberty slogans in Josephus, an influence made possible by the parallel between the Greek and the Jewish understandings of liberty. It is unlikely that the Greek influence was merely literary. It may be that during the Greco-Roman period, the Greek political notion of liberty came in contact with the Jewish concept of national liberty, the latter the result of an internal Jewish impetus. So while it is true that "the story of the exodus from Egypt speaks of slavery but says nothing about freedom,"[8] and the Hebrew noun "freedom" (חופש) is not attested in the Bible, "the ideal of emancipation from political oppression exists, indeed is prominent, in the accounts of the exodus . . . and the same is true of the return from the Babylonian exile and the proclamations of future redemption."[9] The yearning for liberty is, then, an important Jewish accomplishment, and its roots are undoubtedly ancient. At the same time, it is clear that the Jewish concept of liberty evolved over time, until ultimately crystallizing in the ideology of the zealots. That said, the slogan of liberty was not unique to the anti-Roman rebels, whether those of the first revolt or of the Bar Kosiba revolt.[10]

Already in the liberation from the Egyptian bondage we find the kernel of the liberty ideal, and it stands to reason that at some point in the Second Temple period the Jewish conception of liberty developed in new ways. For it

6. Pines, "Jewish Thought," 128, and see idem, "The Concept of Liberty," 248, 251-255.

7. See Jones, *Freiheit*, 48-52, 175-178.

8. Pines, "Jewish Thought," 128.

9. I. Tishby, responding to Pines' article, "The Concept of Liberty," 135-136. See also Pines, "The Concept of Liberty," 247, discussing Leviticus 26:13. It is worth noting the statement issued at Vatican II, concerning the relationship of the church to non-Christian religions, that "the exodus of the chosen people from the land of bondage (Egypt) symbolically prefigures the redemption of the church" (*salutem ecclesiae in populi electi exitu de terra servitutis mystice praesignari*).

10. See, e.g., Schürer, *History*, 1.605-606. On the coins of the first revolt there appeared the inscription "liberty of Zion" and "for the redemption of Zion"; the coins minted in the first year of Bar Kochba's reign were inscribed "for the redemption of Israel," those minted in the second, "year 2 of the liberty of Israel," and those of the third year, "for the liberty of Jerusalem."

was during this period that this internal Jewish contribution came in fecund contact with the Greek concept of liberty. We will have occasion to speculate below as to when precisely the critical shift in the Jewish understanding of national liberty occurred. It appears that since the crystallization of the religious view that the Jewish people was born into liberty, this term was understood as signifying political independence. Very little material is extant from the earlier periods, so it is hard to know how exactly this political-religious view took shape, but it is clear that by the late Second Temple period there were many Jews — not only the zealots — who understood Roman political domination as illegal and, indeed, unnatural.[11]

Needless to say, we cannot outline all the nuances within this ideology — from the most radical rebels to those promoting reconciliation and compromise. It is also difficult to ascertain how the Sadducees responded to this ideology of liberty in different periods. The Qumran writings clearly indicate that the Essenes were of the opinion that the Jewish people should be free, though they adopted a different conceptual tack than the sages.[12] True, they believed Israel to be "the nation redeemed by God,"[13] but, such statements notwithstanding, there is no evidence in the Qumran literature of the idea, so typical of the Pharisees, that the Jewish people are by their nature free. This may be due to the dualistic worldview of the Qumran community, which pits the forces of light against those of darkness. The latter will be destroyed in the endtime, along with the wicked nations, but the present era is — socially and politically — under the government of evil, which must then be God's will. Thus, "in this time," the Essenes are commanded "everlasting hatred for the men of the pit in clandestine spirit. To them he should leave goods and handmade items like a servant to his master and like one oppressed before someone domineering him" (1QS 9.21-23).[14] The member of the community further promises "my soul shall not crave wealth by violence, nor shall I be involved in any dispute with the men of the pit until the day of vengeance" (1QS 10.19-20). These passages shed new light on the statement of Josephus in *War* 2.140, that the Essenes are commanded to remain loyal to the powers that be

11. See G. Alon, "The Pharisees' Position Concerning Roman and Herodian Rule" (Hebrew) in *Studies in Jewish History*, 1.26-47.

12. See D. Flusser, "The Dead Sea Sect and Its Worldview," *Judaism of the Second Temple Period: Qumran and Apocalypticism*, 1-24.

.13. 1QM 1.12, and see also 1QM 14.5; 15.1; 18.10, and compare 1.5, and 11.8-9. On the inconsistent dialectic between the separatist tendencies of the Qumran community and the expectation of national redemption, see J. Licht, "Eternal Deceit and the Nation of God's Redemption," in *Studies in the Dead Sea Scrolls* (Hebrew), (Jerusalem, 1961), 49-75.

14. See also 1QS 11.1-2.

— no ruler, after all, ascends to that position without God willing it so — a position tantamount to conditional pacifism, a kind of "militant defeatism."[15] In practical terms, the Essene behavior was not much different than the peace-seeking faction within the rabbinic circles, even if from an emotional-religious perspective the difference between the groups is dramatic.[16] In his *Jewish Antiquities,* Josephus recounts that during Herod's siege of Jerusalem, Hillel and Shammai convinced the people to accept Herod as legitimate king, but on account of their sins they could not be saved from him.[17] As we will see, this position is strikingly close to that of the peace party within the rabbis, who argued that were it not for the sins of Israel, no foreign nation could conquer the Jewish people.

Herod most likely did not consider those unwilling to accept the rule of a sinful government as a threat to his throne. When he demanded that the nation swear an oath of fealty to him, he tried to convince Hillel, Shammai, and their disciples to take the oath, but though they refused they were not punished. The Essenes too refused to vow fealty to Herod, though their motives were different from those of the Pharisees. It appears that the refusal of the Houses of Hillel and Shammai was rooted in the conviction that his reign was illegitimate. Mishnah Nedarim 3.4 indicates that both Hillel and Shammai questioned the legitimacy of Roman rule over Israel.

While it is true that the broad and varied group known as the Pharisees generally resisted Roman rule and yearned for political freedom,[18] we must take a wider view: the notion of political liberty did not come about as a result of the unbearable burden of Roman rule. Foreign rule was viewed by most Jews as an unnatural state in the eyes of both God and man: "I shall not

---

15. See Flusser, "The Dead Sea Sect and Its Worldview," and idem, "The Jewish Origins of the Early Church's Attitude toward the State," in *Judaism of the Second Temple Period: Qumran and Apocalypticism,* 299-304.

16. One of the outstanding characteristics of the Qumran texts is the absence of the root גאל in the positive sense of liberation. For example, the Hodayot (1QH 10.34-35) passage "but you, my God, have freed the soul of the poor and needy from the hand of someone stronger than him" is a gloss of Jeremiah 31:11: "For the LORD has ransomed Jacob, and *redeemed* (וגאלו) him from hands too strong for him." The avoidance of the secular sense of *g-'-l* may be due to the particularly sacred sense it enjoyed among the Qumranites, but I tend to the view that they were distancing themselves from the rabbinic understanding of גאולה as "redemption" or "liberation."

17. Josephus, *AJ* 14.176; on the Essenes see 15.371-379. See also Schürer, *A History of the Jews,* 2.362-363. There are strong arguments for identifying the sages as Hillel and Shammai and not, as some propose, as Shema'yah and Avtalion, e.g., the fact that *AJ* 15 refers to the many disciples each had.

18. See Alon, "The Pharisees' Position," 47.

appoint nor delegate any one else, so to speak, to rule over you."[19] The fact that this is, ultimately, the meaning of liberty for the Jews of the time, sheds new light on the rabbinic sources, which contain discrete statements that amount to an interesting and cohesive ideology. In what follows, we cite a number of rabbinic dicta, beginning with those that refer to the biblical verses that, by their very nature, anchored the Jewish ideology of liberty.

We have already discussed the liberation from the Egyptian exile. We have also seen that God, and not the foreign nations, is the legitimate ruler over Israel, as the last rabbinic citation makes clear — an interpretation of Exodus 19:6: "but you shall be for me a priestly kingdom and a holy nation." The broader context, however, includes the preceding verse: "Now therefore, if you obey my voice and keep my covenant, you shall be my treasured possession (עם סגולה) out of all the peoples. Indeed, the whole earth is mine" (Exod 19:5). In his study, S. A. Löwenstamm demonstrates that the word סגולה[20] is a master's term of endearment for a beloved vassal. If Israel obeys the words of the Lord, it will be a סגולה, a beloved vassal, from among the nations, presumably enjoying a privileged status. This last suggestion is strengthened by the second cola of the verse: "Indeed, the whole earth is mine." Rabbi Yehoshua ben Korcha develops this idea, saying: "This phrase is used to penetrate the ear. Just as a wife treasures what her husband gives her, and a son treasures what his father gives him, so might it be the case that Israel should treasure what they receive from the nations. Scripture teaches, saying, 'Indeed, the whole earth is mine.'"[21]

Another biblical verse that lends itself to the later discussion of political liberty is Leviticus 25:55: "For to me the people of Israel are servants; they are my servants whom I brought out from the land of Egypt: I am the Lord your God."[22] The rabbis learned from this verse that since the Israelites are slaves of the Lord, they cannot be slaves to slaves: "'they are my servants whom I brought out from the land of Egypt' — it was on that condition that I

---

19. Mekhilta of Rabbi Ishmael, Bahodesh 2, Lauterbach 2.204.

20. S. A. Löwenstamm, "עם סגולה" (Hebrew), in *Linguistic Studies Presented to Ze'ev Ben-Hayyim* (Jerusalem, 1983), 321-328.

21. Mekhilta of Rabbi Shimon ben Yohai (Epstein-Melamed, 139), and also *Midrash Hagadol* to Exodus (Margaliot, 379). A different reading is attested in Mekhilta of Rabbi Ishmael, Bahodesh 2 (Lauterbach 2.204), as well as in Pesiqta Rabbati (Friedmann, 46b). For a discussion of this reading see the discussion in Löwenstamm, "עם סגולה" and W. Bacher, *Die Agada der Tannaiten* (Strasbourg, 1890), 317, n. 2.

22. See also verses 23, 38, and 42 in the same chapter. Most of the midrashim that deal with the topic at hand are to be found in *Midrash ha-Gadol* to Leviticus, ad loc. (Steinsaltz edition [Jerusalem, 1976], 724). On the teaching of Rabban Yohanan ben Zakkai, see Bacher, *Aggadot ha-Tannaim*, 1.27, n. 2.

brought them out of Egypt; on the condition that they not be enslaved. 'I am the Lord your God' — why is this stated? To teach that whoever is enslaved in the world below, it is as though he is enslaved in the world above."[23] Rabban Yohanan ben Zakkai refers to this very verse in his well-known statement:[24]

> "And his master shall pierce his ear with an awl" (Exod 21:6): Why was the ear specified of all limbs? Because it heard at Sinai "For to me the people of Israel are servants" (Lev 25:55), yet cast off the yoke of [the kingdom of] heaven and accepted the yoke of flesh and blood. Thus Scripture states: Let the ear come forward and be pierced, for it has not obeyed what it heard. Another interpretation: he did not want to be enslaved to his creator, let him be enslaved to his [the creator's] sons.[25]

Rabban Yohanan ben Zakkai's statement is important for a number of reasons. First, it reiterates the view that the Children of Israel may not be ruled by another nation,[26] a position clearly not limited to the zealots of the late Second Temple period as it was shared by such a prominent member of the peace-seeking faction. Second, it appears that both sages linked the concept of liberty with "the kingdom of heaven," and this phrase likely played an important role in the zealot ideology. However, the contrast between "the kingdom of heaven" and foreign rule over Israel is only one aspect of the phrase, the other being the exclusive rule of God over the whole world. The zealots, then, marginalized the universal aspect of the kingdom of heaven, focusing instead on its political and the nationalistic dimensions. Third, an interesting dialectic is evident in Rabban Yohanan ben Zakkai's polemic against the zealots' nationalistic interpretation of the concept of liberty. For he recognizes that establishing a foreign government over Israel entails casting off the yoke of the kingdom of heaven. However, the same is true for those who would be ruled by Jewish potentates. Here is the midrash of Rabbi Hananiah the prefect of the priests, a man known for his pacifism (the midrash is also attributed to Rabbi Nehuniah ben ha-

23. Sifra Ba-Har, pereq 9.4, following the reading of *Midrash Hagadol*. There we find a daring interpretation of the end of Leviticus 25:55, in the spirit of Rabbi Aqiva.

24. Tosefta Baba Kama 7.5-6 (pages 29-30 in Lieberman's edition of the Tosefta [New York, 1988]); see also S. Lieberman, *Tosephta ki-feshuta: Neziqin* (New York, 1988), 66-67; Bacher, *Aggadot ha-Tannaim*, 1.27, n. 2.

25. According to Lieberman, "to his sons" (לבניו) should be read לכנותיו, "to his slaves."

26. The Hebrew phrase *shi'abud malkhuyot* is first attested in the words of Rabbi Yohanan in b. Pesahim 118a. On Shmuel's famous statement, "The political domination of Israel is the only difference between this world and the messianic era" (b. Berakhot 34b) see W. Bacher, *Die Agada der babylonischen Amoräer* (Frankfurt, 1913), 43, and A. Büchler, *Studies in Sin and Atonement* (New York, 1967), 76.

Kanah): "'My mother's sons were angry with me; they made me keeper of the vineyards, but my own vineyard I have not kept' (Song of Songs 1:6): This refers to the councils of Judea, who disregarded the yoke of heaven and established the yoke of flesh and blood."[27] Rabbi Hananiah is responding to the changes that occurred when the zealots and their allies gained political control. A similar tone, and similar language, appear in the sharp, almost apocalyptic words of Rabban Yohanan ben Zakkai in chapter 14 of Tosefta Sotah. Most of this chapter — at least up to mishnah 9 — appears to be aimed at the difficult times that came about after the zealots came to power, and his account certainly fits that of Josephus. Based on the similarity to the midrash of Rabbi Hananiah (or perhaps Rabbi Nehuniah ben ha-Kanah), it is clear that Rabban Yohanan ben Zakkai is referring to the miscarriages of justice perpetrated by the zealot courts: "When the partial judges grew numerous, the verses 'you must not be partial in judging' and 'you shall not be intimidated by anyone' (Deut 1.17) were no longer observed, they cast off the yoke of heaven and established for themselves the yoke of flesh and blood."[28] We see, then, that the "yoke of flesh and blood" referred to in the sayings of Rabban Yohanan ben Zakkai and of Rabbi Hananiah is the yoke of the zealots.[29] After the destruction of the temple, Rabban Yohanan repeated his view: "You were unwilling to be subject to God, behold now you are subjected to the most inferior of nations, the Arabs. . . . Because you did not serve the Lord your God with love, therefore you will serve your enemy with hatred. . . ."[30]

This, then, is the two-yoke argument: whoever casts off the yoke of the kingdom of heaven, ultimately accepts the yoke of flesh and blood. The corollary is also true — whoever casts off the yoke of flesh and blood accepts the

---

27. Avot de-Rabbi Nathan (A), 20 (page 72 in the Schechter edition [New York, 1945]), and see the variant readings ad loc. See also G. Alon, *"Ga'on, Ge'im,"* in his *Studies in Jewish History*, 316-318. Alon is right that all other references to the "councils of Judea" involve the Bar Kochba revolt, while the words of Rabbi Hananiah are aimed at the zealots' rise to power, as I argue in the present article. On the attribution of the saying to Rabbi Nehuniah ben ha-Kanah, see Schechter, 71. My friend, M. Kiester, notes that this name also appears in MS New York.

28. The image of the two yokes is attested as early as 2 (Slavonic) Enoch 34. See F. I. Andersen's comments in *The Old Testament Pseudepigrapha*, ed. J. H. Charlesworth, 1.158-159. See also the French translation with variant readings and the original Slavonic text in *Le livre des secrets d'Henoch*, ed. A. Vaillant (Paris, 1952), 34-45. The use of the two yokes is, however, distinct from that of the sages. According to 2 Enoch, God sent the flood because of the wickedness of mankind: they cast off the yoke of God, taking on a second yoke and worshipping false gods. Clearly there is a connection between the two yokes of Slavonic Enoch and the teachings of the sages. For similar statements see Büchler, *Sin and Atonement*, 82-83.

29. See also Büchler, *Sin and Atonement*, 65.

30. Mekhilta Bahodesh 1, Lauterbach 2.194.

yoke of the kingdom of heaven — though this view is not attested in the ancient sources. Nonetheless, it seems to be the position of the activist zealots.[31] Indeed, both the zealots and the peace-seeking sages base their views on the same assumptions, though they reach different conclusions. The zealots hold that if you accept foreign rule you are sinning before God, while the sages hold that the foreign rule came about as a result of earlier sins. If Israel repents and returns to God, no nation can rule over them:[32]

> "If they were wise they would understand this" (Deut 32:29): If Israel would but look closely at what their father Jacob had said to them, no nation or kingdom could dominate them. What did he say to them? Accept upon yourselves the kingdom of heaven, vie with each other in fear of heaven, and act toward each other in loving-kindness.[33]

According to the Aramaic Targum to Ezekiel 2:10, if Israel transgresses the laws of the Torah, they will be ruled by foreign nations, but if they abide by the Torah "lamentation and mourning and woe" will be eliminated.[34] A similar view is found in the midrash to the biblical commandment to wear fringes, "So you shall remember and do all my commandments, and you shall be holy to your God" (Num 15:40): "Scripture should not have said 'you shall be holy to your God' but rather 'you shall be holy like your God.' Why, then, was this said? [It is as though God is saying:] Just as no creature can touch my divine presence, so too when you sanctify yourselves, no creature will be able

31. See especially Josephus, *AJ* 18.4-5, and *BJ* 2.118, 433; 7.323, 410. *BJ* 7.254-255 is of particular importance. The Sicarii view of liberty cited there is not materially different from the views of most of the sages, nor indeed from that view that is lauded by Josephus, on which see Michel and Bauernfeind, *De Bello Judaico*, 267-268. Also significant are Josephus's comments (*BJ* 7.417-419) on the spirited resistance of the zealots who were captured in Egypt after the war: "Nor was there a person who was not amazed at the endurance and — call it what you will — desperation or strength of purpose, displayed by these victims. For under every form of torture and laceration of body, devised for the sole object of making them acknowledge Caesar as lord, not one submitted nor was brought to the verge of utterance; but all kept their resolve, triumphant over constraint, meeting the tortures and the fire with bodies that seemed insensible of pain and souls that well nigh exulted in it. But most of all were the spectators struck by the children of tender age, not one of whom could be prevailed upon to call Caesar lord." See the parallels to this description in Michel and Bauernfeind, *De Bello Judaico*, 282, to which should be added Josephus's description of the Essenes at *BJ* 2.152-153, who were tortured in order to force them to curse their lawgiver and eat prohibited foods.

32. See P. Volz, *Die Eschatologie der jüdischen Gemeinde* (Tübingen, 1934), 166-167; Büchler, *Sin and Atonement*, 36-52, 60-101.

33. Sifre Deuteronomy §323, translated by Reuven Hammer (New Haven, 1986), 334-335.

34. "For if Israel transgress the law, they will be ruled by the nations, but if they keep the law, [God] will end all mourning, and misery, and grief for them."

to touch you."[35] And in more general terms: "Israel received the Torah so that no nation and no language could rule over them."[36]

A classical midrash relevant to the present theme interprets Deuteronomy 33:3 as follows:

> "Indeed, O lover of nations, all his holy ones are in your charge" — is interpreted as follows: Moses said to the Holy One Blessed Be He, "You place two yokes on your children. The yoke of Torah and the yoke of foreign rule." The Holy One Blessed Be He said to him: "Whoever studies Torah, 'all his holy ones are in your charge.'"[37]

According to this midrash, "all his holy ones are in your charge" because whoever studies Torah is spared foreign domination. If, however, Israel casts off the yoke of Torah, the Lord becomes a "lover of nations," and places Israel under the yoke of foreign rule.

The worldview embodied in these and other passages — that Israel's political liberty is contingent upon their adherence to Torah — may have served as a damper against the rebellious activism of various zealot groups. At the same time, this is of necessity a utopian view — absolute acceptance of the Torah by all Israel is an ideal that cannot be measured, much less achieved — and thus dulls the political force of the idea of Jewish liberty. As a result, we find an increasing tendency to interpret the dual-yoke ideology in individual rather than national terms. This is not surprising, since as a practical matter, every individual Jew can live in keeping with the Torah:

> Whoever takes upon himself the yoke of Torah, which was likened to fire, the yoke of foreign rule is cast off him, which was also likened to fire. And whoever casts off himself the yoke of Torah, which was likened to fire, the yoke of foreign rule is placed upon him, which was also likened to fire. As Scripture states:[38] "I will set my face against them; although they escape from the fire, the fire shall still consume them." (Ezek. 15:7)[39]

---

35. Sifre Zuta to Numbers 15:40 (page 289 in the Horovitz edition [Jerusalem, 1966]).

36. B. Avoda Zarah 5a.

37. This midrash appears in *Magen Avot*, Rabbi Shimon bar Tzemach Duran's commentary to m. Avot 3.5 as a citation from the Sifre Deuteronomy. And while the passage does not appear in our editions of the Sifre, it stands to reason that it once did. It is also found in Yalqut Shimoni ad loc., §951, in the Tanhuma (both the Buber edition and the print edition), and in Deuteronomy Rabbah ad loc. (page 130 of the Lieberman edition [Jerusalem, 1940]). See also b. Bava Batra 8a.

38. See also Targum Jonathan to this verse.

39. Mekhilta of Rabbi Shimon bar Yohai to Exodus 19:18 (page 144 in the Epstein-Melamed edition [Jerusalem, 1955]).

It appears that already in the late Second Temple period this shift found expression within the various Jewish concepts of liberty. Not only does liberty come to be understood as an individual quality, it undergoes a radical interiorization, largely due to the close link between the acceptance of the yoke of Torah and the notion of internal liberty:

> "The tablets were the work of God, and the writing was the writing of God, engraved *(harut)* upon the tablets" (Exod 32:16): Do not read engraved *(harut)*, rather liberty *(herut)*. For no one is as free as one who studies Torah.[40]

According to this view, the four cubits of Torah law become an enclave of sorts, free from the rule of any foreign nation. As Nehuniah ben ha-Kanah states: "Whoever accepts the yoke of Torah is released from the yoke of foreign rule and of proper conduct *(derekh 'eretz);* whoever casts off the yoke of Torah is burdened with the yoke of foreign rule and proper conduct."[41] It is difficult to ascertain whether this dictum has practical ramifications, namely, that one who accepts the yoke of Torah thereby changes his social status.[42] In either case, Nehuniah ben ha-Kanah's statement has far-reaching theoretical implications, so much so that the concept of liberty in his and similar statements has an almost existential dimension.[43] Moreover, we find ourselves much closer to abstract Greek philosophy, since the three yokes (Torah, political rule, and proper conduct) parallel the tripartite division of ancient philosophy: theoretical, political, and practical life. Note, too, that many ancient thinkers argued that the true philosopher should devote his life to contemplation and be relieved of the political and practical aspects of human existence. Moreover, both the Stoics and the Epicureans held that only the philosopher can be truly free.[44] As Epicurus states: "One must be a slave to philosophy to achieve true liberty."[45] The similarity to the rabbinic saying is striking. Note,

40. Mishnah Avot 6.2. See also the parallels cited in H. L. Strack and P. Billerbeck, *Kommentar zum Neuen Testament* (Munich, 1926). 3.508-509, as well as the Epistle to James 1:25 and 2:12.

41. Mishnah Avot 3.5.

42. On which see Büchler, *Sin and Atonement,* 89-92.

43. Compare the secondary version preserved in Avot de-Rabbi Nathan version A, chapter 2 (pages 70-71 in the Schechter edition), and version B, chapter 32 (page 68).

44. For a discussion of this view among the Greek and Roman philosophers, see Pines, "The Concept of Liberty," 254-255.

45. Cited in Seneca's eighth epistle to Lucilius, §7. See also the ninth epistle attributed to Heraclites (page 84 in the Attridge edition [Missoula, 1976]): "Only wickedness enslaves and only virtue *(aretē)* liberates."

moreover, that neither the rabbinic view that accepting the yoke of Torah is true liberty nor the philosophical notion that enslavement to philosophy is itself freedom poses a direct threat to the existing social and political order.

Let us return to the earlier stages of the Jewish concept of liberty, one of the key foci of which involves the interpretation of Deuteronomy 32:8-9:[46] "When the Most High apportioned the nations, when he divided humankind, he fixed the boundaries of the peoples according to the number of the gods;[47] the Lord's own portion was his people, Jacob his allotted share." In other words, God divided the other nations to the lesser gods, but kept Israel as a personal patrimony. In Jubilees 15:31-32 we find an explanation of these verses that reflects the spirit of this work: ". . . for there are many nations and many peoples, and they all belong to him, but over all of them he caused spirits to rule so that they might lead them astray from following him. But over Israel he did not cause any angel or spirit[48] to rule because he alone is their ruler. . . ." These verses are based on the notion that every nation is overseen by a particular angel who is their שׂר, prince.[49] A similar explanation of Deuteronomy 32 is offered in Ben Sira 17.17: "He appointed a ruler for every nation, but Israel is the Lord's own portion."[50]

---

46. S. A. Löwenstamm has devoted two important articles to these verses: "The Lord's Portion" (Hebrew), *Shmuel Deem Volume* (Jerusalem, 1958), 120-125; "The Lord's Portion" (Hebrew), *Bible Studies: In Honor of the One Hundred Year Anniversary of the Birth of M. D. Cassuto* (Jerusalem, 1987), 149-172. I accept the position set forward in the first article, while noting the important material cited in the second. See also, D. Flusser, *Judaism and the Origins of Christianity*, 288, n. 33.

47. The Masoretic Text reads: "according to the number of the Children of Israel." On this question see the two articles by Löwenstamm (cited in the pervious note), as well as *Biblica Hebraica* (Stuttgart, 1983), 345; E. Qimron, "A Review Article on Songs of the Sabbath Sacrifice," *HTR* 79 (1986), 369-370; C. Newsom, *Songs of the Sabbath Sacrifice* (Atlanta, 1985), 89.

48. This phrasing may be an allusion to Isaiah 63:9: "In all their distress, it was no messenger or angel but his presence that saved them; in his love and in his pity he redeemed them." This reading, which follows the Septuagint and not the Masoretic Text, may indeed be the more original (even Buber, who usually adheres to the Masoretic reading, uses it in his translation). This reading also underlies 1QM 13.14 and is reflected in rabbinic dicta, and see Flusser, *Judaism and the Origins of Christianity*, 252, n. 24. Regarding 1QM 13.14, see the Rule of Blessings (1Q28b) 4.23-24: ". . . of your hand the men of the council of God and not by the hand of the prince. . . ." On Isaiah 63:7-14 see J. Morgenstern, "Heavenly Host," *HUCA* 23 (1950-1951), 183-203.

49. See Y. Licht, *Biblical Encyclopedia* (Hebrew) (Jerusalem, 1954), 5.387-388, *s.v.* שׂר.

50. This passage was not preserved in Hebrew. In some of the Greek manuscripts this verse is preceded by the words "When he divided up the nations of the earth," and this is most likely a secondary expansion, similarly based on Deuteronomy 32. The "Book of Dream Visions," an independent composition preserved in 1 Enoch (chapters 83-90), composed during the days of Judah Maccabee, is in accord with the view that each nation has its own angel. In this apocalyptic work, they appear as seventy sheep. God gives them dominion over Israel after the

These interpretive traditions are developed in a midrash preserved both in Pirke de-Rabbi Eliezer §24[51] and in Targum Jonathan to Genesis 11:7-8 and to Deuteronomy 32:8.[52] The following is from Pirke de-Rabbi Eliezer:

> Rabbi Simeon said: The Holy One, blessed be He, called to the seventy angels, who surround the throne of his glory, and He said to them: Come, let us go down and confuse the seventy nations and the seventy languages. Whence (do we know) that the Holy One, blessed be He, spoke to them? Because it is said, "Let us go down" (Gen 11:7). "Let me go down" is not written, but "Let us go down." And they cast lots among them. Because it is said, "When the Most High apportioned the nations, when he divided humankind" (Deut 32:8). The lot of the Holy One, blessed be He, fell upon Abraham and upon his seed, as it is said, "the Lord's own portion was his people, Jacob his allotted share." The Holy One, blessed be He, said: The portion and lot which fallen to me, is what my soul desired, as it is said, "The boundary lines have fallen for me in pleasant places; I have a goodly heritage" (Ps 16:6). The Holy One, blessed be He, descended with the seventy angels, who surround the throne of His glory, and they confused their speech into seventy nations and seventy languages. Each nation had its own writing and its own language, and He appointed an angel over each people. And Israel fell unto His lot and portion, as it is said: "the Lord's own portion was his people."[53]

As these sources indicate, the ancient interpreters continued to develop the idea already found *in nuce* in Deuteronomy: God appointed angelic princes over the rest of the nations, but kept Israel as his own lot, suggesting, perhaps, that foreign rule over Israel is fundamentally illegitimate.

---

destruction of the First Temple (89.59), but in the end of days sentences these seventy shepherds to the fires of hell (90.22-26), and all the nations of the world "fall down and worship those sheep [Israel], making petition to them and obeying them in every respect" (90.30). The princes of the nations also appear in Daniel 10, but there (verse 21) Israel too is assigned a prince, the angel Michael. It seems this was also the view of 1QM and of 1 Enoch 20.5. And see S. Löwenstamm, *Biblical Encyclopedia* 4.881-882, *s.v.* מיכאל.

51. It is also cited in Yalqut ha-Mekiri to Psalm 55:10 (page 290 in the Buber edition [Jerusalem, 1964]), and in Yalqut Shimoni to Genesis, §62 (page 234 in the Hyman-Shiloni edition [Jerusalem, 1973]), and see the comments therein. See also Midrash Tehillim to Psalm 16:10.

52. Though Targum Jonathan appears to draw directly from Pirke de-Rabbi Eliezer, here it clearly reflects sources not preserved in that collection. In the translation to Deuteronomy 32:8 the Targum mentions the nations born of the sons of Noah, and the seventy "sons of Israel" who went to Egypt. The latter clearly alludes to the Masoretic reading "according to the number of the children of Israel" and not "according to the number of the gods."

53. *Pirke de Rabbi Eliezer,* translated by Gerald Friedlander (New York, 1965), 176-177.

We noted above the connection between Jewish political freedom and the kingdom of heaven. They differ, however, in that the former — ultimately a religious concept anchored in Israel's election — leads to the idea of political independence and the illegitimacy of foreign rule. As such, the eschatological dimension is less pronounced in the ideal of liberty than in that of the kingdom of heaven. To be sure, the yearning for liberty may be channeled toward the future, as a result of the present state of political domination. Only then will Israel be free of foreign rule and only then will the kingdom of heaven be fully manifest. Another difference between the two terms is that while the ideal of political liberty is limited to the Jewish people, already in the Bible we find a universalistic (and starkly eschatological) understanding of the kingdom of heaven. And yet the kingdom of heaven does not refer only to a future state: God's kingdom is already upon us, though only potentially, while in the end of days it will be fully realized.[54] As Targum Jonathan renders the conclusion of the Song of the Sea (Exod 15:18), God has "a crown of kingship and he is the king of kings in this world, and the kingship of the world to come is his and will be for all eternity."[55]

The Song of the Sea ends with the words: "The Lord will reign for ever and ever." From the perspective of the later readership, this phrase — the tense of which is unclear in the Hebrew — appears to refer to a future time, when the kingdom of God will be revealed. This despite the fact that, philologically, the verse may well be stating that God's kingship is temporally unlimited, that is, exists even now. This was the understanding of the Targum Jonathan rendering cited above, and it is in this sense that the verse is cited in Mishnah Avot 6.11. The Septuagint too translates the verse into the Greek present ("The Lord rules forever and ever" [Exod 15:18]), as does Onkelos.[56] We cannot ascertain whether these translations adopted the present tense in order to discourage a misunderstanding of the biblical verse. After all, the "future" reading of Exodus 15:18 is guided not only by the linguistic norms of the day, but also by the powerful eschatological dimension inherent in the notion of the kingdom of heaven. In any case, there is no question that Rabbi Yose the Galilean, in his discussion of this verse,[57] undertakes an open polemic against those who would locate the revelation of the kingdom of heaven

---

54. See D. Flusser, *Das Christentum — eine Jüdische Religion* (Munich, 1990), 39-44; B. H. Young, *Jesus and His Jewish Parables* (New York, 1989), 189-199 and 222-229.

55. See the full text of Targum Jonathan to Exodus 15:18, as well as the other Aramaic targumim, all of which are enlightening.

56. Jerome, however, uses the future: *regnabit*. See also, The Wisdom of Solomon 3.8.

57. See the Mekhilta of Rabbi Ishmael, Shirata 10, Lauterbach 2.80; see also Mekhilta of Rabbi Shimon bar Yohai (Epstein-Melamed, 100); Bacher, *Aggadot ha-Tannaim*, 360.

in the future: "Rabbi Yose the Galilean says: Had the Israelites at the sea said, 'The Lord is king for ever and ever,' no nation or kingdom would ever have ruled over them. But they said, 'The Lord will rule forever and ever' — in the future."[58] According to Rabbi Yose the Galilean, then, Israel received the kingdom of heaven while on the shore of the Red Sea, but they committed an error: by stating "the Lord will reign forever and ever" instead of recognizing God's present kingship. Had they done so, no nation or language would ever have dominated them. Against whom is this polemic aimed? Undoubtedly against those who exaggerate the eschatological dimension of the kingdom of heaven, and/or those who turn away from the present aspect of God's kingdom (e.g., apocalyptic prophets and seers), expecting it to be revealed at some future time without taking any action toward this end. The importance of Rabbi Yose's dictum lies in the way it weaves together political independence and foreign subjugation with the notion of the kingdom of heaven. He clearly does not state that had the Children of Israel stood on the shores of the Red Sea and accepted the kingdom of heaven in its fullest sense, the eschatological redemption would already have been attained. Rather, no nation or language would have been able to subjugate Israel politically.[59]

This midrash is evidently based on an existential understanding of the kingdom of heaven, an understanding that allowed some circles to individualize and interiorize this ideal. Needless to say, we cannot know if the zealots used the terminology of the kingdom of heaven, but there is no question that the rejection of foreign rule and striving for political independence were, for them, not deferred to a future time; the establishment of the kingdom of heaven was a current, pressing task. It follows that both the peace seekers among the sages and the zealots would accept Rabbi Yose the Galilean's midrash. The difference between them lay, most likely, in the sages' view that the kingdom of heaven could not be manifested in the present time due to the sins of Israel, while the activist zealots saw the acquiescence to foreign rule a grave sin in its own right since it was, to their mind, forbidden to accept any master other than the Lord.

If we set aside any preconceived notions and examine Josephus's statements alongside those of the sages, the picture is clear enough. However, the influence of Josephus's *The Jewish War* created a one-sided portrait in mod-

58. In Psalm 146:10 ("The Lord will reign for ever, your God, O Zion, for all generations. Praise the Lord!"), the Hebrew *yimlokh* (which is, here too, temporally ambiguous in Hebrew) is translated in the future tense in the Aramaic Targum, the Septuagint, and in the two Latin versions of Jerome.

59. This is the midrashic interpretation of the verse "The Lord will reign forever and ever."

ern scholarship. Josephus defines the concept of liberty promulgated by the group revolting against Rome, but he says nothing about the sages' views on liberty. He could not have acted otherwise, since this was an apologetic presentation aimed at silencing the critics who characterized the Jews as a rebellious nation, so Josephus downplayed the yearning for redemption and the messianic hopes of the Jewish populace as a whole. Indeed, before the discovery of the Dead Sea Scrolls, the portrait of the Essenes as outright pacifists appeared quite reliable. Josephus was able to purify the sages of the taint of anti-Roman animus; he nowhere mentions an ideological commitment to liberty. On this point, there is no real difference between *War* and *Antiquities*. But while the former discusses an ideology of liberty only in the context of the zealots, the latter speaks of liberty as an ancient Jewish ideal,[60] so much so that he describes Israel as a nation of liberty-lovers *par excellence*:[61] liberty given them by God.[62] According to *Antiquities* 6.20, the prophet Samuel addresses the people, encouraging them in their war against the Philistines, by saying that "it is not enough to yearn for liberty, one must act so that it comes about." This position is not far removed from the activism of the zealots.

Of particular note are Josephus's descriptions of Mattathias the Hasmonean, and his son Judah. According to *Antiquities*, prior to his death Mattathias told his sons, *inter alia*, that they must be prepared to die for the laws of the Torah: "[Bear] in mind, that when the Deity sees you so disposed, He will not forget you, but in admirations of your heroism will give [the laws] back to you, and will restore to you your liberty, in which you shall live securely and in the enjoyment of your own customs."[63] Judah's speech to his warriors, which appears later in the book, is even more fascinating. Josephus attributes to him the following: "If you now fight bravely, you may recover that liberty which is loved for its own sake by all men, but which to you most of all happens to be desirable because it gives you the right to worship the Deity."[64] According to Judah, fierce battle is now required in order to regain liberty, and thus return to a life of happiness, that is, to a life governed by the Torah and the ancestral customs. The battle is over the most precious of possessions: "liberty, country, ancestral laws, and religion."[65] In both these

---

60. On the difference between these two works with regard to the representation of liberty, see Hengel, *Die Zeloten*, 117-119; Michel and Bauernfeind, *Flavius Josephus: De Bello Judaico* 2.2, 267-268, which lists all the differences.

61. *AJ* 2.281; 3.19.

62. *AJ* 2.327; 3.64; 7.95.

63. *AJ* 12.281, and see also 285.

64. *AJ* 12.302-304.

65. On the political meaning of the phrase "ancestral laws," see Hans G. Kippenberg,

speeches political liberty is tied with a life lived according to the Torah. Full political independence, then, is a *sine qua non* for Israel's worship of God and fidelity to Torah laws.

It is no coincidence that Josephus attributes the most important passages on liberty to Judah Maccabee and his father. Is it significant that Josephus himself was, from his mother's side, of Hasmonean lineage?[66] We cannot discount the possibility that Josephus received his information about the early Hasmonean view of liberty via family tradition. All the same, it may be that Josephus attributed these statements to Mattathias and Judah because it seemed appropriate to connect a desire for liberty with the first fighters for Jewish independence. In any case, if the Hasmonean revolt was, in fact, a critical moment in the formation of a Second Temple ideology of liberty, this was no doubt widely recognized.

Even absent more concrete data, it is quite likely that this new ideology emerged as a result of the Hasmonean revolt, and perhaps was an initiative of the first Hasmoneans. Historical considerations, as well as the contours of the ideology, suggest it predates the Roman conquest, and may be tied to the early Hasmonean period. It was during this time, after all, that Israel achieved political independence. Such an ideology could not predate the Hasmoneans, since during the Persian and early Hellenistic periods any claim that Israel should be independent and that foreign rule was illegitimate would have appeared fantastical and absurd. In locating the genesis of the liberty ideology in the early Hasmonean period, we do not claim that its content was, at that early point, as fixed as it would become in the late Second Temple period. There was undoubtedly an evolutionary process that occurred prior to its ultimate crystallization, though the precise nature of this process cannot be recovered.

There is some evidence that points to the early Hasmoneans as the source of the liberty ideology, and to Judah Maccabee's political worldview playing an important role. We have already cited the rallying speeches Josephus attributes to Mattathias and Judah Maccabee. A similar statement is attributed to Judah in 2 Maccabees 13.10-14, where he asks his troops to fight to the death "for the laws, temple, city, country, and commonwealth *(politeia)*" (2 Macc 13.14). This term, *politeia*, appears also in *Jewish Antiquities* 12.280, in the last words of the dying Mattathias, who asks his sons to "preserve our country's customs, and to restore our ancient form of government *(politeia)*."

"Die Jüdischen Überlieferung als πάτριοι νόμοι," *Die Restauration der Götter* (Würzburg, 1986), 45-54.

66. Josephus, *Vita*, 3.4.

It is, of course, possible that both Josephus and 2 Maccabees attribute these words to the Hasmoneans *ex post facto*. But this cannot be for 1 Maccabees, where we learn that during the days of Simon, Judah's brother (142 B.C.E.), "the yoke of the Gentiles was removed from Israel and the people began to write in their documents and contracts 'In the first year of Simon the great high priest and commander and leader of the Jews'" (1 Macc 13.41-42). We have already encountered the image of the "yoke of the Gentiles," and I believe this verse refers to winning political independence.[67] In the opening of the "Declaration of Independence" in 1 Maccabees, we are told that Simon and his brothers "repulsed Israel's enemies and established its freedom" (1 Macc 14.26). This formulation undoubtedly stems from the circles of Simon himself.

Another source is the epistle of Judah Maccabee, preserved in the beginning of 2 Maccabees (2 Macc 1.10–2.18). While the word liberty does not appear in the letter, it is an important document for the Second Temple concept of liberty, not least because its author is Judah Maccabee himself.[68] The epistle was, of course, written in Greek, but the style suggests it was originally composed in Hebrew. In order to understand the novelty of Judah's address, I first cite a passage from this epistle that deals with the end of Nehemiah's prayer, following the dedication of the Second Temple:

> Accept this sacrifice on behalf of all your people Israel and preserve your portion and make it holy. Gather together our scattered people, set free those who are slaves[69] among the Gentiles, look on those who are rejected and despised, and let the Gentiles know that you are our God. Punish those who oppress and are insolent with pride. Plant your people in your holy place, as Moses promised. (2 Macc 1.26-29)

---

67. See Schürer, *History*, 1.190, and n. 4 there. Note the statements of Pompeius Trogus (cited by Justinus) on the Jews: "They won their liberty in battle" and "They were the first among the eastern nations to win their liberty"; Stern, *Greek and Latin Authors* 1.334-342, §137.

68. Though some scholars argued the epistle is a forgery, there is a growing consensus that this is, in fact, the letter sent by Judah Maccabee to the Jewish community in Egypt, a few days before the rededication of the temple. See D. Flusser, "Jerusalem in Second Temple Literature," in the present volume; B. Z. Wacholder, "The Letter from Judah Maccabee to Aristobulus," *HUCA* 49 (1978), 133-189; Schürer, *History*, 3.533-534; H. W. Attridge, "Historiography," *Jewish Writings of the Second Temple Period*, M. Stone (ed.) (Assen and Philadelphia, 1984), 182-183. On the concept of liberty, see the fascinating discussion of the ideological backdrop of 1 and 2 Maccabees in J. W. Van Henten, *Die Entstehung der jüdischen Martyrologie* (Leiden, 1989), 149-161.

69. This word, which corresponds to the Hebrew עובדים ("workers," "slaves"), may be the result of an error by the Greek transcriber, who confused it with its homonym אובדים ("those who wander," "those who are lost"), in which case the verse alludes to Isaiah 27:13.

These requests reflect the desires of Israel at that time. Similar motifs appear at the end of the epistle, where Judah addresses the Jews of Egypt as follows:

> Since, therefore, we are about to celebrate the purification, we write to you. Will you therefore please keep the days? It is God who has saved all his people, and has returned the inheritance to all, and the kingship[70] and the priesthood and the consecration, as he promised through the law. We have hope in God that he will soon[71] have mercy on us and will gather us from everywhere under heaven into his holy place, for he has rescued us from great evils and has purified the place. (2 Macc 2.16-18)

This formulation provides insight into Judah's goals in purifying the temple.[72] Judah hoped that the rededication of the temple would pave the way for a new and critically important era in the history of the Jewish people. Up to that point, the Jews both within Israel and without were subjugated by foreign nations, the land was oppressed by the Romans, the priesthood was illegitimate, and the temple was desecrated. But now God's promises to His people have been fulfilled. It should be noted that the author represents the dedication of the temple as God's saving and returning the inheritance to *all* Israel. That is, also to the Jews living in the Diaspora. The author further states that the Lord gave kingship to his people. True, full independence has not yet been attained, but Judah Maccabee believes the purification of the temple paves the way for it, so that the present event is like a harbinger of national redemption. Now, then, is the time that God's second promise can come to fruition, namely, the ingathering of exiles. If so, Judah Maccabee believes this process may, in the future, culminate in ultimate redemption, but even so the practical-political goal remains paramount. And while the yearning for political independence is evident in the epistle, there is no indication that the Jewish people are — by their nature and their religion — congenitally free from foreign rule.

Further confirmation that the understanding of liberty as political independence originates with Judah Maccabee and his circle is found in the Book of Dream Visions (chapters 83–90 of 1 Enoch).[73] In this apocalypse,

---

70. The Greek term used here is *basileion,* "a thing that belongs to the royal house." The same word appears in the Greek translation of Exodus 19:6 — "a kingdom of priests and a holy nation." There is a link between the epistle and the Greek version of this Exodus verse.

71. On the meaning of this term see Flusser, *Judaism and the Origins of Christianity,* 101.

72. The following discussion is based on my "Jerusalem in Second Temple Literature," pp. 60-61 in the present volume.

73. See Appendix B, below.

Enoch witnesses the entire history of Israel in a dream. Israel is represented as a herd, while the Gentile nations are wild beasts and birds of prey, and the seventy heavenly princes of the nations are the shepherds of the herd. According to this text, God gave the princes of the nations authority over Israel as a punishment for the sins of the people, but at the same time determined that any injury to Israel beyond what has been commanded will result in the shepherds — i.e., the princes — being punished (1 Enoch 89.59-64). And so it was: the shepherds killed more of the flock than was permitted, showing them no mercy, and for this the heavenly princes of the Gentile nations will be sent to the fires of hell in the end of days (1 Enoch 90.22-25). The content of this vision indicates that Israel was given over to the Gentile nations during the Assyrian conquest of the northern kingdom, a time that, as a matter of historical fact, marks the first step in the loss of Jewish political sovereignty. The historic survey in the Book of Dream Visions ends with the wars of Judah Maccabee, wars in which the enemies of Judah "gather and battle with him and seek to remove his horn, but without any success" (1 Enoch 90.12). At this point, the author shifts from his own historical time, which is also the time of Judah Maccabee, to the end of days, where he describes the future attack on Judah and his warriors by the enemies of Israel (1 Enoch 90.15-16), God's direct intervention, and, ultimately, Israel's victory over the nations of the world (1 Enoch 90.17-19). Finally, there will come a great day of judgment, which immediately precedes the coming of the messiah, in which God sentences the princes of the Gentile nations (1 Enoch 90.22-25). Clearly, the Book of Dream Visions, which was composed in the very days of Judah Maccabee, dates the beginning of Israel's political subjugation to the conquest of Samaria, and its end to the eschatological battles of Judah Maccabee. This view stands in remarkable agreement to the position outlined in Judah Maccabee's own epistle, though his approach was undoubtedly less "messianic" and more practical.

The importance of Judah Maccabee's epistle — as noted above — lies in the fact that in it he communicates his motives in rededicating the temple, which are anchored in the political view that would guide him throughout his life. Judah understood that after Antiochus's decrees it was no longer possible to return to the earlier status quo and merely annul the decrees. This was probably a minority opinion at the time, but the subsequent events proved it to be correct, as the fate of the priesthood of Alcimus demonstrates.[74] Upon his appointment, the scribes and Hasidim gathered and made peace with him, though the Hasidim were not necessarily pacifists or even moderate,

74. See 1 Maccabees 7, and especially verses 12-17; Schürer, *History* 1.169.

rather a group of warriors that had joined Mattathias when he ruled it permissible to fight on the Sabbath.[75] Now that the decrees of Antiochus were annulled and a legitimate priest installed, they believed the status quo had been restored and there was no longer any reason to revolt. Nonetheless, Alcimus seized sixty of them and had them executed.[76]

We see, then, that the attribution of these statements to Mattathias and Judah was done with a clear knowledge of the thought process of these early heroes of the revolt. Josephus, a descendent of the Hasmonean house, is correct when he states that Mattathias and his sons exhorted their men "to preserve our country's customs and to restore our ancient form of government, which is in danger of passing away,"[77] since liberty was a *sine qua non* of a full and meaningful Jewish life. From Judah's epistle (2 Maccabees 2.16-18) it appears that it was he who established full political independence as the goal of the struggle, a goal finally attained by his brother, Simon, in 142 B.C.E. This is evident from the fact that documents were dated to the onset of Simon's reign,[78] and from the "Declaration of Independence" found in chapter 14 of 2 Maccabees. This book further indicates that this ideology did indeed guide Simon when he conducted the (failed) negotiations with Antiochus VII Sidetes. The latter demanded of Simon the territories he had conquered, but Simon answered: "We have neither taken foreign land nor seized foreign property, but only the inheritance of our ancestors, which at one time had been unjustly taken by our enemies. Now that we have the opportunity, we are firmly holding the inheritance of our ancestors" (1 Macc 15.33-34). However, Simon was willing to pay Antiochus one hundred talents for Yaffo (Joppa) and Gezer (Gazara). In short, Simon considered the territories that were formerly, before the Babylonian exile, part of Judea, to be "the inheritance of our ancestors," an integral part of the independent Jewish state.[79]

Simon, too, saw the link between national liberty and political inde-

75. 1 Maccabees 2.42.

76. 1 Maccabees 7.16-18. On the Jewish legend that reflects these events and its significance for the death of the Masada rebels, see below, n. 96.

77. *AJ* 12.280-282, 302-304.

78. 1 Maccabees 13.41-42.

79. See F. M. Abel, *Les Livres des Maccabées* (Paris, 1949), 272; J. A. Goldstein, *I Maccabees* (New York, 1976), 516. Note that the primary function of the opening section of 1 Maccabees, up to the death of Mattathias and the encomium of Judah Maccabee (3.9), is to justify the armed rebellion. See, e.g., the words attributed to Mattathias (2.19-22), putatively spoken out loud before the murder. In this sense, the opening of 1 Maccabees plays a similar role to the legends surrounding the figure of Wilhelm Tell and the liberation of Switzerland and, as such, should be treated with great caution. I hope to return to the question of the historic reliability of 1 Maccabees in a future study.

pendence as self-evident. But note that his argument is historical; he does not know the super-historical ideology so typical of the later Second Temple of the sages and, most prominently, the zealots. This concept, in its most sublime formulation, is (like any ideological abstraction) impressive; but by its nature this clear and elevated slogan contains real dangers. This is what happened among late Second Temple thinkers, who, in their zeal, understood liberty as an ideal unto itself. As such, they divorced it from any practical considerations, and from the yoke of justice and law. This development yielded not political independence, but a national calamity whose consequences are still felt today. The closing chord of this tragedy was the suicide of the Masada fighters.

II

Scholars who study the depths of the human soul rightly recognize that sadism and masochism are two sides of the same coin. It is no surprise, then, that when violent and even deadly aggressions aimed outward are frustrated, they may be turned back inward, toward the aggressor. In extreme cases, this dynamic may lead to suicide,[80] which may explain the not infrequent occurrence of suicide among the zealots.

This is the explanation offered for the earliest of these events, the old man who killed his family and took his own life in one of the caves in Arbel during Herod's Galilean campaign against Antigonus.[81] According to Josephus, the king encountered an old man, the father of seven children, and asked that he exit the cave, thus saving his life and the life of his family members. The old man, however, killed his wife and children, threw their bodies into the ravine, then jumped after them to his death. When Gamla fell to the Romans, and the defenders despaired of saving their own lives, they hurled their families and themselves into the ravine below the fort.[82] Four thousand died in battle with the Romans, and five thousand took their own life. In Josephus's telling, the siege of Gamla turned against the defenders when a storm arose and blew in the direction of the city, thus tilting the outcome in the Roman favor — a hint that the storm was a sign from heaven. As we will see below, a similar event is told concerning the fall of Masada.

80. For a general discussion of the suicide at Masada see Stern, "Masada," 375-387.

81. *BJ* 1.311-313 and *AJ* 4.429-430. On this event see Stern, "Masada," 386. According to Stern, Josephus's source for this story is Nicholas of Damascus.

82. *BJ* 4.76-83, and see Stern, "Masada," 384.

Another suicide is related from the battle of Bet She'an, whose Gentile residents rose up and began to kill their Jewish neighbors.[83] One of the Jews of Bet She'an was Simon ben Saul, a military hero who had gained a name for himself in battles against rebellious Jews, and was now receiving his punishment for the deaths he had caused to his fellow Jews. Seeing the Gentile slaughter of the Jews of Bet She'an, he drew his sword, but not in order to attack the enemy. Wishing to atone for his crimes, and to deny the Gentile fighters the glory of slaying him, he killed his wife and children, as well as his elderly parents, and then fell on his sword.

III

We have cited a number of Jewish suicides during the great revolt, as they may help us understand the events at Masada.[84] We also discussed the Jewish liberty ideal and the special form it takes in the zealot circles, including the Masada fighters. At this point, we move to another topic, no less important than the conceptual history. Namely, we will try to reconstruct how the contemporaries of the Masada warriors justified the latter's horrific deed. Our primary source is the speech Josephus attributes to Elazar ben Yair, the leader of the Masada rebels. As a preliminary statement I suggest that the death of the defenders of Masada was understood as an act of atonement for their sins. If we apply this hypothesis to the conceptual framework of Second Temple Judaism, we will be able to shed light on the spiritual world of the period. But first, let us examine once again the death of Simon ben Saul, of Beth She'an.

The similarities between the tragic death of this figure and the suicide of the Masada defenders are, to be sure, striking. In both cases, the fighters killed their families and only then committed suicide, in part so that they not fall into enemy hands. More importantly, both cases are then justified as self-inflicted punishment for earlier transgression.[85] There is also an interesting parallel between the Masada story and the fall of Gamla, as a sudden change in the direction of the wind presages a turn to the worse for the besieged Jews

83. *BJ* 2.466-467.

84. We should also mention the suicide of the Yodfat defenders.

85. In the speech Josephus attributes to Simon ben Saul (*BJ* 2.472-473), the latter admits his guilt and announces he will carry out the punishment himself. Note the similar statement Josephus places in the mouth of Elazar ben Yair in his first speech (*BJ* 7.329): "But did we forsooth hope that we alone of all the Jewish nation would survive and preserve our freedom, as persons guiltless towards God and without a hand in crime . . . ?"

— a change Josephus presents as divine intervention in favor of the Romans.[86] Josephus even has Elazar ben Yair allude to this event in his first speech:

> For it was not of their own accord that those flames which were driving against the enemy turned back upon the wall constructed by us; no, all this betokens wrath at the many wrongs which we madly dared to inflict upon our countrymen. The penalty for those crimes let us pay not to our bitterest foes, the Romans, but to God through the act of our own hands.[87]

Now, in late Second Temple Judaism, carrying out a divine death sentence by suicide was seen as consistent and positive, since it was assumed that the act was a form of atonement. This view is part of a robust, organic worldview concerning sin and atonement,[88] the core of which being that if one admits guilt and accepts full responsibility for his transgressions, proclaiming the punishment just, he atones fully for his sins.

Our starting point will be the earliest such statement — dating back to Hasmonean times — the dictum of Yehudah ben Tabbai in Mishnah Avot 1.8: "When the litigants stand before you, consider them guilty, but when they depart from you, consider them innocent, for they have accepted the judgment." This suggests that Yehudah ben Tabbai is promoting a humane treatment of the condemned, that is, that they not be considered guilty because "they have accepted the judgment." This is not, however, the final word in the matter, and the trend toward empathy with the other — so typical of the Judaism of those days — intensified in later sources until it became a new Jewish humanism. Thus, for example, we find a midrashic interpretation of Deuteronomy 25:3, preserved only in Midrash Hagadol:

> "Your brother will be degraded" (Deut 25:3): Before he was degraded, he is called guilty, as it is written, "If the person in the wrong deserves to be flogged" (Deut 25:2). But once he is flogged, he is your brother. Before he was degraded, one may treat him with disdain, but once he has been degraded, one may not treat him with disdain. Beloved are the lashes, for they atone for sins, as it is written, "according to his offense" (Deut 25:2)

---

86. *BJ* 7.318-319.

87. *BJ* 7.332-333.

88. For a discussion of death as atonement see E. Lohse's fascinating *Märtyrer und Gottesknecht* (Göttingen, 1963). For a broad treatment of these themes, see Büchler, *Sin and Atonement*.

— so that the lashes are fitting to atone for his offense. Beloved are the lashes, for they make one beloved in the eyes of his heavenly father. As it is written, "And if anyone asks them, 'What are these lashes on your chest?' the answer will be 'The lashes I received in the house of my beloved.' That is, these lashes caused me to love [the] heavenly father. . . ."[89]

This interpretation represents a profound shift relative to the dictum of Yehudah ben Tabbai. We are no longer dealing with humane treatment of the condemned, but with a belief that punitive measures as such are cathartic: "Beloved are the lashes, for they atone for sins. . . . Beloved are the lashes, for they make one beloved in the eyes of his heavenly father." Needless to say, the same sentimental view holds also for the most severe punishment, the death sentence. And so the rabbis teach that one who accepts his death sentence is absolved of all his transgressions! "It is typical of the condemned to make confession, for every one that makes his confession has a share in the world to come. . . . If he knows not how to make his confession they say to him, 'say, May my death serve as atonement for all my sins.'"[90] Elsewhere we find views that provide a still more merciful perspective, namely, that it is not capital punishment but death as such that atones for sins: "Death and Yom Kippur atone when one repents."[91] And similarly: "The purification offering (חטאת) and the reparation offering (אשם) and death and Yom Kippur cannot atone in the absence of repentance . . . if one repents, he is atoned for, if not, he is not atoned for."[92] But Rabbi Yehudah states: "Death and Yom Kippur atone with repentance; repentance atones with death; and the day of death counts as atonement."[93] The statement that those executed by the courts are atoned by confession is deeply humanistic.[94] The balance between crime and punish-

---

89. Midrash Hagadol, Deuteronomy (page 560 in the Fisch edition [Jerusalem, 1973]), whence it was copied into D. Hoffmann's Midrash Tannaim (Berlin, 1909), 164. This midrash was known to Rabbi Nathan, who applied it to martyrdom (see Mekhilta of Rabbi Ishmael, Tractate Bahodesh, 6 (page 226 in the Horovitz-Rabin edition).

90. M. Sanhedrin 6.2, and also t. Sanhedrin 9.5.

91. M. Yoma 8.8.

92. T. Yoma 4.9.

93. T. Yoma 4.9. See also the parallels cited in S. Lieberman, *Tosephta ki-feshutah* (New York, 1962), 4.826-827. I cannot accept Lieberman's non-literal understanding of Rabbi Yehudah's statement ("the day of death counts as atonement"). Such statements were never intended as normative guidance for God.

94. The present article will not deal with the idea that God purifies one through suffering, a classical formulation of which is already found in the apocryphal Psalms of Solomon 10.1-2 (dating back to the days of Pompey). We also will not discuss the related idea that the death of a righteous man atones for others, on which see my "Martyrology in the Second Temple Period and Early Christianity," pp. 248-57 in the present volume.

ment — so dear to Jewish teachings — is preserved, but judgment is somehow transformed into mercy.

From this soil emerges the radical notion that one who has committed a capital offense can atone for his crimes by recognizing his guilt and executing the punishment himself, i.e., commiting suicide. We have already noted that Josephus interprets the suicide of Samuel ben Saul of Bet She'an in this way.[95] In terms of the Masada martyrs, a more telling story is that of the suicide of Alcimus, the Hasmonean high priest who served in the early days of the dynasty.[96] The legend regarding his death has no basis in fact, since Alcimus never took his life; he died of a stroke.[97] Nonetheless, there is one historical element it preserves, namely, that sixty of the Hasidim were captured and executed with his knowledge, and perhaps even on his command.[98] It further appears that Yose ben Yoezer — who was, according to the midrash, Alcimus's uncle — was one of those executed.[99] According to the legend, as Yose ben Yoezer was about to be crucified, Alcimus (known by his Hebrew name, Yakim), rode by his relative on horseback, on the Sabbath. When Yose ben Yoezer explained to the wicked priest the punishment God metes out to those who anger him, "the words entered [Alcimus] like the venom of a serpent, and he went to fulfill by his own hand the four forms of capital punishment. . . . Yose ben Yoezer was sleeping [on the cross] and saw the death of Alcimus rising through the air. He said: 'He preceded me to Paradise by a whit.'"

The sages derive the same lesson from the story of King Saul's death.[100] Already Josephus was taken with Saul's bravery in deciding to go into battle, even though Samuel had foretold his death.[101] Saul did not flee, choosing instead his own death and the death of his sons. Rabbi Simon ben Lakish offers similar praise of Saul: "At that moment the Holy One Blessed Be He said to the ministering angels, 'Come see a creature that I created in the world, a form that I formed! Generally, a man goes to the inn without his sons so as

---

95. See above, n. 85.

96. The legend is found in Bereshit Rabbah 65.22, to Genesis 27:27 (pages 742-744 in the Theodor-Albeck edition), in Yalqut Shimoni, §115 (pages 553-554 in the Mossad Harav Kook edition), and in Midrash Tehillim to Psalm 11:7 (pages 103-104 in the Buber edition).

97. See 1 Maccabees 9.54-56; Josephus, *AJ* 12.413.

98. See 1 Maccabees 7.16-17. On the possibility that Alcimus commanded the killings, see 2 Maccabees 14.6-10.

99. The Mishnah refers to Yose ben Yoezer as "a Hasid (or: a pious man) among the priests" (m. Hagigah 2.7). I am aware of the chronological difficulties this identification entails.

100. Leviticus Rabbah 26.7-9 (pages 605-606 in the Margaliot edition [Jerusalem, 1972]), and also in Pirke de-Rabbi Eliezer 33.

101. *AJ* 6.344-345.

not to make an improper impression, while this one [Saul] goes into battle knowing he will be killed, takes his sons with him, and rejoices in the harsh judgment meted to him."[102]

The end of this midrash hints that King Saul chose his death and the death of his sons in order to fulfill the judgment, though the idea is not developed further. Another midrash, however, emphasizes Saul's acceptance of the divine judgment against him, and his self-castigation as a way of atoning for his sins. Prior to his final battle, Saul consulted the recently deceased prophet Samuel through a medium. According to the sages, after Samuel informed the king that he would fall in the battle, Saul asked if he might not flee. To this Samuel replied: "If you flee you will be saved, but if you accept the divine judgment, tomorrow you and your sons will be with me."[103] Flight, then, will prolong Saul's earthly life, but he will lose his place in the world to come; but if he and his sons die on the battlefield, thus accepting God's judgment, his death will be an act of atonement and he and his sons will enter heaven.[104] And so the prophetic words of Samuel were fulfilled: "'Tomorrow you and your sons are with me' (1 Sam 28:19) — what is the meaning of 'with me'? Rabbi Yohanan says, 'with me, that is, in my presence.'"

The attribution to Rabbi Yohanan indicates the midrash was composed no later than his lifetime, and there are clear indications it may be significantly earlier as a dictum attributed to Jesus in the Gospel of Luke appears to be dependent upon it. Jesus was crucified between two criminals,[105] who, according to Mark (15:32) and Matthew (27:44), derided Jesus and cursed him. But according to Luke, only one of them derided Jesus, and was then rebuked by the second criminal, who said: "'Do you not fear God, since you are under the same sentence of condemnation? And we indeed have been condemned justly, for we are getting what we deserve for our deeds, but this man has done nothing wrong.' Then he said, 'Jesus, remember me when you come into your kingdom.' He replied, 'Truly I tell you, today you will be with me in Paradise'" (Luke 23.40-43).[106]

---

102. Leviticus Rabbha, 606. See also Bacher, *Aggadot ha-Tannaim*, 1.388.

103. Leviticus Rabbah, 26.

104. Compare Yose ben Yoezer's statement regarding the death of Alcimus: "He preceded me to Paradise by a whit."

105. The criminals were most likely zealots.

106. A striking aggadic parallel to the Luke narrative (already noted by Billerbeck, *Kommentar zum Neuen Testament*, 2.264) is found in Sifre Deuteronomy to Deuteronomy 32:4. "When they apprehended Rabbi Hananiah ben Teradion, he was condemned to be burned together with his Torah Scroll. When he was told of it, he recited this verse: 'The Rock, his work is perfect' (Dt 32:4). . . . A philosopher protested to the prefect, saying, 'My master, do not boast

What does this conversation mean, and why did Jesus speak as he did? His promise was an affirmative answer to the criminal's request, as the latter had admitted his guilt and the justice of his punishment; his words are a confession of sorts[107] and precisely for that reason Jesus informs him that he has a place in Paradise, for "it is typical of the condemned to make confession, for every one that makes his confession has a share in the world to come."[108] By confession and death, the criminal atoned for his sins.

The narrative in Luke 23:40-43 is a "Hasidic" tale par excellence (both in the contemporary sense and in the spirit of Second Temple Hasidism).[109] Ultimately, the story of the two criminals, one righteous the other wicked,[110] constitutes an independent narrative unit not necessarily related to Jesus. Both with regard to its content and to its genre, the story is similar to the legend concerning the death of Yose ben Yoezer and the evil Alcimus.[111] Both stories refer explicitly to Paradise (Luke in Jesus' words to the repentant criminal), and both are related to the story of Samuel's words to Saul. Here are the conclusions of all three stories, along with that of the death of Hananiah ben Teradion:

Luke 23:43	Truly I tell you, today you will be with me in Paradise
Samuel to Saul	Tomorrow you and your sons are with me

---

that you have burned the Torah, for it has now returned to the place whence it had come — its Father's house.' The prefect replied, 'Tomorrow your fate will be the same as theirs,' whereupon the philosopher said to him, 'You have conveyed good tidings to me, that tomorrow my portion will be with them in the world to come [or: Paradise]" (Sifre Deuteronomy §307, page 312 in the Hammer edition). There is a clear connection between this legend and the derashah about the death of King Saul in Leviticus Rabbah, most visible in its last sentence. Billerbeck also cites the Leviticus Rabbah legend in his discussion of Luke.

107. Lohse, *Märtyrer und Gottesknecht,* 38 n. 2, cites K. Borkhauser, *Das Wirken Christi* (Gütersloh, 1924), in this context. The latter rightly saw (p. 228) that according to Luke 23:41, the criminal admits that his punishment is justified, and thus his death atones for his sins.

108. M. Sanhedrin 6.3

109. The story of the death of Hananiah ben Teradion also belongs to this genre.

110. The image of a criminal and a righteous man being crucified (or hanged) serves Rabbi Meir in enunciating his wonderfully humane view — one rooted in the teachings of Rabbi Aqiva, his master — that God is with Israel "in all their distress" (see Isaiah 63:9). To m. Sanhedrin 6.5 we can add t. Sanhedrin 9.7: "Rabbi Meir said, When a man is in pain, what does the Divine Presence say? 'My head aches, my arm aches!' What does Scripture teach with the verse '[for anyone hung on a tree] is God's curse' (Deut 21.23)? It is akin to two identical twin brothers. One was ruler of the entire world, the other became a brigand. After some time, the brigand was captured and hanged, and all the passersby said: 'It appears the king has been hanged.' Thus Scripture states, 'for [it] is God's curse.'" See Bacher, *Aggadot ha-Tannaim* 3.59, n. 4 and 3.64, n. 3.

111. Discussed above, n. 96.

Sifre to Deut 32:4   tomorrow my portion will be with them in the world to come [or: Paradise]

Alcimus the Priest   He preceded me to Paradise by a whit

The term "Paradise" (עֵדֶן גַּן) is common to Luke and the Alcimus narrative, though the commonality is not necessarily indicative of a literary connection, since it is so self-evident in a discussion of the resting place of the souls of the righteous. However, there are two striking linguistic affinities between Jesus' response and the response of the prophet Samuel, and it is clear that the former is dependent upon the latter.[112] Indeed, Samuel's statement that "tomorrow you and your sons are with me" (1 Sam 28:19) is, in a daring exegetical twist, alluded to in Jesus' saying. The entire thrust of the Luke narrative here is similar to the story of the death of King Saul, though of course the author had to change Samuel's "tomorrow" to "today," as Jesus was to die that same day. Clearly, then, the midrash about Saul's encounter with Samuel's spirit predates the composition of Luke's account of Jesus and the criminals. This is also apparent from the words of Jesus, "Truly I tell you, today you will be with me in Paradise." For there is a clear tension between this assertion and the belief of the early Christians — including the author of Luke — that Jesus' soul did not ascend to heaven since he was resurrected on the third day.[113] The upshot of all this is that the conversation between Jesus and the good criminal cannot be considered historical, but since the tension between Jesus' words and standard Christian belief is relatively subtle, the narrative found a home in Luke's gospel. We are dealing with an independent narrative that was only later reworked into the crucifixion of Jesus.

We are dealing with a "Hasidic" narrative about two crucified men, one righteous, the other wicked, a story meant to demonstrate the general rule that "those executed by the courts have a place in the world to come, since they confess all their sins."[114] But if the sinner who repents his crimes and justifies his punishment before his death is forgiven and accorded a place in the world to come, a more daring possibility arises. Namely, that a sinner who realizes he has committed a capital offense will be forgiven if he executes the

---

112. A similar literary dependence is evident in the conclusion of Hananiah ben Teradion's death.

113. On this crux see E. Klostermann, *Das Lukasevangelium* (Tübingen, 1975), 229; H. Marshall, *Commentary on Luke* (Grand Rapids, 1979), 873. It seems to me that these internal difficulties caused Marcion to pass over Luke 23:43.

114. T. Sanhedrin 9.5, with parallel at m. Sanhedrin 6.2.

punishment himself, that is, commits suicide. This is the explicit lesson of the aggadic tales about the deaths of King Saul and Alcimus.[115]

It may well be that this is the way the contemporaries of the Masada martyrs — perhaps even Josephus himself — interpreted their act as their taking their lives to atone for their sins, the many sins they committed against their fellow Jews. Josephus alludes to this very interpretation,[116] which was, as we have seen, his understanding of the suicide of Simon of Beth She'an in the early days of the revolt against Rome.[117] Needless to say, Josephus does not explicitly say that these deaths served as atonement for sin. One of the reasons for this silence is undoubtedly that atonement through suicide would appear odd to any outsider not accustomed to the special mode of thought that typifies Jewish ethics. Moreover, how could Josephus even suggest that the Masada zealots, who so despised him, won, through their suicide, a place in Paradise?

In summary, it is clear that the notion that death atones for a criminal's sins is fundamentally similar to the idea that a righteous man may die for sinners — a cornerstone of Jewish martyrology.[118] The difference is that the

---

115. Another story that touches on this theme, albeit indirectly, is the tragic death of the sons of Aaron, Nadab and Abihu. The Torah itself treats the event with ambivalence: on the one hand they sinned and were punished, on the other hand their death was a sanctification of God (Lev 10:1-3). Aaron's sons are mentioned in the Qumran War Scroll (1QM 17.2): the priest refers to their death in rallying the sons of light after a temporary defeat and promises them ultimate victory, for the deaths they have suffered in battle are nothing more than a crucible, that is, as an example of suffering that purifies. God, then, tests his people in a crucible (1QM 16.13), a people referred to as "tested by a crucible" (1QM 17.1). The priest then addresses the warriors as follows: "And you, remember the trial of Nadab and Abihu, sons of Aaron; by judging them God showed his holiness to the eyes of all the people" (1QM 17.2). Unfortunately, there is no further discussion of the meaning of the death of Aaron's sons. If we could ascertain that the War Scroll believed that the death of Nadab and Abihu atoned for their transgressions, this would be another example of atoning death, albeit with one critical difference — they did not justify God's judgment. On the positive approach to the death of Nadab and Abihu in Philo and rabbinic midrash see D. Flusser and S. Safrai, "Nadab and Abihu according to Philo and the Rabbis," pp. 286-296 in the present volume.

116. *BJ* 7.332-333.

117. *BJ* 2.466-476.

118. It is well established that this idea — that a righteous man can, through his death, atone for the sins of others — emerged following the anti-Jewish decrees of Antiochus IV. See the essays collected in J. W. van Henten (ed.), *Die Entstehung der jüdischen Martyrologie* (Leiden, 1989), particularly the studies of Henten (127-161), who deals with the earliest martyrological narratives, and H. S. Wersnel (162-196), on Greek and Roman parallels to martyrological motifs. See also Flusser, "Martyrology in the Second Temple Period and Early Christianity." K. Koch (*Deuterokanonische Zusätze zum Danielbuch* [Neukirchen, 1989]) argues that verses 14-17 of Azariah's prayer, which are a late addition to Daniel, contain the idea of atoning death in lieu of

death of an individual condemned by the court atones for his sins, while a martyr atones for the sins of others. Both cases are no doubt rooted in a primordial religious view that atonement can be acquired at the price of life itself — a form of "life in place of death" and so a form of the view that gives rise to the phenomenon of cultic sacrifice. It may well be that the antiquity of this view allowed it to produce such special fruit, and the dark idea was transformed, in unexpected circumstances, into a beacon of light. On the one hand, the notion of atoning death gave rise to the sublime "sanctification of God," that is, to Jewish martyrology — one of the summits of Jewish (and, later, Christian) religious thought. The idea of martyrdom, of self-sacrifice, allows one to overcome opposing forces and attain victory. At the same time, the idea that a criminal's death atones for his sins belongs to a very different realm of Second Temple Jewish thought. The forgiveness of sins, even for one convicted of capital offences, is part of an organic worldview, a Second Temple Jewish humanism that seeks to increase love of one's fellow man.

We have suggested that the contemporaries of the Masada martyrs interpreted the latter's suicide as a self-imposed death sentence aimed at atoning for their sins. This suggestion is supported by part of the first oration of Elazar ben Yair in Josephus, and parallels those from Josephus and the sages. Our argument is also based on the view that the zealots, including those at Masada, were considered by most Jews as sinners whose deeds had caused a great deal of suffering.[119] As for the Masada fighters themselves, it appears they (and the other zealots) shared the ideal of liberty with the sages. However, the peace-seekers among the sages believed that political independence is contingent upon moral purity, while the zealots thought that subjection to foreign rule is itself an unpardonable sin. This led to the zealots' activism and rebellion, with its calamitous results for the Jewish people.

---

cultic sacrifice, but this is doubtful. The author seems, rather, to hold that prayers are a fitting substitute for sacrifices, following Psalm 51:17-19. The argument, then, is that our supplication be pleasing to you like a burnt offering or sacrifice.

119. See *BJ* 7.254-258.

Emperor Julian on the Tower of Babel

In the course of our essay we cited a midrash, preserved in Pirke de Rabbi Eliezer 24 and Targum Jonathan to Genesis 11:7-8 and to Deuteronomy 32:8, on the confusion of tongues. According to this interpretation, God's plural address "Come, let us go down" (Gen 11:7) means that God descended to the Tower of Babel along with the seventy angels that circle his heavenly throne, and "they confused their speech into seventy nations and seventy languages. Each nation had its own writing and its own language, and He appointed an angel over each people. And Israel fell unto His lot and portion, as it is said: 'the Lord's own portion was his people' (Deut 32:9)." The midrash, then, understands the confusion of tongues at the Tower of Babel as the event described in Deuteronomy 32:8-9. There we find (following the ancient version):

> When the Most High apportioned the nations,
> when he divided humankind,
> he fixed the boundaries of the peoples
> according to the number of the gods;
> the Lord's own portion was his people,
> Jacob his allotted share.

Not only — reasons our midrashist — did the seventy angels allot seventy different languages to humanity, thus creating a confusion of tongues, they were appointed as ministers of these nations. Only Israel was "the Lord's own portion."

We cited this midrash because of its underlying argument regarding Israel's election and absolute dependence on God, while the other nations are governed by angelic ministers. Interestingly, Julian, the last pagan emperor of Rome, uses the same biblical passage to justify polytheism. Indeed, the story serves as proof that Moses erred in identifying one of the angelic ministers,[120] the (lowercase) god of Israel, with the highest divinity, creator of heaven and earth.[121]

In his critique of the Hebrew Bible, Julian adopts the religious views of the pagan philosophers that preceded him, and refers to them as "our authors." According to these writers, there is a god who created all things, who is a common father and king over all, but he divided all things among the deities that govern the nations and defend isolated cities.[122] "These gods gave each nation the laws that suit its character. This fact explains the fixed differences in the mores of different religious traditions, as well as the devotion of different nations to the laws of their forefathers and the worship of the god that defends them."[123] At this point, Julian turns to the biblical account of the confusion of tongues, but while he cites Genesis 11:1-8, he considers the plain meaning of the story a contradiction of reason and plain sense. Julian further notes that Moses omits discussion of the different characters and mores of human beings, even though they are more significant than linguistic differences. Julian suggests that Moses is writing esoterically: when he writes "let us go down," he was not attributing the confusion of tongues to God alone — others descended with him and effected the confusion, and these others were obviously similar to him. The result was not only the proliferation of languages, but also the differences in human character. In short, the Torah of Moses contains a contradiction: on the one hand it reveres a

120. Julian argues that the Jewish god is particular, as opposed to the universal deity of higher paganism. I assume that the modern accusation that Judaism is particularistic ultimately stems from Julian, though "particularism" has a different meaning for him.

121. Julian's argument is found in his *Against the Galileans* and is here cited according to *The Works of the Emperor Julian*, ed. W. C. Wright (Harvard, 1980), 3.344-359. I also rely on Yohanan Lewy, "Julian the Apostate and the Building of the Temple," *Jerusalem Cathedra* 3 (1983), 70-96, and see G. Alon, *Studies in Jewish History* (Tel Aviv, 1958), 2.315-316.

122. Julian, *Against the Galileans*, 344-345.

123. Lewy, "Julian the Apostate," 233-234. It is an open question to what extent this Neoplatonic view was influenced by the position, cited by Philo of Byblos as part of the Phoenician religion, that individual gods are assigned to particular cities and lands. This view may be part of the background of the biblical view that finds expression in Deuteronomy 32. See Eusebius, *Praeparatio Evangelica* 1.10.10, 32-42; Philo of Byblos, *The Phoenician History*, ed. H. W. Attridge (Washington, 1981), 54-57. See also S. A. Löwenstamm, "Sanchuniat(h)on," *Paulys Realencyclopaedie*, Supplement 14 (Munich, 1974), 597-598.

minor, national god, and on the other hand attributes to this god dominion over all things.[124]

It seems to me that the similarity between Julian's interpretation of the biblical Tower of Babel story, and that of the midrash, cannot be chalked up to coincidence. There is no reason to think that Julian's knowledge of Jewish sources was limited to the Bible.[125] As a former Christian, Julian presumably read Philo, who, like many other authors, interpreted "let us go down" as an indication that God descended with an entourage who helped him in the confusion of tongues (*De Confusione Linguarum* §§168-179). This interpretation, however, is almost self-evident. More significant is that both Philo and Julian link the Tower of Babel narrative with *Odyssey* 11.314-315. But here too, the two stories are so similar that many readers could have used the Homer legend to interrogate the biblical story. Moreover, the points of similarity between Julian and Philo are not the most important overlap between Julian and the midrash, namely, that both identify those who descended with God to confuse the tongues with the angelic ministers of the nations that came into existence. The midrash represents this conclusion as the confusion of tongues occurring at the same time that God "fixed the boundaries of the peoples according to the number of the gods" (Deut 32:8). But Julian does not mention the Deuteronomy narrative. It is hard to believe that Julian could identify the confusers of tongues with the angelic ministers without some knowledge of the similarity between the biblical passages in Genesis and Deuteronomy.

Did this interpretive tradition reach Julian in writing, or orally? From a Jewish source or perhaps a Christian source dependent on rabbinic midrash? How similar was this source to our midrash, or perhaps to one that preceded it? Did the Jewish tradition that reached Julian still link the Tower of Babel to Deuteronomy 32, or was this motif blurred or even effaced? One thing is clear: in the midrash preserved in Pirke de Rabbi Eliezer, as in any hypothetical midrash similar to it, the citation from Deuteronomy was an organic part of the interpretive argument. This was the time that "the Most High apportioned the nations," and thus established the angelic ministers of each people, but "the Lord's own portion was his people, Jacob his allotted share." Ultimately, the midrash announces Israel's election by God most high, and thus is diametrically opposed to Julian's argument, that the god of Israel is but one of these ministers, subservient to the almighty creator of heaven and earth.

---

124. Julian, *Against the Galileans*, 356-359. This is an attempt to summarize Julian's somewhat unwieldy argument.

125. As noted by G. Alon, *Studies in Jewish History*, 2.315-316.

The encounter between elite pagan thought, represented by Julian, and Judaism, is fertile and its study may yield far-reaching conclusions. From a purely scholarly perspective, it is fascinating to trace the pagan theology regarding the almighty god and the minor divinities charged with the other nations, a view already attested in the pre-Sinaitic strata of the Bible and that continues into apocalyptic literature and rabbinic midrash. It is further worth noting that the encounter between late antique Hellenistic thought and the Torah leads Julian to conclusions similar to those of modern Bible critics as to the status of biblical monotheism, though to my mind his conclusions are more accurate than those of his modern colleagues. All the same, one could argue that it is the tension, the *coincidentia oppositorum,* between God as the ruler of all and creator of the world, on the one hand, and as the one who took Israel as "his own people," on the other, that animates the Torah. The god of the philosophers is also the God of Abraham, Isaac, and Jacob.

APPENDIX B:
Enoch's Vision of the Seventy Shepherds and Judah Maccabee

The vision of the shepherds dates to the time of Judah Maccabee's wars and is preserved in 1 Enoch 83-90. The present discussion deals only with those aspects that affect the topic at hand.[126] The seventy ministers of the foreign nations appear as seventy shepherds who are charged with the herd (Israel) by the owner of the herd (God) (1 Enoch 89.59-60). The event immediately preceding this momentous event is Elijah's ascent to heaven (89.52). If so, the dominion of the nations over Israel began after Elijah's ascent and before the destruction of the First Temple (89.66). If follows, then, that according to the author of the vision, Israel lost its independence during the Assyrian conquest of the northern kingdom. Israel's domination is divided into four:

i. From the Assyrian conquest to the destruction of the First Temple (89.61-71);

ii. From the return of the exiles to the beginning of the Second Temple period (89.72-77);

iii. From the days of Alexander the Great to the conquest of Israel by the Seleucid dynasty (90.1-5);

iv. From the Seleucid rule to the Hasmonean revolt (90.6-16).

126. For a fuller analysis see D. Flusser, "Seventy Shepherds, Vision of," *Encyclopaedia Judaica* (Jerusalem, 1978), 1198-1199; J. T. Milik, *The Books of Enoch* (Oxford, 1976), 254-259; S. Uhlig, *Das äthiopische Henochbuch* (Gütersloh, 1984), 700; Y. Licht, "The Relationship between Past Events in the Bible and Apocalyptic Literature" (Hebrew), *Tarbiz* 60 (1991), 7-16.

This division was likely influenced by the idea of four kingdoms, although the content of the individual chapters does not bear this hypothesis out. The time of Greek dominion differs from its two predecessors in the symbolic representation of Israel's enemies: in the former they are birds of prey, while in the preceding periods they were represented as wild animals. The vision of the shepherds was composed during the wars of Judah Maccabee, since all the events that occur after the middle of the battles are described in eschatological terms, including Israel's ultimate victory over its enemies, the great day of judgment, and the messianic era. The judgment will take place in Israel, and all seventy shepherds — the ministers of the nations — will be condemned to the fires of Gehenom (90.22-25). In short, the author believes that Israel will be freed of the yoke of foreign oppression in the eschaton, a period that will begin in the days of Judah Maccabee.

5. "What Is Hanukkah?":
The Historical Setting of the
Hasmonean Temple Dedication

This study is dedicated to the memory of Menahem Stern, not only out of friendship and admiration for the man and the scholar, but because of his important contributions to the study of the Hasmonean period, which is central to my own research interests.[1] Immediately after the Six Day War and the reunification of Jerusalem, I re-read Judah Maccabee's letter (2 Macc 1.10–2.18), since at that time many felt that God again saved us from a great danger (see

1. Of particular importance is his book *Documents on the History of the Hasmonean Revolt* (Tel Aviv, 1973). Other sources consulted in preparing this article include M. Avi-Yonah, "The Battles in the Books of the Maccabees" (Hebrew), *The Yohanan Levy Festschrift*, ed. M. Schwabe (Jerusalem, 1949), 13-24; D. Flusser, "The Image of the Masada Martyrs in Their Own Eyes and in the Eyes of Their Contemporaries," and "Jerusalem in Second Temple Literature," both in the present volume; F.-M. Abel, *Les livres des Maccabées* (Paris, 1949); J. A. Goldstein, *I Maccabees* (New York, 1973), 161-174; E. Schürer, *The History of the Jewish People* (Edinburgh, 1973); O. Mørkholm, *Antiochus IV of Syria*, Diss. 8 (Copenhagen, 1966); E. Bickermann, "Ein jüdischer Festbrief vom Jahre 124 v. Chr.," *ZNW* 32 (1933), 233-254, especially p. 234; Ben Zion Wacholder, "The Letter from Judah Maccabee to Aristobulus," *HUCA* 49 (1978), 89-133; A. L. Oppenheim, "A Seleucid King List," *ANET*, ed. J. Pritchard (Princeton, 1969), 566-567; J. Schaumberger, "Die neue Seleukiden-Liste BM 35603 und die Makkabäische Chronologie," *Biblica* 36 (1955), 423-435; Chr. Habicht, "2. Makkabäerbuch," *Jüdische Schriften aus hellenistisch-römischer Zeit*, 1.3 (Gütersloh, 1979), 167-284; idem, "Royal Documents in Maccabees II," *Harvard Studies in Classical Philology* (Harvard, 1976), 1-18; E. Meyer, *Ursprung und Anfänge des Christentums* (Berlin, 1921), 2.454-462; F. R. Stephenson and C. B. F. Walker (eds.), *Halley's Comet in History* (London, 1985). I want to thank Dr. Dov Gera for his valuable assistance.

2 Macc 9.11). But upon reading the research literature I found that most scholars thought the letter was not authentic.[2]

I. The Authenticity of Judah Maccabee's Epistle to the Jews of Alexandria

The authenticity of Judah's letter to the Alexandrian community has significant ramifications for two issues in Second Temple historiography.[3] Indirectly, for the historical circumstances surrounding the dedication of the temple, and, more directly, for Judah's political and ideological leadership. It seems the main argument against the authenticity of the letter is that it contains a report of Antiochus's death (2 Macc 1.13-17), while in 1 Maccabees Antiochus' death follows the dedication of the temple (1 Macc 4.36-61; 6.1-17). But even prior to the discovery of new evidence — the subject of this study — this difficulty was more imagined than real. After all, not only the epistle, but 2 Maccabees itself (9.1-29) accepts this sequence of events. If so, the dating that putatively undermines the authenticity of the letter appears only in 1 Maccabees, while the other view is supported by the letter, 2 Maccabees itself, and, as we now see, archaeological evidence.[4] Today, scholars agree that Antiochus did in fact die before the dedication of the temple, though for some reason most do not draw the necessary conclusions regarding the authenticity of Judah Maccabee's letter and the historical circumstances that preceded this event.

The difficulty in reconstructing the historical events leading up to the dedication lies in the deficiences of 1 and 2 Maccabees. Needless to say, neither book is objective as they were composed (both circa 100 B.C.E.) out of deep sympathy for Judah Maccabee and the Maccabean wars. Still, they are not cut from the same cloth. 2 Maccabees was composed in Greek and is an abridgment of a much longer work by Jason of Cyrene. The book, not all of which survived, belongs to the genre of Hellenistic historiography composed in the form of dramatic, pathos-laden adulation. For example, both books

2. See Wacholder, "The Letter from Judah Maccabee," 90-92. Wacholder believes the letter is authentic, and see also my two articles cited in the previous note.

3. According to critical scholarship, the name "Judah" at the end of the list of authors in 2 Maccabees is a late addition. However, the name also appears in 2 Maccabees 2.14. Thus, the absence of the name Judah at the opening of the letter has no bearing on its composition. See also Habicht, "2. Makkabäerbuch," 202, and n. 53, below.

4. See especially Mørkholm, *Antiochus IV of Syria;* Wacholder, "The Letter from Judah Maccabee"; and Schaumberger, "Die neue Seleukiden-Liste." See also below, n. 8.

describe the death of Antiochus according to the conventions of a tyrant who atones his sins on his deathbed (1 Macc 6.1-17; 2 Macc 9.1-29), undoubtedly with no factual basis. However, 2 Maccabees develops this narrative in the fashion of the Greek rhetorical tradition concerning the death of truly evil men.[5] But let me note already that the letter of Antiochus preserved in this chapter (2 Macc 9.19-27) is probably authentic but was not addressed to the Jews — their mention is a later addition to an epistle originally written to "honored citizens."[6] As for the literary pathos of 2 Maccabees, Jason of Cyrene's dramatic tendencies are in full view in his description of the martyrdom of Elazar (chapter 6) and the mother and her seven sons (chapter 7).[7] Despite all this, the pathos-filled exaggerations of Jason of Cyrene do not undermine the historical value of 2 Maccabees, since it demonstrates expertise regarding the administrative working of the Seleucid court and military, and its contribution to the study of Hellenistic terminology and broader culture has long been recognized. Moreover, as ongoing discoveries demonstrate, 2 Maccabees is often the most accurate historical source in terms of the historical events it represents. For example, "There were those who argued against the book on the grounds that it wrongly placed the death of Antiochus Epiphanes (chapter 9) prior to the dedication of the temple (10.1-8), unlike 1 Maccabees, where the order is reversed . . . however now it appears the new of Antiochus' death reached Babylonia no later than December 164, so Antiochus must have died prior to that date. Since the temple was purified in Kislev of that year, it appears the sequence in 2 Maccabees is historically accurate."[8] We have already mentioned the date of Antiochus's death,[9] and will have opportunity to discuss its importance for the dedication of the temple and the authenticity of Judah Maccabee's epistle. Unfortunately, in other places the original order of Jason of Cyrene has been reversed by the abridger, and perhaps by other, later editors.[10]

---

5. See Abel, *Les livres des Maccabées*, 400; Habicht, "2 Makkabäerbuch," 245. Also, the death of Herod according to Josephus, *BJ* 1.656-658 and *AJ* 17.168-170; the death of Agrippa in Acts 12:23; and the death of Judah Iscariot according to Papias (see *Neutestamentliche Apokryphen*, ed. W. Schneemelcher [Tübingen, 1989], 2.25).

6. See Abel, *Les livres des Maccabées*, 402, and Meyer, *Ursprung und Anfänge*, 460-461. But see also Habicht, "Royal Documents," 2-7, and "2 Makkabäerbuch," 172.

7. Habicht, "2 Makkabäerbuch," 171, 176, and 233, where he argues that the latter episode is a secondary addition. Be that as it may, the chapter was already part of 2 Maccabees when 4 Maccabees was composed. On this story see I. Gutman, "The Mother and Her Seven Sons in Rabbinic Legend and in 2 and 4 Maccabees" (Hebrew), *The Yohanan Levy Festschrift*, 25-37.

8. Stern, *Documents*, 21-22, as well as Habicht, "2 Makkabäerbuch," 190-191.

9. See above, n. 4.

10. According to Habicht, "2 Makkabäerbuch," 175, Jason of Cyrene was a contemporary

Having established the accuracy of 2 Maccabees (and of Judah Maccabee's epistle) with regard to the death of Antiochus, and the error of 1 Maccabees, many scholars are now more inclined to accept the historical witness of Jason of Cyrene. This shift should have brought about a reassessment of the *Tendenz* of 1 Maccabees, especially regarding the details provided in its first chapters (which overlap with the historical period narrated by 2 Maccabees). After all, it is clear that the author seeks to lionize Judah and his brothers, "the glorious brothers," and to establish the legitimacy of Hasmonean rule, whose sons are "those men through whom deliverance was given to Israel" (1 Macc 5.62).[11]

II. The Reliability of 1 Maccabees

Those who viewed 1 Maccabees as a straightforward and "realistic" historic source, and thus to be preferred to the drama and pathos of 2 Maccabees, were led astray by the apparent and largely artificial immediacy of 1 Maccabees' style. We find a parallel case in the very tendentious legends surrounding the early days of Swiss independence and its struggle against tyranny.[12] These historical narratives give the impression of a truly epic struggle. So it is no wonder that 1 Maccabees' tales of the early stages of the revolt, like the tales of Swiss independence, inspired authors, composers, artists and sculptors from one generation to the next.[13] But scholars have already established that

---

of Judah Maccabee and composed his work after Judah's death but before Jonathan's installation as high priest in 152 B.C.E. This hypothesis assumes a number of editorial strata.

11. See Schürer, *History*, 3.180-192; Goldstein, *1 Maccabees*, 72-78. This is also an argument in favor of those who suggest 1 Maccabees was once called *spr byo qr bny-al*, 'The Book of the House of the Commander and Prince of God's Children.' See the discussion in D. Flusser, "The Roman Empire in Hasmonean and Essene Eyes," *Judaism of the Second Temple Period: Qumran and Apocalypticism*, 175-206.

12. The earliest source for these legends is *Das Weisse Buch von Sarnen*, ed. B. Beyer (Kanton Obwalden, 1984). My thanks to the heads of this canton who presented me with this book. The historical documents that pertain to Swiss independence have been collected in *Die Bundesbriefe zu Schwyz*, ed. A. Castell (Einsiedeln, 1976). An openly apologetic approach is adopted by B. Meyer, *Weisses Buch und Wilhelm Tell* (Weinfelden, 1984), though the book remains important for the material it contains. For an objective description of Swiss history to the year 1499, see Gui P. Marchal, *Geschichte der Schweiz* (Munich, 1991), 7-22 and 177-178. For a comprehensive survey of the idea of Swiss independence see Marchal, "Die 'alten Eidgenossen' im Wandel der Zeit," *Innerschweiz und frühe Eidgenossenschaft* (Olten, 1990), 2.309-403, and especially 321-326.

13. The only parts of 2 Maccabees that lend themselves to graphic representation are the story of the sin and punishment of Heliodorus (chapter 3) and the martyrdom of the mother and her seven sons. On Judah Maccabee in the arts see *EJ* 10.382-383.

the legends of the harsh anti-Swiss decrees and the daring deeds of the Swiss in their struggle are not historically accurate but first and foremost richly imagined. As for 1 Maccabees, with its religious decrees and the beginning of the Hasmonean revolt, it appears we are today at the beginning of a rethinking process. Issues of historical methodology, along with the comparison to 2 Maccabees and external evidence, are slowly undoing the putatively solid structure of 1 Maccabees' narrative, and it seems the account of Antiochus's religious decrees requires the utmost caution. Increasingly, 2 Maccabees is accepted as more historically reliable.

1 Maccabees states: "Then the king wrote to his whole kingdom to be as one people, and that all should give up their particular customs; and all the nations accepted the command of the king" (1 Macc 1.41-43). Already the sublime biblical style elevates the content beyond historical accuracy. The phrase "to be as one people" recalls the Shechem story in Genesis 34, where the same phrase is spoken by Hamor and his son, Shechem (Gen 34:21), who is repeating the words of Jacob's sons (Gen 34:16). The repetition in 1 Maccabees is no coincidence. As for the historical accuracy of the odd command itself — such a cosmopolitan decree is highly suspect, despite the opaque allusion in Daniel 11:37-38.[14] There is no evidence to suggest that Antiochus preferred one god over all others, or that he sought to effect religious reform in all the countries of his dominion. To be sure, it is clear that Antiochus did indeed issue cruel decrees against the temple, the Jews, and the Torah (see 2 Macc 6.1-7),[15] and they gave rise to a new phenomenon — Jewish martyrology. Still, it is difficult to know what constitutes that historical kernel of 1 Maccabees' account of the decrees and the early revolt, led by Mattathias the Hasmonean (1 Macc 1.54–2.28). The story of Mattathias killing those willing to offer foreign sacrifices is, in any case, cut from the same cloth as the Swiss tales. As recounted in 1 Maccabees, the king's men came to the town of Modi'in to force its residents to make pagan offerings and sought to entice Mattathias to lead by example:

> Now be the first to come and do what the king commands, as all the Gentiles and all the people of Judah and those that are left in Jerusalem have done. Then you and your sons will be numbered among the Friends of the king, and you and your sons will be honored with silver and gold

14. See Goldstein, *1 Maccabees*, 119-121; Mørkholm, *Antiochus IV of Syria*, 130-133, and 186; M. Hengel, *Judentum und Hellenismus* (Tübingen, 1969), 516-525.

15. I think Goldstein is right to suggest that Antiochus's anti-Jewish decrees — so unusual in the Hellenistic world — were an imitation of Roman anti-religious legislation. The report in 1 Maccabees 1.56 that Torah scrolls were seized and burned is confirmed in 2 Maccabees 2.14.

and many gifts. But Mattathias answered and said in a loud voice: Even if all the nations that live under the rule of the king obey him, and have chosen to obey his commandments, every one of them abandoning the religion of their ancestors, I and my sons and my brothers will continue to live by the covenant of our ancestors. We will not obey the king's words by turning aside from our religion to the right hand or to the left. (1 Macc 2.18-22)

After issuing this declaration, Mattathias approached a Jewish man who had come forward to offer a sacrifice, and slew him on the altar, along with the royal official, and then destroyed the altar. The story, in its present form, is highly unlikely. Mattathias's dramatic pronouncement that while all nations have betrayed their ancestral laws he and his sons will be faithful to the customs of their fathers, is thoroughly apologetic.[16] And the same apologetic impetus underlies the earlier report that Antiochus had commanded all the nations to abandon their laws (1 Macc 1.41-42). Incidentally, it is at least possible that the Jewish chauvinism that characterizes the author of 1 Maccabees is one of the reasons Antiochus's death comes after the liberation of the temple — to exclude the possibility that the dedication came about because of the death of the king, rather than the heroics of Judah Maccabee and his forces.

III. The Date of Antiochus Epiphanes' Death

We again had occasion to mention the date of Antiochus Epiphanes' death. As noted, there is today no doubt that this event preceded the rededication of the temple, and that Judah's epistle, and 2 Maccabees more generally, are in the right in this respect. The question that must occupy us now is, when exactly in 164 B.C.E. (i.e., 148 by the Seleucid reckoning), prior to the purification of the temple, did the king die. According to a Babylonian list of Seleucid rulers,[17] the

16. Fidelity to ancestral customs was highly prized during that time. See H. G. Kippenberg, "Die jüdischen Überlieferung als 'patrioi nomoi,'" in R. Faber and R. Schlesier (eds.), *Die Restauration der Götter* (Würzburg, 1986), 45-60; A. Fuks, *The Ancestral Constitution* (London, 1953).

17. The Babylonian list appears in Oppenheim, "A Seleucid King List," 556-557, and, partially, in Stephenson and Walker, *Halley's Comet*, 21, and see also 18. See, *inter alia*, Schaumberger, "Die neue Seleukiden-Liste"; Stern, *Documents on the History of the Hasmonean Revolt*, 57, and n. 12, and p. 22, where Stern conjectures that the news of Antiochus's death "reached Israel only after the purification, thus explaining the chronology of 1 Maccabees." See also Goldstein, *1 Maccabees*, 83.

news of Antiochus's death arrived[18] in Kislev of 148. It is significant that this was an intercalated year in Babylonia. We know nothing of the condition of the local Jews, nor can we determine with certainty how much time passed from the death of the king until the news reached Babylonia some time between November 18th and December 20th of that year. Some scholars have suggested, on the comparative evidence of Greek chronological texts, that Antiochus died in the second quarter of 164.[19] According to Babylonian astronomical tablets,[20] the king was still alive between the 26th of Nisan, and the 15th of Iyar. However, the same type of material suggests that Antiochus's corpse was brought to Babylonia — along with his son, Antiochus V — toward the end of the 10th month, i.e., of Tevet, which suggests Antiochus had died in the Babylonian month of Kislev or even a little earlier. As noted, according to the Babylonian calendar, 164 B.C.E. was a leap year, which included two months of Adar. It is, then, possible, that the Babylonian Kislev during which the news of the king's death reached Babylonia, was *earlier* than that year's Kislev in Jerusalem. Even so, we cannot know how much time passed between the death of Antiochus and the dedication of the temple by Judah Maccabee. What is clear, is that the news could have reached Judah and his troops (who were undoubtedly very interested in fresh news regarding Antiochus's whereabouts) before the dedication, just as his epistle suggests.[21] It is even possible that this news factored into Judah's decision to take this action.

As for the accounts of Antiochus's death (1 Macc 6.1-17; 2 Macc 1.13-17 and 9.1-29),[22] let me add a brief comment to the one found in Judah Maccabee's letter. If, in fact, the news of Antiochus's death reached Judah shortly before the dedication of the temple, it is small wonder that the narrative becomes a bit fantastic at that point.[23] Antiochus had indeed tried to sack a temple dedicated to Artemis in Elam,[24] but was not killed by the locals, as

18. On the significance of this Babylonian phrase, see Oppenheim, "A Seleucid King List," and Stephenson and Walker, *Halley's Comet,* 21.

19. See Schürer, *History of the Jewish People,* 128.

20. See Stephenson and Walker, *Halley's Comet,* 34-35.

21. Wacholder, "The Letter from Judah Maccabee to Aristobulus," who accepts the authenticity of the epistle, argues that it was composed a year after the dedication of the temple. It is true that the language of the epistle does not contradict this assumption, but neither does it support it. On the epistle itself, see also Habicht, "2 Makkabäerbuch," 199-201, who argues that it is not authentic.

22. See also the sources cited above, notes 5 and 6.

23. On the historical fact see Mørkholm, *Antiochus IV of Syria,* 166-180, and especially 171, which discusses the idea that Antiochus died as punishment for his desecration of the temple.

24. Mørkholm, *Antiochus IV of Syria,* 170-171.

Judah's letter claims. The letter further states (2 Macc 1.14) that Antiochus burst into the temple in order to wed a woman — the goddess Artemis who was, according to the Greek traditions, an eternal virgin — and to confiscate the temple funds as a dowry. A similar story, also involving Antiochus and a temple of Artemis, is found in the writings of a second century c.e. Roman historian,[25] whose account is of some relevance to the present discussion.[26] It is, of course, possible that the letter of Judah Maccabee has incorporated an event that took place at another temple of Artemis, or perhaps the Roman historian erred, identifying the Elam temple with another, more famous temple of the goddess. In any case, the historical errors may in fact strengthen the case for the epistle's authenticity, as its author did not yet possess accurate information concerning the death of Antiochus.

IV. 1 Maccabees and 2 Maccabees

Antiochus' death is not the only event whose dating is a matter of controversy between 1 and 2 Maccabees. A striking difference is the date and nature of the two invasions of the Seleucid general Lysias.[27] The historical reconstruction is so fraught with difficulty that some scholars doubt the very historicity of these invasions.[28] The question which of Lysias's military excur-

25. See *Granius Licinianus*, ed. M. Flemisch (Leipzig, 1904), 5-6. A new edition has appeared under the editorship of N. Criniti (Leipzig, 1981), and see the following appendix. According to Licinianus, Antiochus died during the second consulship of Graccus, i.e., in the year 591 *ab urbe condita* (= 163 b.c.e.). Habicht, "2 Makkabäerbuch," 202, states that fictive matrimonies between kings and goddesses were a common way to extract funds from the temple treasury. See also Mørkholm, *Antiochus IV of Syria*, 132.

26. Licinianus's account contains a second parallel to 2 Maccabees. 2 Maccabees 9.7-8 attributes to Jason of Cyrene the information that Antiochus fell to the earth from a galloping chariot, was crushed, and was later carried on a litter. According to Licinianus, Antiochus died of a night terror, but "when they brought his body to Antioch, the mules were suddenly startled and his body fell into the river, never to be recovered." One of the Babylonian astronomical charts (Stephenson and Walker, *Halley's Comet*, 32) preserve the words "the men came with the king's body . . ."! 2 Maccabees 9.29 states that Philip, a Syrian noble, led Antiochus's body. Habicht, "2 Makkabäerbuch," 248-249, rightly notes that the meaning of 2 Maccabees 9.29 is unclear.

27. See the chronological order in the two books as summarized by Schürer, *History of the Jewish People*, 1.161, n. 61.

28. See Schürer, *History of the Jewish People*, 1.160, n. 59; Mørkholm, *Antiochus IV of Syria*, 152-154. It is clear, in any case, that the account of Lysias's invasion in 1 Maccabees 4.28-35 — during the reign of Antiochus IV and before the dedication of the temple — parallels 2 Maccabees 11.1-15, where it occurs after Antiochus's death and the dedication of the temple. The

sions really occurred is not particularly important for a historian of the Seleucid empire, but is very significant for the historical context of the dedication of the temple. In any case, all three of the invasions that (between them) 1 and 2 Maccabees date after the dedication, ended with Lysias reconciling with the Jews. 1 Maccabees (6.58-61) tells of Lysias's proposal to make peace with the men of Beth-zur and "with all their nation," allowing them "to live by their laws as they did before," a proposal accepted by the king. In the parallel account in 2 Maccabees (13.1-26) the peace reached between Lysias and the Jews is further emphasized. The sources differ, however, in that 2 Maccabees describes an earlier invasion undertaken by Lysias and the heir of Antiochus IV, an invasion that also ended with a peace accord. As we will see, to this account were appended four authentic letters involving peace negotiations with the Jews (2 Macc 11.16-38).[29] Of these, only the second (2 Macc 11.22-26) is cited in the proper context. In it, Antiochus V, son of Antiochus Epiphanes, writes to Lysias that the Jews' "temple be restored to them and that they shall live according to the customs of their ancestors." The other three letters predate the events described in 2 Maccabees 11, having been composed during the reign of Antiochus IV, but were attached to the second letter by accident as they too deal with reconciliation between the Seleucids and the Jews. However, the organic connection between the second letter and the events of chapter eleven does not prove that Lysias's first invasion, accompanied by young Antiochus V, is a historical fact.

V. The Letters in 2 Maccabees

We saw above that 1 and 2 Maccabees differ regarding the date of Antiochus Epiphanes' death, as well as the military excursions of Lysias. We also alluded to a more substantive difficulty: even though 2 Maccabees 11 relates events that follow Antiochus's death, two or three of the letters preserved in the chapter were written during his reign. These clearly indicate that the negotiations that resulted in the annulment of the decrees began under Antiochus and, indeed, were initiated by him — prior to the dedication of the temple.

---

latter source states that Lysias's defeat ended the war (followed by the important letters which will be discussed in what follows). This part, however, parallels 1 Maccabees 6.28-63, which places these developments (and the end of the conflict) after the temple dedication and the death of Antiochus.

29. On these four letters see Habicht, "Royal Documents in Maccabees II," and idem, "2 Makkabäerbuch," 179-185. See also Stern, *Documents*, 56-58, 66-73, where they are numbered as letters number 5-8.

1 Maccabees is silent about the annulment of the anti-Jewish decrees during the reign of Antiochus, as are Josephus and, most surprisingly, 2 Maccabees. It is only from the documents preserved in 2 Maccabees 11 that we learn of these events — events that contradict the historical narrative of the book itself.[30] Is it possible that the Jewish authors of the day preferred to ignore the fact that Judah conquered the temple and purified it only after the decrees had been annulled?[31] Perhaps they feared that publicizing the connection between the peace negotiations and the dedication of the temple might dull the glory of this historic event. To my mind, however, the fact that Judah Maccabee had more room to maneuver only underlines the boldness of his decision to conquer the temple and renew the sacrifices.

As noted, the second of the four letters (2 Macc 11.22-26) was written by Antiochus V, after his father's death. The young emperor writes to Lysias, whom he addresses as "my brother," saying:

> We have heard that the Jews do not consent to our father's change to Greek customs, but prefer their own way of living and ask that their own customs be allowed them. Accordingly, since we choose that this nation also should be free from disturbance, our decision is that their temple be restored to them and that they shall live according to the customs of their ancestors.[32]

The letter is undated. Were it possible to predate the letter to the rededication of the temple, Judah's seizure of the temple and renewal of the sacrifices would have been the direct result of Antiochus V's decision "that their temple be restored to them and that they shall live according to the customs of their ancestors."[33] However, recent discoveries make such an early dating untenable. True, the Babylonian documents state that news of the death reached Babylonia only in Kislev of 164 B.C.E. and that men arrived with the body of the king on the 24th-26th of Tevet, when Antiochus V is already referred to as king.[34] However, it is clear that Antiochus was still among the living in the

---

30. See Stern, *Documents,* 56.

31. It should be noted that these psychological and ideological difficulties did not prevent Jason of Cyrene from following the literary conventions of the day and representing the regrets of the evil emperor who, having been bested by God, was even willing to convert to Judaism (2 Macc 9.11-18). The author even includes a royal letter (2 Macc 9.19-27) that, in fact, was not originally addressed to the Jews. See above, n. 6.

32. See Stern, *Documents,* 72-73.

33. This is indeed possible following the chronology proposed by Schürer, *History of the Jews,* 1.128, who locates the death of Antiochus IV in the second quarter of 164 B.C.E.

34. See Stephenson and Walker, *Halley's Comet,* 32 (line 17), 34 (line 20), and 35 (line 21).

previous Nisan and Iyar. Even if we account for 164 being a Babylonian leap year, and the attendant one-month lag relative to the Palestinian calendar, it appears that no more than forty days elapsed between Antiochus IV's death in Elam and the dedication of the temple. It is highly unlikely that during that short time, the new king could have written a letter that overturned his father's decrees and returned the temple to faithful Jews, and that the letter could have reached Israel and caused Judah to pursue the rededication, now permitted by the new king! So even though news of Antiochus IV's death may well have reached Jerusalem prior to the dedication, and mention of it was made in Judah Maccabee's letter to the Jews of Alexandria, the *plan* to retake the temple must have been formulated earlier, under the influence of the peace negotiations that took place toward the end of Antiochus IV's life.

To better understand the significance of Judah Maccabee's rededication of the temple, we must examine the three remaining letters preserved in 2 Maccabees 11. The dating and interrelations of these letters have been examined at length by scholars, and we will base our discussion on their conclusions.[35] Clearly, the second letter, in which Antiochus V writes Lysias, overturning his father's decrees and returning the temple to the Jews, is chronologically latest, most likely written after the rededication of the temple. As such, the letter probably does little more than ratify the existing status quo.

Of the remaining letters, the earliest, number 1, is likely the third (2 Maccabees 11.27-33; number 7 in Stern's list). In it, Antiochus addresses the senate *(gerousia)* of the Jews (i.e. an official body that represents the Jewish nation) as follows:

> Menelaus has informed us that you wish to return home and look after your own affairs. Therefore those who go home by the thirtieth of Xanthicus will have our pledge of friendship and full permission for the Jews to enjoy their own food and laws, just as formerly, and none of them shall be molested in any way for what may have been done in ignorance. And I have also sent Menelaus to encourage you. (2 Macc 11.29-32)

---

35. The difficulty in dating the letters can be traced back to the author of 2 Maccabees, who placed three of them in an unconnected chapter (probably "dragged" there by epistle 2, which does belong there). Habicht, "Royal Documents," 13-14, and "2 Makkabäerbuch," 179-180, rightly argues that the date given at the end of the third and fourth letters (2 Macc 11.33 and 11.38, respectively) — the 15th of Xanthicus in both cases — is unconvincing, while the month cited at the end of the first (2 Macc 11.21) is textually corrupt. However, the year cited in all three, 148 of the Ptolemaic rule, i.e. between the falls of 165 and 164 B.C.E., is quite plausible, indicating that these were composed during the reign of Antiochus Epiphanes. See also the references cited above, n. 29.

The Menelaus in question was the infamous Hellenized high priest, ultimately executed by Antiochus V after Lysias demonstrated that he, the priest, was to blame for all the tribulations (2 Macc 13.3-8). However, Menelaus was still alive when the letter was composed, and in fact represented the Jews to the throne. In this letter, Antiochus Epiphanes proposes a pardon for anyone who will return to their daily life by a certain date. Moreover, he grants "full permission for the Jews to enjoy their own food and laws, just as formerly." The notion that the letter offers religious freedom only to those that cease their revolt has no basis in the language of the epistle.[36] Such a qualified pardon seems to me quite unrealistic, though there is some ambiguity concerning the rights of the Jews to live according to the Torah. Perhaps this ambiguity regarding the annulment of the religious decrees reflects the doubts of the author himself.

It should be noted that Antiochus IV offers a pardon to the Jews who lay down their arms by the 30th of Xanthicus, while the letter itself is dated to the 15th of Xanthicus. But while the date of the pardon is quite reasonable,[37] the two-week grace period is clearly too short. Moreover, the 15th of Xanthicus is also the date of the fourth letter (2 Macc 11.38), which addresses the Roman envoys. Both dates, then, are suspect, and may be the result of an error by Jason of Cyrene's editor. In any case, it is best to set aside the dates attached to the letters and focus instead on their content.

This approach leads us to conclude that the chronological order of the letters is as follows:[38] number 1 is from Antiochus Epiphanes to the Jewish senate, where the high priest Menelaus is the Jewish representative; number 2 is Lysias's epistle to "the people of the Jews" (2 Macc 11.16-21; Stern, document n. 5), in which he addresses Judah Maccabee's men; number 3 is the letter of the Roman envoys also "to the people of the Jews" (2 Macc 11.34-38). All were written in the year 148 of the Ptolemaic rule (fall of 165 to fall of 164 B.C.E.), the final year of Antiochus Epiphanes' life. In his letter, Lysias, who was Antiochus's viceroy, states that he has made it clear to John and Absalom, Judah's emissaries, that a number of questions would be decided by the king himself. However, this was no longer possible since Antiochus Epiphanes had shuffled off this mortal coil. The latest letter was composed by Antiochus V Eupator, and annuls the religious decrees of the now dead Antiochus IV (2 Macc 11.22-26; Stern, document no. 8).

36. Thus Habicht, "2 Makkabäerbuch," 181, and "Royal Documents in Maccabees II," 14-15; Stern, *Documents on the History of the Hasmonean Revolt*, 56.

37. See the discussion in Habicht, "2 Makkabäerbuch," 259, n. 30.

38. See Habicht, "2 Makkabäerbuch," 180-182, and n. 77, and idem, "Royal Documents in Maccabees II," 13.

Stern has already provided a detailed analysis of the historical dynamics that underlie these documents, pointing rightly to the odd fact that we know of the negotiations for the annulment of the decrees — negotiations started by Antiochus IV himself — only from the epistles preserved in 2 Maccabees 11. We have already raised the possibility that this silence stems from a Jewish reluctance to admit that the situation had changed so dramatically for the better under the reign — and by the initiative — of the villain who enacted the decrees. This hypothetical *Tendenz,* however, was certainly not consistent, for in 2 Maccabees (9.11-27) we learn of Antiochus's repentance on his deathbed (albeit in accordance with the literary conventions of the day), and a letter he wrote to the Jews.[39]

VI. The Political Process Reflected in the Letters

Let us apply these new findings to an examination of the political process reflected in the letters. Number 1 presents us with unexpected facts. For instance, we would not expect Menelaus, who is traditionally portrayed as a wicked Hellenizer, to write his Syrian master as an intermediary between the Jewish anti-Hellenists and the Seleucid court, essentially to arrange a pardon in matters of religion. His success was evidently quite limited, but even this tentative retreat from the Draconian decrees was a hopeful sign for the Jews. The ultimate failure of this attempt was, however, foreordained, not only on account of its lack of clarity, but because the Jews were represented by the pro-Hellenistic Jews, headed by Menelaus the priest. The Seleucid court realized its first attempt to placate the Jews had failed, and opened channels of communication to the rebel forces (2 Macc 11.16-21). Antiochus was already on his final journey, far from Antioch, so Lysias, the viceroy, undertook the negotiations with the Jews. John and Absalom were sent to Lysias and he promised that the matters that require royal sanction will be sent to the king, while responding generously to matters in his jurisdiction. At the same time, the two Roman emissaries were on their way to Antioch, hoping to join in the negotiations of the Palestinian Jews with the Seleucid court, and perhaps exert some influence in favor of the Jews. In their letter (vv. 34-38), the Romans ask the Jews to send an ambassador so they can learn of the Jews' demands. This letter also mentions that Lysias decided that certain matters "are to be re-

---

39. See above, n. 6. That the letter in 2 Maccabees 9 is authentic — though not addressed to the Jews — is evident from the fact that the dying king does not offer any concessions to the Jews.

ferred to the king." The king's response could no longer arrive, as he had died in a foreign land.

At this point, after the death of Antiochus IV and just before the complete annulment of the anti-Jewish decrees, in the midst of negotiations with the Seleucid court — Judah and his men conquered the temple, purified it, and renewed the Jewish temple cult. It stands to reason that Judah planned this operation before he learned of the king's death, but the news may have encouraged him — perhaps Lysias would be more eager now to successfully resolve the negotiations, for the new king was young and Lysias's survival more precarious.[40] Indeed, Menelaus was eventually executed on the king's command,[41] and Lysias made peace with the Jews. There is a broad consensus among scholars that all this occurred after Lysias's journey with the nine-year-old Antiochus V, immediately following the death of Antiochus IV,[42] and after the dedication of the temple. At this point the last of the epistles in 2 Maccabees, number 4, was composed. It fully annulled the anti-Jewish decrees (11.24-25), because "the Jews do not consent to our father's change to Greek customs, but prefer their own way of living and ask that their own customs be allowed them." The letter also returned the temple to the Jews, affirming, in effect, the status quo that existed after Judah seized the temple and rededicated it.

Judah Maccabee's letter in 2 Maccabees, which, I believe, was composed at the outset of the purification process, reflects not only Judah's motives for seizing the temple, but the political worldview that prohibited him from reaching a truce with the Seleucid court even after the decrees of Antiochus IV were annulled. This position established the force of Israel's resistance, but also engendered Judah's relative isolation and, ultimately, brought about his tragic death. His political convictions were first tested when the Seleucids appointed Alcimus (Hebrew: Yakim) high priest, in place of the executed Menelaus.[43] Along with Alcimus, Antioch sends to Judea a general, Bacchides, with his troops. The response of the Jews was as follows:

40. See Schürer, *The History of the Jewish People*, 1.128-129; Habicht, "2 Makkabäerbuch," 248-249, n. 29, and see especially 2 Maccabees 13.23.

41. See 2 Macc 13.3-8, and Habicht's comment ("2 Makkabäerbuch," 267, n. 4), ad loc.

42. See 2 Macc 13 and 1 Macc 6.28-62. See also Schürer, *The History of the Jewish People*, 1.166-167. On the confusion surrounding Lysias's invasions, see above, notes 27 and 28; Habicht, "2 Makkabäerbuch," 183; B. Isaac, "A Seleucid Inscription from Jamnia-on-the-Sea: Antiochus V Eupator and the Sidonians," *IEJ* 41 (1991), 132-134. The date there is June-July, 163 B.C.E.

43. See 1 Macc 7.1-25; 2 Macc 14.1-10; Stern, *Documents on the History of the Hasmonean Revolt*, 74-75; Schürer, *The History of the Jews*, 1.168-169; Habicht, "2 Makkabäerbuch," 270-272; Goldstein, *I Maccabees*, 167.

"Then a group of scribes appeared in a body before Alcimus and Bacchides to ask for just terms. The Hasideans were first among the Israelites to seek peace from them, for they said, 'A priest of the line of Aaron has come with the army, and he will not harm us'" (1 Macc 7.12-14). The Hasideans in question are the community of warriors who joined Mattathias and his cohort, when they decided to fight on the Sabbath (1 Macc 2.39-42). This important group believed that the annulment of the decrees signaled a return to the status quo under the king's auspices. They agreed to the appointment of Alcimus, even as Judah and his brothers continued their revolt. As it happens, the latter were in the right — at least at that moment — as Alcimus seized sixty of the Hasideans and had them executed (1 Macc 7.16-18). Judah and his allies gained strength and eventually defeated the forces of Nicanor on the 13th of Adar, 161 B.C.E. A few months after his brilliant victory, however, Judah fell in battle against a more powerful army (1 Macc 9.1-21).

VII. Judah Maccabee's Political Worldview

We have briefly surveyed the events that occurred between the dedication of the temple and Judah Maccabee's death, with an aim to identify his unique political worldview. He worked toward full political independence,[44] because he thought it was impossible to turn back the hands of time. When did Judah reach this conclusion? If we read his epistle in light of the political events that helped him seize the temple, we find that already then he believed that Israel must be freed of foreign rule, and that this view guided his decisions.

Both the letters preserved in 2 Maccabees 11 and the recently published Babylonian documents clearly indicate that *Judah Maccabee dedicated the temple in the midst of ongoing negotiations with the Seleucid court.* Did the negotiations mean there was a de facto armistice? 1 Maccabees states that Judah "detailed men to fight against those in the citadel until he had cleansed the sanctuary" (1 Macc 4.41),[45] but perhaps this is an exaggeration since 2 Maccabees makes no mention of such military action. The rapprochement likely influenced the muted Syrian response to the dedication of the temple. As noted, epistle number 4 not only annuls the decrees of

---

44. See Schürer, *The History of the Jews*, 1.171. "[Judah] believed political independence was a goal to be attained by any means possible. He viewed the establishment of political ties with Rome (1 Macc 8.23-32; *Jewish Antiquities* 14.233) as one of the means toward this end" (Stern, *Documents on the History of the Hasmonean Revolt*, 75).

45. *Jewish Antiquities* 12.318 is dependent on 1 Maccabees here.

Antiochus IV, it returns the temple to the Jews and validates the new status. I do not think we can rule out the possibility that Lysias gave silent assent to Judah's actions.

Be all that as it may, Judah could plot his political moves with relative freedom. He likely had some time in which to set an appropriate date for the renewal of the proper temple rituals, and it is no wonder the purification occurred on the anniversary of the day the temple was first defiled.[46] Antiochus IV probably desecrated the temple on a day of some pagan ritual importance, perhaps related to the winter solstice.[47] It should be recalled that during the first Hanukkah celebration the Jews "celebrated it for eight days with rejoicing, in the manner of the festival of booths (Sukkot), remembering how not long before, during the festival of booths, they had been wandering in the mountains and caves like wild animals" (2 Macc 10.6), and as early as 124 B.C.E. the celebration was referred to as "the festival of booths in the month of Kislev."[48] Even to this day, the holiday of Hanukkah lasts eight days, just like Sukkot. It appears, then, that Judah chose to rededicate the temple on the date of its desecration as an act of religious and political defiance.

VIII. The Letter to the Jews of Egypt in Light of Judah's Political Worldview

The letter to the Jews of Egypt was itself a political calculation: Egypt had the largest Jewish community, and the Egyptian court was not fond of the Seleucids, the enemies of Israel at that time. The letter is addressed "[t]o Aristobulus, who is of the family of the anointed priests, teacher of King Ptolemy, and to the Jews in Egypt," a festive opening that may constitute proof for the letter's authenticity. The reference to Aristobulus as "teacher of King Ptol-

46. 2 Macc 10.5; 1 Macc 4.54. And see Habicht, "2 Makkabäerbuch," 249-250.

47. See Goldstein, *I Maccabees*, 155. 1 Maccabees 1.54 states that "on the fifteenth day of Kislev, in the one hundred and forty-fifth year, they erected a desolating sacrilege on the altar of burnt-offering." This statement does not, in and of itself, contradict the fact that the pagan cult was officially initiated only ten days later, as we find in 1 Macc 1.59 (and is implied in 1 Macc 4.54 itself and 2 Macc 10.5). See also Schürer, *The History of the Jews*, 1.155. The connection to the winter solstice may be responsible for the proximity of Hanukkah and Christmas. And see b. 'Avodah Zarah, 8a, the legend regarding Adam's fear of the shortening days.

48. Thus in the letter sent by the Jews in that year (2 Macc 1.9). See also Judah Maccabee's letter in 2 Macc 1.18. It should be noted that there are scholars who accept the authenticity of the letter, but believe that beginning at 2 Maccabees 1.18 there is a long, and late, addition. See also below, n. 52.

emy" is probably hyperbolic, but it is clear that he was an important Jew in Alexandria.[49] Of course, the scholars who question the authenticity of the epistle doubt that it was really addressed to Aristobulus,[50] but the exaggerated praise the Jerusalemites heap on Aristobulus is understandable. If indeed Judah had the letter written while preparing for the renewed dedication of the temple, this would only point to his political wisdom. All the same, we must admit a certain difficulty: the time between the composition of the letter and the actual dedication was quite short — how could the Jews of Egypt assent to this request and celebrate the days of dedication together with their brethren in Jerusalem? Some scholars have suggested that the letter was written prior to the first anniversary of the dedication, but while this hypothesis cannot be disproved, there is nothing in the letter itself to recommend it. Others point out that the actual year of the dedication is a matter of controversy.[51] But we require no recourse to such speculations, since nothing in the epistle calls its authenticity into question.

There are some who believe the broad historical narrative of 2 Maccabees 1.18–2.15 is a late addition.[52] I am not convinced of this, especially in light of the striking similarity between the concluding verses of the epistle (2.17-18) and the prayer at 2 Maccabees 1.24-29.[53] For the present discussion, however, we may omit the descriptive elements, citing only the core of the epistle's argument:

> 1.10The people of Jerusalem and of Judea and the senate and Judas, To Aristobulus, who is of the family of the anointed priests,[54] teacher of King

49. See Schürer, *The History of the Jews*, 3.579-587; Hengel, *Judaismus und Hellenismus*, 295-307. See also Y. Amir, "Monotheistische Korrekturen heidnischer Texte," *Festschrift für Heinz Schreckenberge* (Göttingen, 1993), 9-11. The extant fragments of Aristobulus's epistles were published by A. M. Denis, *Fragmenta pseudepigraphorum quae supersunt Graeca* (Leiden, 1970), 217-228, and in English by A. Y. Collins, in *Old Testament Pseudepigrapha*, J. H. Charlesworth (ed.) (Garden City, 1985), 2.831-842.

50. See Habicht, "2 Makkabäerbuch," 202; Stephenson and Walker, *Halley's Comet*, 261-262; Hengel, *Judentum und Hellenismus*, 297, n. 367. Wacholder, "The Letter of Judah Maccabee," 93-95, who believes the letter is authentic, holds — rightly, to my mind — that the titles attributed to Aristobulus in the opening are not implausible.

51. See Habicht, "2 Makkabäerbuch," 249-250, commenting on 2 Macc 10.5.

52. See Habicht, "2 Makkabäerbuch," 199-201. If this is in fact the case, it is possible that the original version did not mention Judah Maccabee by name. His name appears in 2 Macc 2.14 and in the salutation at 2 Macc 1.10 (a possible addition, as mentioned above, n. 3). As noted, these are speculative hypotheses that, even if correct, do not substantively alter the argument.

53. See the comparison in "The Image of the Masada Martyrs," in the present volume.

54. The phrase is taken from Numbers 3:3 and is in keeping with the florid rhetoric of the day. It does not mean that Aristobulus was of a family of high priests. See J. Licht, *Commentary to Numbers [1–10]* (Jerusalem, 1985), ad loc.

Ptolemy, and to the Jews in Egypt, Greetings and good health. 11Having been saved by God out of grave dangers we thank him greatly for taking our side against the king, 12for he drove out those who fought against the holy city. 13When the leader reached Persia with a force that seemed irresistible, they were cut to pieces in the temple of Nanea by a deception employed by the priests of the goddess Nanea. 14On the pretext of intending to marry her, Antiochus came to the place together with his Friends, to secure most of its treasures as a dowry. 15When the priests of the temple of Nanea had set out the treasures and Antiochus had come with a few men inside the wall of the sacred precinct, they closed the temple as soon as he entered it. 16Opening a secret door in the ceiling, they threw stones and struck down the leader and his men; they dismembered them and cut off their heads and threw them to the people outside. 17Blessed in every way be our God, who has brought judgment on those who have behaved impiously. 18Since on the twenty-fifth day of Kislev we shall celebrate the purification of the temple, we thought it necessary to notify you, in order that you also may celebrate the festival of booths and the festival of the fire given when Nehemiah, who built the temple and the altar, offered sacrifices. . . .

2.16Since, therefore, we are about to celebrate the purification, we write to you. Will you therefore please keep the days? 17It is God who has saved all his people, and has returned the inheritance to all, and the kingship[55] and the priesthood and the consecration, 18as he promised through the law. We have hope in God that he will soon[56] have mercy on us and will gather us from everywhere under heaven into his holy place, for he has rescued us from great evils and has purified the place.

If we read the epistle in the context of the surrounding historical events, bearing in mind what we know of Judah Maccabee the man, we find that it speaks for itself.[57] The epistle conveys a sense that God "rescued us from great

---

55. The Greek word appears three times in the Septuagint as a translation of the Hebrew ממלכה, and twice in the remains of a prayer for the well-being of the Hasmonean king John, uncovered at Qumran. See E. Eshel, H. Eshel, and A. Yardeni, "A Qumran Composition," *IEJ* 42 (1992), 199-229, and especially 209-210. It may be that this verse alludes midrashically to Exodus 19:6 ("a kingdom ממלכה of priests and a holy nation"), since it contains terms that may refer to all four of these elements: nation, kingdom (ממלכה), priesthood, and holiness.

56. On this term see D. Flusser, *Judaism and the Origins of Christianity* (Jerusalem, 1988), 101.

57. See also my "Jerusalem in Second Temple Literature," and "The Image of the Masada Martyrs," both in the present volume.

evils and has purified the place" (2 Macc 2.18, and see also 1.11). These concluding words express a "double causality" typical of the Jewish worldview.
God has rescued his people and purified the temple, yet it is Judah and his
men who undertake the purification.

IX. Judah Maccabee's Political and Religious Worldview

The epistle also affords us insight into what Judah Maccabee considered the
political and religious goals of the temple's dedication. After all, even prior
to the recent discoveries it was evident that the capture of the temple was not
motivated by military needs. Now it appears that the purification and dedication of the temple were undertaken under relatively conducive conditions,
and the main motivation was Judah Maccabee's worldview. Namely, he
hoped that this act would usher in a new and decisive era in Jewish history.
Up to that time, the Jewish people in Israel and abroad were under foreign
rule, and the land of Israel part of the wicked Roman Empire. The priesthood was a sham, and the temple desecrated. But now God had fulfilled his
promise to his people, "saved all his people, and returned the inheritance to
all, and the kingship and the priesthood and the consecration, as he promised through the law" (2 Macc 2.17-18).[58] Many elements of the divine promise were fulfilled — the Hellenizing priests expelled and a true priesthood
instated, and the temple was once again a sacred site for all Jews. Note that
the author states that through this God "saved *all* his people, and returned
the inheritance to *all*." The divine inheritance now belongs to the Jewish
people as a whole and, as a result, all are affected by the salvific events in Jerusalem, even the Jews of Egypt. Among the gifts God has bestowed upon his
people, the epistle mentions the ממלכה, "kingdom" or "kingship."[59] There is
no doubt that the term here indicates that the dedication of the temple was
understood as a necessary step on the way to full political independence, a
preliminary step on the way to the ultimate redemption. There remain, however, a number of elements that have not yet been fulfilled: "We have hope in
God that he will soon have mercy on us and will gather us from everywhere
under heaven into his holy place" (2 Macc 2.18).[60] After the Hellenized
priests were removed, the proper cult restored, and the temple once again
holy for all Jews, it could become the site of pilgrimage for the Jews of the

58. On the possible allusion to Exodus 19.6, see above, n. 55.
59. On this word, see above, n. 55.
60. See also Flusser, "Jerusalem in Second Temple Literature," in the present collection.

Diaspora. It is not surprising, then, that Judah alludes to the biblical promise of the ingathering of exiles.

Pilgrimage, especially mass pilgrimage, was a tenuous proposition not only because of the difficulties the pilgrims faced, but also because of the possible response of the imperial masters.[61] Judah, like all Jews, hoped for a future ingathering of exiles, another of the divine promises, some of which were already realized with the dedication of the temple. If so, we may assume that Judah Maccabee saw the dedication of the temple as, at least in some sense, an eschatological event, or, at the very least, a harbinger of salvation. I have elsewhere discussed the two eschatological hopes that have animated Israel's spirit since the destruction of the First Temple:[62] the rebuilding of Jerusalem in all its former glory, such that "the latter splendor of this house shall be greater than the former" (Haggai 2:9); and the ingathering of exiles.[63] Both motifs are evident in Judah Maccabee's epistle: the temple has been purified and dedicated as God "promised through the law," so it is possible that the second hope, the ingathering of exiles, will similarly come true. The epistle as a whole testifies to the powerful bond between Jerusalem and the temple, on the one hand, and the Jews of the Diaspora, on the other, a bond not reducible to eschatological yearning. The solidarity of Jerusalem and the Diaspora finds expression in the prayer for the well-being of King Jonathan, i.e., Alexander Jannaeus.[64] The author of the prayer pleads on behalf of "King Jonathan, and the whole assembly of your people, Israel, who are in the four winds of heaven." It appears, then, that when an independent Hasmonean state was established in Israel, the bond with Diaspora Jewry not only did not falter, it grew stronger, as we see from Philo's statement that while Jews reside in many cities and consider them their homeland, they consider Jerusalem,

---

61. This problem was clearly recognized by Philo. In his discussion of Deuteronomy 30:4, he states: "For even though they dwell in the uttermost parts of the earth, in slavery to those who led them away captive, one signal, as it were, one day will bring liberty to all. This conversion in a body to virtue will strike awe into their masters, who will set them free, ashamed to rule over men better than themselves" (*On Rewards and Punishment*, §164).

62. See my "Jerusalem in Second Temple Literature" in the present volume, and "4QMMT and the Benediction Against the *Minim,*" *Judaism of the Second Temple Period: Qumran and Apocalypticism*, 70-118. It should be noted that the apocalyptic composition preserved in 1 Enoch 83–90 links eschatological Jerusalem with the ingathering of exiles. This work was composed during the period of Judah Maccabee, as I discuss in the *Encyclopaedia Judaica* 14.1198-1199.

63. These found expression in two of the Eighteen Benedictions, the only two eschatological benedictions.

64. On this prayer see my "A Comment on a Prayer for the Welfare of King Jonathan," *Judaism of the Second Temple Period: Qumran and Apocalypticism*, 170-174.

which houses the sanctuary of God most high, to be their capital.[65] Other sources similarly indicate that the political independence attained by the Maccabees strengthened the ties between Israel (and Jerusalem in particular) and the Jewish Diaspora, ties reflected in the epistle of Judah Maccabee.

X. Conclusion

Though my conclusions may help confirm the authenticity of Judah's letter in 2 Maccabees, this was not the goal of the present study. A renewed examination of the relevant material — some of which has only come to light in recent years — allows us to situate Judah Maccabee's dedication of the temple as part of a broader trend leading to the annulment of Antiochus IV's anti-Jewish decrees, and to better understand the role of Judah Maccabee the man in this process. We found that Antiochus IV died *before* the dedication, and that news of his death probably reached Jerusalem shortly before the event. Still, the plan to recapture and purify the temple was formulated earlier, as a result of ongoing negotiations between Judah and Antiochus IV himself. These negotiations are not mentioned in Maccabees 1 or 2, though 2 Maccabees 11 contains four epistles that bear clear witness to contacts with Antiochus Epiphanes toward the end of his days, which eventually came to fruition when his son annulled the decrees.

The four epistles suggest that in his final days Antiochus understood that the decrees and the desecration of the temple provoked such resistance among the Jews that they were damaging the Seleucid throne. After the mediation of Menelaus, the high priest and head of the Jewish Hellenizers, did not yield fruit (vv. 27-33), Antiochus had no choice but to deal directly with Judah and his men (vv. 16-21). The Seleucid throne was represented by Lysias, the viceroy, since Antiochus himself had already set off on his final campaign into Asia. Lysias, who was interested in a quick and successful end to the entire affair, promised the Jews that if they maintained a positive attitude toward the throne, he would try to secure for them additional benefits, but that the final decision rested with the king (v. 19); the king, however, could no longer render his decision, as he had "gone on to the gods" (v. 23). It was at this point that Judah and his men seized the temple and rededicated it. Ultimately,

65. Philo, *Contra Flaccus* 46; and cf. *The Embassy to Gaius,* 281. The terms *patria* (homeland) and *metropolis* (capital) are ultimately derived from the Greek words for "father" and "mother," respectively. By juxtaposing the two, as he does in both passages, Philo may be alluding to the different roles Jerusalem and the native cities play for diaspora Jews.

Lysias — now serving Antiochus V — annulled the decrees altogether, and declared the Jews' temple "be restored to them and that they shall live according to the customs of their ancestors" (v. 25).

As the above summary indicates, it is almost certain that there was a de facto armistice at the time, and it may be that the seizure of the temple was undertaken with Lysias's silent consent. Judah Maccabee also drew encouragement from the support of Rome, the superpower of the day, who considered Judah and his forces representatives of the Jewish people (v. 34).[66] Judah, then, rightly estimated that Rome's favor would provide support for him in time of need.[67] The circumstances, then, were quite favorable for this act, which was to change the course of Jewish history. Indeed, they were so favorable that Judah could plan the details of the renewal of the temple cult and even write the epistle to the Jews of Egypt. If the letter is authentic, its purpose was, *inter alia,* to provide additional support for Judah.

The epistle's portrait of the political situation as a whole is in striking agreement with everything we know about Judah Maccabee's personality and worldview — another argument for its authenticity. Judah believed that through the dedication of the temple, an act he initiated, God "has saved all his people, and has returned the inheritance to all, and the kingship and the priesthood and the consecration" (2 Macc 2.17). Judah was true to this view up to his tragic death on the battlefield. Most of his hopes were, in fact, realized — so much so that his Hasmonean heirs adopted the ways of the now waning Hellenistic world, even daring to commit the crimes so typical of kings.[68] Our task here, however, is not to examine the fulfillment or atrophy of ideals. We wish only to shed light on the true and largely unknown historical background of Judah's temple dedication, and in so doing, to point to the stature of this great leader.

---

66. See Stern, *Documents on the Histories of the Hasmonean Revolt,* 68-70.

67. On the first treaty between Judah and Rome, which was forged later, in 161 B.C.E., see Stern, *Documents on the History of the Hasmonean Revolt,* 74-83.

68. See Tacitus, *Historiae* 5.8.3. It is true that Tacitus was hostile to the Jews, but the passage is on the whole quite accurate and fits well with what the Dead Sea Scrolls recount of "the last priests of Jerusalem." On the Jewish nationalism of the day, see D. Mendels, *The Rise and Fall of Jewish Nationalism* (New York, 1992).

Granius Licinianus on Antiochus Epiphanes

The account provided by Granius Licinianus appears to be part of the same narrative tradition concerning Antiochus IV reflected in Judah Maccabee's letter and in 2 Maccabees 9.7-8. The Roman author, like Judah Maccabee, states that Antiochus sought to rob the temple of Artemis under the guise of a fictive matrimony with the goddess. Moreover, he adds, Antiochus actually removed the precious vessels of the temple and used them for a festive meal, then confiscated them as a dowry. He did return a single ring to Artemis. This form of desecration parallels the description of the feast of Belshazzar in Daniel 5, while Licinianus's account of Antiochus's body falling from the carriage echoes 2 Maccabees 9.7-8, but with an interesting difference: in the latter the king falls out while alive, in the former it is his corpse that plunges into the river and disappears. To my mind, it is the Roman historian's version that is more plausible and, considered in light of the Babylonian source text about men carrying off the body,[69] may even contain a historical kernel of truth. Unfortunately, the Babylonian tablet is broken after these words.

Interestingly, Licinianus's description is very similar to that of Josippon (10th century C.E.), which is based on 2 Maccabees: "So (Antiochus) rode on the chariot and entered with his army, a very great multitude, and with him many elephants and a very mighty host. And it happened, en route, that the chariot passed before the elephant, and the elephant bellowed and disturbed the horses. The horses bolted and overturned the chariot, and Antiochus fell

69. See Stephenson and Walker, *Halley's Comet*, 12.

from the chariot, breaking all his bones, for he was heavy and fat."[70] This is not the only place where Josippon's imagination manages to penetrate beyond the surface of his sources.

To complete the picture, it is necessary to cite the scholion to *Megillat Ta'anit*, on the 28th of Shevat, the death of Antiochus Epiphanes, who sought to destroy the Jews: "But bad news from his land startled him (see Daniel 11:42), and he fell on the spot." Some scholars argue that the Antiochus in question is Antiochus VII Sidetes, while others suggest it is Antiochus V Eupator. However, the citation from Daniel proves that it is Antiochus Epiphanes.

70. See *Sefer Josippon* (Hebrew), ed. David Flusser (Jerusalem, 1979), 84.

6. Did the Jewish People Obscure the Memory of the Maccabees in the Middle Ages?

In one of his studies, the late Gedalyahu Alon examined whether the sages of late antiquity sought to obscure the memory of the Hasmonean dynasty.[1] He attacks the then current view that the memory of Maccabee victories and bravery was reduced to "small jugs" of oil.[2] The goal of the present study is rather simpler: we argue that the Mediaeval period witnessed an increased glorification of Judah Maccabee and his brother, even beyond what is alluded to in the writings of the sages. This occurred as a result of external influence, as well as internal development in Jewish historiography. Throughout, the famous oil jug remained a secondary motif intended as an etiology of Hanukkah.[3]

Hanukkah

Of all the dates mentioned in Megillat Ta'anit, only Purim and Hanukkah are still celebrated.[4] Purim is well-established, for it recalls events from biblical

---

1. G. Alon, "Did the Nation and Its Sages Obscure the Memory of the Hasmoneans?" in his *Studies in Jewish History* (Tel Aviv, 1978), 1.15-25. Alon's article paved the way for the present study.

2. See Alon, "Did the Nation and Its Sages?" 15. And see my two articles on the Maccabees, "The Image of the Masada Martyrs," and "What Is Hanukkah?" both in the present collection.

3. B. Shabbat 21b.

4. B. Rosh Ha-Shana 19b. On Megillat Ta'anit see H. Lichtenstein, "Die Fastenrolle," *HUCA* 8-9 (1931-1932), 257-351. And see also V. Noam, "The *Scholion* to *Megillat Ta'anit*: Towards an Understanding of Its Stemma," *Tarbiz* 62 (1993), 55-99; idem, "*Megillat Ta'anit* and the

times and is anchored in the canonic Scroll of Esther. Hanukkah, however, involves events that took place after the cessation of prophecy, and so no biblical work is devoted to it. The Aramaic "Scroll of Antiochus" — about which more below — could not play a parallel role to the Scroll of Esther, if only because of its impoverished content.[5] The Jewish sages of Israel believed that only works composed in Hebrew (or Aramaic) during the time of the prophets — which ended in the early Second Temple period — could be counted as Scripture.[6] This is the main reason the original Hebrew text of 1 Maccabees is no longer extant, even though Origen (who died in 253 C.E.) testified to its existence. As for the Talmudic sources, they were not primarily interested in preserving Jewish history — even the great rebellion against Rome is poorly documented and would be almost unattested were it not for Josephus and a number of foreign sources. Still, the Talmud does preserve some statements in praise of the Maccabee heroes, at least up to the point when the Hasmoneans broke with the core tenets of Israel and its sages and became Sadducees.[7] We need not enter into a detailed discussion of the rabbis' accounts of the Hasmonean dynasty and its struggles; our focus is rather on what they passed on to medieval Jewry and how this heritage was transformed through encounters with non-Jewish sources.

The jug of oil is never mentioned during the Hanukkah candle lighting ceremony, nor in the Hanukkah liturgy that begins with the words "In the days of Mattathias son of John. . . ." In the version of this prayer preserved in Tractate Soferim,[8] the miracles God performed in those days are not speci-

---

Scholion, Their Nature, Period and Sources, Accompanied by a Critical Edition" (Ph.D. Dissertation; Hebrew University, 1997).

5. A critical edition of the original Aramaic text, along with a Hebrew translation, is found in M. Z. Kedari, *Bar Ilan* 1 (1963), 81-105. The "Antiochus Scroll" will be cited according to this edition. And see also Kedari's discussion of the language of the scroll in *Bar Ilan* 2 (1962), 178-214.

6. See Josephus, *Contra Apionem* 1.40-41; Urbach, *The Sages: Their Concepts and Beliefs* (Hebrew), 502-503.

7. Even Tacitus, no philosemite, saw the late Hasmonean period as a time of atrophy. See *Historiae* 5.8.3, cited in M. Stern, *Greek and Latin Authors on Jews and Judaism* (Jerusalem, 1980), 2.21, 28, 48. Stern rightly compares Tacitus's account with the testimony of the Dead Sea Scrolls. See also D. Flusser, "The Roman Empire in Hasmonean and Essene Eyes," in *Judaism of the Second Temple Period: Qumran and Apocalypticism*, 175-206.

8. See Tractate Soferim 20, 8: "In the benediction for Thanksgiving we include [on Hanukkah] 'and thanks for the wonders and salvation of your priests you performed in the days of Mattathias, son of Yohanan, High Priest, and the Hasmoneans his sons. So also, O Lord our God and God of our fathers, perform for us miracles and wonders, and we will give thanks to your name forever. Blessed are you, O Lord, who is all-good'" (*Minor Tractates* 1.313). It appears the same principle applies to Purim as well: "The miracles of the days of Mordechai and Esther are

fied. The alternate version, which has gained acceptance throughout the Jewish world, speaks of the bravery of the Maccabees in their battle against the wicked Greeks and the decrees of Antiochus IV. The entire passage is very much in the spirit of 1 Maccabees — a distillation of the historical events aimed at presenting the Maccabees in the most positive light possible. Unfortunately, we cannot determine when and under what circumstances this passage was composed, only that it represents the medieval Hanukkah message.

"John the High Priest"

The positive spirit of our Hanukkah liturgy is in no way anomalous. There are those who suggest that John Hyrcanus, who late in life turned his back on the sages, was referred to in a positive way in Targum pseudo-Jonathan to Deuteronomy 33:11. There, at the end of the blessing of Levi, Moses states, "let his adversaries not rise again," which Pseudo-Jonathan renders: "The enemies of John the High Priest will not have a leg to stand on."[9] Already Geiger proposed that the High Priest Jonathan in question is John Hyrcanus,[10] though this is a matter of controversy.[11] It is difficult to endorse the claim that John Hyrcanus is praised by Targum Pseudo-Jonathan, a late composition that incorporates material from similarly late sources.[12] Still, it is possible that "John the High Priest" in question is, in fact, a Hasmonean figure, since the midrash

---

also mentioned [on Purim] in the benediction for Thanksgiving" (ibid.). The prayer book of Rav Saadia Gaon states that there are those who append an additional statement to the Hanukkah liturgy, "Just as you performed miracles for our ancestors, so too will you perform for us and redeem us in the present days just as in the past days. . . ." See *Siddur Rav Saadia Gaon* (Hebrew), ed. Davidson, Assaf and Yoel (Jerusalem, 1941), 256. See also the important comment of Abudraham in *Commentary on the Benedictions and the Prayers* (Hebrew) (Jerusalem, 1962), 202. See also: *Rabbenu Yehudah ben Yaqar, Commentary on the Benedictions and the Prayers* (Hebrew) (Jerusalem, 1979), 2.8, n. 43; *Mahzor Vitry* (Jerusalem, 1963), 68, 198-199, and the note therein. Similar addenda are found in the liturgical traditions of Italy, Yemen, Persia, and more, but, nonetheless, it is probably a secondary addition to the Babylonian liturgy, echoing the language of Tractate Soferim. See also D. Goldschmidt, *Studies in Prayer and Piyyut* (Hebrew) (Jerusalem, 1979), 405.

9. See *Targum Pseudo-Jonathan* (Aramaic with Hebrew translation), ed. D. Reider, 157 (the annotated Hebrew translation) and 306 (Aramaic).

10. See A. Geiger, *The Bible and Its Translators* (Hebrew) (Jerusalem, 1970), 314.

11. See A. Shinan, *The Embroidered Targum* (Hebrew) (Jerusalem, 1993), 194-195. To the list of adherents to Geiger's view add Schürer, *The History*, 1.215, n. 33; to the detractors, L. Ginzberg, *The Legends of the Jews* (Philadelphia, 1946), 6.156, n. 925.

12. Though it is nonetheless possible that the encomium to John Hyrcanus appears in Pseudo-Jonathan's Targum.

interprets Deuteronomy 33:11 as referring to the Hasmonean victory over the Seleucids. Perhaps a fragment of this midrash — in a version that is otherwise unattested — found its way into Pseudo-Jonathan.

The midrash in question,[13] includes the words of Rabbi Yohanan, who interpreted Jeremiah 5:6 as a reference to four kingdoms: "'Therefore a lion from the forest shall kill them,' this refers to Babylonia; 'a wolf from the desert shall destroy them,' these are the Medes and the Persians; 'A leopard is watching,' this is Greece; 'everyone who goes out of them shall be torn in pieces,' this is Edom, and Edom is Rome." Rabbi Yohanan's interpretation integrates the four animals mentioned by Jeremiah, with the four beasts in Daniel 7:4-7 — even appearing in the same order — with the wolf (זאב) of Jeremiah substituted for the bear (דב) of Daniel. The substitution is relatively unproblematic since the Aramaic word is written with *defectiva* orthography "and דיבא can be a translation of זאב (wolf), which also refers to the Persian empire."[14]

As noted, Rabbi Yohanan's derashah is part of a broader midrashic framework,[15] and it may be that the entire passage — discussed below — originated with this sage.[16] The passage in question is tied to Genesis 49:27: "Benjamin is a ravenous wolf, in the morning devouring the prey, and at evening dividing the spoil," and involves the four kingdoms, two of which are alluded to in the blessing of Jacob, and the remaining two in the blessing of Moses. Here is the passage in its entirety, as it appears in Bereshit Rabbati:

> Jacob and Moses saw four kingdoms, and when they came to bless the tribes, Jacob gave two of his sons to take revenge upon them and Moses similarly gave two. Jacob saw Babylonia as a lion, as it is written, "the first was like a lion and had eagles' wings" (Dan 7:4), and called Judah "lion's whelp" (Gen 49:9). Jacob said: When Babylon arises, Judah will set himself against her, as it is written "And from the tribe of Judah . . ." (Dan 1:6). Into the hand of whom does Babylonia fall? Into the hand of Daniel, a Judean.[17] He saw the Medes as a wolf . . . and called Benjamin "a ravenous wolf" (Gen 49:27). Jacob said: When the Medians and Persians — who are likened to a wolf — come, Mordechai and Esther will set themselves

---

13. Bereshit Rabbah 99.2 (pages 1273-1274 in the Theodor-Albeck edition); Bereshit Rabbati 49.27 (pages 252-253 in the Albeck edition). See also Midrash Tanhuma, Va-Yehi 14; Tanhuma (Buber), Va-Yehi 13 (106a); Rashi's comments to Deuteronomy 33:11.

14. Thus Rashi, *ad loc.*

15. See above, n. 13.

16. See below, n. 26.

17. The phrase "who is a Judean" is from Bereshit Rabbah, 1273.

against them, as they are descendents of Benjamin. Moses saw Greece [see "as a tiger" in Daniel 7:6] and gave them Levi. As it is written: "Bless, O Lord, his substance, and accept the work of his hands" (Deut 33:11). Levi was born third, and Greece is the third kingdom. Levi has three letters (לוי), and Greece has three letters (יון).[18] The one sacrifices bulls, while the other writes with the bull's horn.

We saw above that Targum Pseudo-Jonathan applies the words "let his adversaries not arise again" (Deut 33:11) to Jonathan the high priest. It is worth noting that the above derashah is preceded by the verse "crush the loins of his adversaries, of those that hate him, so that they do not rise again," an allusion to the Hasmonean victory over the Hellenistic kingdom. It stands to reason, then, that Pseudo-Jonathan preserves a different and most likely earlier tradition of the midrash, which was linked to the phrase "let his adversaries not arise again," understood as a reference to some Hasmonean John, perhaps John Hyrcanus. As Rabbah, the great Babylonian sage stated: "John is righteous at heart."[19]

We find, then, two verses from the blessing of Jacob (Gen 49:9 and 27) and two from the blessing of Moses (Deut 33:10 and 11) that purportedly allude to Daniel 7:4-7. The same is true of the fourth and final kingdom, that of Edom, i.e., Rome:

He saw the final kingdom coming with its horns, as it is written: "it had ten horns" (Dan 7:7); and he knew that Esau would not be felled except by the descendents of Rachel, as it is written, "Surely the little ones of the flock shall be dragged away; surely their fold shall be appalled at their fate" (Jer 49:20). Thus he blessed Joseph with horns, as it is written, "His horns are the horns of a wild ox" (Deut 33:17). Moses said: When someone bearing horns arises, horned-Joseph will set himself against them. And into the hand of whom does the kingdom of Edom fall? Into the hand of the Messiah, who is a descendent of Joseph.[20]

The man who will defeat the fourth kingdom is, then, the Messiah son of Joseph.[21]

---

18. In Bereshit Rabbah there follows here an important statement comparing the Levites and the Greeks. It is absent from Bereshit Rabbati, though it undoubtedly is an integral part of the midrash. See the important notes in the Theodor-Albeck edition, 1274.

19. B. Berakhot, 29a.

20. The phrase "into the hand of whom" etc. is from Bereshit Rabbah.

21. On the Messiah son of Joseph, and the allusion to him in this passage, see D. Flusser, "Hystaspes and John of Patmos," in *Judaism and the Origins of Christianity*, 46, n. 124.

As noted, it is possible that this entire midrash was composed by Rabbi Yohanan, to whom another midrash that characterizes the Maccabees as redeeming Israel from the Greeks is attributed:

> They were enslaved in Egypt, Moses rose up and redeemed them. Again they were enslaved in Babylonia, Daniel and Hananiah and Mishael and Azariah rose up and redeemed them. Again they were enslaved in Elam and in Media and in Persia, Mordechai and Esther rose up and redeemed them. Again they were enslaved in Egypt, the Hasmonean and his sons rose up and redeemed them. Again they were enslaved by the wicked kingdom of Edom, and the Children of Israel said . . . this time we do not ask for human redemption. . . .[22]

Two more derashot follow the same pattern, celebrating the Maccabees' victory over Greece:

> "Awake, my soul! Awake, O harp and lyre! I will awake the dawn" (Ps 57.8): [The verse] refers to the four kingdoms. "Awake" to Babylonia, against whom Hananiah, Mishael, and Azariah will set themselves. "Awake" to the Medes, against whom Mordechai and Esther will set themselves. "Awake" to Greece, against whom the Hasmoneans set themselves. "Awake" to Edom, against whom the king messiah will set himself in future days.[23]

The second is preserved in a relatively late collection, and has been reworked to fit the number four:

> God set four righteous men in each of the four kingdoms, to redeem them and cause Torah to reside in their midst: In Babylon — Daniel, Hananiah, Mishael, and Azariah; in Persia — Haggai, Zechariah, Malachi, and Nehemiah; in Greece — the four Hasmonean sons, the elder of which, Judah, already having been killed; in Edom — Rabban Gamaliel, Rabbi Yehoshua, Rabbi Elazar ben Azariah, and Rabbi Aqiva.[24]

The same pattern — four saviors for the four kingdoms, with the Hasmoneans cast as the saviors of the Greek period — appears in a midrash to Leviticus 26:44:

---

22. Midrash Psalms 36:10 (page 250 in the Buber edition). See also Bacher, *Die Agada der palästinensischen Amoräer* (Strasbourg 1892-1905), 1.248, n. 3.

23. Midrash Psalms 32:9 (page 185 in the Buber edition).

24. *Mishnat Rabbi Eliezer*, ed. H. Enelow (New York, 1936), 102-103.

"I did not spurn them" refers to the days of the Chaldeans, when I established for (Israel) Daniel, Hananiah, Mishael, and Azariah; "or abhor them" refers to the days of the Greeks, when I established for them Simon the Righteous, and the Hasmonean and his sons, and Mattathias the high priest; "to destroy them" refers to the days of Haman, when I established for them Mordechai and Esther; "and break my covenant with them," the days of the Romans,[25] when I established for them the house of Rabbi (Judah) and the sages of the day;[26] "for I am the Lord their God" refers to the future days, when no nation and no language will have dominion over them.[27]

Another interpretation of this type is found in the Targum to three verses in Hannah's prayer (1 Sam 2:3-5), which are correlated to the four kingdoms, and here too the Maccabees are mentioned. Verse three ("Talk no more so very proudly, let not arrogance come from your mouth, etc.") is linked with the Babylonians who will rule over Israel but ultimately suffer for their sins. Verse four ("The bows of the mighty are broken, but the feeble gird on strength") is Hannah's prophecy concerning the Greeks: the bows of the Greeks will be broken, while the feeble Hasmoneans will be girded by strengths (i.e. miracles). Verse five, "Those who were full have hired themselves out for bread, but those who were hungry are fat with spoil," refers to Haman and Esther, respectively. The conclusion — "The barren has borne seven, but she who has many children is forlorn" — is a prophecy concerning Jerusalem, which is barren but will be filled with the ingathering of exiles, and Rome, which is filled with many nations but will eventually be razed. The placement of the Greeks before the Persians is midrashically motivated: the reference to "the feeble" in verse four lends itself to the Maccabees, since the Hanukkah liturgy states that God delivered "mighty warriors to the hand of the feeble."

The Hasmonean Dynasty in Megillat Ta'anit

Vered Noam has recently published two important studies on the Hasmoneans in the Hebrew part of Megillat Ta'anit.[28] Noam concludes that the He-

---

25. So in the manuscripts and the earlier printed editions.

26. So in MS Munich and *Aggadot Ha-Talmud* (Jerusalem, 1961), 25a.

27. B. Megillah, 11a.

28. On the characterization of Judah Maccabee in the Aramaic part of the scroll, see Lichtenstein, "Die Fastenrolle," 273-280.

brew section is, in fact, two separate compositions that have been appended to an earlier Aramaic work. Not merely separate, they are radically different in content, structure, and style. Each is attested in a single witness: MS O (from the Bodleian Library, Oxford) and MS P (Parma), respectively.[29] As a result, it becomes necessary to discuss each of these works, with their traditions and style, individually. The remaining witnesses to the Hebrew section of Megillat Ta'anit belong to the common version that is nothing more than an intentional hybrid of MSS O and P.[30] The following discussion is intended to pave the way to new questions, only some of which bear directly on the topic at hand. However, in order to examine the place of the Hasmoneans in medieval Jewish literature it is necessary to examine how much of the relevant material in Megillat Ta'anit is a reworking of earlier material, and how much a product of later speculation. We need, then, to examine what parts of Ta'anit are drawn from known rabbinic sources, and what parts are of primary historical value.

One example of this question involves the Hanukkah etiology offered in Megillat Ta'anit.[31] The miracle story is, of course, recounted in b. Shabbat 21b, where we find the Aramaic and the Hebrew of Megillat Ta'anit. Nonetheless, detailed analysis suggests that the Ta'anit passage was not taken from the Babylonian Talmud. For neither MS P nor the citation from MS O in 'Or Zaru'a mentions the miracle of the oil.[32] We cannot know, of course, if the author of 'Or Zaru'a knew a version that predates the Talmud's, or perhaps he omitted mention of the miracle of oil. As for the rest of the Hanukkah narrative in Ta'anit, it has no parallel in the Talmud and contains interesting historical material.[33]

Both the Hebrew and Aramaic portions of Ta'anit contain important and otherwise unattested historical material concerning the 23rd of Iyar. MS O

29. See Noam, "The Scholion to Megillat Ta'anit," 67, 92-93.

30. Noam, "The Scholion to Megillat Ta'anit," 67.

31. See Noam, "Megillat Ta'anit and the Scholion," 22-23, 46-56. Aside from b. Shabbat 21b, Noam mentions (p. 46) b. Rosh Ha-Shana 24b (parallels at b. 'Avodah Zarah 43a and b. Menahot 28b); Pesikta Rabbati §2 (5a in the Friedmann edition).

32. 'Or Zaru'a, laws of Hanukkah, 2.321; discussed in Noam, "Megillat Ta'anit and the Scholion," 22-23.

33. For a parallel of Ta'anit's Hebrew account of the temple dedication in the days of Solomon, see 2 Maccabees 2.8-12, and the discussion in Noam, "Megillat Ta'anit and the Scholion," 49. Similar material appears in Judah Maccabee's epistle, which I believe to be authentic. MS O's discussion of the construction of the altar parallels 1 Maccabees 5.9, as Noam rightly points out. And see her fascinating comparison (pp. 51-52) of the seven steel spikes the Hasmonean brothers held during the dedication of the temple and the passage in b. Rosh Ha-Shana 24b (and parallels).

preserves an authentic tradition that describes the non-Jews abandoning the Hakra fortress during the Hasmonean period.[34] Another important passage in MS P discusses the dedication of the temple in the days of Judah Maccabee and the 23rd of Marheshvan, with a parallel in 1 Maccabees 4.44-46.[35] Interestingly, 1 Maccabees states that the altar stones that were defiled by Antiochus were "the stones in a convenient place on the temple hill until a prophet should come to tell what to do with them" (1 Macc 4.45-46), while Ta'anit states that the stones were set aside until Elijah returns to testify if they are impure or pure. Elijah here plays the role of the eschatological prophet, as is common in rabbinic literature.[36]

Megillat Ta'anit and Antiochus IV

Finally, there is a particularly interesting passage in MS O regarding the 28th of Shevat: "On the 28th, Antiochus was taken from Jerusalem, for he had set out to destroy and raze Jerusalem. But bad news from his land startled him, and he fell on the spot."[37] There are a number of theories as to what events are here alluded to, but we must bear in mind the linguistic similarity to Daniel 11:44: "But bad news from the east and the north shall startle him, and he shall go out with great fury to bring ruin and complete destruction to many." The following verse relates that the wicked king will meet his end "in the beautiful holy mountain." It is only Megillat Ta'anit that teaches us that Antiochus set out to destroy "Jerusalem," that the bad news came "from his land," and that he ultimately fell "on the spot." It should be noted that the figure described in the Book of Daniel is none other than Antiochus Epiphanes, a fact widely-known among Pagan philosophers from the time of Porphyry on, and recognized in Jewish circles no later than the 14th century.[38] As for the information concerning the 28th of Shevat in the Hebrew and Aramaic sections of Ta'anit (according to MS O), there is no doubt that the Hebrew correctly glosses the Aramaic, especially in light of the close proximity between Ta'anit and Daniel 11:44. For here too the text seems to refer to Antiochus Epiphanes, and if this

---

34. See Noam, "*Megillat Ta'anit* and the Scholion," 1-4, who does not cite the parallels. See also Lichtenstein, "Die Fastenrolle," 286-287, 327.

35. Noam, "*Megillat Ta'anit* and the Scholion," 8-9; Lichtenstein, "Die Fastenrolle," 273-275. And cf. m. Middot 1.6.

36. Elijah is cast in this role only by the rabbis and Jesus!

37. See Noam, "*Megillat Ta'anit* and the Scholion," 13; Lichtenstein, "Die Fastenrolle," 299-301, 339.

38. See H. A. Ginsberg, *Biblical Encyclopedia* (Hebrew), 687-688 (s.v.: דניאל).

is a sign of Taʿanit's dependence on Daniel, the former's author must have known to whom Daniel was referring.

There is another difficulty involving Daniel 11:44. It appears that the author of Daniel presents as prophecy events that he had already seen; however, beginning with 11:40, he leaves behind him the historical account and tries to prophesy the future. Alas, his prophecy did not come true.[39] To the modern reader, then, Daniel 11:44 is not a historical account (irrespective of its presentation as prophecy), but a future event as imagined by the author. This distinction was foreign to the author of Megillat Taʿanit, who thought of Daniel 11:44 as an authentic prophecy. Thus, he reworked the biblical verse to suit the known facts regarding Antiochus's decision to leave Jerusalem on the 28th of Shevat. He provides a new datum — that Antiochus was startled by bad news "from his land," and whereas Daniel's account of the king's death implies (wrongly, as it turns out) that he will meet his end in Israel, Megillat Taʿanit states only that he "fell on the spot," an obscure statement that may be interpreted as an allusion to the fact that Antiochus died far from Jerusalem, on his final campaign. According to Taʿanit, then, Antiochus set out on his final campaign on the 28th of Shevat, a date that is by no means implausible.[40] It seems, then, that the author of Taʿanit believed that the statements in Daniel 11:40 and following are also authentic prophecies, and reworked 11:44 to the historical facts surrounding the death of the wicked king. Porphyry too was incapable of distinguishing the historical (up to Daniel 11:40) from the ahistorical, and he, like Taʿanit, interpreted verses 44-45 as a description of Antiochus's final campaign.[41]

Later Midrashim and the Tale of Judith

Aside from Megillat Taʿanit we should also mention the later midrashim that deal with the dedication of the temple.[42] These tales have no truck with the historical facts, contain few allusions and often inaccurate allusions to the Books of Maccabees, and have been shaped by the rich imagination of the medieval

---

39. See D. Flusser, "The Apocalyptic Elements in the War Scroll," *Judaism of the Second Temple Period: Qumran and Apocalypticism*, 140-158.

40. On the final campaign of Antiochus Epiphanes see O. Mørkholm, *Antiochus IV of Syria* (Copenhagen, 1958), 166-171.

41. Porphyry's interpretation was preserved in Jerome's commentary to Daniel, ad loc. See A. von Harnack, *Porphyrius gegen die Christen* (Berlin, 1916), 71-72.

42. The midrashim in question are collected in A. Jellenick, *Bet Ha-Midrash* (Jerusalem, 1938), Room I, 132-136, 137-141; Room VI, 1-3.

authors. The stories of Hasmonean bravery are filled with hyperbole and certainly do not suggest a marginalization of their bellicose and heroic aspects. In these midrashim,[43] we find an interesting combination of the *jus primae noctis*[44] and the origins of the Hasmonean revolt. The daughter of Mattathias son of John (or the daughter of John) was engaged to one of the Hasmoneans, who rescued her from a wicked Greek governor, whom he then killed. The linkage between this legend and the origins of the revolt is secondary and relatively late. The story of the "Decree of the Virgins" appears in the Jerusalem Talmud,[45] with an important parallel in MS O, under the 17th of Elul.[46] But the story of Mattathias's daughter is late, not attested in MS O.[47] The tale appears in later midrashim and is mentioned in a number of liturgical poems, as well as the two versions of the Antiochus Scroll.[48] Still, it is clear that we are dealing with a late addition that stems from medieval Hanukkah midrashim.

Medieval Jewish sources also linked the apocryphal story of Judith with the Hasmonean revolt, and many came to believe that Judith's actions occurred during the decrees of Antiochus. This connection is already attested in the most important Hanukkah midrash, which was composed no later than 1000 B.C.E.[49] From these midrashim, the story of Judith found its way into two Hanukkah-themed liturgical poems. The earlier, composed for the first night of Hanukkah, is by Rabbi Yosef bar Shelomo,[50] who lived in the 14th century, and the later composed for the second night, by Rabbi Menahem ben Rabbi Mekir.[51]

43. Jellenick, *Bet Ha-Midrash*, Room I, 133, 135, 137; Room VI, 2.

44. That is, the right of the master to have intercourse with the bride of his subjects prior to the wedding. The motif appears in Beaumarchais's *The Marriage of Figaro*, and from there made its way into Mozart's opera.

45. P. Ketubot 1, 5, 25c.

46. Lichtenstein, "Die Fastenrolle," 304-305, 335-336.

47. For a general discussion of the matter see Noam, *Megillat Ta'anit and Its Scholion* (Hebrew University diss., 1997), 38-41.

48. See the Kedari edition; the tale appears following §40. See also the *Encyclopaedia Judaica* s.v.: "Scroll of Antiochus," 14.1045-1047, and Jellenick, *Bet Ha-Midrash*, Room VI, ix.

49. See Y. M. Grintz, *The Book of Judith* (Hebrew) (Jerusalem, 1957), 197-208. The Hanukkah midrash in question appears in Jellenick, *Bet Ha-Midrash*, Room I, 132-136. See also the Tosafot to b. Megillah 4a, where Rabbi Shmuel ben Meir (the Rashbam) is cited to the effect that the Hanukkah miracle occurred primarily for the sake of Judith. See also the textual comments *(hagahot)* of Rabbi Meir Isserless (the Rama) to *Shulchan Arukh* §670, 5, which are based on *Sefer Kol-Bo*.

50. Published in Seligmann Baer, *Siddur Avodat Yisrael* (Redelheim, 1868), pp. 637-640, and in *Mahzor Italiano* 1.66-69. See D. Flusser, *Sefer Josippon* (Jerusalem, 1981), 2.64-66 and n. 185.

51. Published in Baer, *Siddur Avodat Yisrael*, 643-646. On the author see A. Grossman,

The Hasmoneans in Liturgical Poems *(piyyutim)*

With regard to the Hanukkah midrash discussed above, we can say with certainty that it was composed before 953 C.E., the date of Sefer Josippon.[52] The latter text states that Antiochus commanded his ministers: "Indeed you shall blot out the memory of Judah from the face of the earth, and whoever maintains a Jewish name, you shall kill him; but whoever agrees to belong to our nation and to call himself a Greek, him you shall let live."[53] While the Hanukkah midrash states: "Evil Greece came and decreed . . . saying that whoever mentions the name of God will be run through with a sword."[54] It stands to reason that the author of *Josippon* was familiar with this late midrash — or one very similar to it — but altered the threat to "whoever maintains a Jewish name."[55] The medieval *paytanim,* the liturgical poets, were familiar with the original language of the midrash.[56] According to Shelomo Ha-Bavli, a contemporary of Josippon, the Greek states: "He who mentions the most precious name will be run through."[57] Similarly, the benediction following the Shema known as *birkat ha-yotzer* for the second Sabbath of Hanukkah by Rabbi Menahem the son of Rabbi Mekir, reads: "This is the angry king of Shashaq . . . so too a decree passes in a scroll in the name of the Macedonian, to say: 'Hush! We must not mention the name of the Lord.'"[58] The last author who draws from the midrash that predates *Josippon* is Rabbenu Gershom Meor Ha-Golah.[59] In his *piyyut 'Atah mi-qedem 'Elohenu* (you are our God since eternity) he writes: "The foolish Greek and his wicked ministers/sought to drive from your people the memory of your beloved name/he sought to turn astray, trifling child/but he fell broken and died in terrible agony."[60] The author of *Josippon* may have come to know the

---

The Early Sages of Ashkenaz (Hebrew) (Jerusalem, 1981), 361-386, and, on his poetic oeuvre, p. 37, n. 63.

52. On this date see Flusser, *Josippon,* 2.74-84. I published the text of *Josippon* as the first volume of my edition (Jerusalem, 1979), including Josippon's discussion of the composition, chapter 40, lines 42-45. Citations of *Josippon* follow this edition.

53. Flusser, *Josippon,* chapter 16, lines 2-4.

54. Jellenick, *Bet Ha-Midrash,* Room I, p. 134.

55. On the significance of this change, see my comments, *ad loc.*

56. See Flusser, *Josippon,* 114, n. 342.

57. See E. Fleischer (ed.), *The Piyyutim of Shelomo Ha-Bavli* (Hebrew) (Jerusalem, 1973), 244 and the notes therein. The *piyyut* was also published in *Siddur Avodat Yisrael,* 641.

58. The language here echoes Amos 6:10.

59. On Rabbenu Gershom see Flusser, *Josippon,* 4-6.

60. Published by A. M. Haberman, *Rabbenu Gershom Meor Ha-Golah: Poems of Penitence and Hymns* (Jerusalem, 1944), 21.

motif of the prohibition against uttering God's name indirectly, from a *piyyut* for the Hanukkah Sabbath. But whatever his source, he altered its language as part of a clear nationalist *Tendenz*. Rabbenu Gershom's poem reflects not only the Hanukkah midrash, but *Josippon*'s description of the death of Antiochus Epiphanes.[61]

An outstanding example of the various channels by which information regarding the early days of the Hasmonean revolt found its way to medieval Jewry is the story of those who martyred themselves in a cave on the Sabbath.[62] The story is preserved in The Antiochus Scroll,[63] from which it was adapted to one of the Hanukkah midrashim.[64] It also appears in an ancient Hebrew translation of 1 Maccabees,[65] and *Josippon* includes the tale as well.[66] Only *Josippon* and the ancient Hebrew translation of 1 Maccabees include Mattathias' critical response — and concomitant qualification of the cave martyrdom — a view already attested in 2 Maccabees.

The Antiochus Scroll

I will not discuss the Antiochus Scroll at length here, since I have done so elsewhere.[67] The Aramaic scroll enjoyed wide circulation among the Jews of the Middle Ages, and had a significant impact on the literature of the day. The date and circumstances of its composition are elusive. Like the second translation of the Scroll of Esther, it is an Aramaic work marked by its author's lively imagination and dependence on the Greek version of ancient Jewish sources,[68] and so not sui generis. As for its unfettered imagination, in this it is similar to some of the non-Jewish "historical" works written in late antiquity and the early medieval period, both in the west and the east, such as the

61. See *Siddur Avodat Yisrael*, at the bottom of 644, and compare *Josippon*, chapter 18, lines 12-14. It further appears that the conclusion of Rabbi Menahem the son of Rabbi Mekir's Antiochus story is based on Megillat Antiochus §60.

62. See 1 Maccabees 2.29-38; 2 Maccabees 6.11.

63. See Kedari, "The Antiochus Scroll," vv. 37-40.

64. Jellenick, *Bet Ha-Midrash*, Room I, p. 139.

65. This translation was published by Chavelsohn as *"Sarid u-Falit,"* in *Qovetz 'Al-Yad* 7 (1906), 1-14; S. Hartum, *The Apocryphal Books* (Hebrew) (Tel Aviv, 1959), 1.78-88, as an appendix to 2 Maccabees, and see also the introduction to 1 Maccabees, at p. 9. For the passage under discussion see *Qovetz 'Al-Yad*, 7-8, and Hartum, 81.

66. Flusser, *Josippon*, chapter 16, lines 15-21.

67. Flusser, *Josippon*, 150, 160.

68. For a discussion of the epistles incorporated into the additions of the Greek Esther translation, see Flusser, *Josippon*, 149, n. 424.

chronicles of Malalas, a Greek composition from the sixth century. According to the Antiochus Scroll, the wicked king sought to annul the Jewish covenants: the Sabbath, the new month, and circumcision.[69] Antiochus sent his viceroy, Nicanor, to the Jews, and the latter erected an idol in the temple, then slaughtered a pig and had its blood brought into the temple courtyard.[70] John the son of Mattathias assassinated Nicanor and then defeated the Greeks. In response, Antiochus sent Bagras (perhaps a corruption of Bacchides, the Greek general) to persecute the Jews — including the killing of two women who had their sons circumcised,[71] and here appears the narrative of the cave martyrdom mentioned above. The battle against the Greeks was waged by Mattathias's five sons: Judah, the eldest, then Simon, Jonathan, John, and Elazar.[72] Judah fell in battle, as did Elazar, who was crushed by an elephant. The composition further alludes to 1 Maccabees' account of Mattathias's deathbed address,[73] though in the Antiochus Scroll we find only words of encouragement.[74] After their victory, the Jews burn the wicked Bagras, while Antiochus flees in shame. Finally, the author cites the miracle of the oil as the reason for the Hanukkah celebration.[75] Even this brief survey demonstrates how far removed the imaginative narrative of the Antiochus Scroll is from the historical facts, and we have focused here only on the details that the author knew indirectly, probably from Greek sources. I believe that the origins of this work lie in 1 Maccabees.

The Ancient Hebrew Translation of 1 Maccabees

We have already mentioned the ancient Hebrew translation of 1 Maccabees and parts of 2 Maccabees. It is an important document dealing with the Hasmonean period, but unfortunately not all of it is extant. Its first editor referred to it as "a remnant," and the second "part of the Book of Maccabees."[76] It is preserved in MS Heb 325, in the Bibliothèque Nationale in Paris.[77] The

69. Antiochus Scroll, verse 8.

70. Antiochus Scroll, verses 10-12.

71. Antiochus Scroll, verses 33-40.

72. Antiochus Scroll, verse 52.

73. 1 Maccabees 2.49-68.

74. Antiochus Scroll, verses 51-52.

75. Antiochus Scroll, verses 61-64.

76. See Chavelsohn, "Sarid u-Falit," and Hartum, Apocryphal Books.

77. Pages 101b-110b. According to the first editor, 3, "There is a twelve page gap following these pages, which no doubt contained the rest of the Hebrew translation."

manuscript appears to date to the 13th century, while the translation may be from the 10th. It is hard to say if it was done from the Greek original, or from a Latin translation of Maccabees, since all three versions are very similar, no doubt because the Latin translation follows the Greek quite literally. Nonetheless, there are indications that the Hebrew translation was made from the Latin, and this is generally the more plausible hypothesis.[78]

The Hebrew translation is based largely on 1 Maccabees, and incorporates a number of brief passages from 2 Maccabees. The composition is stylistically sophisticated — similar to the style of *Josippon* — and bears witness to the scientific achievement of the translator. The first editor, then, seems justified in suggesting the translation was undertaken in Italy, and the translator "lived among the sages who produced the original *Sefer Josippon*." That there is a connection with the Hebrew translation of 1 Maccabees is evident, though the nature of the connection is not completely clear. It appears the Maccabees translation is earlier than *Josippon* and served as one of the latter's sources. Elsewhere I have even hypothesized that the translator himself composed *Josippon*.[79] In both works Lysias is called "Lyseia" and Judah Maccabee's name is spelled with two *yod*s.[80]

In the Hebrew translation we find that when Mattathias died, "Judah Maccabee arose in his place, and his brothers aided him, anointing him for battle in lieu of his father." What are the origins of this fascinating detail? In part, it was likely historical speculation on the part of the translator. But clearly the Latin translation played a part, for there we find (*ad* 1 Maccabees 3.2-3): *et adiuvabant eum omnes fratres eius et universi qui se coniunxerant patri eius* ("and his brothers aided him and all those who had joined his father"). Apparently, the Hebrew translator read *unxerant* ("anointed") for *coniunxerant* ("joined").[81] And, strikingly, we find the same reading in *Josippon*, who renders Mattathias's farewell words as follows: "Be the military leader of this nation, and its anointed for battle. And [Mattathias] took the [horn] of oil and poured it on his head, anointing him for battle. And all the people cheered and blew their trumpets and said, 'Long live the anointed one' . . . and so there arose under [Mattathias] his son Judah, who is called Maccabee, and he was

78. According to 1 Maccabees 1.13, Antiochus authorized the Hellenized Jews "to observe the ordinances of the Gentiles." The Latin translation states that the king *dedit eis potestatem ut facerent iustitiam gentium*. The Hebrew translator erroneously rendered this "gave them authority to judge the gentiles."

79. Flusser, *Josippon*, 2.132-133.

80. On this form see my comments to *Josippon*, chapter 16, line 56.

81. See my comments to *Josippon*, chapter 16, line 61. Judah is also referred to as "anointed for battle" in chapter 19, line 14.

aided by his brothers and the entire household of his father, and by those faithful to him."[82] A comparison of the different versions reveals that *Josippon* here reworks the ancient Hebrew translation of 1 Maccabees which, again, may have been written by the author of *Josippon* himself.[83]

The ancient Hebrew translation does not mention the miracle of the oil jug, since neither 1 nor 2 Maccabees knows of this story.[84] The miracle of the oil is similarly absent from *Josippon,* primarily because the author did not find it in his Latin sources, this despite the fact that when he describes the Maccabees' temple dedication he suggests — perhaps due to a misunderstanding of his source[85] — that the lighting of the fire was somehow supernatural. *Josippon* writes: "And they built the new altar and placed on it the sacrificial meat and the timber, but fire could not be found. Then they called out to the Lord and fire emerged from the stones of the altar and they placed the timber upon it. And this fire lasted until the third exile."[86] *Josippon's* source was, as noted, 2 Maccabees, which states: "They purified the sanctuary, and made another altar of sacrifice; then, striking fire out of flint,[87] they offered sacrifices." *Josippon* is also dependent on his own account of the sacred fire in the days of Nehemiah.[88] Overall, then, *Josippon* draws an analogy between the Hasmonean dedication and the original dedication of the Second Temple, and he does not incorporate the miracle of the oil.

Josippon and the History of the Hasmonean Dynasty

Josippon was written in Hebrew, but was based on the primary sources available at the time (in Latin translation), including the writings of Josephus and

82. Chapter 16, line 61–chapter 17, line 2.

83. Another example of the literary connection between the ancient Hebrew translation and *Josippon* is the latter's reworking of 2 Maccabees 15.3 — the request by the Jews accompanying Nicanor to respect the Sabbath. In the translation they say: "Give honor to the LORD who commanded that we keep and respect the Sabbath." In *Josippon* they say: "Give honor to the giver of the Sabbath" (chapter 27, line 48).

84. Judah Maccabee's epistle, preserved in the beginning of 2 Maccabees, alludes to the dedication fire in his mention of the story of the search for fire in the days of Nehemiah (2 Macc 1.18-33) and to the heavenly fires in the days of Moses and Solomon.

85. 2 Maccabees 10.2.

86. *Josippon,* chapter 18, lines 31-34.

87. In Latin: *de ignitis lapidibus igne concepto.*

88. "They built the altar according to the law and they set the timber upon the altar and on the timber the meat, but they could not find the sacred fire. Then they prayed to the Lord . . ." (chapter 7, lines 13-15).

1 and 2 Maccabees.[89] As such, the book was a central source of information about the Second Temple period for medieval Judaism.[90] In this sense — and in others — the Hebrew translation of 1 Maccabees and *Josippon* belong to the by no means negligible number of works by which Jewish authors who knew Greek and Latin provided their brethren with information about Jewish and general history; *Josippon* is the largest, most comprehensive, and most respected of the lot.[91] A closer examination of medieval Jewish literature will show a meaningful shift beginning with *Josippon* and its contemporary works. This is relevant to the subject at hand because the return to primary Jewish sources paved the way for a fuller understanding of the Hasmonean period, as *Josippon* became the primary source of information on the period.

As noted, *Josippon* deals extensively with the Hasmonean wars and subsequent dynasty. Though no author stands outside his own period, *Josippon* approaches his sources with rare historical and analytic acuity. One example of *Josippon*'s healthy instincts involves the death of Antiochus Epiphanes — which (following 2 Maccabees) he locates *after* the dedication of the temple.[92] All the same, *Josippon* contains statements that do not hold up under critical scrutiny. Thus, *Josippon* connects Eleazar who died during the Antiochean decrees with Eleazar the Priest who was involved in the translation of the Septuagint, and writes: "This is the Eleazar whom we mentioned above, who went to Egypt during the reign of Ptolemy."[93] In his earlier discussion of the Septuagint (which relies heavily on Josephus) he writes: "Thus the priest sent him [Ptolemy] seventy priests under the charge of Eleazar, the same Eleazar who was tested during the days of Antiochus and martyred himself for the sake of the Lord God."[94]

---

89. *Josippon* is explicit about his sources: "The rest of the tales of Judah, his wars and his mighty deeds, are recorded in the book of Yosef Ben Gurion (= Josephus), and in the Book of the Hasmoneans and the Book of the Roman Kings" (chapter 26, lines 2-4, and see also lines 30-33). The Book of the Roman Kings is Jerome's Chronicle.

90. The halakhic compendium *Qitzur Shulchan Arukh* recommends reading *Josippon* during Hanukkah. Solomon Maimon, the renowned Jewish philosopher (1753-1800), writes in chapter 3 of his autobiography *(Lebensgeschichte)* that *Josippon* was one of the "secular" books he read in his youth (along with *Tzemach David* and *Shevet Yehudah*).

91. The active engagement with the "classical" Jewish past is also to be viewed in light of broader trends within medieval thought. For beginning with the ninth century, we find a renewed interest in ancient sources among non-Jewish scholars as well. See Flusser, *Josippon*, 2.153-154.

92. See my "Jerusalem in Second Temple Thought," and "What Is Hanukkah?" both in the present volume.

93. *Josippon*, chapter 14, lines 1-2, and see 2 Macc 6.18-31.

94. On "testing" as a martyrological term see my comments to chapter 12, line 13, and in volume 2, 113, n. 340.

A detailed discussion of the literary and historiographic nature of *Josippon* — even limited to his discussion of the early Hasmonean history — lies beyond the purview of the present discussion. The germane issues are those aspects of *Josippon*'s worldview which influenced the medieval Jewish understanding of the Maccabees. We saw above that *Josippon* did not discuss the miracle of the oil (since it is absent from the historical sources he used) but recorded the putatively miraculous account in 2 Maccabees. *Josippon* described other supernatural events during the time of Judah Maccabee,[95] but while it appears throughout that he takes pleasure in rendering them in a vivid style, they remained of secondary importance to him. In contrast, national pride was clearly important to *Josippon,* and, in keeping with the spirit of the time, he admired bravery, including on the battlefield. This is his poetic description of the beginning of the revolt: "And all were fortified by the words of Mattathias, and they turned to one another, saying, 'To your tents, Judah. Take rule over your country! Enough of King Antiochus! Brandish your sword with Judah and fear for your life, on nation of Macedon!' And from that day forth, the nation of Macedon parted ways with the Jews."[96] *Josippon* uses the same elevated language to describe Judah: "Blessed is his memory for the Jewish people. Let peace reside on the bed of his righteousness, on the resting place of his holiness, for he spared not his life for the sake of Israel, the nation of the Lord."[97]

Judah Maccabee in Medieval Judaism

In its admiration for Judah and his brothers, *Josippon* is undoubtedly a product of its time, the days of medieval chivalry. The gentile world admired not only those who martyred themselves during the decrees of Antiochus, but Hasmonean bravery enjoyed iconic status in Christian Europe. In this, then, *Josippon* exemplifies the shared values of the Jewish and non-Jewish world.[98]

This is not the place for a comprehensive discussion of the similarities and differences in the Jewish and Christian approach to this period. Much depends on the shared cultural heritage of particular thinkers, as well as their

95. See chapter 13, lines 10-12; chapter 18, lines 18-22; chapter 20, lines 14-18; and the discussion of Heliodorus in chapter 11.

96. *Josippon*, chapter 16, lines 11-14, and see also my suggestion at lines 22-24.

97. *Josippon*, chapter 17, lines 8-10.

98. Another example is the portrait of Judah Maccabee found in MS Rothschild 24, 139a, a reproduction of which may be found in volume one of my *Josippon* edition. The portrait does not refer to *Josippon*, but to a Hanukkah *piyyut* found on the same page.

social and political standing. Martyrology was, of course, very much a living issue for the Jews, but not so for the dominant Christian society. Also, Jews were generally prevented from engaging in acts of military heroism, so their yearning for past deeds of bravery were less realistic than those of their Christian neighbors. Finally, we must bear in mind that the Books of the Maccabees were included in the Catholic canon, while the Jews knew these texts primarily through the mediation of *Josippon*. As a result, Jewish authors (beginning with the Antiochus Scroll) developed imaginary tales of Hasmonean bravery — a trend that continued even after the publication of *Josippon*. This does not mean that from the Talmudic period on the Jews sought to obscure the bravery of the Maccabees or chose to remember them as merely legendary figures. As we saw above, the miracle of the oil played only a minor role among those authors, and it would be fair to say that it became a secondary motif.

7. "Love Your Fellow Man"

To My Son, Yohanan

I

In the last centuries of the Second Temple period, Judaism underwent structural changes which shaped it for centuries to come. In earlier studies, I discussed one post-biblical development, namely the emergence of a new attitude toward the other, and toward humanity in general, what might be called a "Jewish humanism."[1] Needless to say, the formative Judaism of that time contained other views as well, but more needs to be said on ancient Jewish *philanthropia*. The present study is a modest contribution in this direction, though much remains to be done.

Relatively early material on our topic is preserved in a Jewish-Hellenistic composition, namely the Letter of Aristeas.[2] Most scholars date the letter to the second century B.C.E., and it describes the formation of the Greek translation of the Torah, the Septuagint, on the order of Ptolemy II, king of Egypt.[3] According to Aristeas, the translators were sent from Jerusa-

1. See D. Flusser, "A New Sensitivity in Judaism," in *Judaism and the Origins of Christianity,* 469-493; idem, *Jesus,* 81-82.

2. For the Greek text see H. S. Thackery, "The Letter of Aristeas," ed. H. B. Swete, *An Introduction to the Old Testament in Greek* (Cambridge, 1914), 531-606. An English translation, by H. Andres, is found in R. H. Charles (ed.), *The Apocrypha and Pseudepigrapha* (Oxford, 1913), 2.1-31, and see also N. Meisner, *Aristeasbrief* (Gütersloh, 1977), 57-85; M. Hadas, *Aristeas* (New York, 1973).

3. For a discussion of the letter see E. Schürer, *The History of the Jewish People in the Age of Jesus Christ,* 3.677-687; A. Tcherikover, *Encyclopaedia Judaica* (Jerusalem, 1972), volume 3, col-

lem to Egypt under the leadership of Eleazar, the High Priest. The Egyptian king was impressed with the wisdom of the translators, and questioned each and every one. The answers they provided include much of the Jewish wisdom of the day.[4] The "rabbinic" material is readily distinguished from the basic stratum of Jewish-Hellenistic thought: though the author incorporated fragments of these motifs in his work because they fit his general argument, the integration is not smooth. There is almost always some tension between the "rabbinic" statements and the Hellenistic apologetics of the author, though of course it is precisely this tension that allows us to identify the different strata, as rabbinic sources contain clear parallels to the incorporated material. It should be noted that the author selected from the internal Jewish sources precisely those motifs and fragments whose universalist tendency suited his own Jewish-Hellenistic apologetics. Clearly, then, the "rabbinic" material within the Letter of Aristeas represents only one aspect of the internal Jewish thought of the period.[5]

A synopsis, or perhaps a leitmotif, of the Jewish gospel teaching love of humanity is found in §254, where the king asks what he must do to avoid anger. The Jewish interlocutor responds both that anger is harmful and that "God governs the whole universe with his kindness and without any anger, and you, O King, must follow him." In §208 the author explains how the king is to love his fellow man: "it is your duty neither to inflict punishments easily nor to submit men to torments, knowing that the life of mankind is constituted in pain and punishment. If you bear in mind each set of facts, you will be inclined to mercy, even as God is merciful." The conclusion is well known as it occurs in Luke 6:36, though in a slightly different formulation.[6] The same principle occurs in the Mekhilta of Rabbi Ishmael to Exodus 15:2: "Abba Shaul says: Be like Him! Just as He is gracious and merciful, so too you be gracious and merciful."[7]

---

umn 439; G. W. Nickelsburg, "Epistle of Aristeas," in M. Stone (ed.), *Compendia Rerum Iudaicarum ad Novum Testamentum* (Assen, 1989), 2.75-80.

4. Aside from the questions and answers, there is a very interesting section (§142) in which Eleazar explains to the Alexandrian why the Torah includes practical commandments: God uses the laws governing food, drink, contact, hearing and sight to place boundaries around the Jewish people lest they come into corrupting contact with others. The discussion recalls motifs attested in rabbinic thought.

5. It appears that §196 can also be traced back to internal Jewish thought. There we are told that God grants humanity power and wealth. This is a universalist Jewish idea, whose (Greek) formulation is similar to Didache, 1.5.

6. See Flusser, *Jesus*, 83.

7. Mekhilta of Rabbi Ishmael, Shirata 3, Lauterbach 2.25.

Clearly, in these conditions there developed a tendency to believe that God is merciful not only toward the righteous, but toward the sinners as well, so if a man wishes to be like God, he too must be merciful toward *all* people. A similar view is found in §207, in response to the king's question "What does wisdom teach?": "Insofar as you do not wish evils to come upon you, but to partake of every blessing, it would be wisdom if you put this into practice with your subjects, including the wrongdoers, and if you admonished the good and upright also mercifully." Scholars have noted that the passage alludes to the "golden rule."[8] The author is aware that the notion of universal mercy does not fit popular morality, and he addresses this in §227, in explaining who is worthy of generosity: "It is the general opinion that it is a man's duty to be generous toward those who are amicably disposed toward us. My belief is that we must also show liberal charity to our opponents so that in this manner we may convert them to what is proper and fitting to them. You must pray God that these things be brought to pass, for he rules the minds of all."

We have, I believe, accomplished the first goal of the present study, namely to uncover the internal Jewish stratum within the Letter of Aristeas and to sketch its character. Most of this material suggests that already in the second century B.C.E. there was a Jewish ideology of *philanthropia*, toward the righteous and the sinner alike — a universalist mercy of sorts. The demand to behave with supreme mercy was tied with the view of God as merciful and compassionate. The final testament in the Testament of the Twelve Patriarchs, i.e., the Testament of Benjamin (chapters 4–6),[9] enjoins one to behave with compassion toward the wicked as well as the good and not try to distinguish between people, for then you yourself become, as it were, divided. There are other examples of this fascinating approach.[10] Jesus too represents this Jewish view. For it was among the adherents of universal love and compassion that there emerged an ideology of love and (qualified) forgiveness toward those who have caused you personal injury.[11] We will examine this view in the next section.

8. See P. S. Alexander, "Jesus and the Golden Rule," in J. H. Charlesworth and L. L. Johns (eds.), *Hillel and Jesus* (Minneapolis, 1997), 372-373.

9. See Flusser, *Jesus*, 98-99, and chapter five.

10. It is not the goal of the present essay to discuss the various Jewish views of gentiles in antiquity.

11. See also the well-known story of Beruriah's response to Rabbi Meir in b. Berakhot 10a. Rabbi Meir was being harassed by local ruffians and he wished for their death. Beruriah then offered an interpretation of Psalm 104:35: "Let sin be consumed from the earth" emphasizing the reading "sin" as opposed to "sinners," who will, apparently, remain. This legend does not represent historical reality, first because Beruriah appears as Rabbi Meir's wife only in late Babylonian sources, and second because (as we will see below) Rabbi Meir would never wish death upon sinners.

II

The God of Israel was also the creator of the world and thus of all mankind. It stands to reason, then, that the group that emphasized love of all Jews, would be open to an ideology of love toward mankind as such, toward human solidarity as such. The most striking expression of this view is found in m. Sanhedrin 4.5:

> Therefore but a single man was created in the world, to teach that if any man has caused a single soul to perish,[12] Scripture imputes it to him as though he had caused the whole world to perish. And if any man saves a single soul, Scripture imputes it to him as though he had saved the whole world. . . .[13] For man stamps many coins with the one seal and they are all like one another, but the King of kings, the Holy One blessed be He, has stamped every man with the seal of the first man, yet not one of them is like his fellow.

This mishnah clearly expresses the unique nature of this Jewish humanism, which is rooted in the belief that every individual is considered equal to all of creation, for the world was created for his sake.[14] This Jewish view is not to be confused with a positive view toward mankind that nonetheless allows for the harming of individuals or groups even in the name of this very view. The Jewish humanism (which influenced Christian humanism) cannot be transformed into a political ideology without considerable difficulty.

Rabbi Meir is the exemplar of this Jewish view. According to the Tosefta (Sanhedrin 9.7),[15] he states: "What does Scripture instruct with the verse '[his corpse must not remain all night upon the tree; you shall bury him that same day, for anyone hung on a tree] it is God's curse' (Deut 21:23)? It is like two identical twins, one is the king of the entire world, and the other became a bandit. After a while, the bandit was captured and hanged, and all the passersby said, 'It appears the king has been hanged.' Thus Scripture states, 'it is God's curse.'" In the same spirit of humanism he states (m. Sanhedrin 6.5): "When man is sore troubled, what does God's presence *(Shekhinah)* say? My

---

12. Some editions have a secondary addition, "of Israel," and again below. See Hanoch Albeck's comments ad loc., 445.

13. This idea was known to Philo (*De Decalogo,* 37) and to Jesus (Luke 6:9; Mark 3:4); see Flusser, *Jesus,* 63.

14. See also the discussion in *Avot De-Rabbi Natan,* ed. S. Schechter (New York and Jerusalem, 1997), version A, chapter 31, which parallels the mishnah discussed above.

15. Also preserved in *Yalqut Ha-Mekiri,* ed. S. Buber (Jerusalem, 1964), 126.

head is ill at ease, my arm is ill at ease! If God is sore troubled at the blood of the ungodly that is shed, how much more at the blood of the righteous?" In other words, God suffers with the executed criminals, without distinguishing between righteous and wicked. Human beings should adopt this approach, since "man was created by himself. Why? So that the righteous not say, We are the sons of a righteous man, and the wicked not say, We are the sons of a wicked man" (t. Sanhedrin 7.4). This approach is always related to the fact that man was created in God's image. Already Jesus links the call for human acceptance toward righteous and wicked alike with God's fundamental openness toward all mankind (see Matt 5:44-45) — and this teaching did not occur in a vacuum.[16] It appears that Rabbi Meir was influenced on this point by the teachings of his master, Rabbi Aqiva, who taught, "Whoever sheds blood diminishes the divine image, as it is written: 'Whoever sheds the blood of a human, by a human shall that person's blood be shed (for in his own image God made humankind)' (Gen 9:6)" (t. Yebamot 9.4). The entire issue is discussed in greater detail in the Mekhilta of Rabbi Ishmael: "Scripture states that whoever sheds blood it is accounted to him as though he diminished the divine image. To give a parable: A king of flesh and blood entered a province and the people set up portraits of him, made images of him, and struck coins in his honor. Later on they upset his portraits, broke his images, and defaced his coins, thus diminishing the likenesses of the king. So also if one sheds blood it is accounted to him as though he had diminished the divine image. For it is said, 'for in his own image God made humankind' (Gen 9:6)."[17] It appears Rabbi Aqiva understands Genesis 9:6 as though it means "Shedding the blood of man is akin to shedding the blood of God, for in his own image God made humankind."[18]

And if you are going to have compassion on the wicked, mercy — even extreme mercy — must be shown toward those who injure you personally. Thus we find in the Tosefta:[19] "whoever injures another, even if the injurer has not asked for forgiveness from the injured party, still he must pray for divine mercy for him, as it is written, 'Then Abraham prayed to God' (Gen 20:17), and similarly we find in Job, as it is written, 'Now therefore take seven bulls and seven rams, and go to my servant Job, and offer up for yourselves a burnt-offering; and my servant Job shall pray for you' (Job 42:8). And what

16. See Flusser, *Jesus*, 83.

17. Mekhilta of Rabbi Ishmael, Yitro 8, Lauterbach 2.262. See also Bereshit Rabbah, section 32 (page 326 in the Theodor-Albeck edition), and W. Bacher, *Aggadot der Tannaiten*, 1.279, n. 3.

18. This is Shmuel Safrai's correct interpretation.

19. T. Bava Kama 9.29-30. See also j. Bava Kama 6c; Bacher, *Aggadot*, 92, n. 2.

do we find is the response? 'And the Lord restored the fortunes of Job when he had prayed for his friends; and the Lord gave Job twice as much as he had before' (Job 42:10). Rabbi Judah says in the name of Rabban Gamaliel: Scripture states, 'the Lord may turn from his fierce anger and show you compassion, and in his compassion multiply you' (Deut 13:17). Let this be a mnemonic — whenever you show compassion, God is compassionate toward you."[20] The idea that the injured party pray for divine mercy for the injurer is not far from Matthew 5:44: "Pray for those who persecute you."[21]

In summary, the Letter of Aristeas bears witness to the fact that already in the second century B.C.E. there was a Jewish demand to be merciful toward all people, because God too is merciful toward all. This special approach to the other finds its expression in the second century B.C.E. Book of Ben Sira (27.30–28.7),[22] and this attitude of love toward every individual was adopted by Jesus. We could even say that when Jesus states that one must love not only one's friends but also one's enemies (Matt 5:43-44), he was no different than any other Jew; for him too this was an outgrowth of an ideology of *imitatio Dei* (Matt 5:45-48). To be sure, there is a certain tension between this ideology and the fundamental Jewish views of God as a god of justice, who repays the righteousness of the righteous and metes out punishment to the wicked, and of the chosenness of Israel.

---

20. The conclusion follows the Palestinian Talmud. Bacher argues that Rabban Gamaliel's teaching is based on Psalm 2:5-6.

21. See also Luke 6:28; Rom 12:14; 1 Cor 4:12.

22. See Flusser, *Jesus*, 84-85.

8. "But Who Can Detect Their Errors?" (Ps 19:13): On Some Biblical Readings in the Second Temple Period

Habent sua fata verba. The Hebrew words שגיאה (Ps 19:13) and משגה (Gen 43:12), both of which mean "error" today, are biblical *hapax legomena* and are not to be found in rabbinic literature. It would appear that both were dormant for a very long period: שגיאה to medieval times, משגה to modern. But the discovery of the Dead Sea Scrolls demonstrates that משגה awoke from its slumber at least twice, and took on a different sense in each case. In the Scrolls, it is a technical term that designates a religious error.[1] Referring to the temptation of the community's enemies, the Hodayot state: "But they have changed them for an uncircumcised lip and a weird tongue of a people without understanding, and so they will be ruined by their mistake (במשגתם)" (10.18-19). And in the Damascus Document we find: "Jacob's sons strayed because of them and were punished in accordance with their mistakes (משגותם)" (3.4-5). 4Q Florilegium (1.8-9) speaks of "The sons of Belial, those who make them fall, to destroy them on account of their sins when they come with the plan of Belial to make the sons of light fall, and to plan against them wicked plans so that they are trapped by Belial because of their guilty error (במשגה אשמה)."[2] The same sense is also attested in the so-called Apocryphal Psalms of David (3.18), a significant section of which was preserved in the Cairo Genizah.[3] There we are told that in the end of

1. See David Flusser and Shmuel Safrai, "The Apocryphal Psalms of David," in Flusser, *Judaism of the Second Temple Period: Qumran and Apocalypticism*, 258-282.
2. See also the phrase ארור במשגה עור בדרך in the Damascus Document fragment published in B. Wacholder and M. G. Abegg, *A Preliminary Report* (Washington DC, 1991), 23, 37, 51.
3. See Flusser and Safrai, "Apocryphal Psalms," 262, Psalm III.18.

days Israel "will put their trust in the Lord for he has done mighty deeds, no longer going astray after vanity and error (משגה)," i.e., idolatry. The appearance of משגה in a sense so similar to that found in the Qumran texts may strengthen our hypothesis that the Apocryphal Psalms belong to the Qumran library. As noted, משגה then fell into disuse, until it was revived by modern Hebrew authors, though with a slightly altered sense, namely, an error that occurs as a result of miscalculation. Still, the basic sense of the root ש-ג-ה (error) is preserved.

Like משגה, שגיאה is a biblical *hapax legomenon*, but it is not clear that, like its sister term, it preserves the same basic meaning. To phrase it differently, is the semantic sense of this word since medieval times the sense we encounter in Psalm 19:13? To be sure, already the Septuagint understands שגיאות as "errors."[4] But this is not the view of N. H. Tur-Sinai, who writes: "This is the meaning according to the Masoretic vocalization and the later Hebrew usage. But it is odd that the word is written with an *aleph* (and not שגיה, with a *heh*). The context of the passage suggests, moreover, that the psalmist intended to write שגיאות, i.e., "great and wondrous deeds who can comprehend," as in "marvelous things without number" (Job 5:9) and "he does great things we cannot comprehend" (Job 37:5)."[5] Tur-Sinai's hypothesis is buttressed by the word שגיא, which occurs only twice in the Bible, both times in the Book of Job: "Surely God is great (שגיא), and we do not know him; the number of his years is unsearchable" (Job 36:26) and "The Almighty — we cannot find him; he is great (שגיא) in power and justice" (Job 37:23).

Though the late Tur-Sinai could not have known it, his hypothesis is not only reasonable, but there is now definitive evidence that both readings of שגיאות existed during the Second Temple period. The one, reflected in the Septuagint, identifies the word with the root ש-ג-ה, "err," and the other with שגיא. According to the latter, the meaning of the verse is, roughly, "who can comprehend the wondrous deeds of the Lord? Purify me of the desire to know that which is hidden from me!"

This is undoubtedly a textual variant and not a later midrash, for Ben Sira 3.21-22 assumes this reading of Psalm 19:13. Here is the passage in question, following the Hebrew version discovered in the Cairo Genizah:

> Neither seek what is too difficult for you, nor investigate what is
> beyond your power.

---

4. There it is translated παραπτώματα.

5. N. H. Tur-Sinai, *The Dictionary of the Hebrew Language, Ancient and Modern* (Jerusalem, 1952), 6894, n. 1.

> Reflect upon what you have been commanded, for what is hidden is not your concern.

Ben Sira's words played an important role in the literature of the sages, and were understood as an admonition against excessive mystical speculation. But it is clear that Ben Sira only intended to further develop an idea that he thought was already present in Psalm 19:13, following the vocalization that was before him, i.e., the vocalization proposed by Tur-Sinai. But, as the Septuagint demonstrates, the vocalization that identifies שגיאות with "errors" was also current during the Second Temple period. Which of the two readings better clarifies the sense of the verse within the context of the psalm? It seems to me that the traditional reading — "errors" — is to be preferred. Nonetheless, Ben Sira's reading cannot be discarded, as there were objective difficulties that led Tur-Sinai to propose the same vocalization. Indeed, who can comprehend great matters?

Now we turn to another case, though here the Masoretic reading will not be upheld. First, I note that the root כ-ע-ר, which is not found in the Bible but common in rabbinic literature, appears twice in the Hebrew fragments of Ben Sira. Once (13.22) it refers to the improper or unseemly words of the rich man, and once (11.2) it refers to a man who is physically ugly — the meaning of the root in modern Hebrew as well. Further, *Derekh 'Eretz,* one of the so-called minor tractates, admonishes the reader to "stay clear of that which is מכוער (ugly or unseemly) and from what is similar to it" (1.12 and 7.2). And in a Jewish treatise preserved in the Didache we find "My child, flee from all evil and from everything like it" (3.1).[6] Our focus, however, is on the root כ-א-ר (with an א), and particularly its biblical usage, where it appears twice.[7]

We begin with a passage from Pesher Nahum (3.1-4):

> "I will throw filth at you and treat you with contempt, and make you repulsive. Then all who see you will shrink from you" (Nah 3:6-7): Its inter-

6. See the discussion in G. Alon, "The Halakhah in the Didache," *Studies in the History of Israel* (Tel Aviv, 1978), 1.282-284; D. Flusser, "Which is the Straight Way That a Man Should Choose for Himself?" pp. 232-247 in the present volume.

7. On this root see, *inter alia,* L. Ginzberg, "Beiträge zur Lexikographie des Jüdisch-Aramäischen," *MGWJ* 78 (1934), 10-11. On the occurrence in Psalm 22:17 see, e.g., W. Baumgarten and Y. Kutscher, *Hebräisches und aramäisches Lexicon zum AT* (Leiden, 1974), 474; H. J. Kraus, *Psalmen* (Neukirchen, 1966), ad. 2. On the occurrence in Nahum 3:6 see R. Weiss, "A Comparison between the Masoretic and the Qumran Texts of Nahum III,1-11," *Revue de Qumran* 4 (1963), 437; M. P. Horgan, *Pesharim* (Washington DC, 1979), 1.49, 2.164, 2.185-186. Oddly, the 1984 *Biblica Hebraica* does not mention the reading כאורה in Pesher Nahum to Nahum 3:6!

pretation concerns those looking for easy interpretations *(dorshei halakot)*,[8] whose evil deeds will be exposed to all Israel in the final time; many will fathom their sin, they will hate them and loathe them for their reprehensible arrogance.

But where Pesher Nahum reads ושמתיך כאורה ("I will make you repulsive"), the Masoretic Text reads ושמתיך כראי ("and I will make you a spectacle"). This reading was before the translator of the Septuagint,[9] while the Aramaic Targum is identical with Pesher Nahum.[10] Moreover, the Pesher's biblical citation is based on the biblical text the Qumran author had before him,[11] since the interpretation that follows states "many will fathom their sin, they will hate them (וכארום). . . ." Thus, the root כ-א-ר recurs in the Pesher itself.

In light of all this, it appears we ought to reject the Masoretic כראי ("as a spectacle") in favor of כאורה ("repulsive"). True, the Masoretic reading was already extant when Nahum was translated to Greek, but it undoubtedly came about because the word כאורה was foreign to most Hebrew speakers. Nahum 3:6 is, after all, one of only two biblical verses that contain (in their original form) the root כ-א-ר. The other is Psalm 22:17, where a parallel dynamic is in evidence: the corrupt reading won out because כאר is so rare.[12]

The Masoretic reading of Psalm 22:17 is: "For dogs are all around me; a company of evildoers encircles me like a lion (כארי)." True, the reference to the lion (ארי) may be connected to the lion in verses 13 and 21 of the psalm, but nonetheless the syntax is difficult, since the last third of the verse lacks a verb. This difficulty is overcome if we follow other Hebrew witnesses and read "a company of evildoers encircles me, my hands and feet are pierced (כרו)." Today, most scholars prefer the reading כרו, because it is attested in the Septuagint.[13] Despite this weighty argument, there is no doubt in my mind that כארו is the superior reading: "a company of evildoers encircles me, my hands

---

8. This epithet refers to the Pharisees. See my "Pharisees, Sadducees, and Essenes in Pesher Nahum," *Judaism of the Second Temple Period: Qumran and Apocalypticism*, 214-257.

9. LXX: καὶ θήσομαί σε εἰς παράδειγμα. The Vulgate reads: "ponam te in exemplum."

10. The Targum reads: וארמתי עלך קוצין ואנבליניך מכערא לעיני כל חזק.

11. This is not always the case in the Pesher literature. See Bilhah Nitzan, *Megillat Pesher Habakkuk* (Jerusalem, 1986), 46-51.

12. It is odd that the scholars who discussed כאר in Pesher Nahum make no reference to the occurrence of the root in the variants to Psalm 22:17, and vice versa!

13. ὤρυξαν. Onkelos translates "bound" (ἐπέδησαν), while Symmachus renders it "as if seeking to bind" (ὡς ζητοῦντες δῆσαι), and I do not know what motivated these translations. The same division is reflected in the two Latin translations of Jerome. In the translation that follows the Septuagint we find "foverunt manus meas et pedes meos," while in the translation that is based on the Hebrew he follows Onkelos, "vinxerunt manus meas. . . ."

and feet have been shriveled (or: made ugly)." I prefer this reading not only because the corruption of כארו to כארי is easy to explain, but also because of the appearance of the root כ-א-ר in Nahum 3:6.

The above discussion of כ-א-ר in the two biblical verses contains, I believe, a lesson of sorts. It appears that the root כ-א-ר was attested twice in the Bible, but today does not appear even once in any of the widely available versions. This is due to the fact that the root appeared odd and foreign, even though it is widely attested in rabbinic literature in its alternate spelling, כ-ע-ר. The scribes who did not recognize it believed earlier copyists had erred and "corrected" the reading: in Psalm 22:17 they wrote כארי for כארו and in Nahum 3:6 כראי for כאורה. It is fascinating that in both instances the original reading fights for its life, as it were, and refuses to surrender. In the case of Nahum 3:6, the "corrected" version, כראי, is already attested in the Greek translation, but both Pesher Nahum and the Aramaic Targum preserve כאורה, the more original reading. As for Psalm 22:17, the vitality of כארו is more pronounced still, as it survives in a number of manuscript traditions (alongside כרו, which was before the Greek translator of the Psalms).[14] The survival of the root כ-א-ר, despite great difficulties, exemplifies an interesting phenomenon in the study of the biblical text: despite a gradual distancing from the original reading, occasionally exempla do cross all the historical hurdles and survive to the present day — sometimes in far-flung corners.

Our discussion thus far has focused on readings attested in the Second Temple, which may be original even though they are not to be found in the Masoretic text. We now turn to an ancient reading that — despite its likely secondary status — is of great significance for the history of Judaism. The Gospels of Matthew and Luke tell of three temptations Satan placed before Jesus, all of which Jesus successfully met. In one (Matt 4:8-10; Luke 4:5-8), Satan offers Jesus all the kingdoms of the world if he bows down before him, but Jesus replies: "Away with you, Satan! for it is written, 'Bow down[15] to the Lord your God, and you shall serve him alone,'" a reference to Deuteronomy 6:13 and 10:20. Now, neither Deuteronomy verse contains the word "alone," but without it Jesus' response lacks punch: Satan demands that Jesus worship him, but is rebuffed by a verse that demands that man worship *only* God.[16]

---

14. The Masoretic reading, כארי, is attested in the Aramaic Targum.

15. The verb "bow down" has been adopted as a response to Satan's offer. The original reading most likely attributed to Jesus the words of Deuteronomy 6:13, "the Lord your God you shall fear." See also below, n. 18.

16. I have no explanation as to why New Testament interpreters have failed to notice this significant issue.

The word "alone," then, justifies Jesus' refusal to bow before Satan, and thus it cannot be that the gospel has Jesus quoting Scripture and adding of his own accord the most critical word! We must, then, suppose that the relevant verse in Deuteronomy did contain the word "alone," as quoted by Jesus. In what follows we demonstrate that the reading "the Lord your God you shall fear and you shall serve him alone" once existed.

At the outset it must be admitted that the main Septuagint witnesses lack the word "alone." However, there are Greek manuscripts of Deuteronomy — along with numerous citations from early Christian literature — that read "alone" (μόνον). It is unlikely that the word was added due to the influence of the Gospel version,[17] since the rest of the verse shows not such influence.[18] Still, we can only determine the existence of a Hebrew "serve him alone" reading in the two Deuteronomy passages on the basis of Jewish material.

Such sources are found in abundance. Aside from the Greek manuscripts, the most important witness to the "serve him alone" reading is the original conclusion of the Temple benediction.[19] This is a pre-70 benediction, that was said by Israel as a whole, and in the temple both by the priests and the pilgrims,[20] and by the high priest.[21] Today, the benediction concludes המחזיר שכינתו לציון, "Who returns his glory to Zion." But when God's glory still resided in Jerusalem, the conclusion was a shortened version of our Deuteronomy phrase. This, at any rate, is the case with the conclusion of the benedictions spoken by the people and the high priest (we do not have any direct evidence regarding language of the priests in the temple service). The Palestinian Talmud (Yoma 44b) records the high priest's prayer as אותך נירא ונעבוד ("we will fear and worship you"), but that reading has been altered to accommodate the biblical phraseology. In j. Sotah 22b we find the correct reading, שאותך לבדך ביראה נעבוד ("you alone shall we worship with fear").

---

17. This is untrue of MS Alexandrinus, which appears to exhibit the influence of the New Testament, since along with the addition of "alone" both instances of the phrase read "bow down" (rather than "fear"), as in Matthew and Luke.

18. It is likely that the gospels' adjustment of the language to suit Satan's demand occurred in the Greek stage of the shared source of Matthew and Luke, since both read "bow down" and not "fear." See also the apocryphal Epistle of Jeremiah, verse 6. As for the Greek manuscripts that contain the word "alone" but are not otherwise influenced by the language of the gospels, it is likely that the copyists added the word because they were familiar with a Hebrew manuscript with that reading. This is a common occurrence in the Septuagint and well-attested in the scholarly literature.

19. See Elbogen, *Jewish Liturgy*, 51.

20. See m. Tamid 5.1.

21. See j. Sotah 22a.

The same dynamic is evident in two Palestinian Genizah fragments.[22] In one, the conclusion is ברוך אתה ה' שאותך ביראה נעבוד ("blessed are you Lord, whom we will worship in fear"), a reading that is biblical in that it lacks "alone." The second fragment reads ברוך אתה ה' שאותך לבדך ביראה נעבוד ("blessed are you Lord, you alone will we worship in fear") — most likely the correct reading. This hypothesis is buttressed by Yalqut Shimoni to Samuel, §80, where an early Palestinian midrash is cited, Midrash Yelamdenu. The passage deals with the Eighteen Benedictions, and the Temple Benediction is cited thus: "you alone will we worship in fear." This is the original conclusion of the benediction, and is attested in the Jewish prayer book to this day,[23] as it occasionally takes the place of its successor (המחזיר שכינתו לציון, "who returns his Glory to Zion").[24]

Aside from the ancient conclusion of the Temple Benediction, there are two additional witnesses to the Deuteronomy readings in the Gospels and the Greek manuscripts. The first is Pseudo-Philo's *Biblical Antiquities* (23.14), which was composed in Hebrew at the end of the first century C.E., but preserved only in a Latin translation. There we find "Dominus est Deus noster et ipsi soli serviemus" (The Lord is our God and Him alone do we serve). The second is from Josephus's *Jewish Antiquities* (3.91), where the first commandment of the Decalogue is defined as follows: "The first word teaches us that God is one and that He alone must be worshipped."[25] These varied sources point to the high probability that at least one of the Deuteronomy verses reflected the Palestinian reading את ה' אלהיך תירא ואותו לבדו תעבוד ("the Lord your God you shall fear and him alone shall you serve"). Unfortunately, we cannot determine the version in the Qumran literature since neither Deuteronomy 6:13 nor 10:20 is attested in the Scrolls.[26]

Despite the antiquity of the "him alone" version in some of the biblical traditions, this was surely not the original reading, rather a secondary addition.

22. See J. Mann, "Geniza Fragments of the Palestinian Order of Service," *HUCA* 2 (1925), 309-310.

23. See Elbogen, *Jewish Liturgy*, 50-51. Elbogen did not pay attention to the word "alone" in his discussion. See also E. Fleischer, "On the Temple Benediction" (Hebrew), *Sinai* 60 (1957), 269-276.

24. This occurs in the Ashkenazi holiday liturgy outside of Israel, when the priests take their place on the bimah. But according to the prayer book of the Gaon of Vilna, "who returns his Glory to Zion" is used here as well, even though the repeated prayer does include the conclusion ושם נעבדך ביראה ("and there we will worship you in fear").

25. Ὅτι θεός ἐστιν εἷς καὶ τοῦτον δεῖ σέβεσθαι μόνον. Another possible source is the Testament of Joseph 6.5, where Joseph addresses Potiphar's wife, asking "How can you say, 'I do not go near the idols, but only to the Lord?" (κυρίῳ μόνῳ).

26. Frank Cross provided me with this information.

Most probably, this was done under the influence of the Temple Benediction, since movement in the opposite direction — from Scripture to the temple service — is problematic. After all, the liturgical conclusion "you alone will we worship in fear" is not a proper biblical citation but a paraphrase. But while we cannot know the ideological motivation for the insertion of "alone" into the biblical text, we can propose a reasonable hypothesis. To wit, the desire to emphasize the monotheism of the Jewish God: God and God alone is to be worshipped in the Jerusalem temple. A single God for whom, fittingly, there is a single holy city, in it a single sanctuary,[27] with a single altar. No other city or temple or altar can be allowed since God is one and Israel is one.[28] This is most likely the ideological backdrop to the change in the biblical text, i.e., that of the Jerusalem temple, which emphasizes the singularity of God, the city, the worship and the temple, where "you shall serve him alone." This hypothesis also fits the earlier suggestion that the change in the biblical text came about under the influence of the Temple Benediction, and not vice versa.[29] Of course, the main textual tradition of Deuteronomy remained untouched by this change, though the language of Matthew and Luke suggests there were Hebrew manuscripts (and not only Greek) that read "the Lord your God you shall fear, and you shall serve him alone."[30] Since Jesus' response is introduced with "it is written," we conclude that the addition of "alone" to the verse occurred in the first century C.E., at the latest.[31] If, moreover, we are right that the formula was shortened under the influence of the Temple Benediction, the biblical text must have been changed earlier, though the precise time cannot be determined. Finally, we have shown that the "alone" reading, with all of its conceptual weight, was not original to Deuteronomy. The extant witnesses do, however, open before us a window to the glorious days when the temple still stood.

In all the cases discussed in the present study, we find biblical readings attested in the Second Temple period that left no traces in the Masoretic text. The addition of "alone" to the two verses in Deuteronomy was surely attested in the Hebrew readings of the day, as we clearly see, inter alia, from the words of Jesus in Matthew and Luke. But while the addition is very significant for

---

27. Josephus, *Against Apion* 2.193.

28. Josephus, *Jewish Antiquities* 4.200-201.

29. Needless to say, we cannot determine whether Pseudo-Philo's *Biblical Antiquities* and Josephus's *Jewish Antiquities* are influenced by the temple liturgy or by the altered reading of Deuteronomy.

30. It goes without saying that the story of Jesus' temptation was not composed in Greek, but only translated into it. As for the biblical citation attributed to Jesus, the conclusion of the Temple Benediction indicates that the word "alone" was attested among those writing in Hebrew.

31. This is the time of the common source of Matthew and Luke.

the history of Jewish thought during the time of the Second Temple, it is late and not part of the original text of Deuteronomy. The first case discussed, however, does lead us to conclude that the MT should be emended to include the root כ-א-ר in both Nahum 3:6 (כאורה in place of כראי) and Psalm 22:17 (כארו in place of כארי). It is interesting to follow the persistent struggle of כ-א-ר in these verses. It is found in a number of manuscripts to Psalm 22, while כאורה is found in the text of Nahum preserved in the Dead Sea Scrolls and was the *Vorlage* of the Aramaic Targum.

The matter is not so clear regarding Psalm 19:13 ("Keep back your servant also from שגיאות"). Are we to understand the *hapax legomenon* שגיאות as derived from the root ש-ג-ה, or perhaps Ben Sira was correct to understand it as "great and wondrous acts"? I cannot say that the MT is definitively to be preferred. The question, in any case, has far-reaching ramifications, for it raises the question of the authorized vocalization of Scripture.[32] More accurately, we find that in a number of cases there are two normative traditions, two "mothers" that determine the reading of a single verse. A famous example is found in b. Berakhot 64a: "Rabbi Elazar said in the name of Rabbi Hanina: 'Students of the sages increase peace in the world, as it is written, "All your children shall be taught by the Lord, and great shall be the peace of your children [בניך]" (Isa 54:13). Do not read "your children" (בניך) but rather "those who build you up" (בוניך).'" This passage would no doubt be understood as a tendentious midrash aimed at bolstering the status of the sages, were it not for the Qumran Isaiah scroll. There we find, instead of the word בניך, the form בוניכי, with a superlinear *vav*.[33] Thus, at the time the scroll was copied there were two possible readings: בניך along with בוניך! The Isaiah scroll provides a second example at Isaiah 49:17.[34] The MT reads "Your sons (בניך) outdo your destroyers, and those who laid you waste go away from you," while the Isaiah scroll scribe writes "Your builders (בוניך) outdo your destroyers, and those who laid you waste go away from you." I believe this is the original version, and was the reading of the MT version as well, but the *plene* orthography of the Isaiah Scroll preserved the original pronunciation. Finally, consider an obscure verse from Psalms (110:3): "From the womb of the morning, like dew, your youth (יְלְדֻתֶיךָ) will come to you."[35] In some

---

32. See N. Aminach, "אם למקרא and אם למסורת as Normative Phrases" (Hebrew), in the Grintz Memorial Volume, 43-56.

33. See *Biblia Hebraica Stuttgartensia* (Stuttgart, 1984), 761.

34. See my discussion in "The Text of Isa. xlix,17 in the DSS," *Textus* 2 (1962), 140-142, and D. Flusser, "Melchizedek and the Son of Man," *Judaism and the Origins of Christianity* (Jerusalem, 1988), 99-101.

35. See *BHS*, 1197. I discussed this verse in "Melchizedek and the Son of Man," 192.

Hebrew editions one finds ילדתך (without the second *yod*), but the better manuscripts follow the above reading, which was current already in Jerome's time. However, it appears to be a scribal emendation of sorts, for the Greek reflects the reading יְלִדְתִּיךָ, that is, "I birthed you," and this reading was known to Origen from the Jews of his day. The image is taken from the mythology of the ancient near east,[36] and when it became a source of discomfort was changed.

---

36. See the poetic reworking of the image of the god birthing the hero in, e.g., Psalm 2:7: "He said to me, 'You are my son; today I have begotten you.'"

9. The Decalogue and the New Testament

Christianity is famously an offshoot of Judaism, and the Hebrew Bible is (along with the New Testament) canonical for all Christian churches. It goes without saying, that Jesus and his disciples were Jews who were intimately familiar with the Hebrew Bible. The church inherited its esteem of the Decalogue from Judaism and, beginning with the early church fathers, valued it even more highly than did the synagogue. The reason for this change is to be found, paradoxically, in the increasingly tense attitude toward the Torah: the gentile Christians were not obligated to adhere to the biblical commandments. In order to distinguish itself from Judaism, Christianity concluded that its doctrine surpasses the Torah of Israel, and some extremists even claimed that the advent of Christ annulled the Torah altogether. The Catholic Church's position found its outstanding expression in Thomas Aquinas's (13th century) liturgical hymn — which, like all his work, was considered authoritative — which begins with the words *pange lingua*. According to this hymn, when Jesus participated in his last Passover meal, he meticulously observed the Jewish commandments, but when he broke the matzah he gave himself as food to his apostles, saying "this is my body." At that moment, the matzah turned into his flesh and the wine to his blood, and a new sacrament emerged: "the more ancient testimony must make way for the new ritual." Here St. Thomas expresses poetically one of the main motifs in the Church's attitude toward the Hebrew Bible — that its power dissipated with the advent and crucifixion of Jesus; the Jewish ritual commandments not only did not apply to Christians, their observance was outright prohibited on several occasions.

It is not our aim to trace the various permutations of this attitude over the centuries, though one matter should be mentioned: the Church did not hold a positive view of the Decalogue as such. Rather, it was the universal nature of the Ten Commandments that was used by the Church as a counterweight to the Jewish commandments.

Christians view the Ten Commandments as the words of the living God, and their force is not dulled by the explicit mention of Sabbath observance. Church writers overcame this difficulty by offering a spiritual or allegorical interpretation of the Sabbath as cleaving to God. When, from the time of Constantine, Sunday became the day of rest, the fourth commandment was interpreted as referring to the Christian day of rest.[1] In modern times, a number of Christian groups keep the Sabbath in their own way because, inter alia, it is mentioned in the Decalogue and is thus binding for the Church. Nor is it our aim to discuss the status of the Ten Commandments in ancient Judaism, even though such an investigation — aided by New Testament and early Christian scholarship (including Jewish-Christian and Gnostic literature) — would yield fascinating conclusions. The present study is merely a modest step in this direction.[2]

The phrase "the Ten Commandments" does not appear in the New Testament. Moreover, whenever the Decalogue is cited it is only the latter five commandments that are mentioned, namely the commandments governing social norms. There is, however, one interesting exception. A passage (Matt 19:16-22; Mk 10:17-22; Luke 18:18-25) that involves a dialogue between Jesus and a rich man,[3] who approaches Jesus and asks: "Teacher, what good deed must I do to have eternal life?" This, in any case, is how the question is phrased in Matthew 19:16. According to Luke (18:18) and Mark (10:17), however, the man asks: "Good Teacher, what must I do to inherit eternal life?" The addition of the adjective "good" is typical of the Greek style but neither Hebrew nor Aramaic knows forms of address such as "good teacher."[4] Matthew's

1. For a discussion of various texts pertaining to the Sabbath and Sunday from the earliest Christian times to the end of the Patristic era, see Willy Rordorf, *Sabbat und Sonntag in der Alten Kirche* (Zurich, 1972).

2. During the Second Temple period, there existed traditions that reversed the order "Thou shalt not kill," "Thou shalt not commit adultery." These are attested in the Septuagint, the Nash Papyrus, and pseudo-Philo's *Biblical Antiquities* (11.10-11), which survives only in Latin translation but was originally composed in Hebrew. See D. Flusser, "Do Not Commit Adultery, Do Not Murder," *Textus* 4 (1964), 220-224.

3. Note that the rich man is characterized as young only in Matthew 19:20 and 22. According to Luke and Mark, the man says "I have kept all these since my youth" and I believe this to be the better reading.

4. See the halting discussion of V. Taylor, *The Gospel According to St. Mark* (London,

reading, then, is to be preferred: "Teacher, what good deed must I do . . . ?" Luke and then Mark were led astray by their Greek linguistic sensibilities in referring to a "good teacher," even when such a phrase would have been impossible in Jesus' surroundings.

According to Luke (18:19) and Mark (10:18), this odd address determined Jesus' response, as Jesus says to the rich man: "Why do you call me good? No one is good but God alone." But according to Matthew (19:17), Jesus' response to the question "Teacher, what good deed must I do . . . ?" is clear enough: "Why do you ask me about what is good? There is only one good." The "one" in question is grammatically masculine in Matthew, suggesting that the Greek translator of the Hebrew original assumed Jesus to be speaking of God. Now we see that it was not only Luke's linguistic intuitions (and Mark follows him in this regard) that caused them to misunderstand the rich man's question. If Jesus answered the man that there is but one good and that is God, this is tantamount to a rejection of the man's address of Jesus as "Good Teacher"! But it is much more plausible that the Greek translator erred here and that Jesus' statement "there is only one good" refers not to God but to the Torah and its commandments. This becomes clear from the question that follows: "Do you know the commandments?" (Luke 18:20; Mk 10:19). Or, in Matthew's case: "There is only one good. If you wish to enter into life, keep the commandments." The gist of the conversation is clear enough in Hebrew, but the error arose because Hebrew does not distinguish between the masculine and the neuter. As a result, the translator thought Jesus was speaking of God (and used the Greek masculine), though the broader context indicates he is speaking of the Torah.[5] Moreover, the rich man's question echoes the words of Micah: "What does the Lord require of you but to do justice, and to love kindness, and to walk humbly before your God?" (Mic 6:8). Jesus' response, on the reading proposed here, reflects a famous midrash to Proverbs 4:2, "for I give you good precepts: do not forsake

---

1957), 425, and E. Klostermann, *Das Markusevangelium* (Tübingen, 1971), 101. Both scholars try to justify the Greek reading, but do so from the widespread but mistaken belief in Marcan priority and the dependence of Matthew and Luke on Mark. See Kenneth E. Bailey, *Through Peasants' Eyes: More Lucan Parables* (Grand Rapids, 1981), 162. Fragment 11 of the apocryphal Gospel According to the Hebrews cannot be invoked in favor of our argument, since it is dependent on the Greek version of Matthew. W. R. Farmer, *The Synoptic Problem* (London, 1964), 160, comes close to the truth.

5. My friend, Robert Lindsey, who accepts this argument, even goes so far as to suggest that Luke and Mark reflect mistranslations of Jesus' original response, which should read: מה אתה אומר לי טוב. The reader is encouraged to examine the Greek of the relevant verses (Luke 18:19; Mk 10:18).

my teachings."[6] Even the phrase "There is only one good" reminds us of the phrase "Only the Torah is good" in m. Avot 6.3.[7]

We find, then, that Jesus answers the rich man's question as to what he must do to have eternal life as follows: "why do you ask me about what is good? There is only one good. Do you know the commandments?[8] You shall not murder; you shall not commit adultery;[9] you shall not steal; you shall not bear false witness;[10] honor your father and your mother."[11] In short, the rich man seeks eternal life and Jesus directs him to the biblical commandments. The same link, between the Torah and eternal life, finds expression in the ancient blessing recited after the Torah reading in the synagogue: "Blessed are You our God who gave us the Torah of truth, and planted eternal life in our midst."[12] Let us further recall that the phrase תורת חיים ("Torah of life") is already attested in Ben Sira 17.11 (the Hebrew of which is not extant), and in 45.5 (which is) we find: "and gave [Moses] the commandments face to face, the Torah of life and knowledge." If so, the conversation between Jesus and the rich man is of a piece with the Jewish concepts current in that time.

We find, then, that in the passage in question, Jesus mentions the second half of the Decalogue. All three synoptic gospels mention honoring one's father and mother, but this commandment appears at the end of the list and it is likely that it is an interpolation. That is, a later hand added this commandment to Jesus' reply because it too belongs to the social sphere, even though it appears in the first half of the Decalogue.

Paul too regularly cites the second half of the Decalogue. Thus, in Romans 13:8-10 we find: "Owe no one anything, except to love one another;

---

6. See the citations in Strack-Billerbeck 1.803, to which add Midrash Psalms 90a.

7. Thus the rabbinic dictum helps us to reconstruct the original words of Jesus. Matthew reads "There is only one good" and Luke and Mark "No one is good but God alone."

8. This question is attested in Luke and Mark. According to Matthew 19:17-18, Jesus says "If you wish to enter into life, keep the commandments." The rich man then asks "which ones," and Jesus said. . . ." It is clear that Matthew's reading is the result of later expansion.

9. Luke (18:20) cites these prohibitions in the opposite order, following the Septuagint. See above, n. 2.

10. The gospels contain only the first Greek word of the commandment, while in the Sermon on the Mount (Matt 5:33) we find a different word ("You shall not swear falsely"). Moreover, Mark's gospel adds here "you shall not defraud" (Mk 10:19). See the various textual witnesses and Farmer, *The Synoptic Problem*, 160-161.

11. Matthew (19:19) concludes with "you shall love your neighbor as yourself." We will see below that this is a significant addition.

12. On the antiquity of this benediction and its original meaning see D. Flusser, "Sanktus und Gloria," in O. Betz, M. Hengel, and P. Schmidt (eds.), *Abraham unser Vater: Festschrift für Otto Michel* (Leiden, 1963), 141-143.

for the one who loves another has fulfilled the law. The commandments, 'You shall not commit adultery; You shall not murder; You shall not steal; You shall not covet'; and any other commandment, are summed up in this word, 'Love your neighbor as yourself.' Love does no wrong to a neighbor; therefore, love is the fulfilling of the law." Already here we find that loving one's neighbor as one's self was understood as a general instruction, whose applications are enumerated in the second half of the Decalogue, which deals with social justice. Elsewhere, Paul states that the whole Torah is summed up in the commandment to love one's neighbor as one's self (Gal 5:14).

One could argue that Paul's emphasis on the latter half of the Decalogue is part and parcel of his tense relationship with the practical commandments more generally. However, the same pattern is evident in the Epistle of James, which endorses the practical commandments and which some scholars interpret (rightly, I believe) as a polemic response to Paul's critique of the commandments. All the same, the Epistle of James cites only the second half of the Decalogue: "You do well if you really fulfill the royal law according to the scripture, 'You shall love your neighbor as yourself.' But if you show partiality, you commit sin and are convicted by the law as transgressors. For whoever keeps the whole law but fails in one point has become accountable for all of it. For the one who said, 'You shall not commit adultery', also said, 'You shall not murder.' Now if you do not commit adultery but if you murder, you have become a transgressor of the law" (James 2:8-11).[13]

It is worth noting that the Epistle of James also ties the last five commandments of the Decalogue with the commandment to love your neighbor as yourself.[14] This passage also contains another Jewish idea: that whoever transgresses a single commandment is counted as though he transgressed all the commandments.[15] Moreover, the next verse (2:11) reduces the Decalogue to its final five commandments, a statement based on the following midrash: "One might think he is not culpable unless he has transgressed all of them

13. James defines the commandment to love one's neighbor as "the royal law" while Rabbi Aqiva calls it "a great principle in the Torah." As we will see below, Jesus already characterizes it thus. It appears, then, that the Greek phrase is nothing more than a Hellenized version of the Hebrew counterpart, whose origins are most likely in Hellenistic Judaism.

14. In the passage from Romans cited above (13:8-10), the commandment "you shall not covet" is followed by the phrase "*and any other commandment*, are summed up in this word, 'Love your neighbor . . .' etc." In Matthew's version of Jesus' response to the rich man, the second half of the Decalogue is followed by the phrase "you shall love your neighbor" (Matt 19:19).

15. See, e.g., M. Dibelius, *Der Brief des Jakobus* (Göttingen, 1957), 135. See also Yitzhak Beer, "The Historical Foundations of Halakhah" (Hebrew), *Zion* 27 (1962), 127-128. Beer does not cite the Epistle of James. Jewish parallels would include Philo, *Legatio ad Gaium* 115-117, and 4 Maccabees 5.20.

[i.e. all the commandments of the Decalogue]. Scripture teaches, saying, 'You shall not murder. You shall not commit adultery. You shall not steal. You shall not bear false witness. You shall not covet.' One is culpable for each and every one in and of itself. If so, why does Scripture later repeat 'You shall not murder. You shall not commit adultery. You shall not steal. You shall not bear false witness. You shall not covet' (Deut 5:17-21)? This tells that all of them affect each other. If someone transgresses one of them, he will ultimately transgress all of them."[16] This midrash is based on the different formulation of the first and second halves of the Decalogue: in Exodus each is stated as a self-standing prohibition, but in Deuteronomy they appear in a syndetic chain, linked by the conjunction *vav*. Indeed, "all of them affect each other. If someone transgresses one of them, he will ultimately transgress all of them," precisely parallels James 2:10-11.

We have seen, then, that both in the synoptic Gospels and in other books of the New Testament, the second half of the Decalogue is cited and tied with the commandment to love one's neighbor as oneself.[17] The latter commandment, moreover, is represented as the summary or epitome of the last five commandments of the Decalogue: James calls it "the royal law," while Paul states that "one who loves another has fulfilled the Law. The commandments, 'You shall not commit adultery; You shall not murder; You shall not steal; You shall not covet'; and any other commandment, are summed up in

---

16. Mekhilta of Rabbi Shimon bar Yohai to Exodus 20:14 (*Mekhilta de-Rabbi Shimon bar Yohai*, translated by W. David Nelson [Philadelphia, 2006], 252).

17. A fascinating passage from an ancient Jewish-Christian work, preserved in two Pseudo-Clementine texts, ties the second half of the Decalogue with the golden rule. Both the texts are, in fact, reworkings of an earlier composition based on the Jewish-Christian Ebionites. See the Pseudo-Clementine *Homilies* 8.4.3-4, and the *Recognitions*, 8.56.7-8. The former cites the golden rule in its positive form, the latter in its negative form, and it appears the negative is the more original. In the Homilies we read that "as the God-fearing Jews have heard, do you also hear, and be of one mind in many bodies; let each man be minded to do to his neighbor those good things he wishes for himself." And in the *Recognitions* that ". . . almost the whole rule of our actions is summed up in this, that what we are unwilling to suffer we should not do to others. For as you would not be killed, you must beware of killing another; and as you would not have your own marriage violated, you must not defile another's bed; you would not be stolen from, neither must you steal; and every matter of men's actions is comprehended within this rule." The different content of the Jewish-Christian text suggests it is not dependent on the New Testament passages cited (Rom 13:8-10; James 2:8-11; the story of the rich young man as it appears in Matt 19:18-19). This passage represents, then, an independent tradition linking the love of one's neighbor (here replaced with the golden rule) and the last five commandments of the Decalogue. The mention of "the God-fearing Jews" in the context of the golden rule may suggest that not only the rule as such but the entire passage reached the Jewish-Christian author via a Jewish source.

this word, 'Love your neighbor as yourself'" (Rom 13:8-9).[18] All of which suggests the commandment to love one's neighbor is understood both as a summary of the last five commandments of the Decalogue and as a summary of the Torah itself.

The first of these views is attested in several rabbinic dicta. As noted, Rabbi Aqiva glosses the biblical exhortation to "love your neighbor as yourself" (Lev 19:18) with the statement: "This is a great principle in the Torah."[19] Even though "great principle" does not mean a summary of the entire Torah, it stands to reason that this is what Rabbi Aqiva had in mind. Moreover, the famous Talmudic story (b. Shabbat 31a) tells that Hillel the Elder said to the gentile that "what is hateful to you do not do to your friend — this is the entire Torah. All the rest is commentary. Go learn." The Fathers According to Rabbi Nathan attributes this saying — which came to be known as the golden rule — to Aqiva, not Hillel, who then characterizes it as "a general principle of the Torah."[20] If so, Judaism turned the golden rule into a somewhat different formulation of "love your neighbor as yourself," which was also understood as a summary of the Torah. In the New Testament too we find Jesus saying: "For with the judgment you make you will be judged, and the measure you give will be the measure you get" (Matt 7:2). Here, then, we have the golden rule in its positive formulation standing as a general principle of the Torah, in contradistinction from Hillel and Rabbi Aqiva. The positive formulation is also attested in Jubilees — a Hebrew work composed circa 150 B.C.E. — which has Abraham exhorting his children "that they should guard the way of the Lord so that they might do righteousness and each one might love his neighbor, and that it should be thus among all men so that each one might proceed to act justly and rightly toward them upon the earth" (20.2). Though the precise meaning of the Ge'ez is unclear, it is nonetheless evident that the commandment to love one's neighbor is here integrated into a positive formulation of the golden rule. The confusion is the result of the failure of the Ethiopic translator, or perhaps the Greek translator that preceded him, to understand the original Hebrew of Jubilees. The combination of loving one's neighbor with the golden rule is here characterized as "the way of the Lord," although it is not the only one since Abraham then enumerates other commandments. Nonetheless, the testimony of Jubilees is significant in that it expresses the idea that the love of one's neigh-

18. See also Gal 5:14: "For the whole law is summed up in a single commandment, 'You shall love your neighbor as yourself.'" Here there is no mention of the Decalogue.

19. Sifra Qedoshim, parashah 2. See S. Safrai, *Rabbi Aqiva ben Yosef* (Hebrew) (Jerusalem, 1971), 239.

20. Avot de Rabbi Nathan B, chapter 26 (page 53 in the Schechter edition).

bor is one of the primary commandments of the way of the Lord. Since we have also seen — thus far on the basis of New Testament passages — that some considered this dictum to be a summary of the final five commandments of the Decalogue, it appears there were two distinct views concerning love of one's neighbor.[21]

The issue at hand can be clarified if we recognize that in the time of the temple there were those who believed that the entire Torah could be expressed through two principles. The first, "You shall love the Lord your God with all your heart, and with all your soul, and with all your might" (Deut 6:5) encompasses the commandments between man and God, while "love your neighbor as yourself" (Lev 19:18) deals with the commandments that govern human interrelations. Jesus says as much quite clearly: "which commandment[22] in the law is the greatest? . . .[23] 'You shall love the Lord your God with all your heart, and with all your soul, and with all your mind.' This is the greatest and first commandment. And a second is like it: 'You shall love your neighbor as yourself.' On these two commandments hang all the law and the prophets" (Matt 22:34-40).[24] Jesus' juxtaposition of these two principles is apt, since both verses begin with the word ואהבת "you shall love." And if he says that the entire Torah hangs on these two principles, we find the same language in the Torah concerning the biblical pericope *Qedoshim* (which includes the second of Jesus' two principles), "for most of the fundaments (literally: bodies) of the Torah depend on it." And Hillel the Elder says of the golden rule that "this is the entire Torah. All the rest is commentary (פרוש)." That is, that the Torah is summarized in the golden rule and the rest of the commandments are enumerations (פרוט), for "enumeration" is the sense of the Hebrew פרוש during this period.

The earliest witness that cites the two great principles side by side is Jubilees 36, when Isaac adjures his sons to "be loving of your brothers as man loves himself, with each man seeking for his brother what is good for himself" (36.4),

---

21. I note in passing a section from the ancient Hebrew translation of *The Parables of Sandabar* (critical edition by Morris Epstein [Philadelphia, 1967], 296). At the end of the book, the hero offers advice to the king. In one family of manuscripts, the advice is "that which you hate for yourself do not do to your friends, and love your people as you love yourself." This is clearly a translation. In a second family of manuscripts, the golden rule and the love of the neighbor have been corrected: "that which is hateful to you do not do, and love your neighbor as yourself."

22. The Greek translator was unable to find a proper rendering of the Hebrew כלל (general principle) and consistently used the Greek word for commandment. An examination of Roman 13:9 and Galatians 5:14 indicates that Paul overcame this linguistic difficulty.

23. In the gospels the question is posed by others, and this may indeed have been the case.

24. The author of Matthew adds here "and the prophets."

and calls this "a great oath" (36.7).[25] This in and of itself is a fascinating phrase, since Rabbi Haninah the prefect of the priests states that the commandment to love one's neighbor is so important that this is "a statement upon which the entire world depends," and "a great oath."[26] The same phrase, "a great oath," also appears in the name of Rabbi Shimon ben Elazar in the parallel version: "Under a great oath was this statement pronounced, You shall love your neighbor. . . ."[27] And we have already seen that Jubilees itself characterizes love of one's neighbor as an important commandment, part of the way of the Lord.

The same two principles, the love of God and the love of one's fellow man, are juxtaposed in another apocryphal work, the Testament of the Twelve Patriarchs, which records Jacob's dying testament to his sons.[28] In addition, the two principles and the golden rule are presented as the desired way of life in the beginning of the Didache, a reflection of its Jewish source. All these works were composed within the spiritual and ideological environment that gave rise to the Essene sect. Thus far, we have discussed the world of the Jewish sages, who characterize the love of the neighbor (or the golden rule) as the summary of the entire Torah. Might it be, then, that Jesus received the concept of the two principles not from the sages but from the Essenes?[29]

25. See also the statements attributed to Noah in Jubilees 7.20.

26. The Fathers According to Rabbi Nathan B, chapter 26 (page 53 in the Schechter edition). The dictum is textually corrupt and it may be that the correct reading is "a statement upon which the entire Torah depends." This, in any case, is likely the more ancient reading since it fits the dicta cited thus far. It is, however, possible that Rabbi Haninah was the first to change the language of the saying to "a statement upon which the entire world depends"; see Matthew 5:18 and the parallel sayings in rabbinic literature.

27. The Fathers According to Rabbi Nathan A, chapter 16 (page 86 in the Goldin translation).

28. The Testament of Dan 5.3; Testament of Issachar 5.2 and 7.6; Testament of Zebulun 5.1; Testament of Joseph 11.1. For what follows see the discussion in Flusser, "The Two Ways," (Hebrew) in the Hebrew edition of *Judaism and the Origins of Christianity* (Tel Aviv, 1979), 235-252. Aside from the Greek Testament of the Twelve Patriarchs (and the Hebrew and Aramaic fragments discovered at Qumran and in the Cairo Genizah), there is a medieval Hebrew translation of the Testament of Naphtali from either Latin or Greek. This may be ascertained from the very first chapter of the work, where the two great principles are presented in the following language: "I do not command but to fear God, to worship and cleave to him . . . and that you should not do to one another that which one does not want for himself." Instead of loving one's neighbor, we have here the golden rule translated from a foreign language.

29. It should be noted that there does exist a late rabbinic text that echoes Jesus' words concerning the two great principles, namely *Sefer Pitron Torah*, ed. E. E. Urbach (Jerusalem, 1978), 79-80 (and see Urbach's comments ad loc.). This, however, is a late text and may have been indirectly influenced by the New Testament. We will discuss this work, and its relevance to the Ten Commandments, in what follows.

It is most likely a matter of chance that rabbinic literature proper preserved direct and indirect evidence only for the view that there is a single summary of biblical morality, namely, love of one's neighbor. It is certainly possible that the other view — that there were two great principles — is not attested in the extant rabbinic literature because of the great authority of Rabbi Aqiva, who sided with the single summary camp. After all, the sages distinguish between transgressions between man and God and transgressions between man and man (m. Yoma 8.9).[30] Furthermore, it is clear that juxtaposing two verses that begin with the word ואהבת, as Jesus does in Matthew 22:36-40, accords with the midrashic techniques of the sages. And the love of God and love of man are often found in contiguity in rabbinic dicta. In m. Avot we are told that one should "love God and love mankind" (6.1 and 6.6).[31] If we did not already know of the doctrine of two principles, we might have posited one based on the following sayings in the Testaments of the Patriarchs: "Love the Lord and the neighbor" (Test. Issachar 5.2); "The Lord I loved with all my strength, likewise I loved every human being as I love my children" (Test. Issachar 7.6); "keep the Lord's commands, show mercy to your neighbor, have compassion on all" (Test. Zebulun 5.1), and others like them. Perhaps, then, an otherwise innocuous statement such as m. Avot's command to love God and love mankind is an indication that some sages explicitly upheld the view that there are two great principles in the Torah, both of which begin with the word ואהבת. The first commands love of God, the second, love of mankind.

Let us return now to the sayings of Jesus and, through them, to the Ten Commandments.[32] The encounter with the rich young man (Matt 19:18-20) is of interest to us because Jesus there cites only the second half of the Decalogue, but it is only in Matthew that the commandment to love one's neighbor is appended. Not so in the Sermon on the Mount (Matt 5:17-47 and parallels). True, Matthew added material from other sources (including, I believe, the divorce dicta at 31-32), but on the whole this constitutes a single unit that was probably preached by Jesus at a particular time. After the proem, in which he introduces his interpretive method (Matt 5:17-20), Jesus discusses the commandments "you shall not murder," and "you shall not commit adultery,"[33] followed by

30. Josephus (*BJ* 7.260) says that the zealots competed as to who will accrue more transgressions between man and God and between man and man.

31. The phrase "love mankind" is already attributed to Hillel the Elder in m. Avot 1.12.

32. For a detailed discussion of what follows see "The Two Ways," and "The 'Torah' in the Sermon on the Mount," both in the Hebrew edition of *Judaism and the Origins of Christianity* (Tel Aviv, 1979), 235-252, and 226-234, respectively.

33. I omit the discussion of divorce since, as noted, I do not believe it to be an original part of the section.

"You shall not swear falsely, but carry out the vows you have made to the Lord." The opening words allude to Leviticus 19:12, part of the pericope *Qedoshim*, which we have had occasion to mention above. This is no coincidence, as *Qedoshim* is tied to the Ten Commandments, as ancient Jewish thinkers well recognized. As a result, discussions of verses from *Qedoshim* often combine with discussions of the Decalogue (a matter that requires separate analysis). Here too, then, despite the allusion to *Qedoshim*, Jesus' discussion deals with the commandment "you shall not bear false witness."

After the matter of false oaths (Matt 5:33-37), Jesus discusses the verse "an eye for an eye, a tooth for a tooth" (Exod 21:24), and it is not the present study's goal to examine why Matthew places this discussion here. At its end, though, Jesus turns to "love your neighbor as yourself." Again, then, we find the last five commandments of the Decalogue juxtaposed with love of one's neighbor, and it is clear that Jesus is linking the two. True, the list of commandments is not complete, but we already saw that the *Qedoshim* verses may have influenced the understanding of the Decalogue, and that there is, as a rule, some flexibility in the citation of the Decalogue commandments.

The passage as a whole deals with commandments that govern the relations between man and man, concluding with the verse "you shall love your neighbor as yourself." In the introduction, however, Jesus discusses the Torah as a whole and all its commandments. The overall effect, then, is similar to his statement of the golden rule, "you shall love your neighbor as yourself" (Matt 7:12). This is also the view expressed in the New Testament epistles, in the pseudo-Clementine literature, and by Hillel the Elder and Rabbi Aqiva. At the same time, we already saw that Jesus characterizes the entire Torah by two great principles — the love of God and the love of one's fellow man (Matt 22:34-40 and parallels). This view too is attested in other Jewish sources.

Jesus begins the sermon by stating that his interpretations are meant to fulfill the original sense of the Torah, "For truly I tell you, until heaven and earth pass away, not one letter, not one stroke of a letter, will pass from the law until all is accomplished."[34] Even the smallest part of the Torah, then, sustains the world and thus it is dangerous to annul even the slightest commandment. "Therefore, whoever breaks one of the least of these commandments, and teaches others to do the same, will be called least in the kingdom of heaven; but whoever does them and teaches them will be called great in the kingdom of heaven." Jesus demands of his disciples that they be stricter than the scribes, and what follows indicates that he is referring to the realm of moral behavior,

---

34. The original version is preserved not in Matthew 5:18 but in Luke 16:17, though he forgets to mention the *yod*.

these being the commandments Jesus refers to as "least." Throughout the sermon Jesus employs קל וחומר arguments, at least as far as the second half of the Decalogue is concerned. The Bible says only that "you shall not kill," but even "if you say, 'You fool', you will be liable to the hell of fire"; the Bible says "you shall not commit adultery," but "everyone who looks at a woman with lust has already committed adultery with her in his heart"; and if the Torah forbids lying under oath, Jesus believes one should avoid oaths altogether: "Let your word be 'Yes, Yes' or 'No, No'; anything more than this comes from the evil one."[35] One might say that the entire sermon is an expression of Jesus' righteousness, his *hasidut,* perhaps even in the technical sense that it bespeaks a similarity to the moral outlook of the contemporary Hasidim.

There is another Jewish composition that is worth noting, since the similarities between it and the Sermon on the Mount are so great that it may be justified to speak in terms of literary influence. Known as "The Two Ways," it is the Jewish source for the Didache, an early Christian work written in Greek.[36] Already with its initial publication, scholars rightly surmised that the first six chapters of the Didache are a Christian reworking of a Jewish source. And while the Hebrew "The Two Ways" is extant in a (poor) Latin translation, the discovery of the Dead Sea Scrolls advanced our understanding of this text, first and foremost because of its similarity with 1QS. Apparently, "The Two Ways" was composed in the same Jewish circles that produced the Essene Qumran sect.

"The Two Ways" proposes a dualistic understanding of the universe as containing two ways:

> There are two ways in the world, one of life, the other of death, one of light, the other of darkness; upon them two angels are appointed, one of righteousness, the other of iniquity, and between the two ways there is a great difference. (1.1)[37]

The first four chapters deal with the way of life, the fifth sketches the way of death, and the sixth is a conclusion of sorts. Immediately following the passage

35. Jesus, then, was familiar with the midrash to Leviticus 19:36 in the Sifra: "Rabbi Yose in the name of Rabbi Yehudah . . . why does Scripture state 'You shall have an honest *hen* [a measure of volume]' (Lev 19:36)? A 'no' of justice and a 'yes' *(hen)* of justice." Bacher, *Aggadot ha-Tannaim* mentions Jesus' saying. From the Sermon on the Mount and the word "justice" it appears that the midrash does not pertain only to the abstract moral realm, but primarily to legal debates.

36. See my discussion in "The Two Ways."

37. See H. van de Sandt and D. Flusser, *The Didache: Its Jewish Sources and Its Place in Early Judaism and Christianity* (Assen and Minneapolis, 2002), 128.

just quoted, the way of life is defined as follows: "Now the way of life is this: you shall love first the God who created you, then your neighbor as yourself, and do not yourself do to another what you would not want done to you. . . . You shall not murder. You shall not commit adultery. . . . You shall not fornicate. . . . You shall not covet what belongs to your neighbor" (Didache 1.2–2.2). This is a striking passage as it contains the two great principles — love of God and love of one's fellow man. The latter is presented in two ways: as a citation of the biblical verse, and immediately following — the golden rule.[38] The author then characterizes the way of life by saying "Here is the teaching that flows from these words" (Didache 1.3), much as Hillel the Elder added to the golden rule the assertion that "the rest is commentary." Hillel meant that the entire Torah is, in some sense, an enumeration of the golden rule. "The Two Ways" suggests that the explanation of the two great principles (the second of which is expressed in the golden rule) is presented in the composition itself.

The characterization of the way of life is complex and draws on a wide range of sources and traditions. After presenting this part of his teachings, the author of "The Two Ways" could summarize the way of death through a list of the bad traits that are to be avoided. From the passage cited above it is evident that the second half of the Decalogue plays an important role. All five prohibitions are mentioned in chapters 5 and 2, while at 3.6-7 (which will be discussed at length below) we find a prohibition against false vows, which appears in the first half of the Ten Commandments (and appears in the Sermon on the Mount; Matt 5:33).

The second five commandments also play an important role in Didache 3.1-6, an interesting discussion which apparently once constituted an independent unit.[39] However, it is hard to ascertain the unit's original form, since it has been heavily influenced by the list of negative traits in Didache 5.[40] Roughly, then, the original version appears to have gone something like this: "My child, flee from all evil and everything like it. Do not be an angry person, for anger leads to murder; do not be a person given to passion, because passion leads to fornication; do not be a liar, because lying leads to theft; and do not be a grumbler, because this leads to slander" (based on Didache 3.1-6). If my reconstruction is correct, we have here another passage built around the

---

38. Note the similarity to Jubilees 36, which contains the two principles, alongside Abraham's instruction to his sons to keep the way of God, i.e., to love their neighbors and live by the golden rule (20.2).

39. It is followed by a new unit (Didache 3.7-10) which opens with a Greek version of a list of positive traits enumerated in 1QS 4.3-4: "It is a spirit of meekness, of patience, generous compassion, eternal goodness." The Didache even cites the traits in the same order!

40. For a detailed discussion see Flusser, *Judaism and the Origins of Christianity*, 249-252.

last five commandments of the Decalogue — with the exception of bearing false witness.

This is an important text, not only in its relevance to the question of the Decalogue, but because it is based on the same traditions — or even, perhaps, the very same source — that informed the passage from the Sermon on the Mount (Matt 5:17-48). Here are the parallels, side by side:

Didache	Matthew 5:17-28
"My child, flee from all evil and everything like it.	Minor and severe commandments (vv. 17-20)
Do not be an angry person, for anger leads to murder;	"You shall not murder . . . if you are angry with a brother or sister . . . you will be liable to the hell of fire." (vv. 21-22)
do not be a person given to passion, because passion leads to fornication."	"You shall not commit adultery . . . everyone who looks at a woman with lust has already committed adultery with her in his heart." (vv. 27-28)

To the shared interest in the last five commandments of the Decalogue, we can add another common point. In its opening lines, "The Two Ways" invokes the verse "love your neighbor as yourself" to characterize the way of life, the same verse Jesus interprets at the end of the passage (Matt 5:43-48).

The entire discussion in "The Two Ways" 3.1-6 is based on the view that one must avoid evil and anything that approximates evil, since the latter inevitably leads to the former: "My child, flee from all evil and everything like it!" This idea is repeated in the literature of the sages.[41] Thus we find in "Fear of Sin," one of the so-called minor tractates: "Distance yourself from that which causes sin, distance yourself from that which is unseemly and all that is like it; be wary of a slight sin lest it lead you to grave sin, and run to perform a slight commandment since it will lead you to great commandments." This appears to be the source of the rule קלה כחמורה, "the slightest commandment no less than the most grave."[42] Indeed, the latter is a different version of the exhorta-

---

41. See G. Alon, "The Halakhah in the Didache," *Studies in the History of Israel* (Tel Aviv, 1978), 1.297-302.

42. The earliest extant occurrence of the term קלות is found in the opponents of the Pharisees. In the Pesher to Psalm 37:7 (4Q171 1.27) the Essene author claims against the Pharisees that "they have chosen worthless things (קלות)."

tion to "distance yourself." The same elevation of the minor commandments, which serve as moral safeguards, is found in the opening of the Sermon on the Mount. So much so that one could summarize the content of Matthew 5:17-20 as "My child, flee from all evil and everything like it." This opening statement serves as a definition of sorts to the entire discussion in "The Two Ways," which ultimately consists of a moral קל וחומר. Combined with the strikingly similar interpretations of "you shall kill" and "you shall not commit adultery," the shared opening statements provide further evidence for a literary connection between this part of the Sermon on the Mount and "The Two Ways."

In summary: we have addressed two interrelated conceptions. The first is that all the commandments of the Torah are contained in either a single principle or in two principles. Some sources argue for one principle, namely "love your neighbor as yourself" (i.e. the golden rule), others for two principles adding "You shall love the Lord your God with all your heart, and with all your soul, and with all your mind."[43] The second holds that loving one's neighbor is an expression of the second half of the Decalogue. There are sources that discuss the last five commandments without mentioning "love your neighbor," among them Didache 3.1-6, and the story of the rich young man according to Mark and Luke (but Matthew 19:18-19 does mention love of the neighbor). Other sources juxtapose the last five commandments with love of the neighbor, among them the Sermon on the Mount (Matt 5:17-45), Romans 13:8-10, James 2:8-11), and the Pseudo-Clementine sources. The Jewish source of the Didache begins with a statement concerning the two principles (together with the golden rule), but much of the work is devoted to the second half of the Decalogue, which tends to be associated with the commandment to love one's neighbor. This survey suggests that in pre-70 Judaism there was a fairly widespread tendency to tie the second five commandments with "love your neighbor" or the golden rule. This conception is clearly tied to a religious worldview similar to that of Hillel the Elder and Rabbi Aqiva. It stands to reason that according to the anthropocentric views of Hillel and his school, the love of one's neighbor incorporates the other principle, the love of God.

It further appears that the idea that the commandment to love one's neighbor summarizes the latter half of the Decalogue, is tied to the view that the entire Torah is somehow dependent upon the Ten Commandments.[44] It

---

43. As noted, Jubilees seems to advocate both positions; see 20.2 and chapter 36, especially verses 6-7.

44. See E. E. Urbach, *The Sages: Their Concepts and Beliefs,* translated by Israel Abrahams (Cambridge, MA, 1979), 360-366.

seems to me that this view was much more widespread than the extant sources suggest, but weakened over time because of the danger of over-emphasizing the Decalogue at the expense of the practical commandments. That there was at some point such a view seems almost undeniable. After all, we have already established that there were those who posited that the Torah depends on the laws of pericope *Qedoshim,* or on the two principles, or on love of one's neighbor. But one view is missing, and we may assume that there were those who linked the Torah to the first five commandments of the Decalogue with love of God (epitomized in the verse "you shall love the Lord your God with all your heart") and the second five with love of one's fellow man (epitomized in "love your neighbor as yourself"). In any case, there is substantive evidence for the view that the entire Torah hangs on the Decalogue. Let us also recall that "love your neighbor as yourself" was under-stood not only as the epitome of the Torah, but of the latter half of the Decalogue. Interestingly, the view that the Torah depends on love of one's neighbor — the view attributed to Hillel the Elder and Rabbi Aqiva — is most common in the New Testament, and it gave rise to the tendency to link the last five commandments to the verse "love your neighbor as yourself" or to the golden rule.

We turn now to a later, medieval midrash, a passage from *Sefer Pitron Torah,* a collection of midrashim surrounding the pericope *Qedoshim.*[45] The relevant passage reads: "You shall love your neighbor as yourself. This is the Principle of all the prohibitions commanded man, for whenever you love your neighbor as yourself, you shall not commit:[46] you shall not take God's name in vain, you shall not kill or commit adultery or steal or bear false wit-ness or covet, and all such things. For the rabbis say that all the command-ments in the Torah depend on two verses. The one — 'You shall love the Lord your God with all your heart, and with all your soul, and with all your mind,' the other — "Love your neighbor as yourself." For all two hundred and forty eight positive commandments depend on 'you shall love the Lord your God.' For whoever loves God loves himself and will perform them. And all the neg-ative commandments depend on 'Love your neighbor as yourself,' for when-ever you perform 'love your neighbor as yourself,' you will not do all these others, and the same holds for the proselyte and the resident alien, for Scrip-ture states 'The alien who resides with you shall be to you as the citizen

---

45. It was first published, in an annotated edition, by E. E. Urbach (Jerusalem, 1978). The passage in question is found on pages 79-80.

46. The printed edition reads "you shall act," but I am emending following the advice of my friend Menahem Kiester.

among you; [you shall love the alien as yourself]' (Lev 19:34). Thus the sages say: 'what is hated unto you do not do to your companion.'

If we could establish that *Pitron Torah* does not preserve ancient material, or even that it was not indirectly influenced by the Gospels, its significance would be greatly diminished. As it stands, we have here a midrash that revolves around the two principles, a view that, while congruent with rabbinic thought, is not attested in the literature of the sages. Since (as the editor rightly mentions) this view is attested in the teachings of Jesus (Matt 22:34-40 and parallels), might this late midrash have been influenced by Jesus? This is possible but, to my mind, unlikely. For one thing, the medieval midrash ties the second half of the Decalogue to "love your neighbor," a connection absent in the sayings of Jesus but attested elsewhere in the New Testament as well as in the Jewish source of the Didache. If we assume that *Pitron Torah* preserves an ancient midrash not attested in earlier rabbinic sources, this still does not mean the midrash is preserved in its original form. For *Pitron Torah* offers an interesting innovation — that the first principle, the love of God, includes all the positive commandments, while "love your neighbor" the negative. On this reading, love of God is, at its root, an exhortation to action, while loving one's fellow man entails avoiding wrong and unjust behavior. Is this too part of the hypothetical midrashic *Urtext?* I find this difficult to accept. Even so, it could be that the juxtaposition of the positive and negative commandments to the two great principles, respectively, occurred over the course of the Middle Ages, motivated by the fact that the second five commandments are formulated as prohibitions, and all begin with the word לא (a view already attested in Second Temple literature). This view forced our author to place לא תשא, "do not take God's name in vain," in the second half, since it too is a prohibition that begins with the word לא. Even if *Pitron Torah* reworks an earlier midrash, we cannot reconstruct the various stages in the evolution of the midrash. Still, the *Pitron Torah* passage does provide the heretofore missing piece, confirming the conclusions we reached based on other sources. Note further that *Pitron Torah* ends with the golden rule (as phrased by Hillel). But even with the new light *Pitron Torah* sheds on the subject of our study, we are still missing an important link in our chain, as it does not state explicitly that the first half of the Decalogue is summarized in the commandment "love your neighbor."

In our discussion of the Ten Commandments and the New Testament we have touched on ancient Jewish ethical beliefs and literary forms. We have seen that the early sages tried to distill the essence of the Torah, but our study is far from complete, and the same is true of the role of the Decalogue in Judaism. We have taken a preliminary and tentative step toward clarifying this topic, and hope to explore it further in future studies.

APPENDIX

There are two important passages dealing with the two great principles whose authors appear to have learned the matter only indirectly.[47] The first is Philo in *De Specialibus Legibus* 2.63, where he speaks of two outstanding principles, two main heads: "one of duty to God as shown by piety and holiness, one of duty to men as shown by humanity and justice." Philo clearly attests to the two great principles, but it is unclear whether he authored its details, since he apparently heard the interpretation from another and remembered only its theological content. It is interesting that Philo (apparently following the language of the original interpreter) refers to the principles as *kephalaia*. This Greek term is the most appropriate rendering of כלל in this sense, and Paul uses the same Greek root when he says that "love your neighbor as yourself" epitomizes the second half of the Decalogue (Rom 13:9). In Matthew, however, the Hebrew כלל גדול בתורה is rendered "a great commandment in the Torah" (22:36), an obviously wanting translation. Anyone familiar with the simplistic approach of the Greek translators of the gospels will know why כלל could not be translated *kephalaion*: the Greek word was too bombastic!

Another author familiar with the doctrine of the two great principles, though apparently only indirectly, was Lactantius, whose principal work, *Divinae institutiones*, was composed circa 300 c.e. In this work, Lactantius draws on many important sources, but his knowledge of Scripture — both Jewish and Christian — is weak. One of the most lovely passages in this work,

---

47. For a list of studies dealing with the two great principles, see J. Becker, *Die Testamente der Zwölf Patriarchen* (Gütersloh, 1974), 94.

which appears to be based on the works of an earlier Christian author who was steeped in Greek philosophy, uses Stoic arguments for the brotherhood that binds humanity to argue for love of one's neighbor (*Divinae institutiones* 6.10).[48]

In the beginning of Book 6, Chapter 9, Lactantius states that "the first dogma[49] of this law is to know God, to serve him alone, to worship only Him."[50] While in the opening of chapter 10 he asserts: "I have spoken about what is owed to God. Now I will tell what ought to be bestowed upon man, although that which you bestow upon man is bestowed upon God, for man is the image of God."[51]

Lactantius preserves for us here an echo of the two great principles, together with a very interesting argument. Namely, that the commandments that govern the relations between people are, by their very nature, related to God. Behavior towards our neighbors is, ultimately, directed at God since man was created in the image of God. I assume this idea guided the Jews (as well as the early Jewish-Christian) to include the principle of love of God in the second, love of the neighbor, and focus on the second half of the Decalogue. This is explicitly stated by Lactantius. And if Lactantius did not arrive at this conclusion independently, we will have to assume he derived it from Jewish midrashic thought. If Lactantius's source was a Hellenistic-Jew, or a Christian thinker familiar with Jewish-Hellenistic literature, we can readily understand how the view that "love your neighbor" summarizes the entire Torah is attested in the work of Lactantius. In any case, both passages, those of Philo and Lactantius, shed new light on the doctrine of the two principles.[53]

48. Lactantius's source may not even be Christian, rather a Hellenistic Jew, for there is nothing explicitly Christian in the passage. Still, it is most likely that we are dealing with a Christian author who drew on Jewish-Hellenistic sources.

49. *Primum caput*. Lactantius's Greek source undoubtedly had *kephalaion*, which can mean "head," and "chapter," and "summary."

50. Lactantius, *Divine Institutes* 6.9, translated by Sister Mary Francis MacDonald (volume 49 in the series *The Fathers of the Church* [Washington D.C., 1964], 413). The discussion is tied to Jesus' response to the devil (Matt 4:10; Luke 4:8): "Away with you, Satan! for it is written, 'Worship the Lord your God, and serve only him.'" The verses in question are Deuteronomy 10:13 and, particularly, 10:20: "You shall fear the Lord your God; him alone you shall worship; to him you shall hold fast, and by his name you shall swear." In both these passages an important LXX manuscript reads "him alone." See my discussion in "'But Who Can Detect Their Errors?' (Ps 19:13): On Some Biblical Readings in the Second Temple Period," pp. 162-171 in the present volume.

51. Lactantius, *Divine Institutes* 6.10 (page 417 in the MacDonald translation).

52. On the Decalogue in ancient Christian literature see also W. Rordorf, "Beobachtungen zum Gebrauch des Dekalogs in der vorkonstantinischen Kirche," *The New Testament Age: Essays in Honor of Bo Reicke* (Macon, GA, 1984), 431-442.

10. "Who Sanctified Our Beloved from the Womb"

With Shmuel Safrai

In Philo of Byblos' work on Phoenician history we find the following:

> It was a custom of the ancients in great crises of danger for the rulers of a city or nation, in order to avert the common ruin, to give up the most beloved of their children for sacrifice as a ransom to the avenging daemons; and those who were thus given up were sacrificed with mystic rites. Kronos then, whom the Phoenicians call Elus, who was king of the country and subsequently, after his decease, was deified as the star Saturn, had by a nymph of the country named Anobret an only begotten son, whom they on this account called Ιεούδ (יחיד), the only begotten being still so called among the Phoenicians.[1]

S. A. Löwenstamm has already recognized the importance of Philo's statement for understanding the biblical Abraham narratives.[2] The story is evidently a Canaanite etiology meant to explain why boys are circumcised and why some children are sacrificed, preferably only sons. Both customs stem from a single event and serve a common cause. El sacrificed his son as ransom to vengeful Shaddai when the land was in great danger, even dressing his son in royal garb prior to the sacrifice. Since El himself was a king,[3] the clothing drew imminent death away from him to his slaughtered son, and thus he was able to ward calamities off himself and off those bound to him by the cove-

---

1. Preserved in Eusebius, *Praeparatio Evangelica* 1.10.33 (Gifford translation).
2. See S. A. Löwenstamm, *Philo of Byblos* (Hebrew) (Jerusalem, 1971), 326-327.
3. Eusebius, *Praeparatio Evangelica* 1.10.18.

nant of circumcision. It is worth noting that in the Phoenician traditions both these motifs, the circumcision of the household and the sacrifice of the single, beloved son, are tied to El. Genesis ties both to Abraham, though the original apotropaic function of these acts is wholly absent: the sacrifice of Isaac culminates with the salvation of the beloved son, and circumcision is presented as a mark of the covenant with God. There is, however, an allusion to the apotropaic significance of circumcision in the "Bridegroom of Blood" narrative (Exod 4:24-26), where circumcision wards off imminent death.[4] Did the primary role of circumcision, i.e. to mark the covenant with God, obscure this second function of the act?

The ancient apotropaic function of the Paschal sacrifice is explicit, as the blood on the doorposts of the house protects its inhabitants.[5] "For the Lord will pass through to strike down the Egyptians; when he sees the blood on the lintel and on the two doorposts, the Lord will pass over that door and will not allow the destroyer to enter your houses to strike you down" (Exod 12:23 and see also 12:13). The sacrifice was made to protect Israel from the destroyer that descended on Egypt that night. "It is thus no surprise that the paschal laws emphasize that only circumcised men could participate in the sacrifice (Exod 12:48): like circumcision itself, the paschal sacrifice is explicitly apotropaic."[6] The material Löwenstamm cites demonstrates that the sages recognized the apotropaic function of circumcision, and referred to it in their discussions of the paschal blood (whose apotropaic powers are explicitly stated in Exodus). Both midrashic texts and the targums indicate that the sages sensed the common role of the blood in these two rituals, and linked the two in their discussions,[7] and preserved the apotropaic meaning of circumcision that was largely suppressed in the Abraham cycle. For example, the Targum to Song of Songs 3:8 glosses "each with his sword at his thigh because of alarms by night" as follows: "and each one of them has the mark of circumcision on their flesh just as it was marked on the flesh of Abraham, their father, and they are strengthened by it like a man bearing a sword on

---

4. See S. A. Löwenstamm's discussion in *Biblica* 50 (1969), 429-430.

5. On the original apotropaic function of the paschal sacrifice see S. A. Löwenstamm, *The Evolution of the Exodus Tradition*, translated by B. J. Schwartz (Jerusalem, 1992), 80-94.

6. Löwenstamm, *Exodus Traditions*, 87-88.

7. Perhaps the word אות, "a sign," which occurs in the context of circumcision (Gen 9:12: "This is the sign of the covenant that I make between me and you") and of the paschal sacrifice (Exod 12:13: "The blood shall be a sign for you on the houses where you live") once had an apotropaic meaning. M. D. Cassuto, in his *Commentary on the Book of Genesis (From Adam to Noah)*, ties the protective mark (אות) of the Passover with Genesis 4:15 (the mark of Cain) and Joshua 2:12.

his thigh, and on account of it they do not fear the spirits and the demons that roam at night."

Judaism underwent two deep transformations during the Second Temple period. There emerged a theoretical, theological understanding of the Torah, and the mythical aspect of Judaism grew much stronger. But even in the mythical realm the theoretical impetus was evident, as the mythical forces came to be understood as concrete manifestations of good and evil. The demonic forces of destruction became part of an evil kingdom which encompasses *Gehenom* (hell). Thus, Jubilees (49.2-7) states that God sent the soldiers of the demonic Mastema to slay the firstborn of Egypt.[8] The Qumran scrolls identify Mastema with Belial, about whom the War Scroll says: "You have made Belial for the pit, angel of enmity; in darkness is his domain, his counsel is to bring about wickedness and guilt. All the spirits of his lot are angels of destruction, they walking the laws of darkness" (1QM 13.10-12).

It appears that the Damascus Document passage that refers to Mastema (16.4-6) refers to the apotropaic power of circumcision: "And on the day on which one has imposed upon himself to return to the law of Moses, the angel Mastema will turn aside from following him, should he keep his words. This is why Abraham circumcised himself on the day of his knowledge." Though the sentence about Abraham appears to be textually corrupt, it is nonetheless clear the author links entrance into the covenant of the Qumran community with entrance into the covenant of circumcision. The notion that the wicked are under the dominion of Belial, while those who live a righteous life are protected from him, is also attested in the Testament of the Twelve Patriarchs, where Naphtali says to his sons: "If you achieve the good, my children, men and angels will bless you; and God will be glorified through you among the gentiles. The devil will flee from you; wild animals will be afraid of you; and the angels will stand by you. . . . The one who does not do the good, men and angels will curse. . . . Every wild animal will dominate him and the Lord will hate him."[9] The similarity to the Damascus Document's statement — that he who joins the community "the angel Mastema will turn aside from following him" — suggests that the apotropaic understanding of circumcision is at work here. All this accords with the apotropaic view of circumcision found in rabbinic sources, as discussed above.

8. See Löwenstamm, *Evolution of the Exodus Tradition,* 91.

9. Test. Naphtali 8.4-6, and see also Test. Issachar 7.7; Test. Dan 5.1; the Epistle of James 4:7-8; The Shepherd of Hermas 45.2-5, 47.6-7, 48.2, 49. The affinity between the Testament of Naphtali and Mark 1:13 was noted by G. G. Montefiore, *Synoptic Gospels* (1927), 1.9. I hope to discuss the relevant Christian sources elsewhere.

The passage from the Damascus Document cited above sheds light on another area as well, namely the Jewish source of baptism. Both Josephus and the Scrolls indicate that when someone joined the Qumran community they were required to immerse themselves in water.[10] Baptism, then, was part of the entrance into the Qumran community, a moment that some considered the instant that Mastema gets behind the new member (and thus analogous to circumcision). In Christianity too, the baptized individual is freed from the dominion of Satan and his destructive angels. Though the Christian baptism contains other elements as well (many of which can be traced to Essene roots), the CD passage suggests that the idea that one is freed of Satan's dominion by baptism was influenced by the Qumran community and is ultimately related to the apotropaic power of circumcision, the paradigmatic entrance into a covenant. I hope to discuss this in greater detail elsewhere.

We now come to the most significant testimony to the apotropaic power of circumcision, which dates back to the time of the sages, namely, the blessing said when the infant is circumcised:[11] "Who sanctified our beloved from the womb, and placed his statute with the family, and sealed his descendents with the sign of the holy covenant, and the reward for this, living God, is that we redeem the beloved of our family from the pit."[12]

The poetic and stylized language of the benediction suggests it may be

---

10. Josephus, *BJ* 2.138; 1QS 5.7-14, and see J. Licht, *Megillat ha-Serachim* (Jerusalem, 1965), 128-129. And see my article, "John the Baptist and the Dead Sea Sect," in the Hebrew edition of *Judaism and the Origins of Christianity*, 81-112; J. Ysebaert, *Greek Baptismal Terminology: Its Origins and Early Development* (Nijmegen, 1962).

11. That is, "that the reward for fulfilling the commandment of circumcision is our lot in protecting the newborn from harm." There are some who emend to "let it be our lot," while others have erroneously thought that "our lot" is a reference to God. As a result they had to add an extraneous verb, i.e., "a living God commanded us this lot." The Geonim debated whether the verb was צוה or ציוה, on which see N. Wieder, "An Emendation to a Corrupt Responsum by Rav Hai Gaon" (Hebrew), *Sinai* 54 (1964), 285-289. Though we have cited the best reconstruction of the benediction, this is probably not the original version. The phrase "and the reward for this" is awkward, and the original may have been: "Who sanctified our beloved from the womb and placed his statute with the family, and sealed his descendents with the sign of the holy covenant in order to redeem the beloved of our family from the pit." On the phrase חלק טוב see S. Lieberman, *Greek in Jewish Palestine* (New York, 1942), 72-74.

12. Tosefta Berakhot 6.13; p. Berakhot 9, 14a; b. Shabbat 137b; and also in the prayer books. On the benediction and its various versions see S. Lieberman, *Tosephta Ki-Pheshuta: Zera'im* (New York, 1976), 1.114-115; the comments in *Siddur Rav Saadia Gaon* (Jerusalem, 1963), 99; *Sefer Halakhot Gedolot*, ed. Azriel Hildsheimer (Jerusalem, 1972), 1.215; and especially Wieder, "An Emendation." The version cited here is based primarily on MS Vatican of the Palestinian Talmud (which Wieder does not mention), with minor adjustments in light of the Tosefta, and correction of scribal errors (חי אל instead of אל חי and the addition of ולכן).

early and we will see below that it was probably current in the time of Paul. Moreover, it appears this was once the only benediction said during the *brit*, perhaps by the *mohel* himself, who marks the infant with "the holy covenant" and thus helps "redeem the beloved of our family from the pit." The benediction itself contains a pun: God blesses "our beloved from the womb, and placed his statute with the family" while the infant is referred to as "the beloved of our family." This last phrase is based on Jeremiah 12:7 ("I have given the beloved of my heart into the hands of her enemies"). The circumcision terminology is taken, with one exception, from Scripture: "statute" (חוק) is from Psalm 105:8-10, where God is said to be "mindful of his covenant (ברית) for ever," a covenant "which he confirmed to Jacob as a statute," and the three patriarchs are mentioned as well. The word covenant (ברית) appears in the context of circumcision in Genesis 17:10-11 (and in verse 14), where it is referred to as a sign (אות): "You shall circumcise the flesh of your foreskins, and it shall be a sign of the covenant between me and you." The benediction states that God "sealed" (חתם) the descendents of Abraham with the sacred covenant. The association of this term with circumcision — attested in the Jewish grace after meals ("for your covenant that you have sealed in our flesh") — is very ancient. It is found in the Aramaic Levi Document's account of the Shechem narrative,[13] a copy of which was found at Qumran and dates to roughly 100 B.C.E., which means the composition dates to the second century B.C.E.[14] The term appears in the Targum to Song of Songs 3:8, which was cited above, in Romans 4:11 (see below) and the Epistle of Barnabas 4.6. Baptism is referred to as a seal in Christian sources as early as the Shepherd of Hermes (roughly 100 C.E.).[15]

The benediction states that circumcision saves the infant from the pit (שחת), a clear indication of the apotropaic understanding of the ritual. Indeed, there were sages who believed that circumcision saves the infant from the fires of hell: "Beloved is circumcision, for God swore to Abraham that

13. ....גזורו עורלת בשרכון והתחמיון כ[ואתן] ותהון חתימין כואתן במילת. This is the reading reflected in R. H. Charles, *The Greek Versions of the Testaments of the Twelve Patriarchs* (Oxford, 1908), 245.

14. See D. Flusser, "Qumran and Jewish Apotropaic Prayers," *IEJ* 16 (1966), 195.

15. On circumcision as a seal see Ysebaert, *Greek Baptismal Terminology*, 250-253 (who omits important witnesses), and on baptism as a seal see 281-426. See also Billerbeck, 4, 1.32-33, and W. Bauer, *Griechisch-deutsches Wörterbuch* (Berlin, 1958), 1577. On *signaculum* as a term for baptism see A. Blaise, *Dictionnaire Latin-Français des auteurs chrétiens* (Paris, 1954), 758-759. See also the beautiful parable about circumcision as Abraham's seal in Exodus Rabbah 19.5. On circumcision as a seal see in particular S. Lieberman, "Some Aspects of Life in Early Rabbinic Literature," *H. N. Wolfson Jubilee Volume* (Jerusalem, 1965), 525-527.

whoever is circumcised will not descend into the fires of hell."[16] Indeed, שחת is one of seven words for hell (b. Eruvin 19a). But the blessing "we redeem the beloved of our family from the pit" probably does not refer to a future time in hell. Rather, it appears to be a descendent of the notion that circumcision wards off evil spirits. As we saw above, the Damascus Document preserves the belief that once a child is circumcised "the angel Mastema will turn aside from following him" (16.4-6). And if the benediction states that circumcision serves to keep the child "from the pit," the term probably means the same as the destroyer in the Exodus narrative (Exod 12:23, and also verse 13), and the destroying angel of 2 Samuel (24:16). According to b. Berakhot 16b, Rabbi prayed the following prayer: "May it be your will . . . to save us . . . from a wicked neighbor and a destroying adversary (שטן)." The phrase "destroying adversary" is absent in a number of manuscripts,[17] but there is no question regarding its antiquity since it is found in the Qumran Hodayot: "you threaten every destroying and murderous adversary" (1QH 22.6 and see also "destroying adversary" in 1QH 24. 3). We have already seen that the War Scroll states "You made Belial for the pit, angel of enmity . . ." (1QM 13.10-12). The basic sense of "pit" in the Hodayot is more figurative, as it refers to the place of evil, but the forces of evil burst forth from there: "And she who is pregnant with a serpent is with a racking pang; and the breakers of the pit result in all deeds of terror." It is this sense that gives rise to the author's reference to "the arrows of the pit" (1QM 3.16) and the moment "when all the traps of the pit open" (1QM 3.26) and "all the arrows of the pit fly without return and are shot without hope" (1QM 3.27). It appears, then, that the "pit" of the circumcision benediction is a poetic reference to the region of the harmful spirits, the same spirits mentioned in the Targum to Song of Songs 3:8.

Our hypothesis, that circumcision saves the infant from the dominion of Satan, is confirmed by the opening of the benediction. Some have identified "the beloved" with each of the patriarchs, but in truth it is Abraham and "beloved" (ידיד) is his regular title.[18] The blessing "Who sanctified our beloved from the womb . . ." can be understood in light of a midrash cited by Rabbenu Tam, a 12th century Talmud commentator:[19] "As for the phrase it-

---

16. Tanhuma, Pericope Lekh Lekha, 20. See also Bereshit Rabbah 48.18 (page 483 in the Theodor-Albeck edition), and Yalqut Shimoni 18, §82, and parallels.

17. See *Dikdukei Soferim* ad loc. The phrase is also absent in *Ginzei Talmud Bavli* (Jerusalem, 1976), 9. It is attested in the Venice and Soncino editions, and in the prayer books.

18. See L. Ginzberg, *The Legends of the Jews* (Philadelphia, 1947), 5.207-208, n. 4.

19. Preserved in the Tosafot to b. Menahot 53b, *s.v.: ben yadid.* See also Tosafot to b. Shabbat 137b, *s.v.: yedid mi-beten.* Some of the early commentators cite this midrash as appearing in the Pesiqta, but it is not found in the Pesiqta as we know it and its source is unknown.

self, it is best understood in light of Rabbenu Tam's statement: "As for the benediction of the circumcision 'who sanctified our beloved from the womb' Rabbenu Tam says this refers to Abraham, whom God sanctified from the womb, as we find in Scripture, 'for I have known him' (Gen 18:19), and in Jeremiah (1:5), 'Before I formed you in the womb I knew you.'" The midrash connects God's soliloquy before the overturning of Sodom and Gomorrah: "The Lord said, 'Shall I hide from Abraham. . . .[20] No, for I have known him, that he may charge his children and his household after him to keep the way of the Lord by doing righteousness and justice. . . .'" It is clear that "I have known him" refers to foreknowledge and the same foreknowledge is midrashically linked to Jeremiah 1:5: "Before I formed you in the womb I knew you, and before you were born I consecrated you; I appointed you a prophet to the nations." God, then, sanctified Abraham from the womb and knew him from then.

Why did this idea come about? The midrash is probably trying to explain how Abraham could be righteous when he was still uncircumcised, that is, free from the dominion of evil before his circumcision, before God "sealed his descendents with the sign of the holy covenant." The broader issue that both the midrash and the benediction grapple with involves the righteousness of the patriarchs prior to Sinai. Here the issue is limited to a single commandment, since Abraham was instructed to circumcise himself before Sinai, but after his righteousness was established. The answer is that Abraham was sanctified from the womb so he, unlike his offspring, did not require circumcision to be saved from the pit. What of the biblical figures who came before Abraham? The Fathers According to Rabbi Nathan lists men born circumcised[21] and among those who precede Abraham we find: Adam, Seth, Noah, Shem, and Melchizedeq. Among those born after Abraham we find, *inter alia,* Moses, Balaam, and Jeremiah: "Jeremiah too was born circumcised, as it is written, 'Before I formed you in the womb I knew you, and before you were born I consecrated you' (Jer 1:5)." The very verse that showed Abraham was righteous before his circumcision, now demonstrates that Jeremiah was born circumcised!

All of the above indicates that the righteous who were born before Abraham were born circumcised with no mark on their foreskin. Abraham, of course, could not have been born circumcised since the Bible states explicitly that he circumcised himself. Still, he was saved from the pit from birth be-

20. The Septuagint adds "my servant" (cf. Gen 26:24); Targum Yerushalmi and Neophiti add רחמי, "my beloved."

21. Avot According to Rabbi Nathan A, chapter 2 (pages 12-13 in the Schechter edition).

cause God "sanctified our beloved from the womb." Now we can understand the religious significance of the circumcision benediction. Abraham's righteousness before his circumcision cannot be impugned since God "sealed his descendents with the sign of the holy covenant." But his descendents, including the infant receiving the blessing, require the seal of the covenant to be saved from the pit. At its root, then, the benediction expresses the apotropaic understanding of circumcision.[22]

On this interpretation, there is a dialectic tension between the two halves of the benediction. Abraham's descendents are saved by circumcision, but he himself — throughout his ninety-nine years of uncircumcised life — was completely righteous because God sanctified him from the womb. This conception elicited from Paul the following "Sabbatian" midrash: "We say, 'Faith was reckoned to Abraham as righteousness' (Gen 15:6). How then was it reckoned to him? Was it before or after he had been circumcised? It was not after, but before he was circumcised. He received the sign of circumcision as a seal of the righteousness that he had by faith while he was still uncircumcised" (Rom 4:9-12). It may be that Paul developed this idea based solely on the circumcision benediction, or he may have known the midrashic passages that undergird the benediction. In any case, Paul seems to use the language of the benediction: the biblical word אות (sign) and חותם (seal), which is not attested in the Bible. Paul speaks of "the sign of circumcision . . . a seal of righteousness" while the benediction describes God "sealing" Abraham's descendents "with the sign of the holy covenant." Paul, then, provides the same issue that animates the circumcision benediction with a profound and unexpected interpretation. Since Abraham was righteous prior to circumcision, man does not attain righteousness through circumcision but through faith. There is another Jewish source that Paul utilizes for his own ends. According to the Mekhilta to Exodus 22:20 (page 311 in the Horovitz-Rabin edition), Abraham was not circumcised until the age of ninety-nine "so as not to shut the door to future proselytes."[23] Abraham's act teaches that one can convert even at an old age. Paul concludes that Abraham is the father of all the uncircumcised believers.

---

22. The same understanding is reflected in a midrash attributed to "the school of Rabbi Eliezer" in Midrash Ha-Gadol to Genesis 17:1 (page 269 in the Margaliot edition). Circumcision saves from destruction, and Abraham was worthy of circumcision because he walked in perfection and with an honest heart.

23. Mekhilta of Rabbi Ishmael, Neziqin 18 (Lauterbach 3.140).

11. "He Planted It as Eternal Life in Our Midst"

The Tosefta attributes the following to Rabbi Elazar ben Azariah:

> "The sayings of the wise are like goads, and like nails firmly planted" (Ecc 12:11). Just as the goad directs the cow to bring life in the world [or: into the world], so too the words of Torah are nothing other than eternal life (אף דברי תורה אינן אלא חיין לעולם). As it is written, "It is a tree of life etc." (Prov 3:18). But just as the goad is shaken to and fro, might it be that the words of Torah are thus too? Scripture teaches, saying "like nails firmly planted." Just as the plant increases and multiplies, so too the words of Torah increase and multiply.[1]

I noted some time ago that the background to Rabbi Elazar ben Azariah's reading is the benediction following the Torah reading.[2] In that article I suggested that the blessing is found, in its present version, in the *qedusha de-sidra*, where we find:[3]

> Blessed are You our God who created us for His glory, and separated us from those who *err* and gave us the Torah of truth, and planted it as eternal life[4] in our midst.

1. Tosefta Sotah 7.11, following Lieberman's edition, pages 194-195.
2. See my "Sanktus und Gloria," *Abraham unser Vater: Festschrift für Otto Michel* (Leiden, 1963), 129-152.
3. On the *qedusha de-sidra* see my "Judaism in the Second Temple Period," pp. 27-29 in the present volume.
4. For this reading see below.

There may be an analogy between "separated us from those who err" and "who gave us the Torah of truth" here, and the two parts of the blessing preceding the reading of the Torah: "Who chose us from among all the nations and gave us his Torah." The first part of the latter benediction is attested at a surprisingly early time and is found among the daily prayers of the Dead Sea community:[5] "When the sun ascends to illuminate the earth, they shall bless . . . and say 'Blessed be the God of Israel who has chosen us from among all the nations'" (4Q503 frags. 21-25. 8-9), while the Torah reading begins "Blessed . . . who has chosen us from among all the nations."[6]

Despite the importance of comparative analysis for the history of Jewish liturgy, the parallel in question sheds little light on the theological content of the blessing. A preliminary step in this direction is the identification of "those who err," from whom God has separated the community and whose Torah is evidently not the Torah of truth. Indeed, it appears the blessing is aimed first and foremost at distinguishing the community whose blessing this is from another, who cleaves to a false or erroneous Torah. It is no coincidence that the blessing is located after the reading of the Torah. The very same ideas are evident in the blessing recited after the haftarah: "Blessed are you . . . who chose good prophets and showed favor toward their pronouncements, spoken in truth; blessed . . . who chose the Torah and Moses his servant and Israel his people and the prophets of truth and righteousness."[7] It appears that this blessing, which is recited before the reading from the prophetic writings, seeks to set itself apart from false prophecies and visions, that is, from apocryphal texts containing prophecies and apocalypses, many of which were composed by the Essenes.

It is, of course, common for religious groups to claim that they possess the entire truth and other groups are in error. Thus, Pesher Nahum speaks of the Pharisee sages as "those who misdirect Ephraim, who with their fraudulent teaching and lying tongue and perfidious lip misdirect many" (4QpNah

5. See 4Q503. The Palestinian liturgy knows another version of this blessing: "Blessed are you O Lord, King of the Universe, who gives the Torah from the heavens, eternal life from on high. Blessed are you Lord, who gives the Torah." This version is preserved in Tractate Soferim 40a (*Minor Tractates* 1.273) and in a Genizah fragment. The language of this version was likely patterned on the benediction that follows the reading of the Torah.

6. The Palestinian liturgy preserves a different benediction before the reading of the Torah: "Blessed . . . king of the universe, who gives the Torah from the heavens and eternal life from above. Blessed are you Lord, who gives the Torah," a reading preserved in Tractate Soferim. It appears this version was composed on the basis of the benediction following the Torah reading.

7. A parallel phrase occurs in the first paragraph of the benediction that follows, and see my discussion in "The 'Book of the Mysteries' and the High Holy Days Liturgy," *Judaism of the Second Temple Period: Qumran and Apocalypticism,* 119-139.

2.8). Only the teachings of the Qumran community are true: "And you shall act according to the law which they explain to you and according to the word which they say to you from the book of the Law. They shall explain it to you accurately" (11QT 56.3-5), and so the member of the community is commanded "not to veer from his reliable precepts in order to go either to the right or to the left" (1QS 1.15).[8] And so too in the benediction under discussion, where the true Torah is polemically contrasted to the Torah of those who err and which is to be avoided.[9] In my earlier article, I proposed that the erring community in question is the Sadducees, and while I still stand by that hypothesis, I am no longer sure that my earlier interpretation of the phrase "Torah of truth" is correct. There I argued that the phrase is based on the opening of Malachi 2:6: "True instruction (תורה) was in his mouth," which was interpreted as a reference to the Oral Torah, which — along with the belief in the resurrection of the dead and eternal life (חיי עולם) — the Sadducees rejected. But while this midrash may have influenced the benediction, the phrase "Torah of truth" cannot refer only to the Oral Torah. First, the blessing is recited immediately after the reading of the (written) Torah. Second, the correct reading (on which see below) states that it is the Torah of truth itself (and *not* "eternal life"). The Torah in question, then, must refer to both the Oral and Written Torah, which is precisely the way Rabbi Elazar ben Azariah, in the passage cited above, understood the benediction. The derashah begins with Ecclesiastes 12:11, which speaks of "the sayings of the wise," which are identified with "words of Torah" which are nothing other than eternal life or, on the alternate reading, bring life into the world. If so, the benediction conceives of the Written and the Oral Torah as a single entity, and represents the two core beliefs of the Pharisees: The Torah (encompassing both its Oral and Written aspects) and the belief in eternal life, i.e., in the resurrection of the dead. Those who err, then, must be the Sadducees, a conclusion supported by the paragraph "return our judges as before," found within the benediction "Instruct us" (הבינני), which reads: "And regarding those who err in your way, may they judge according to your knowledge." These who walk in error and refuse to be judged by the Oral Law can only be the Sadducees.[10] We find, then, that the blessing following the Torah reading seeks to distance the sages from the Sadducee understanding of the Torah, while the blessing that precedes the Haftarah distances itself from the apocalyptic texts produced in Essene circles.

---

8. See Y. Yadin, *The Temple Scroll* (Jerusalem, 1983), 2.251.

9. Members of the Essene sect are also enjoined "to convert from all evil and to keep themselves steadfast in all he commanded in compliance with his will" (1QS 5.1 and see also line 10), but the separation there is much more radical than we find among the Pharisees.

10. See D. Flusser, "Jerusalem in Second Temple Literature," pp. 44-75 in the present volume.

Setting aside the internecine religious conflicts and returning to Rabbi Elazar ben Azariah's saying, we find that he interprets "firmly planted" of Ecclesiastes with the Torah increasing and multiplying. This suggests the Torah is planted within us, though the blessing, at least in its current form, states that God planted *eternal life* in our midst (חיי עולם נטע בתוכנו). But this difficulty is only apparent, since the original version reads: ". . . who gave us the Torah of truth and planted it as eternal life in our midst" (חיי עולם נטעה בתוכנו). The language is dense and highly stylized, which is typical of ancient benedictions.[11] It is no wonder, then, that later generations, who did not understand the syntax of the blessing, omitted the *heh* of נטעה, resulting in the present version. Rabbi Ya'akov ben Asher (1270-1340) defends the present version, but clearly knows the earlier: "Torah of truth refers to the written Torah, and 'he planted eternal life in our midst' is the Oral Torah, as it is written 'The sayings of the wise are like goads, and like nails firmly planted' (Ecc 12:11). This refutes those who recite 'who gave us the Torah of truth and planted it as eternal life in our midst'" (*Tur*, Orah Hayyim, §139). Rabbi Yosef Karo also refers to this reading in the Bet Yosef, his commentary on the *Tur*: ". . . this is not the correct reading and also there are those who say 'who gave us the Torah of truth and planted it as eternal life in our midst.'" These passages suggest that the earlier version was fairly current in medieval times.

Having established that "who gave us the Torah of truth and planted it as eternal life in our midst" is the original language of the blessing, we now turn to its meaning. According to this reading, God planted the Torah of truth in the midst of the Jewish people so that it will be for them life eternal. Or, in the formulation of a contemporary sage: "'Who gave us the Torah of truth and planted it in our midst for all eternity' means that the ultimate purpose of the Torah is to provide life eternal."[12] Grammatically, then, "life eternal" is a second object.[13]

---

11. The blessings for circumcision and for matrimony provide additional examples of such language. The former: "Who blessed our beloved from the womb, and placed his statute with the family, and sealed his descendents with the sign of the holy covenant . . . [to] redeem the beloved of our family from the pit"; the latter: "Blessed art thou O Lord our God, king of the Universe, who has created man in his image, in the image of the likeness of his form, and has prepared unto him out of himself a building forever." Both date to Second Temple times. Paul alludes to the former (Rom 4:9-12), while the latter has a fascinating parallel in 1QM 10.14. See D. Flusser and S. Safrai, "Who Sanctified Our Beloved from the Womb," pp. 191-198 in the present volume, and "In the Image of the Likeness of His Form," in *Judaism of the Second Temple Period: Qumran and Apocalypticism*, 50-60.

12. Rabbi Yosef Qafih, from his introduction to Maimonides' *Book of Adoration* (*Maimonides' Mishneh Torah* [Hebrew] [Jerusalem, 1985], 249).

13. See Gesenius and Kautzsch, *Hebräische Grammatik* (Halle, 1929), 117h; cf. Jeremiah 2:21 ("I planted you as a choice vine").

The question that now arises is whether the image of the Torah being planted in the hearts of Israel like a tree is, in fact, attested. The Torah is likened to a tree in many places, among them Rabbi Elazar ben Azariah's *derashah*, an image that draws on Proverbs 3:18 (interpreted as a reference to the Torah). In Ben Sira too we find the Torah likened to a tree, in the verse "I have struck root among a glorious people" (24:12). None of these, of course, indicate that God planted the Torah within Israel, but what we do find is a number of parallels that suggest the Torah is found within each and every Jew. Josephus twice states that the laws of the Torah are "graven on their hearts."[14] An even closer parallel is found in the "Apostolic Constitutions," a Christian work that dates to roughly 380[15] — an important text for Jewish scholarship because its sixth and seventh sections contain Jewish liturgical material.[16] In one (Christian) prayer we find the explicit statement: "You, Lord of Hosts, God of all, created the world and all that is in it . . . and planted the Torah *(nomos)* in our souls."[17] This may certainly be an indirect witness to a common Jewish dictum. A more important witness is the introductory statement to the grace that is common in various communities: "The merciful one will plant his Torah and his love in our hearts."[18] Though the present formulation of the grace after meals is relatively late, this phrase reflects a stage that precedes the Torah benediction, since it contains no signs of the anti-Sadducee polemic:[19] the Torah was not yet referred to as "Torah of truth" and the phrase "life eternal" was not yet introduced. All the same, the phrase from the grace after meals may serve as proof that in the original Torah benediction it was the Torah, not life eternal, that was planted "in our midst." The discovery of the Dead Sea Scrolls has dispelled any doubts regarding the antiquity of the prayer, since in *Sefer ha-Me'orot* the speaker asks of God "to implant your law in our heart."[20]

14. Josephus, *AJ* 4.210, and *CA* 2.178.

15. *Constitutiones Apostolorum, Sources chrétiennes* (Paris, 1987).

16. See D. A. Fiensy, *Prayers Alleged to Be Jewish* (Chicago, 1985), which includes the Greek text along with an annotated translation and analysis.

17. νόμον καταφυτείσας ἐν ταῖς ψυχαῖς ἡμῶν (*Const. ap.* 7.26.3). See also the phrase ὁ ἔμφυτος λόγος in James 1:21, and the parallels to this verse cited in M. Dibelius, *Der Brief des Jakobus* (Göttingen, 1957), 107-108, and F. Mussner, *Der Jakubusbrief* (Freiburg, 1975), 101-103. See also Pseudo-Phocylides, verse 128; the apocryphal Epistle of Barnabas 9.9; and W. Bauer, *A Greek-English Lexicon of the New Testament* (Chicago, 1979), 258 (ἔμφυτος).

18. This phrase, with very minor variations, appears in the liturgies of the Jewish communities in Spain, Italy, Rumania, Kochin, and Persia. See S. Tal (ed.), *The Liturgy of the Jews of Persia* (Hebrew), 215, line 10, and the notes therein.

19. Another example of a relatively late liturgical framework preserving very early material is the *Qedusha de-Sidra*, on which see Flusser, "Sanktus und Gloria," 235-239.

20. See 4Q504 2.13 (*DJD*, vol. 7 [Oxford, 1982], 139). M. Baillet, who edited the volume,

The original benediction recited after the reading of the Torah, then, was "who gave us the Torah of truth and planted it as eternal life in our midst," a reading attested in the *Qedusha de-Sidra*. Another witness is Rabbi Yosef Qafih's comment in his *Shivat Zion* prayer book.[21] Alongside the standard reading he notes: "This is the version in the *Tur*, but according to Maimonides and the ancient liturgical manuscripts, 'he planted it as eternal life' and Saadia Gaon's version is 'he planted eternal life.'" And in his comments to the *Qedusha de-Sidra* he states: "The reading according to Rabbi Yitzhak ben Sheshet (the Riba'sh) 'he planted it,'"[22] — and this is indeed the reading of the ancient Yemenite prayer book *Tichlal ha-Qadmonim*, both in the blessing following the Torah reading and in the *Qedusha de-Sidra*.[23] This, then, was the Yemenite reading, before it was corrupted by external influence. We cannot ascertain whether this was the Yemenite tradition prior to Maimonides' ruling, but it is clear, in any case, that Maimonides did indeed know the version "he planted it as eternal life."[24] This reading is also attested in the early editions of the Aleppo Codex — in both the blessing after the Torah reading and the *Qedusha de-Sidra*. Finally it should be recalled that many medieval authorities changed the reading to "for all eternity," yet another indication that the original reading was "as eternal life in our midst."

After recovering the forgotten original version of the blessing following the Torah reading, we find a strong connection between eternal life and the Torah of truth: the Torah of truth, when it is planted in our midst, is itself eternal life. In this the blessing is in full accord with the traditional Jewish view that the Torah brings eternal life to the world. As the Torah itself fa-

---

dates the scroll to roughly 150 B.C.E. The same scroll states, following Isaiah 43:7, "for your glory (כבוד) you have created us" (4Q504 3.4), just like the opening of our blessing.

21. *Tichlal Shivat Zion*, edited by Rabbi Yosef Qafih (Jerusalem, 1952), 1.181.

22. *Tichlal Shivat Zion*, 1.47.

23. *Sefer Tichlal ha-Qadmonim*, photocopied edition of Y. Chavara (Jerusalem, 1964). The blessing following the Torah reading: 19a; *Qedusha de-Sidra*: 10a.

24. Maimonides cites the blessing after the reading of the Torah in his Codex of Jewish Law *(Mishneh Torah)*, in the *Book of Adoration*, as part of the discussion of the laws of prayer and the priestly blessings (chapter 12, halakhah 5; MS. Vatican [photocopy edition; Jerusalem, 1966], 61). The *Qedusha de-Sidra* is found in *Seder ha-Tefilah*, which is appended to the *Book of Adoration*, MS Vatican, page 89 (See D. Goldschmidt, *Studies in Prayer and Piyyut* (Hebrew) [Jerusalem, 1979], 187-216). The now standard version affected both passages, but in different ways. In MS Vatican the blessing after the Torah reads "he planted eternal life," but the Qafih edition "he planted it as eternal life," while in the *Qedusha de-Sidra* the opposite is the case — MS Vatican preserves the "he planted it as eternal life" reading, and Qafih reads "he planted eternal life." The critical apparatus provided by Goldschmidt (p. 205) indicates that MS Oxford, the manuscript Goldschmidt himself chose as the base manuscript for his edition, reads "he planted it as eternal life" even though in the book we find "he planted eternal life"!

mously states, "You shall keep my statutes and my ordinances; by doing so one shall live: I am the Lord" (Lev 18:5). This concept gave rise to the phrase "Torah of life," which appears twice in Ben Sira (17.11 and 45.5), the second of which is extant in Hebrew, and refers to God giving Moses the Torah: "he gave him the commandments by his hand, the Torah of life and knowledge."[25]

The idea gained a new direction when the belief in life after death gained currency within the Jewish world, as the Torah is identified with eternal life now understood as life in the world to come. "Then someone came to [Jesus] and said, 'Teacher, what good deed must I do to have eternal life?' And he said to him, 'Why do you ask me about what is good? There is only one who is good. If you wish to enter into life, keep the commandments" (Matt 19:16-17). Keeping the commandments guarantees one life eternal. A similar view is expressed in one of the psalms of Solomon, an apocryphal work composed in the first century B.C.E.:

Psalm 14.1-5

Faithful is the Lord to them that love Him in
truth;
To them that walk in the righteousness of
His commandments,
The pious of the Lord shall live by it for ever;
Their planting is rooted for ever;
For the portion and the inheritance of God is
Israel.

To them that endure His chastening,
In the law which He commanded us
that we might live.
The Paradise of the Lord, the trees
of life, are His pious ones.
They shall not be plucked up all
the days of heaven.

Though the imagery in this psalm is somewhat different than in the blessing, the overall similarity between the texts is marked, as both hold that the Torah is a Torah of Life and God's pious will live in it forever. The planting imagery of Psalm 14, however, is taken from Isaiah (60:21 and 61:3), where the pious are like "an eternal plantation" that will never be uprooted all the days of heaven.[26] In the blessing, the Torah is like a tree of life planted in the heart of Israel, providing eternal life to the Jewish people: "Just as the plant increases and multiplies, so too the words of Torah increase and multiply."

25. See P. W. Skehan and A. A. DiLella, *The Wisdom of Ben Sira* (New York, 1987), 282. For a list of sources that refer to the Torah as the source of life see H. L. Strack and P. Billerbeck, *Kommentar zum Neuen Testament* (Munich, 1926), 3.129-132. It appears John's polemic against the *Ioudaoi* (5:37-40) preserves an indirect reference to this prayer: "you do not have his word abiding in you. . . . You search the scriptures because you think that in them you have eternal life. . . ." John's words fit the original language of the blessing.

26. See J. Licht, "Eternal Deceit and the Nation of God's Redemption," in *Studies in the Dead Sea Scrolls* (Hebrew), (Jerusalem, 1961), 49-75, and especially 49-51.

The present study is based on an earlier article,[27] which was further developed following the chance discovery of the original version of the blessing recited after the reading of the Torah, and its various attestations (Yemenite sources, Aleppo Codex, Maimonides). The original version represents a clearer and more coherent theological message, which can be dated on stylistic and conceptual grounds to the Second Temple period.[28] Like other ancient benedictions, it expresses cardinal theological ideas — the true essence of Torah and its blessed effect on the human soul — in highly condensed language.

---

27. Flusser, "Sanktus und Gloria."
28. Moreover, Rabbi Elazar ben Azariah already knew the blessing, as discussed above.

12. Hillel the Elder and His Trust in God

With Shmuel Safrai

Did Hillel's faith in God preserve his house? A "Hasidic" tale in this vein is preserved in the Babylonian Talmud (tractate Berakhot 60a), and for whatever reason no one has challenged its authenticity. The Bavli recounts:

> Our rabbis teach: It happened that Hillel the Elder was walking along the way and he heard a cry within the town. He said, "I am certain that is not coming from my house." Scripture refers to him in saying, "He is not afraid of evil tidings; his heart is firm, secure in the Lord" (Ps 112:7).

Here is the Palestinian Talmud's account:[1]

> Hillel the Elder would say: "He is not afraid of evil tidings; his heart is firm, secure in the Lord" (Ps 112:7). Because he is secure in the Lord he is not afraid of evil tidings.[2]

The Palestinian Talmud cites Hillel's dictum immediately after m. Berakhot 9.3:[3] "One who was walking along the way and heard cries from within the town and said, 'Let it be God's will that no harm come to my household' —

---

1. Tractate Berakhot 14b, following MS Vatican 133. On this manuscript see M. Krupp, "Manuscripts of the Palestinian Talmud," in S. Safrai (ed.), *The Literature of the Sages* (Assen, 1987), 1.320.

2. Hillel's gloss is preserved only in this manuscript.

3. We cite according to MS Kaufmann, which is further attested in MS Cambridge 470.1 (II), MS Parma 138, MS Paris 671, MS Oxford 366, two Genizah fragments (T-S E2.8 and E1.5), the *editio princeps* (Napoli, 1492), and elsewhere.

that is a an empty prayer." The Palestinian Talmud juxtaposes Hillel's dictum to this mishnah because (despite the Mishnah's statement) it expresses Hillel's faith in God even though it would never occur to him that this faith actually protects his family from harm. But this is precisely how the Babylonian Talmud understood the dictum.[4] Indeed, the dictum is transformed into an exemplary tale involving Hillel, a tale that becomes the cornerstone of the discussion of m. Berakhot 9.3. Hillel himself was traveling and heard the cries but was unafraid because he believed his faith in God protected his family from harm. But this is not the thrust of Hillel's original statement in p. Berakhot, which contains no "Hasidic" connotations à la Honi the Circle-Drawer or Hanina ben Dosa. Hillel means only that whoever has faith in God is unafraid of evil tidings because his faith frees him from fear of future events, whether or not the evil tidings turn out to be true. We believe this to be one of the most sublime statements of Hillel's special understanding of the human condition.[5] But an examination of Hillel's dicta reveals a tendency to dull their sting. A case in point is the dictum under discussion: the Babylonian Talmud took a very personal theological statement and, through a literary reworking, transformed it into a "Hasidic" tale, casting Hillel as a Zaddik who possesses unusual attributes.

One final comment. In the Babylonian Talmud, the tale of Hillel is followed by the following statement of Rabbah's:

> One may interpret this verse (i.e. Psalm 112:7) in any manner — from beginning to end or from end to beginning. From beginning to end — why "is he not afraid of evil tidings"? Because "his heart is firm, secure in the Lord." From end to beginning it is interpreted as follows: "his heart is firm, secure in the Lord," and, as a result, "he is not afraid of evil tidings."

The second of these is the midrash the Palestinian Talmud attributes to Hillel the Elder. Was Rabbah familiar with Hillel's interpretation?[6] It appears so. B. Berakhot 63a also cites Rabbah's view that verses can be interpreted from end to beginning, here in the context of Psalm 119:126, "It is time for the Lord to act; for your Law has been broken." At the end of that passage we find

---

4. The Babylonian version is also attested in Yalqut Shimoni to Psalms, §871, and in Yalqut ha-Mekiri to Psalm 112:7, pages 188-189 in the Buber edition (Berditschev, 1900; reprint Jerusalem, 1964).

5. See D. Flusser, *Judaism and the Origins of Christianity* (Jerusalem, 1988), 509-525.

6. On the Palestinian sources of Rabbah's Bible interpretation see W. Bacher, *Die Agada der babylonischen Amoräer* (Frankfurt, 1913), 121-127, and see Bacher's comments on the present derashah at 132, n. 85. See also t. Berakhot 6.24; Tzvi Dor, "The Palestinian Sources in Rabbah's Bet Midrash" (Hebrew), *Sinai* 52 (1963), 128-144; *Sinai* 53 (1963), 31-49; *Sinai* 55 (1964), 306-316.

Hillel's famous discussion of that verse.[7] In both places that Rabbah interprets a verse from the end, there is a connection to Hillel, who interprets the same verses from end to beginning. Taken together, these considerations indicate that Rabbah did indeed know Hillel's original dicta.[8]

Our discussion of Hillel's dictum likely has wider ramifications for the transmission of Hillel's sayings in various Jewish sources. It appears Hillel's unique and strikingly personal voice was progressively weakened, a view corroborated by other of his sayings. Here, for example, Hillel's saying became a "Hasidic" tale, even though this entailed turning the Mishnah's statement concerning empty prayer into a mark of Hillel's greatness.

---

7. On which see Flusser, *Judaism and the Origins of Christianity*, 510; W. Bacher, *Die Agada der Tannaiten* (Strasbourg, 1903), 1.6, n. 2. At the end of m. Berakhot we find the same interpretation of Psalm 119:126 attributed to Rabbi Nathan.

8. Though we cannot determine whether he knew Hillel's interpretation of Psalm 112:7 in its original, Palestinian form, or from the reworked Babylonian story.

13. Hillel's Moderation

Many see a moderate outlook as based on a willingness to concede, to compromise, an opposition to extremism, a softness. Its opponents characterize moderation as defeatism and weakness that may lead to catastrophe, and suggest that it is antithetical to core Jewish values. Let me state at the outset that what follows is not meant to endorse a personal view, since I too admit to certain problems regarding the personal accountability of the moderate. My goal is to examine Hillel the Elder as a moderate, and in so doing perhaps uncover a proper response to some of the above difficulties.

Hillel's philosophy is most clearly seen in the philosophical character of his dicta. Intellectually, Hillel is a unique figure among the sages. His humanism and his moral and halakhic approach are fairly well-known. What has not been examined is his personal philosophy, which is the source of his moderate worldview — not vice versa.

There are many similarities between Hillel's personality and that of Socrates. Both represent a turning point in the intellectual history of their respective nations. The difference lies in the fact that Socrates founded the humanist strain in Greek philosophy by addressing every individual as an end unto himself. Hillel, who shared this view, no doubt contributed greatly to Jewish thought and legal practice, but unlike Socrates he did not need to begin *ab ovo*. The view that values man as man was already developed within the Jewish world and can be traced back to the men of the great assembly. Hillel, then, was able to continue along an established path, while developing it in a unique and highly influential manner.

Our sources recount a story about Hillel that offers a striking parallel to

Socrates' attempt to draw his fellow Athenians to philosophy. Of Hillel we are told:[1]

> He would stand at the gates of Jerusalem while people went off to work. He asked them: "How much will you earn today?" One says a *denarius*, another says two *denarii*. He said to them: "These wages, what do you do with them?" They responded: "We use them to sustain ourselves in this world." He said to them: "Why don't you come and take possession of the Torah, thus taking possession of this world and of the next?" Thus did Hillel do all his days, until he would gather them under the wings of heaven.

It is possible that this story is not authentic, rather transferred from Socrates to Hillel the Elder. It may also be that Hillel consciously adopted the approach of the Athenian philosopher who sought to further learning among his people, or that the story is historically accurate but that there is no connection between it and Socrates' actions. For we know from other sources that Hillel went to great lengths to propagate the study of Torah. On the importance of Torah study he said: "he that does not increase — decreases, and he that does not study is worthy of death" (m. Avot 1.13), i.e., whoever does not study Torah should be put to death. Here we find the outstanding daring and power of Hillel the individual. Though he was humble he was by no means spineless and his moderation in no way entails defeatism.

As for Hillel's patience, we have the testimony of b. Shabbat 30b: "There were two men who entered into a wager, saying: Whoever perturbs Hillel wins four hundred *zuz*." This happened on the Sabbath eve, the time least suited for annoying questions. One of the men then approached Hillel and asked him three questions in succession. Why are the heads of Babylonians oval? Why are the eyes of Tadmorites bleary? Why are the legs of Africans wide? Not only was Hillel unperturbed, he answered each of the questions correctly. Many readers fail to appreciate just how striking this anecdote is. Hillel not only demonstrated his extreme patience, but also his expertise in areas not usually associated with an "orthodox rabbi" and "foolish Babylonian"!

After all, from an internal Jewish perspective these really are nothing more than annoying questions, though they held great interest to the "tabloid readers" of the day, who were influenced by Greek and Roman nonsense. When all was said and done, Hillel consoled the man who lost the wager: "Be moderate in spirit. It is right and meet that you lose four hundred *zuz* on

---

1. Avot According to Rabbi Nathan, §26.

Hillel's account but that Hillel not lose his temper." Note how Hillel does not denigrate himself but, to the contrary, emphasizes his own importance!

What, then, was the true nature of Hillel's ability to accommodate himself to local conditions? The Tosefta (Berakhot 2.21) attributes to Hillel the saying: "Do not appear undressed (among the dressed) nor dressed (among the undressed); do not stand (among the seated); do not be seen laughing (among those crying) nor crying (among those laughing), for Scripture states, 'a time to weep and a time to laugh' (Ecc 3:4)." The parallel to this passage explains this behavior as follows: "As a rule, one should not hold different views than do his colleagues or other people." This is a clear and concise explanation, but does not express Hillel's main justification, and it is doubtful that such a conformist view would have appealed to him. After all, he cites Ecclesiastes, which states "a time to weep and a time to laugh." In other words — following Ibn Ezra's interpretation — one should do every thing in the right time. Phrased differently: there is a time and a place for all things, and these most efficiently determine the proper course of action. If you want to be influential, act in accordance with the *Zeitgeist*. Hillel's dictum has, then, nothing to do with conformism; rather, it expresses his fierce desire to fulfill in the best way possible his historical role. The advice is not intended only for Hillel himself, but rather is incumbent upon all people in their respective activities. This, I believe, is the secret of Hillel's moderation.

The full meaning of Hillel's Tosefta dictum comes to light in another of his sayings, this one from tractate Avot (1.14): "If I am not for myself who is for me? And being for my own self what am I? And if not now, when?" This saying explains the mutual relationship that holds between the individual and the broader community, from which, he counsels elsewhere, one should not separate (m. Avot 2.5). One's success depends on his ability to integrate himself in broader society, but without coming to depend on others. The decision is his alone — an expression of the unique will of every individual not to cast off what is required of him: "If not now, when?" This great saying of Hillel's can be rephrased in more simple language: you must act here and now! This is, in a sense, a daring philosophy, but at the same time Hillel believes that one should not swim against the stream, but work within it and try to direct it.

We have commented on the dialectic unity that exists, according to Hillel, between the general and the individual will, between action and the constraints of one's time and place. Was Hillel aware of the parallel ideas espoused by the Essene members of the Dead Sea community? The members of the sect were commanded to act "according to the times," that is, to direct their individual wills to the exigencies of their time, even to the point of act-ing humbly before a tyrant. Hillel's view is very similar to that of the Essenes, so much so that Hillel may have been influenced by them. Still and all, if such an influence did exist it was merely external, since these ideas played a very different role in Hillel's thought. The Qumran Essenes arrived at these conclusions as a result of their belief in predestination — which determines the development of historical events — and in the absence of free will. Hillel, to the contrary, takes free will as his starting point, and exhorts action in accordance with the spirit of the times in order to change the course of history from within. This active approach — "If not now, when?" — was wholly absent from the Essene world.

There is a well-known example of the importance of the "now" in Hillel's life in b. Beitza 16a, namely, that when Hillel found a "fair animal" he did not keep it for the Sabbath (as did Shammai), but ate of it that very day, as it is written: "Blessed is the Lord day by day" (Ps 68:19). This valorization of the present stems both from his belief that one must act now, and from his faith in God, who provides blessings every moment.

Aside from the valorization of the here and now, Hillel's thought assigns a central role to the individual. This should not be understood as an attempt to elevate himself — Hillel was, in fact, a very humble man — but his daring dicta are couched in terms of "I" and "you." Perhaps one can speak of a type of existential philosophy found in Hillel's teachings. I think this view is not attested in such a robust and vivid manner in the thought of any other Jewish sage. No wonder, then, that the following generations felt the need to gloss his proud statement in Leviticus Rabbah 1.5: "My lying low is my elevation, my elevation is my lying low." How so? "[The Lord] is seated on high [and] lying low to see . . . (Ps 113:5-6)." Hillel seems to be arguing that those who lie low are not just other individuals or even God, but the elevated one himself. Thus, one who raises himself up is, in fact, laying himself low, but one who humbles himself in fact elevates himself. This is not unrealistic and can, indeed, be verified by observing the world around us. As a prooftext, Hillel cites a verse in which the speaker is none other than God himself, a typical occurrence in Hillel's dicta. Hillel is able to make this connection because it was so important to him that man was created in God's image.

Here are two more of Hillel's sayings, sayings so daring that their precise meaning proves elusive. I have discussed these dicta at length elsewhere, but even without detailed analysis their general sense should be clear. The first appears in the context of the *Bet ha-Shoeva* celebration (b. Sukkah 53a): "If I am here everyone is here, but if I am not here, who is here?" And: "My feet lead me to the place I love. If you come to my house, I will come to your house. If you do not come to my house I will not come to your house. As it is written, 'in every place where I cause my name to be remembered I will come to you and bless you' (Exod 20:24)." Taken together, these two sayings express Hillel's paradoxical philosophy of the self. The first characteristically deals with the importance of the individual within the world and for the world. The second, which is the most difficult in Hillel's corpus, treats a similar matter. In light of the discussion thus far, it is clear that the "I" in question is not God but Hillel himself, who represents man as such. But who is the "you"? I believe the addressee is anyone that Hillel (or anyone else) encounters, particularly in the context of Torah study, broadly understood. If so, Hillel is expressing his willingness to enter into the realm of the other, provided the other is willing to enter into his realm. And here we discover the scope and limits of Hillel's moderation. On the one hand he speaks of a great openness, but one that is conditioned upon the openness of the other. Here too we find Hillel's odd propensity for citing the words of God (here the verse from Exodus) in the context of human speech.

A second and apparently interrelated series of Hillel's dicta appears in the Sifre Zuta, pericope *Pinhas*, where they appear in their original form. "'It is time for the Lord to act, for they have broken your Law *(torah)*' (Ps 119:126): This verse should be read 'They have broken your Law so it is time to act for the Lord." Hillel also said: "In the time of those who scatter, gather in, and where none are interested in Torah, withhold it, and where there are no men, be a man."

From the sources cited as well as others, it is evident that Hillel's time was one of crisis — physical and spiritual — for the Jewish people, and we cannot today measure the depth of the crisis. These were the days of Herod's reign, for better or for worse. Hillel argued that because "they have broken your Law" it is now time "to act for the Lord." And again we see the "now" motif so central to Hillel's thinking. He is aware of the crisis in the world of Torah and demands action: "In the time of those who scatter gather in, and where none are interested in Torah, withhold it," concluding with the "where there are no men, be a man." Note the personal daring of Hillel, this being the flip side of his moderation. It is not weakness, rather self-restraint born of prudence, of a desire to integrate himself in the most positive way possible into Jewish history.

In order to recognize the roots of Hillel's view, let us turn to a story preserved in Leviticus Rabbah 34.3:

> Once, when Hillel the Elder concluded his studies with his disciples, he walked along with them. His disciples asked him: "Master, where are you going?" He answered: "To perform a religious duty." "What religious duty

is that?" they asked. "To wash in the bathhouse," he said. "Is this a religious duty?" they asked. "Yes," he replied, "if the statues of emperors, which are erected in theaters and fairs, are scrubbed and rinsed by a man who is appointed to care for them and thus earns a salary — no, indeed, gains entry into the highest social echelons — how much more I, who am created in the image and likeness [of God]. As it is written, 'For in the image of God made he man' (Genesis 9:6)."

The fact that all human beings were created in the image and form of God explains how Hillel could understand the words of God as applying to each and every individual. Moreover, it explains how Hillel could see himself — and everyone else — as possessing such merit and such ability, each according to their time and situation. The emphasis on the ability of every individual to play a key role in human history, suggests that Hillel overemphasized the worth of mankind. This is an understandable error, which Hillel shares with many geniuses, including Socrates, since such geniuses see the rest of mankind as equal in value to them.

Was Hillel's philosophy overly optimistic? Did he not experience the difficulties one encounters when trying to be a good person and fulfill his duties and obligations? There is indeed evidence that Hillel was aware of these difficulties, but the way he resolves them again points to his spiritual greatness. The passage in question is preserved in one of the manuscripts of the Palestinian Talmud: "Hillel the Elder would say: 'He is not afraid of evil tidings; his heart is firm, secure in the Lord' (Ps 112:7). Because he is secure in the Lord he is not afraid of evil tidings." That is, whoever trusts in God need not dread evil tidings because his faith liberates him from fear of future events, irrespective of whether or not they come true. Here, I think, we find one of the most sublime expressions of Hillel's unique understanding of man's relationship with himself and with his place in the world.

I hope my discussion has been sufficiently clear, but whoever did not understand should go forth and learn.

14. Philo of Alexandria

Allow me a few personal memories. When I came to Jerusalem, in the winter of 1939, I had completed three years of Classics (Latin and Greek language and literature) at Prague University. The classical world was then — and to a certain extent has remained to this day — my spiritual homeland. But, of course, not the only one. From early childhood I cherished my Jewish heritage, even though I knew almost nothing of it, and could not live my practical life according to it. When Nazi Germany began to threaten Czechoslovakia, but independently, it seems, of these political developments, I began to take a practical interest in Judaism and discovered the paramount importance of the Second Temple period. Even though I quickly immersed myself in the study of Hebrew, I did not have access to the Hebrew sources of Second Temple and post-70 Judaism. When I decided to immigrate to Israel I knew that my mission was to study the multifaceted glory of the Second Temple period. And despite terrible difficulties, I have not abandoned this mission.

My first scholarly project in Jerusalem was a study of daily life as reflected in the writings of Philo. After all, I had a better command of Philo's Greek than rabbinic Hebrew. Thanks to this work, I read all of Philo's works, and this proved very valuable for future research. I had the honor of studying under an outstanding Philo scholar, Yohanan Levy, who died before his time. As a scholar of Hellenistic culture, Levy emphasized the Greek-philosophical aspect of Philo's thought. I also became friends with another superlative scholar, Gedaliah Alon (who similarly died before his time), an extremely learned man who essentially founded the modern study of the sages. Needless to say, Gedaliah Alon emphasized the internal Jewish aspect of Philo's world.

Thanks to these two teachers I came to recognize the core debate concerning Philo: is he better understood in terms of an internal Jewish dynamic, or did his familiarity with Judaism pale in comparison to his Greek learning? The debate continues and will continue into the future, since a definitive answer is elusive.

In fact, the problem is broader and more complex, and additional research raises new questions. As for Philo, it is clear that he was more thoroughly Hellenized than his compatriots in Alexandria and throughout the Greek-speaking Diaspora, and that his Jewish knowledge was limited. All the same, his writings bespeak a familiarity with the scriptural interpretations of the Alexandrian interpreters, and through him we gain access to internal Jewish midrash. But despite the Hellenization of Philo and of other Alexandrian Jews, it would be a mistake to equate Hellenistic Judaism with the practical and cultural assimilation of modern European (especially Western European) Jewry. One of the outstanding differences between the Jews of the Hellenistic Diaspora and their modern European counterparts is that the latter treat their exilic life almost affectionately, while the former viewed their exile as a curse. Philo himself not only visited Jerusalem time and again and saw in it his spiritual homeland, he even hoped that in the end of days the rulers of the nations would allow the Jews to return to Israel and actively support this enterprise. In this, Philo's position is reminiscent of that of many American Jews after the establishment of the State of Israel.

The Hebrew reader who examines these translations of Philo's works will find that the problem mentioned above is immediately evident. Any reader familiar with the rabbinic midrashim will find parallels in Philo. Some of these parallels are due to the influence of Palestinian sages and, it stands to reason, some due to the nature of the verse that "invited" interpretations independently of the sages. The broader question, then, presents itself anew: did Palestinian Jewry — including the sages, the Essene sect at Qumran, and the Jewish apocryphal literature — and the Jews of the Hellenistic Diaspora, share the same spiritual worldview? It appears the answer is affirmative: during the Second Temple Period and immediately following it, there emerged a particular Jewish outlook shared by the different constitutive groups of ancient Judaism, and which governed not only theoretical issues but, for example, the modes of scriptural interpretation. It is enough that we compare Philo's midrash with that of the sages and the Essenes (as attested in the Pesher literature at Qumran). There were, of course, significant ideological differences between these different groups, but it is necessary to examine the commonalities as well — not to miss the forest for the trees.

We have mentioned the rabbis' influence on Philo's interpretive practices. An examination of the two corpora suggests another possibility, namely, that the Jews of the Hellenistic Diaspora, and Alexandria first and foremost, influenced Palestinian Judaism. The two communities certainly maintained close ties. Jews from the Diaspora visited Israel and some even settled there. We may assume, then, that Alexandrian Jews learned from the sages and that the sages were interested in the intellectual achievements of their Alexandrian brethren. Some Palestinian interpreters probably understood Greek, and there were doubtless midrashists among the Hellenistic Jews that knew Hebrew, certainly among those that immigrated to Israel. Scholars have recognized the unquestioned influence of the famed Alexandrian philology on the editing of the Bible. What must now be considered, is the possibility that this influence did not travel directly from the Pagan philologists of Alexandria to Jerusalem, but rather was mediated by the Jews of Alexandria.

This hypothesis is motivated by the fact that despite the unique standing of Palestinian scholarship, the Jews of Israel were not immune to outside influences. Of course, this does not mean that we accept the fashionable view (and not just among Christians!) to radically overstate the Hellenization of pre-70 Judaism — in the Diaspora and Israel alike. Any level-headed scholar will have to reject this modern view, as the unique nature of Judaism in the ancient period is so readily visible. And let's not forget that Judaism was, at that time, a spiritual superpower, a full-fledged civilization, which eventually gave birth to Christianity as a world religion. Without the uniqueness of Judaism, we will not be able to understand why so many Pagans were willing to alter their worldview and join this new religion, whose roots are Jewish.

But the Greek influence on ancient Judaism is not the topic at hand. I merely wish to alert the reader to the fact that already in Temple times, no later than the early second century B.C.E., there existed a robust Jewish worldview. Though based on biblical foundations, early Judaism had its own unique structure and teaching. The worldview in question encompassed the sages, of course, but also the Essenes of the Qumran community, the apocrypha, messianic and apocalyptic views, and the early Jewish mysticism. And despite the strong Greek influence, the Judaism of the Hellenistic Diaspora too belongs to this group. Here lies the explanation of the similarity between Philo's commentaries and the rabbinic midrashim, even in passages that do not bespeak influence in one direction or the other.

The particular approach to the world, and to the Torah, typical of ancient Judaism, left its imprint on Medieval and Modern Judaism as well, and is to this day dominant in orthodox circles (and elsewhere). Most of the Jewish world, however, has come to accept the "Western" way of thought, with its historic understanding of Scriptures and an interpretive approach that seeks to understand a text from within, using methodological tools based on the achievements of the natural sciences. Unfortunately, this is not the forum for an extended discussion of this question. The new, "Western" approach, and its unmediated approach to the world, is, then, different from the approach formulated during the Second Temple Period and which includes, inter alia, Philo and the sages.

As noted, there are amongst us even today those who have not abandoned the ancient Jewish worldview, but interpretive practices change from generation to generation, and today, in most of the Jewish world, a new "enlightened" orthodoxy has developed a somewhat different approach. To wit, they combine the tried and true approach to the past and, as a "modern" addition, interpretation of modern science, which is read as though it were Scripture. And note how similar these eclectic interpretations — which combine ancient rabbinic midrash with fragments from the modern world of scientific thought — are to Philo's commentaries. He too sought to unite the traditional midrashic approach with the philosophical and scientific thought of the Hellenistic worlds. The result in both cases is a turn toward allegory. When I hear synagogue preachers incorporating Newton or Einstein into their homily I think of Philo, and not necessarily the best aspects of his thought. (By the by, the neo-orthodox combination of tradition and science is more awkward than the Jewish-Hellenistic combination of Jewish and Greek thought. The latter, after all, existed at a time when important streams within Greek philosophy were avowedly interpretive.)

But there are positive aspects to Philo's enterprise as well. Though his commentaries unwittingly reflect a religious crisis that came about as a result of the Jewish encounter with the non-Jewish world, the crisis of his day was far less grave than today's. True, there were in Alexandria Jews who no longer observed the commandments (as Philo himself attests), but we know of only two who converted. One of them, as it happens, was Philo's nephew. Today, in contrast, the "orthodox" are a minority within the Jewish world, and quite a few accept — for various reasons — different religions. This difference is evident in Philo's account, for Philo's Judaism is not on the defensive. To the contrary, he represents a proud Judaism that is understood as a spiritual superpower of sorts.

Second, unlike the modern interpreters, Philo is intimately familiar with Greek thought; he does not use the philosophical material merely to adorn his homilies. Philo was an authentic Jewish philosopher. He did not read Greek philosophy Cliff Notes, but was a permanent resident in that philosophical world. He was a true Jewish thinker, perhaps *sui generis* prior to the Middle Ages and modern era. Still and all we must confess that his writings will not teach much about the original sense of the biblical verses he interprets — even less than the early rabbinic midrashim. In this he differs from Martin Buber (who is often singled out as the most Philo-like of Jewish thinkers), since Buber hoped to uncover the spiritual and religious world of the Bible itself, and avoided fanciful interpretation. This difference is, of course, a reflection of the distinct sensibilities of the ancient and modern period. What Buber and Philo share, though, is an attempt to use the intellectual achievements of Europe to arrive at a fuller understanding of the Jewish spirit.

It appears, then, that while we cannot learn much from Philo about the Bible itself, we can learn about the Jewish world he inhabited and, indirectly, about the Judaism of the sages. In this sense, there is no reason to fear Philo. Philo also provides us with insights into Greek philosophy — not merely for our intellectual edification, but as a way of developing our own thinking. After reading his works, we can better grasp the issues facing all people, issues still very much present for our own time. Though our era seems to become more and more brutal, we can strengthen in our hearts the tendency toward humanism. Most importantly, Philo presents to us a striking understanding of Judaism, one with which we too need to grapple. Like Buber, Philo views Judaism as a spiritual and intellectual system that can successfully compete with those of the non-Jewish world. And like Buber, he believes in the ultimate supremacy of good over the forces of destruction in the world and in the human heart. Both Philo and Buber understand Judaism in fundamentally optimistic terms.

Is Philo's argument foreign to the modern reader? In my opinion, less so than it was to the previous generation. Israel, in particular, seems more receptive to his work, since the Jewish community in Israel — religious and secular alike — is still more accustomed to the traditional midrashic approach than to the simple and immediate intuition of the (Jewish and general) world. For most Israel Jews, philosophy without midrash is more foreign than midrash without philosophy. Philo contains both philosophy and midrash, and so will hopefully stimulate his readers to find in his writings both Jewish and universal themes.

15. Josephus on the Pharisees and the Stoa

Shmuel Hugo Bergman is a scholar of both philosophy and religion, and equally devoted to both. It is not the goal of the present discussion to examine the substantive connections between the two fields. It is enough that we note that the seal of philosophy — like the seal of God — is truth, and here already we can see the link between religious and philosophical thought. So while there are those, on both sides, who would wish to divorce the two, such a break can never be absolute.

The impossibility of religious thought without the aid of philosophy becomes clear in the specific topic that concerns us here, namely the question of divine providence as it appears in Josephus's discussion of the three *haireseis,* the Pharisees, the Sadducees, and the Essenes. This topic has become increasingly important since the discovery of the Dead Sea Scrolls, which scholars have identified with the Essenes. One result has been to demonstrate that Josephus's statements regarding the Essenes are reliable. The Scrolls verify, inter alia, Josephus's claim that the Essenes believed in predestination and, incidentally, that they were the source for the New Testament's belief in predestination, and Paul in particular.[1] True, later generations of Christians forgot that their faith was once based on predestination, and even boasted in the Christian belief in free will. But Augustine revived the old doctrine and in his footsteps followed Luther and Calvin. They were opposed by contemporaries who argued that the Reformation belief in predestination is

---

1. D. Flusser, "The Dead Sea Sect and Pre-Pauline Christianity," *Scripta Hierosolymitana* 4 (1958), 220-227.

nothing more than an old Stoic doctrine. Calvin rebutted this claim by stating that the Reformation belief in predestination is substantively different from the Stoic, since the latter adhere to a worldview of ongoing deterministic natural causes, while the church believes that God determines all matters according to His wisdom, having established all events since time immemorial.[2] Calvin well understood that there is a difference between the consistent philosophical determinism of the Stoa, with its belief in natural causality, and the religious belief in a determinism that flows from the belief in a single, omnipotent God whose will is wholly undetermined.

But despite the core difference that Calvin rightly points to, there is a great deal of similarity between Stoic determinism and the religious belief in divine providence and, more specifically, in predestination. Both, of course, suggest that world events proceed within a fairly limited range and recognize a similarly small number of factors that govern man's fate. This similarity suggests, at a minimum, that the claims leveled against philosophical determinism may be valid for religious predestination as well. Moreover, the religious adherents of divine predestination may find themselves drawing near to philosophical determinism, as appears to have happened to the Qumran community who emphasize the more conceptual aspect of predestination. One of the ancient proofs of philosophical determinism was astrology, i.e., the causal influence of the planets on mankind, an argument championed by a number of Stoic thinkers. And now, with the discovery of the Dead Sea Scrolls, we find that the Qumran community, with its belief in predestination, composed a text in which the external appearance of individuals, as well as their association with the sons of light or the sons of darkness, is correlated to the astrological sign under which they were born.[3] Now, according to the views of this very community, double predestination is based on the doctrine of the two spirits, since God determined in advance the identity of the righteous and the wicked, when he "created the spirits of light and of darkness and on them established every deed, on their paths every labor" (1QS 3.25-26)!

There is also another point of similarity between philosophical determinism and the doctrine of predestination. Although both hold that human decisions are determined by external forces — natural causality for the former, God's will for the latter — both, paradoxically, emphasize the importance of the human will. The important role of individual determination in

2. Calvin, *Institutio Christianae religionis* 1.16, 8: ". . . Non enim cum Stoicis necessitatem comminiscimur ex perpetuo causarum nexu et implicita quadem serie, quae in natura contineatur; sed Deum constituimus arbitrum ac moderatorem omnium, qui pro sua sapientia, ab ultima aeternitate decrevit quod facturus esset, et nunc sua potentia, quod decrevit, exequatur."

3. J. T. Milik, *Dix ans de découvertes dans le desert de Juda* (Paris, 1957), 78-79.

Stoic thought is well-known, and the same tension between the individual's choice and dependence on external forces is found in the Dead Sea Scrolls.[4] The author of the Hodayot, for example, can state that: "But the wicked you have created for the time of your wrath, from the womb you have predestined them for the day of slaughter. For they walk on a path that is not good, they reject your covenant, their souls loathe you [. . .], and they take no pleasure in what you command, but choose what you hate" (1QH 7.20-22). The same sectarian author offers a clear summary of predestination: "But I know that justice does not belong to man nor to a son of Adam a perfect path. To God Most High belong all the acts of justice, and the path of man is not secure except by the spirit which God creates for him to perfect the path of the sons of Adam, so that all his creatures come to know the strength of his power and the abundance of his compassion" (1QH 12.30-33), though none of this prevents the Qumran sectarians from referring to themselves as "those who choose the path" (1QS 9.17).[5] It is interesting that in both the Stoic and Qumranite worldviews the emphasis is on the free choice of the philosophers and the righteous, respectively.

Another similarity between the predestination tradition and philosophical determinism is that both contain a real antinomy. Just as there is no ultimate solution to the philosophical question of natural determinism and freewill, so there is no way for a monotheistic religion to overcome the problem of divine omnipotence and human freedom.[6] Though this cannot be established, there may be a deep connection between the religious belief in predestination and providence, on the one hand, and philosophic determinism, on the other.

It is no wonder, then, that in presenting the different Jewish views concerning predestination and providence, Josephus employs terms taken from Stoic philosophy. But before discussing Josephus's knowledge of Stoicism, let us examine his account of the three groups he surveys, the Pharisees, the Sad-

---

4. On this issue see Licht, "The Concept of Freewill Offering *(nedava)* in the Writings of the Qumran Community," in his *Studies in the Dead Sea Scrolls* (Jerusalem, 1957), 77-84.

5. The dual aspect of human and divine choice is encapsulated in the Rule of the Community 8.6, where the Qumranites refer to themselves as those "chosen by the will (of God)," though the scribe originally wrote "those who choose the will (of God)" and then corrected himself. See K. G. Kuhn, *Konkordanz zu den Qumrantexten* (Göttingen, 1960), 30.

6. One solution, which is enjoying a certain vogue these days, is that God is supertemporal and therefore beyond past, present, and future, while mundane events, including human decisions, are temporal. This solution was first formulated by Boethius in the fifth book of his *Consolation of Philosophy* (pages 399-410 in the Loeb edition). See the arguments against this view in Laurentius Valla, *De libero arbitrio*, ed. M. Antossi (Florence, 1934).

ducees, and the Essenes on its own terms. That is, without comparing Josephus's view with descriptions we have of these groups from other sources.

As Josephus intimates, the question of divine providence was an important element in the Jewish thought of the time,[7] and a source of conflict between the Pharisees, the Sadducees, and the Essenes. Josephus refers to the three Jewish "sects" in three different passages (*BJ* 119-166; *AJ* 13.171-173; *AJ* 18.11-22), but only in *Jewish Antiquities* 13, which deals with the polemic surrounding divine providence, does he delineate the views of all three groups. (In the *Jewish War* he discusses only the Pharisee and Essene views.) It appears the omission is due to the fact that the different views were well known, and so it is understandable that Josephus was careless in two of the three passages and did not provide a full account of the three groups.

As far as the Essenes are concerned, Josephus paints a portrait that has been largely confirmed by the Dead Sea Scrolls, i.e., that they believed in predestination: "The sect of the Essenes declares that Fate is mistress of all things, and that nothing befalls man unless it be in accordance with her decree" (*AJ* 13.172).[8]

The Sadducees, Josephus tells us, take the opposite approach: they deny the existence of divine providence (εἱμαρμένη), to say nothing of its control over human affairs. They believe, rather, that all actions are the result of human will (ἅπαντα ἐφ' ἡμῖν αὐτοῖς κεῖσθαι), with good actions being rewarded and evil deeds punished (*AJ* 13.173). The same view is presented in *War* 2.164-165: the Sadducees deny the existence of providence (εἱμαρμένη) and believe that God does no evil and, indeed, does not even see evil. Good and evil are the result of human actions, and the decisions each individual makes determine his or her share of good and evil.

At first glance it is hard to believe that Josephus's account of the Saddu-

---

7. The echoes of this polemic are already evident in Ben Sira, who emphasizes human accountability and free choice (15.11-16), but also alludes to the doctrine of double predestination (33.7-18). See also Ephraim Urbach's important essay "Studies in Rabbinic Views Concerning Predestination" (Hebrew), *Y. Kaufmann Festschrift* (Jerusalem, 1965), 125-148.

8. τό δὲ τῶν Ἐσσηνῶν γένος πάντων τὴν εἱμαρμένην κυρίαν ἀποφαίνεται. Καὶ μηδὲν ὃ μὴ κατ' ἐκείνης ψῆφον ἀνθρώποις ἀπαντᾷ. Gellius (N.A. 7.2) attributes a similar argument to the opponents of Stoicism, who hold that there is "necessitas quaedam et instantia, quae oritur ex fato, omnium quae sit rerum domina et arbitra, per quam necesse sit fieri quicquid futurum est" (SVF 1000 of II 946). The term ψῆφος in the phrase μηδὲν ὃ μὴ κατ' ἐκείνης ψῆφον ἀνθρώποις ἀπαντᾷ is an interesting example of Josephus as a translator. He uses ψῆφος in the sense of "decision," although its original meaning is "lot," a term that plays an important part in the ideology of the Qumran community (on which see Licht's article in *Bet Miqra* [1956], 90-99). Josephus's statement is based on the sectarian Qumran doctrine that God "cast the lots of every living being" (1QS 4.26).

cees is accurate, and indeed there have been those who argued that he has perverted the Sadducees' views in keeping with his anti-Sadducee animus. For how could a Jewish group utterly deny the existence of divine providence? There are some who argue that the Sadducees believed in an overarching providence but denied God looks over individuals. If this is correct, the Sadducee view is very similar to that of the "wicked."

But I believe it is possible that the Sadducees in fact rejected divine providence altogether in part, at least, because they thought that attributing to God control and supervision over human action is a recipe for disaster. By denying divine providence they freed up a conceptual space in which positive and negative events are the result of good and evil human actions. It appears they believed that God's care for mankind manifested itself in providing man with reason, by which people can arrive at their own decisions and thus determine their reward or punishment. The Sadducees also appear to have believed that the Torah was a divine gift meant to aid us in the time of our decisions. (The Sadducees, after all, famously esteemed the written Torah.) This reconstruction of the Sadducee position is based on conclusions drawn from Josephus's account, without introducing foreign religious motifs. So while it is true that these views are foreign to us, they are attested among contemporary groups such as the deists, though unlike the Sadducees they did not believe the Torah was divine. In any case, it is clear that the Sadducee rejection of divine providence is linked to their denial of corporeal resurrection. If there is not reward and punishment after death, it stands to reason that human actions determine their own fate in this world.

Josephus discusses the Pharisee view of providence in all three passages. In *War* 2.162-163 he says that the Pharisees attribute everything to providence (εἱμαρμένη) and to God, save just or unjust actions that depend on human will, though even here every act is aided by providence.[9] A further clarifica-

---

9. It is worth noting that there is a close parallel to Josephus's account of the Pharisees in the Essene Rule of the Community (3.22-25): "From the Angel of Darkness stems the corruption of all the sons of justice, and all their sins, their iniquities, their guilts and their offensive deeds are under his dominion in compliance with the mysteries of God, until his moment; and all their afflictions and their periods of grief are caused by the dominion of his enmity; and all the spirits of his lot cause the sons of light to fall. However, the God of Israel and the angel of his truth assist all the sons of light." This statement serves as a necessary corrective to the doctrine of double predestination: in a worldview based on good-evil dualism, humanity is divided into the righteous and the wicked, according to God's decree. Thus, the righteous, the sons of light, should live without sin and without suffering or difficulty — though of course this is not the case. The Essene author seeks to explain the gap between ideology and reality by stating that God allows the Angel of Darkness to bring sins and iniquities upon the sons of light. However, this compromise between the sectarian theology and reality could have been interpreted as

tion of the Pharisee position is found in *Antiquities* 13.172: the Pharisees hold that some things are the result of providence (εἱμαρμένη) but not all, as the occurrence of certain matters depend on us (ἐφ' ἡμῖν αὐτοῖς).[10] As we saw in *War* 2.162-163, the only matters not dependent on providence are just and unjust actions (*BJ* 2.162-163). *Antiquities* 18.13 completes the portrait (at least to the extent that his halting formulation can be understood[11]), as Josephus states that all things depend on providence (εἱμαρμένη), though Pharisees do not deny the will of the inclination (ὁρμή) which is within us,[12] and believe[13] that the decision is made by God and the will that helps guide each individual to his righteousness or wickedness.

Even if the difficulty of the text allows for different interpretations, its overall thrust is clear enough and fits with Josephus's other accounts of the Pharisee doctrine of providence. Examining all the relevant sources in Josephus, we can piece together a fairly coherent picture: while the Sadducees reject divine providence, the Pharisees attribute everything but just and unjust actions, and even in this providence plays a part as the decision is ultimately the result of both divine guidance and human inclination. In the realm of good and evil, then, man does have some control over the course of events, influencing whether certain things will occur.[14] This belief is, of

---

though God has handed those who were decreed to be righteous over to the forces of evil. Thus the author adds an addendum to his addendum: the righteous were not wholly given to Belial and his forces; the divine decree still stands since "the God of Israel and the angel of his truth assist all the sons of light." We see, then, that the similarity between the Essene author's attempt to fortify the doctrine of predestination, and Josephus's description of the Pharisee belief in providence's role in human action, is merely superficial.

10. This is the correct reading, attested in several Josephus manuscripts, not ἐφ' ἑαυτοῖς, as we find in other MSS and in the modern scholarly editions, and see the further discussion below.

11. On the poor style of *Antiquities* see M. Hengel, *Die Zeloten* (Leiden, 1961), 81, n. 1. Poor style famously causes scribal errors, and thus the many scholarly attempts to emend this difficult text.

12. The manuscripts read τῆς ἐπ' αὐτοῖς (E: ἀπ' αὐτῆς) ὁρμῆς, which should, perhaps, be read: τῆς ἐφ' ἡμῖν αὐτοῖς ὁρμῆς. And see above, n. 10.

13. Reading δοκήσαντες instead of δοκήσας.

14. The view that an individual can change a divine decree finds its classical expression in the story of Honi the Circle Drawer, which is a "pesher" to Job 22:28-30, following as it does the structure of the Qumran pesharim, which were apparently composed during Honi's lifetime: "'You will decide on a matter, and it will be established for you, and light will shine on your ways.' 'You will decide on a matter' — you decreed from below and the Holy One Blessed be He fulfills your decree from on high. 'Light will shine on your ways' — you lighted with your prayer a dark generation. 'When others are humiliated, you say it is pride' — you made proud with your prayers a generation laid low. 'For he saves the humble' — a humbled generation you re-

course, radically opposed to the Essene doctrine of predestination: "And when they have come into being, at their appointed time, they will execute all their works according to his glorious design" (1QS 3.16-17, and see 1QH 7.15).

We saw above that the Sadducees rejected the notions of divine providence and predestination on the grounds that they place the blame for injustices on the beneficent God, a view that they would identify in the Pharisee formulations as well,[15] although the Pharisees assign to man at least some of the responsibility for good and evil in this world. To my mind, however, the more interesting aspect of their doctrine involves the division between human agency and the role of divine providence. We may posit that the Pharisee position is the result of deep analysis of certain parts of the religious thought of the Bible. For example, the lesson of Jonah is that the repentance of Nineveh cancelled the divine decree against their city. Similarly, the Book of Joel states that "the day of the Lord is coming" but all the same exhorts Israel "Yet even now, says the Lord, return to me with all your heart. . . . Who knows whether he will not turn and relent. . . ." For our purposes, however, it does not matter whether the Pharisee position concerning divine providence is a legitimate heir to certain strains within biblical thought. What matters is that, as portrayed by Josephus, it appears to be a mature and independent theological doctrine.[16] Thus it is clearly not Josephus's fabrication but an authentic transmission of Second Temple Jewish thought.

Those who doubt Josephus's account of the three Jewish "sects" argue that he wrote as he did to find favor with his Greek readers, and so portrayed them according to the conventions of Greek philosophical schools. This view

---

deemed with your prayer. 'He will deliver even those who are guilty' — a guilty generation you delivered with your prayer. 'They will escape because of the cleanness of your hands' — you caused them to escape with the deeds of your blessed hands" (b. Ta'anit 23b, and see p. Ta'anit, 3.12).

15. Philo (*Quod omnis probus liber*, 84) attributes to the Essenes the view that God is the cause of all good deeds but is not responsible for the unjust deeds. Philo's account is clearly erroneous, as a comparison of Philo's description with the Qumran scrolls reveals many inaccuracies on his part. For example, it is odd that Philo states (ibid., 83) that the Essenes "are trained in piety, holiness, justice, domestic and civic conduct, knowledge of what is truly good or evil or indifferent, and how to choose what they should and avoid the opposite." Philo here assigns the Stoic distinction between the good, the bad, and the indifferent to the Essenes, who believed in a radical dualism of good and evil. It would appear Philo heard something regarding Essene dualism, but possessed no firsthand knowledge. This is clear from his statement that the Essenes know "how to choose what they should and avoid the opposite." A similar statement is found in the Rule of the Community: "to hate everything that he rejects . . . and to become attached to all good works" (1QS 1.4-5)

16. To my mind, the Pharisee doctrine is close to the synergism of Luther's colleague Melanchthon. It may also be compared to the semipelagianism of early medieval Christianity.

has been discredited as far as the Essenes are concerned by the discovery of the Dead Sea Scrolls, which verify Josephus's description of this group. I have tried to show that close analysis of his account of the Pharisee doctrine of providence suggests it too is reliable. This argument will find additional support if it can be demonstrated that Josephus employed Greek-Stoic terminology but did not have a deep understanding of Stoic teachings and ultimately his use of these terms is at odds with Stoicism itself.

Josephus employs Stoic terms in his discussion of all three "sects" but particularly with regard to the Pharisees, whom he compares explicitly to the Stoics (*Vita* 2.12).[17] Earlier scholarship has identified one Stoic term in Josephus's discussion of the Jewish groups, εἱμαρμένη (literally: "decree"), that is, the endless chain of causality.[18] This term is central to Stoic determinism and the philosophical parallel of religious "predestination." It is no surprise, then, that Josephus would use εἱμαρμένη when describing the Essene doctrine of predestination (*AJ* 13.172) or the Sadducee denial that God intervenes in the world (*BJ* 2.164; *AJ* 13.173). However, the term appears in all three places where he describes the Pharisee doctrine of divine providence (*BJ* 2.162-163; *AJ* 13.172; *AJ* 18.13). Thus, Josephus uses εἱμαρμένη to refer to divine providence as well as predestination. The other key Stoic term that Josephus uses for all three sects is ἐφ' ἡμῖν, something that depends on us, that is, a willful human decision. According to the Pharisees, there are certain things whose occurrence depends on us (ἐφ' ἡμῖν αὐτοῖς; *AJ* 13.172),[19] and the Sadducees believed that everything depends on us (ἐφ' ἡμῖν αὐτοῖς; *AJ* 13.173). In addition, there are other phrases in Josephus reminiscent of the Stoic term.[20] Two of these statements deserve special attention, as they include additional Stoic terms. As noted, Josephus attributes to the Sadducees the belief that good and evil depend on human volition (ἐπ' ἀνθρώπων ἐκλογῇ; *BJ* 2.165). This term, ἐκλογή (choice), was admittedly common in Stoic discourse from earlier times, but took on a special meaning in the philosophical method of Diogenes of Babylon, the head of the Stoic school in Athens after Chrysippus

---

17. Josephus compares the Essene way of life to that of the Pythagoreans (*JA* 15.371).

18. The "series implexa causarum," in Seneca's terms. See J. von Arnim, *Stoicorum veterum fragmenta* (Leipzig, 1923), 2.1024 (hereafter: SVF).

19. This is the correct reading, and see above, n. 10. On the Stoic ἐφ' ἡμῖν see the SVF index, 4.53.

20. The Pharisees (*BJ* 2.163) hold that τὰ . . . πράττειν τὰ δίκαια καὶ μὴ κατὰ τὸ πλεῖστον ἐπὶ τοῖς ἀνθρωποῖς κεῖσθαι; the Sadducees (*BJ* 2.165) φασὶν δ' ἐπ' ἀνθρώπων τὸ τε καλὸν καὶ τὸ κακὸν προκεῖσθαι; and the Pharisees also do not deny ἡ ἐπ' αὐτοῖς ὁρμή (*AJ* 18.13, and see above, n. 10). We should also note Josephus' statement regarding the Essenes (*AJ* 18.18): Ἐσσηνοῖς δὲ ἐπὶ μὲν θεῷ καταλείπειν φιλεῖ τὰ πάντα ὁ λόγος.

and Zeno of Tarsus. Diogenes understood "choice" in rational terms, i.e., as the process by which we elect those things that agree with nature and reject those that do not.[21] For Diogenes, then, ἐκλογή involves free-will, particularly in relation to the choice between good and evil — the same meaning we find in Josephus.

Another key Stoic term appears in Josephus's account of the Pharisees in *Antiquities* 18.13, where he states that the Pharisees believe we possess an inclination or drive (ὁρμή) that determines for good or for evil. Now, according to Stoic thought, the drive (ὁρμή)[22] is the movement of the soul toward a particular object.[23] Unlike other animals, human beings are endowed with reason, and so can make moral decisions regarding good and evil.[24] It is no surprise, then, that Josephus turns to the Stoic term ὁρμή in discussing free will in matters of good and evil. In all, then, Josephus employs four Stoic terms in discussing the three Jewish "sects": decree (εἱμαρμένη), a decision that depends on us (τὸ ἐφ' ἡμῖν), decision between good and evil (ἐκλογή), and the drive (ὁρμή) that brings about this decision.

Both the Stoic terminology and the explicit comparison between the Pharisees and the Stoa indicate that Josephus crafted the Jewish division regarding divine providence in terms taken from the polemics of the Stoics and their opponents surrounding philosophical determinism and free will. But did Josephus possess a proper understanding of the Stoic philosophy? Phrased differently, do Josephus's Pharisees and their doctrine of providence and free will truly resemble the Stoic view?

From its earliest beginnings, Stoicism emphasized the human capacity for moral choice. According to Chrysippus, there exists a rational law that commands what is right and prohibits what is wrong — righteous and evil behavior deserve, respectively, reward and punishment.[25] In this the Stoic view is indeed similar to Josephus's account of the Pharisees. The main difference is that while the Stoics affirm free will, they assert that such decisions cannot change the course of the world but rather are part of its predestined course. Two types of causes influence human choice: one is external and comes about as a result of the causality of the natural world, which provides the initial stimulus for the ὁρμή. The second and more important involves the character of the man in question, as the choice is largely determined by the individual's education, background, and other similar factors. As a result, the choice is, on

21. See M. Pohlenz, *Die Stoa* (Göttingen, 1959), 1.186-187.
22. See Pohlenz, *Die Stoa*, 1.88-92.
23. See SVF 3.169: τὴν ὁρμὴν εἶναι φορὰν ψυχῆς ἐπί τι κατὰ τὸ γένος.
24. See Pohlenz, *Die Stoa*, 1.105-107.
25. See Pohlenz, *Die Stoa*, 1.92.

some level, free, but also predetermined and so not at odds with the thorough-going determinism of the Stoa.[26] So while Josephus peppers his account of the Pharisees with Stoic terminology and even calls attention to the similarity between the two groups, it is clear that the Pharisee beliefs he describes differ from Stoic philosophy: the Stoics hold that moral choices are ultimately determined, while the Pharisees (according to Josephus himself) hold that moral decisions can alter the course of events. Stoic philosophy, moreover, does not recognize the possibility that just or unjust actions are the result of human choice working in tandem with divine providence. This view — which the Pharisees promoted — does not accord with the Stoic idea of human free will, nor with their commitment to absolute determinism.

The above analysis suggests that the Stoic terminology Josephus employs in describing the three Jewish "sects" is intentional: he wanted to represent the Pharisees as the Jewish Stoics. However, it is clear that Josephus did not properly understand the philosophy whose vocabulary he appropriated. This failure is due not only to his lack of philosophical training, but to a tension among the Stoics themselves, who seek to uphold both free will and determinism. A superficial acquaintance with Stoic philosophy could lead one to the conclusion that it adheres to the middle path between determinism and indeterminism. This is what appears to have happened to Josephus, an error committed by a man with greater philosophical acumen, namely Cicero. According to Cicero, the ancients believed either in determinism or in a free and undetermined human will, but Chrysippus the Stoic stakes out a middle position, with a slight tendency toward the free-will camp.[27] Is Cicero's imaginary division not similar to the real dispute between the three Jewish "sects" regarding divine providence?[28] The Essenes correspond to the philosophical determinists, the Sadducees to the free-will party, and the Pharisees to the middle position that Cicero (wrongly) identifies with Chrysippus and Stoicism more generally. The same error may have led Josephus to identify the Pharisee position with that of the Stoa, even though the similarity between the two is merely superficial.

26. See SVF 2.1002 and 1003.

27. Cicero, De fato (SVF 2.282): Ac mihi videtur cum duae sententiae fuissent veterum philosophorum, una eorum, qui censerent omnia ita fato fieri, ut id fatum vim necessitatis adferret, in qua sententia Democritus, Heraclitus, Empedocles, Aristoteles fuit, altera eorum, quibus viderentur sine ullo fato esse animorum motus voluntarii, Chrysippus tamquam arbiter honorarius medium ferire voluisse, sed adplicet se ad eos potius, qui necessitate motus animorum liberatos volunt.

28. Cicero's list of extreme determinists is largely without basis. Carneades, the head of the Academy, took the free-will position against Chrysippus.

Does the similarity between Cicero's division and Josephus's representation of the three Jewish "sects" not suggest that the latter was in fact trying
to present his account of the three Jewish groups in a way that would appeal
to his Greek readers, and that his testimony is not accurate?[29] A close reading
of Josephus indicates that the Greek elements are merely ornamental and his
historical testimony therefore weighty. Since the discovery of the Dead Sea
Scrolls we can no longer doubt his account of the Essenes — which has been
shown to be generally quite accurate — with regard to their belief in divine
providence and beyond. As for the Sadducees, we do not possess contemporary material against which to measure Josephus's historical fidelity. Nonetheless, Josephus's description of the Sadducees is considered reliable, in part
because of parallels preserved in rabbinic literature. There is, then, no reason
to doubt that the Sadducees believed in absolute free will — not only on the
basis of Josephus's testimony, but because the belief in free will is almost a
logical necessity for a group that denied the world to come.[30] As for the Pharisee view of divine providence, we have seen that Josephus tries to portray
them as Jewish Stoics, but in fact provides a Pharisee position that is radically
different from that of the Stoa. The difference between these groups was not
the result of Josephus's failure to understand Stoic thought. Indeed, Josephus's philosophical ignorance is a blessing in disguise — it prevents him
from distorting the picture and turning the Pharisees into Greek thinkers.
More importantly, the theological position of the Pharisees is profound and
measured, and in no way inferior to that of Jewish and non-Jewish thinkers
who struggled with these questions. In summary, all the evidence points to
the fact that Josephus's account of the Pharisee doctrine of providence preserves one of the summits of Second Temple thought, which itself stands out
as a period in which Jewish religious thought flourished.

29. It is possible that Josephus's discussion of the three views of providence was influenced, directly or indirectly, by a popular account of Greek philosophy that was similar to
Cicero's. It should be noted that Josephus's description of the Essene worldview is very similar
to the definition of Stoicism attributed to its opponents by Gellius (see above, n. 8). This would
explain why Josephus uses four Stoic terms in this discussion, but the entire matter requires further investigation.

30. See my "Sanktus und Gloria," *Abraham unser Vater, Festschrift Otto Michel* (Leiden
and Cologne, 1963), 129-152.

16. "Which Is the Straight Way That a Man Should Choose for Himself?" (m. Avot 2.1)

The following comments are intended as an appendix of sorts to Shmuel Safrai's article, and as a proposal regarding the origin of the term *derekh 'eretz*. This is the preliminary presentation of a broader study. My current comments stem from two core assumptions: first, that the title *derekh 'eretz* is appropriate for the Talmudic tractates — all published by Michael Higger — to which it has been applied, since they represent the earliest stage in the semantic development of the term. The second is that the Derekh 'Eretz tractates are elaborations of an earlier Derekh 'Eretz tractate, whose content and composition can be reconstructed. It appears this hypothetical tractate is a sister text to the Jewish composition preserved in the Didache.[1]

Didache is a short and very ancient Christian treatise, composed in Greek at roughly 100 C.E. In terms of both genre and content it is similar to 1QS ("The Rule of the Community") from Qumran. Like the Qumran text,

---

1. On the Didache see G. Alon, "The Halakhah in the Didache." My analysis is based in part on my earlier study, "The Two Ways" (Hebrew) in the Hebrew edition of *Judaism and the Origins of Christianity* (Tel Aviv, 1979), 235-252. The newer editions of the Didache (with translation and commentary) are: K. Wengst, *Schriften des Urchristentums* (Darmstadt, 1984), 2.1-100; W. Rordorf and A. Tuilier, *La doctrine des douze Apôtres (Didaché)* (*Sources Chrétiennes* 248; Paris, 1978) (and see the appendix at pages 203-210, which is a critical edition of the Latin translation of the Jewish source of the Didache); K. Niederwimmer, *Die Didache* (Göttingen, 1989); R. A. Kraft, *Barnabas and the Didache* (Toronto, 1965). In addition we should mention P. Prigeaut, *Epître de Barnabé* (*Sources Chrétiennes* 172; Paris, 1877), and see also S. Pines, "The Oath of Asaf the Physician," *Proceedings of the Israel Academy of Sciences and Humanities* 5 (Jerusalem, 1975), and, more recently, S. Block, "Two Ways and the Palestinian Targum," *Journal for the Study of the Old Testament*, Supplement Series 100 (*A Tribute to Geza Vermes*) (Sheffield, 1990), 139-152.

the Didache consists of various communal regulations alongside a moral-theological tractate (chapters 1–6); 1QS contains a similar tractate (1QS 3.13–4.26). Modern scholarship has established that the tractate within the Didache is an independent Second Temple Jewish work, which was incorporated into the Christian treatise and underwent some Christian editing. The Jewish work survived as an independent composition in a Latin translation dubbed "The Two Ways."[2] The pre-Christian material in "The Two Ways" is also found in the Epistle of Barnabas (chapters 18–20), composed in the first half of the second century c.e. Most scholars believe that the Jewish work titled "The Two Ways" and Barnabas have a shared source, and some argue that the Barnabas material is the more original since it is supposedly more inchoate and poorly organized. However, there is no doubt that in its original form, the Epistle of Barnabas was essentially identical with "The Two Ways" — save perhaps minor differences in particular words. This is evident not only because "The Two Ways" has a relatively clear and intentional structure, but also because the author of the Barnabas Epistle drew from his source and never claimed to be citing it literally.[3]

All the same, our attempt to uncover the original sense of *derekh 'eretz* has led us to venture behind the present version of "The Two Ways." We have already noted the genre similarity between the Didache and 1QS, and the parallel functions of the theological treatise in 1QS 3.13–4.26 and "The Two Ways" treatise in the Didache. But is there also a literary affinity between these two passages? It appears so, as the list of positive traits in 1QS contains four that parallel — both in their identity and their order — four of the traits listed in "The Two Ways":

1QS 4.3	Didache 3.7-8
Spirit of meekness	Πραΰς
Patience	Μακρόθυμος
Generous compassion	ἐλεήμον
Eternal goodness	ἄκακος

---

2. Didache 6.2-3 is a Christian interpolation with no parallel in the conclusion of "The Two Ways." On the meaning of this short passage see D. Flusser, "Paul's Jewish-Christian Opponents in the Didache," *Gilgul* (Leiden, 1987), 71-90.

3. "But let us pass on to another lesson and teaching. There are two ways of teaching and of power, the one of light and the other of darkness; and there is a great difference between the two ways. For on the one are stationed the light-giving angels of God, on the other the angels of Satan" (Epistle of Barnabas 18.1; translated by J. B. Lightfoot). This opening statement, along with the title of the Latin translation *(Doctrina apostolorum)*, indicates that the ancient Jewish treatise was not called "The Two Ways," but "Didache," like the Christian text that is based on it.

The identity between the two passages is absolute and absolutely significant, especially since lists are usually characterized by irregularity.[4] It is clear that the Greek here depends on the Hebrew, not vice versa. These parallel passages indicate that "The Two Ways" is somehow derivative of the abstract, theological passage in 1QS or of a related text. What follows, then, is an analysis of the composition of the two texts.[5] The author of "The Two Ways" briefly summarized the general introduction of the theological treatise in 1QS (1QS 3.13–4.1) and reworked the lists of positive and negative traits (1QS 4.2-8 and 4.9-14, respectively). He then added another list of negative traits (Didache, chapter 5) and wrote a new section, urging his readers toward a moral way of life (Didache chapters 1–4). That the moral exhortations of the Didache are the result of expansions and elaborations of an earlier source — a source that was (as in 1QS) simply a list of ethical traits — is demonstrated by the exact parallel between Didache 3.7-8 and 1QS 4.3.

"The Two Ways" opens as follows:

> There are two ways in the world, one of life, the other of death, one of light, the other of darkness; upon them two angels are appointed, one of righteousness, the other of iniquity, and between the two ways there is a great difference.[6]

What we find here is a fairly common view (among Jews and Greeks alike)[7] regarding the two paths that lie before man, one a path of life and the other of death. (We will see below that this is the original sense of *derekh* — way or path — in the phrase *derekh 'eretz.*) This view clearly supposes that man enjoys free will, a view famously opposed by the Dead Sea community, who champion a theology of double predestination according to which all is preordained and nothing can be altered. As a result, the theological treatise within 1QS does not present the two ways as options that lie before a human being endowed with free will. Instead, people are forced to proceed along one of the two ways, with no way to choose between them: "In the hand of the Prince of Lights is dominion over all the sons of justice; They walk on paths of light. And in the hand of the Angel of Darkness is total dominion over the

---

4. Rordorf and Tuilier, *La doctrine,* 155, n. 6, rightly remark that Didache 3.7-10 and 4.5-7 have parallels in the Qumran texts.

5. For a fuller discussion see Flusser, "The Two Ways."

6. See H. van de Sandt and D. Flusser, *The Didache: Its Jewish Sources and Its Place in Early Judaism and Christianity* (Assen and Minneapolis, 2002), 128, and the textual discussion therein.

7. See the discussion in van de Sandt and Flusser, *The Didache,* 56-59.

sons of deceit; They walk on paths of darkness" (1QS 3.20-21). And similarly, ". . . for God has sorted them into equal parts until the last time, and has put an everlasting loathing between [their] divisions . . . they can not walk together" (1QS 4.15-18).[8] Another way of reconciling the two ways with the Qumran doctrines is to link the two ways with the two spirits, the Spirit of Truth and the Spirit of Deceit: "[God] created the spirits of light and of darkness and on them established every deed, on their paths every labor" (1QS 3.25-26). Every person *walks* in one of these spirits, according to what has been preordained: "Until now the spirits of truth and injustice feud in the heart of man: they walk in wisdom or in folly. In agreement with man's inheritance in the truth, he shall be righteous and so abhor injustice; and according to his share in the lot of injustice, he shall act wickedly in it, and so abhor the truth" (1QS 4.23-25),[9] and indeed "the reward for all those who walk in [the spirit of the sons of truth] will be healing, plentiful peace in a long life, etc." (1QS 4.6-7) while "all those who walk in [the spirit of deceit] will be for an abundance of afflictions" (1QS 4.12). These opposing spirits, then, have "their paths in the world" (1QS 4.2), with the spirit of deceit leading men "to walk in all the paths of darkness and cunning" (1QS 4.11). For the present discussion, it is important to note that every individual does not proceed along one of these paths, but rather in one of these spirits:

> He created humanity to rule the world, and placed for him two spirits so that he would walk with them. . . . They are the spirits of truth and of deceit. . . . In the hand of the Prince of Lights is dominion over all the sons of justice; they walk on paths of light. And in the hand of the Angel of Darkness is total dominion over the sons of deceit; they walk on paths of darkness (1QS 3.18-21).

Note the parallel with the opening of "The Two Ways" treatise:

---

8. The entire passage ought to be read in its entirety. The dualistic understanding of the two ways predates the Qumran literature. See Ben Sira 33.7-15 (vv. 7-18 according to the numbering in some editions). In Hebrew, see M. Z. Segal (ed.), *The Book of Ben Sira* (Jerusalem, 1969), 206-207; for the Greek, J. Ziegler (ed.), *Sapientia Filii Sirach* (Göttingen, 1965); for an English translation and commentary, P. W. Skehan and A. A. DiLella, *The Wisdom of Ben Sira* (Anchor Bible 39; New York, 1987). The Hebrew fragments of Ben Sira were published by the Academy of the Hebrew Language in *Sefer Ben Sira* (Jerusalem, 1973).

9. Needless to say, the author does not mean that the two spirits are actually fighting in the heart of any individual. Such a view, parallel to the doctrine of the two inclinations, is not attested in the Qumran scrolls. Moreover, the syntax of the Hebrew rules out such an interpretation.

1QS

These are their paths in the world . . . (4.2). In the hand of the Prince of Lights is dominion over all the sons of justice; they walk on paths of light. And in the hand of the Angel of Darkness is total dominion over the sons of deceit; they walk on paths of darkness (3.20-21);

they can not walk together (4.18).

"The Two Ways" in the Didache

There are two ways in the world . . . one of light, the other of darkness; upon them two angels are appointed, one of righteousness, the other of iniquity,

and between the two ways there is a great difference.

Here, then, is another point of similarity between the theological treatise in 1QS and "The Two Ways." Moreover, the extant material allows for a hypothetical reconstruction of the former prior to its sectarian reworking in the hands of the Qumran author — the form that served as the source for "The Two Ways." The author of 1QS — in keeping with the beliefs of the Dead Sea community as a whole — believed in predestination and had to adjust the free-will position of "The Two Ways" doctrine accordingly. Recognizing the editorial hand of the sectarian author allows us to confidently reconstruct one of the key sentences in 1QS:

1QS 3.18-19

He created man to rule the world and placed within him two spirits so that he would walk with them. . . .

Reconstruction

He created man to rule the world and placed with him two ways so that he walk with them.

The reconstruction is certainly correct, since Genesis 1:28 states that God gave Adam dominion over the earth. Furthermore, the language is reminiscent of a midrash to Genesis 3:22, attributed to Rabbi Aqiva: "'Behold, man has become as one of us' (Gen 3:22) . . . [this] means that God put before him two ways, the way of life and the way of death, and he chose for himself the way of death."[10] The same idea also appears in the long recension of 2 Enoch, where

---

10. Mekhilta of Rabbi Ishmael, Beshallah 7, Lauterbach 1.248. The interpretation is based on the Hebrew כאחד ממנו, which is usually rendered "as one of us" but is here understood as referring to "one of them," i.e., of the two ways. The motif of the way of life and the way of death is rooted in the prohibition against eating of the tree of knowledge of good and evil, an act that brings about death. See also Yalqut Shimoni to Genesis (Hymen edition), 115.

God says of the creation of man: "And I gave him free will; and I pointed out to him the two ways — light and darkness" (30.15).[11]

The material adduced thus far indicates that at an early stage in its development, the theological treatise preserved in 1QS did not promote divine predestination. The focus of the treatise was the two ways themselves, and so the author of "The Two Ways" in the Didache did not need to alter anything in that regard. At the same time, the author of 1QS could adopt the same source because of the strong dualistic overtones of the two ways doctrine, introducing only relatively minor changes to reconcile the source to Qumran's doctrine of predestination.[12] We have already shown that according to the pre-sectarian source of "The Two Ways" God placed two ways — one of light, the other of darkness — before man for him to walk on. This is also the opening of "The Two Ways": "There are two ways in the world, one of life, the other of death, one of light, the other of darkness. . . ." I believe all this points to the fact that the "way of life" that we are exhorted to choose is the original sense of *derekh 'eretz*.

Let us return to the "two ways in the world, one of life, the other of death," that God placed before Adam. After his sin, God expelled Adam from the garden: "He drove out the man; and at the east of the garden of Eden he placed the cherubim, and a sword flaming and turning to guard the way to the tree of life" (Gen 3:24). Said Rabbi Shmuel bar Nahmani: *derekh 'eretz* preceded the Torah by twenty-six generations . . . as it is written, "to guard the way to the tree of life." "Way" refers to *derekh 'eretz*, and "tree of life" refers to the Torah."[13] According to this midrash, *derekh 'eretz* preceded the Torah by the twenty-six generations that elapsed from Adam to Moses.[14] Shmuel bar Nahmani then interprets the phrase "to guard the way to the tree of life" as a reference to *derekh 'eretz;* that is, the way that leads to the tree of life, i.e., to

11. J. H. Charlesworth, *The Old Testament Pseudepigrapha* (New York, 1983), 152 (translated by F. I. Andersen). This statement seems to be an addendum to the original text of 2 Enoch, apparently by a Christian hand, as 33.1-2, which mentions the special status of Sunday, would indicate. See Andersen's comments on p. 156. The Christian character of this section does not exclude the Judaism of the midrash on Adam.

12. It is not relevant at this point what passages of the source were used by the author of "The Two Ways." The identity between 1QS 4.3 and Didache 3.7-8 suggests a deep similarity between the source of "The Two Ways" and the theological treatise in 1QS.

13. Leviticus Rabbah §7 (page 179 in the Margaliyot edition), with a parallel at §35 (page 424). See also the opening of Tanna debe Eliyahu, and Yalqut Shimoni to Genesis, §§35-36 (pages 117-118 in the Hyman edition). And see W. Bacher, *Die Agada der Palästinensischen Amoräer* (Hildesheim, 1965), 484, n. 3.

14. The Hebrew קדמה, "preceded," may be midrashically derived from מקדם (לגן עדן), "east (of Eden)."

the Torah. It may be that there is a connection between this midrash and the view that Adam was earlier presented with two ways, the way of death and the way of life. In any case, it is clear that Shmuel bar Nahmani is not suggesting that the Torah is not eternal, only that a general morality was in effect in the time prior to the giving of the Torah, so clearly *derekh 'eretz* does not mean general courtesy and manners, as it is often understood. It is apparently no coincidence that the earliest strata of the tractate Derekh 'Eretz and of "The Two Ways" in the Didache refer only to the general ethical commandments (from a Jewish perspective, of course), and not to the Mosaic laws. Moreover, as we will see below, one of the units in "The Two Ways" (Didache, chapter 3) includes a list of five moral commandments that appear in the Torah "but had they not, should have been written."[15]

As with many other midrashim, Rabbi Shmuel bar Nahmani contrasts Torah and *derekh 'eretz*, a trend that is probably due to the rabbis' gradual recognition of the tension between pure practical ethics and the concrete Torah of Moses. Rabbi Elazar ben Azariah knew that Torah and *derekh 'eretz* are mutually dependent: "If there is no Torah there is no *derekh 'eretz*; if there is no *derekh 'eretz* there is no Torah" (m. Avot 3.17). We must examine the entire catena to better understand the conceptual framework of the text that first links the Torah and *derekh 'eretz*. There is no question that the latter term refers to ethical behavior. But still it appears, especially in light of the link to the Torah, that the scope of the term has narrowed somewhat. A further narrowing is evident in the words of Rabban Gamaliel, the son of Judah the Prince: "Excellent is Torah with *derekh 'eretz*, for toil in them both puts sin out of mind" (m. Avot 2.2). The phrase that immediately follows is "All Torah without worldly occupation comes to naught and brings sin in its train," and one wonders if they are intended as a direct continuation of the earlier statement. Even if the answer is negative — as appears to be the case — and *derekh 'eretz* is not identified with worldly occupation, Rabban Gamaliel does refer to it as a type of activity. The separation of Torah from *derekh 'eretz* gained momentum in the dictum of Nehunia ben ha-Kanah, so much so that one can almost speak of a dichotomy: "He that takes upon himself the yoke of Torah, from him shall be taken the yoke of the kingdom and the yoke of *derekh 'eretz*; but he that throws off the yoke of Torah, upon him are laid the yoke of the kingdom and the yoke of *derekh 'eretz*" (m. Avot 3.5). Here *derekh 'eretz* is understood as practical behavior that is somehow not fitting for the true philosopher![16]

The progressive debasement of *derekh 'eretz* was caused both by the

15. Sifra *ad* Lev 18:4 (page 81a in the Weiss edition); b. Yoma 67b.
16. See my "Image of the Masada Martyrs," in the present volume, pp. 85-86.

ongoing emphasis on the Torah and the internal development of the term *derekh 'eretz*. From the outset the term referred to a practical morality that guides an individual's behavior. Small wonder, then, that this broad concept eventually came to designate the proper behavior of a person in this world.[17] Unfortunately, this narrow sense was later misapplied to many early sources, so much so that in recent times the phrase has come to signify an ideology that is quite distant from its original sense. And it is the original sense to which we return.

We noted that the original sense of *derekh 'eretz* was a particular ethical doctrine, and further assumed that the term finds its full expression in rabbinic *derekh 'eretz* literature. We also proposed a connection between *derekh 'eretz* and "The Two Ways" doctrine: *derekh 'eretz* is the way that one must choose and follow "in the land," i.e., in Israel. This proposal is buttressed by two passages from Mishnah Avot. The first records a conversation between Rabban Yohanan ben Zakkai and his five disciples (m. Avot 2.9),[18] in which the sage turns to his students and says: "Go forth and see which is the good way to which a man should cleave. . . . Go forth and see which is the evil way which a man should shun." The topic of this discussion is, then, the two diametrically opposed ways, replete with the dualistic terminology familiar to us from other sources: a good way to which man ought cleave, and a bad way from which man ought distance himself.[19] The good way is then characterized by the disciples as "a good eye," "a good companion," "a good neighbor," "one that sees what will be," and "a good heart," while the bad way is the opposite: "an evil eye," "an evil companion," "an evil neighbor," "he that borrows and does not repay," "an evil heart." And here is a similar list, one of many, from the *derekh 'eretz* literature: "Fifteen characteristics are mentioned in connection with a scholar: he is decorous in his entering, modest in his sitting, subtle in the fear [of God], shrewd in knowledge, etc."[20] Unlike "The Two Ways" treatise in the Didache and the theological treatise in 1QS, the *derekh 'eretz* literature usually does not include negative lists that might characterize the way which is to be avoided, perhaps because despite its dualist origins, this literature is concerned with the preferred way and not the way of darkness and death. By the by, in its literary form "The Two Ways" preserves a dualist structure, even though it expands its discussion of the way of life.

17. On the different meanings of *derekh 'eretz* (with citations), see M. Higger (ed.), *The Minor Tractates* (New York, 1935), 1-7; W. Bacher, *Die exegetische Terminologie* (Darmstadt, 1965), 1.25.

18. See Flusser, "The Two Ways," 237-239.

19. See also Flusser, "The Two Ways."

20. Derekh 'Eretz Zuta 3.10 (*The Minor Tractates*, 2.576).

The second relevant dictum is attributed to Rabbi Judah the Prince and is found in m. Avot 2.1: "Which is the straight way that a man should choose? That which is an honor to him and wins him honor from other men.[21]" The opening question — "Which is the straight way that a man should choose?" — is identical with that of Rabban Yohanan ben Zakkai (m. Avot 2.9). What follows presents a number of difficulties, and has elicited a number of different interpretations.[22] This is how Rabbenu Natan Rosh ha-Yeshiva interprets the opening of the dictum:[23] "Our Holy Rabbi said, 'Which is the straight way that a man should choose? That which is an honor to him and wins him honor from other men.' Namely, to fulfill the slightest commandment no less than the most grave." In other words, Rabbenu Natan understand the *vav* of והוי זהיר במצוה as marking apposition, and thus he does not need to alter the received text. Rabbenu Bahya offers a similar reading.[24]

Rabbenu Natan is undoubtedly correct, as the rule קלה כחמורה, "the slightest commandment no less than the most grave," is intimately linked with the ideal of *derekh 'eretz*.[25] This connection is alluded to in one of the literary units of "The Two Ways," and is explicit in many passages in the earliest stratum of the *derekh 'eretz* literature.[26] The statement "the slightest commandment no less than the most grave" is no hollow halakhic slogan. It is primarily an ethical rule, whose meaning becomes clear when we set it by another well-known exhortation found in "The Two Ways" (Didache 3.1): "My child, flee from all evil and from everything like it."[27] Already in the earliest

21. This is Rabbi Judah's personal view and does not accord with the overall conceptual framework of *derekh 'eretz*.

22. See I. N. Epstein, *Introduction to the Text of the Mishnah* (Hebrew) (Jerusalem, 1948), 1108-1109; S. Sharvit, "Interpretive Traditions and Their Link to the Mishnah's Textual Traditions" (Hebrew), *Studies in Rabbinic Literature, the Bible, and Jewish History: E. Z. Melammed Festschrift* (Ramat Gan, 1982), 217-218. My thanks to Shmuel Safrai for this last point.

23. "The Commentary of Rabbenu Natan Rosh ha-Yeshiva" in Y. Qafih (ed.), *The Mishnah* (Jerusalem, 1971), 8.9. Natan ben Avraham, the author, died before 1102.

24. See "Pirke Avot," in *The Works of Rabbenu Bahye* (Hebrew), ed. C. Chavel (Jerusalem, 1970), 551-552.

25. It is alluded to, inter alia, in the Sermon on the Mount (Matt 5:19), and is, in fact, a guiding principle of the first part of the sermon (Matt 5.17-48). See also my article "The 'Torah' in the Sermon on the Mount" (Hebrew) in *Judaism and Christian Origins* (Tel Aviv, 1979), 226-234.

26. See similar formulations in Derekh 'Eretz Zuta, 3.3. On the significance of this dictum see D. Flusser, "A Rabbinic Parallel to the Sermon on the Mount," *Judaism and the Origins of Christianity* (Jerusalem, 1988), 469-499.

27. On this statement see G. Alon, "The Halakhah in the Didache," *Studies in the History of Israel* (Tel Aviv, 1978), 1.297-302. In the *derekh 'eretz* literature, this exhortation appears (with some changes) in tractate Derekh 'Eretz 1.12, 2.7, and elsewhere.

strata of the *derekh 'eretz* literature we find this command is linked to the notion of "the slightest commandment no less than the most grave," as the broader context makes clear:[28] "Avoid the ugly and all that is like it. Recoil from even a minor sin lest it lead you to a major sin. Hasten to perform the slightest commandment, for it will lead you to a major one."[29] The imperatives "flee" and "recoil" point to the dualistic roots of the two ways doctrine. The same terms appear in the well-known dictum of Ben Azzai (which does not belong to the *derekh 'eretz* literature): "Run to fulfill even the slightest commandment even as the most grave" (m. Avot 4.2). Ben Azzai's statement inhabits the same conceptual world as "The Two Ways" statement (it is, if anything, more explicit) and develops the idea of "the slightest commandment no less than the most grave" in the same direction as the dictum of Rabbi Judah discussed above (m. Avot 2.1). Rabbi Judah's statement, like ben Azzai's, mentions the reward that attends to commandments. Clearly, then, the tractate Derekh 'Eretz and the dictum of Ben Azzai characterize the straight way that man should choose, according to Rabbi Judah.

The brief passage in tractate Derekh 'Eretz is of utmost importance as it expresses a strong and unique moral view, anchored in a profound fear of sin. The care regarding "the slightest commandment no less than the most grave" is not born of some exaggerated commitment to the commandments, but rather reflects a moral worldview that recognizes no compromises: avoid not only unseemliness but anything that resembles unseemliness. In other words, avoid anything that hints at immoral behavior and might lead to sin. Indeed, the Hebrew word כיעור, which has been translated unseemliness, can mean moral unseemliness.[30] Thus, a Baraita cited in b. Yoma 86a speaks of a scholar who "is not faithful in his commercial interactions, and he does not speak calmly with others. What do people say of him? 'Who is he . . . how corrupt are his actions and how *unseemly are his ways!*'"[31]

The demand to avoid the ugly or the unseemly and anything like it,

---

28. See tractate Yirat Het (pages 75 [version A] and 83 [version B] in Higger, *The Minor Tractates*); tractate Derekh 'Eretz 2.7.

29. The *derekh 'eretz* literature reads "avoid" (רחק); the imperative "flee" is attested not only by the language of Didache 3.1, but also by the dictum of Ben Azzai (m. Avot 4.2).

30. See J. Levy, *Wörterbuch über die Talmudim* (Berlin, 1924), 2.273, 382. See also b. Yebamot 22b, Ketubot 105a, and cf. Ben Sira 13.22. Shmuel Safrai has called my attention to the fact that Tana de-Bei Eliyahu — itself a representative of the *derekh 'eretz* tradition (and see above, n. 13) — frequently speaks of "unseemly matters." See also H. Yalon, *Pirqe Lashon* (Jerusalem, 1971), 211-212.

31. It is on the basis of this Baraita, or one that preceded it, that Paul wrote Romans 2:17-24. And see also Matthew 23:3.

along with the care regarding minor transgressions lest they lead to weightier ones, expresses a superlative piety anchored in an uncompromising moral position. Small wonder, then, that the *derekh 'eretz* texts emphasize the moral aspect of Judaism rather than the practical Torah commandments. As a result, the sages — from a relatively early time — conceived of Torah and *derekh 'eretz* as disparate spheres often understood as complementary, but at times as maintaining a tension. The increasingly narrow purview of *derekh 'eretz*, discussed above, found its expression in the *derekh 'eretz* literature itself, and in later strata we find discussions that deal with daily external behavior. Thus, "A scholar should not eat standing, lick his fingers or belch in the presence of his fellow . . ." (tractate Derekh 'Eretz Zuta, 5.1).

The phrase "avoid the ugly and all that is like it" is, as noted, found in "The Two Ways" treatise (Didache 3.1), where it is the opening statement of an independent unit (3.1-6).[32] Immediately following this unit (3.7-8) we find the literal Greek translation of the four traits cited in 1QS 4.3. The author who introduced the unit into "The Two Ways" reworked the original to better suit the list of sins enumerated in chapter five of the Didache.[33] After the introduction (Didache 3.1) come five structurally and substantively similar units (3.2-6). In the present text, each unit divides into two parallel stichs, but it is clear that the material taken from the list in chapter five is found mostly in the second stich. We may assume, then, that the original version — prior to being reworked by the author of "The Two Ways" — included but one stich that dealt with a slight transgression that leads to a grave one, and which was likely identical with the first stich of our five units. Here, then, is the reconstructed version of the text that underlies Didache 3.1-6:

1. My child, flee from all evil[34] and everything like it.
2. Do not be an angry person, for anger leads to murder.
3. Do not be a person given to passion, because passion leads to adultery.[35]

---

32. On this unit see Flusser, "The Two Ways" (Hebrew) in the Hebrew edition of *Judaism and the Origins of Christianity*, 235-252; idem, "The 'Torah' in the Sermon on the Mount," 229-233; idem, "The Decalogue and the New Testament," in the present volume. See also my discussion with Shmuel Safrai in our "Das Aposteldekret und die Noachitischen Gebote," in E. Brocke and H. Y. Barkenings (eds.), *Wer Torah vermehrt mehrt Leben* (Neukirchen, 1986), 197-190.

33. See Flusser, "The Two Ways," 250-251.

34. It is possible that the original Hebrew read "the unseemly," but that the Greek translator could not find a suitable term.

35. The first stich of the extant version refers to *zenut*, fornication; and *ni'uf*, adultery, appears only in the second. However, the original reading undoubtedly referred to adultery, inter alia, because of the Decalogue.

4. Do not be a necromancer (or: sorcerer), for this leads to idolatry.
5. Do not be a liar, because lying leads to theft.
6. Do not be a grumbler, because this leads to slander.

I have noted elsewhere[36] that this passage in "The Two Ways" plays a key role in understanding the first part of the Sermon on the Mount — in terms of content, argument, and shared moral doctrine. This section of the Sermon on the Mount is close in its spirit to the universal morality of the *derekh 'eretz* worldview, which is why Jesus here deals with questions of morality proper (from a Jewish perspective, of course) and not the Jewish *mitzvoth*. It is immediately apparent that both the Sermon and "The Two Ways" in the Didache list grave sins alongside slight ones, and both echo the second half of the Decalogue, which was understood as the epitome of Jewish morality.[37] The list of transgressions in "The Two Ways" is also important because it is identical with the rabbinic list of "matters addressed in the Torah that, were they not written, it would have been justified to add them." Namely: idolatry, sexual morality, physical injury, theft, and blasphemy. This list appears twice, though in different order, in rabbinic sources,[38] and is in any case not identical with that of the Didache, which includes a different prohibition after the third commandment. It should be noted that these five severe transgressions make up five of the seven Noachide commandments.

Taken together, the material adduced thus far demonstrates that the primary and most original meaning of *derekh 'eretz* is morality in its pure, practical sense. We saw that "The Two Ways" enumerates five prohibitions that appear in the Torah but that would be recognized even were they not written as they are self-evident — a natural morality of sorts. The same approach is found in the midrash to Genesis 3:24, according to which *derekh 'eretz* preceded the giving of the Torah at Sinai by twenty-six generations.[39] It follows that the biblical patriarchs did not keep the precepts of the Torah, but adhered to a refined human morality, *derekh 'eretz*, which was later incorporated into the Torah.[40] In other words, this midrash holds that *derekh 'eretz* refers to or, more accurately, includes the five prohibitions that "were they not written, it would have been justified to add them." And let us not forget that the same five prohibitions are enumerated in "The Two Ways" treatise, it-

36. See Flusser, "A Rabbinic Parallel to the Sermon on the Mount."
37. See Flusser, "The Decalogue and the New Testament."
38. Sifra ad Leviticus 18:4 (page 86a in the Weiss edition); b. Yoma 76b.
39. See above, n. 13.
40. This position stands in contrast to those who hold that the patriarchs kept the entire Torah.

self a *derekh 'eretz* text. It may well be that the early sages who deal with the *derekh 'eretz* doctrine understood the term to refer to a natural, pre-Sinai morality, but I do not think this view has its roots in the midrash to Genesis 3:24. The opposition Torah–*derekh 'eretz* is ancient, but the concept of *derekh 'eretz* itself is rooted in the idea that man must choose the right way here on earth.[41]

Let us return to the well-known exhortation to fulfill "the slightest commandment no less than the most grave," which leads to "the straight way that a man should choose for himself" (m. Avot 2.1). We saw that Jesus alludes to this dictum in the Sermon on the Mount (Matt 5:18-19), that it appears time and again in the *derekh 'eretz* literature,[42] and that it epitomizes the message of "The Two Ways" treatise.[43] This, then, is another connection between the rabbinic *derekh 'eretz* literature and "The Two Ways" treatise, since this same dictum appears as the opening to the important literary unit in Didache 3.1.

The above arguments demonstrate that "The Two Ways" treatise — the source of the Didache — and the *derekh 'eretz* literature of the rabbis constitute a unique literary genre with its own ideological voice. Indeed, had the Didache reached us in Hebrew, we would have been convinced that it is one of the *derekh 'eretz* tractates. And despite the fact that there are a number of unresolved issues concerning the literary development of these traditions, an attentive investigation reveals with relative ease the early stratum of the *derekh 'eretz* tractates. It appears this stratum is represented primarily in Derekh 'Eretz Zuta (also known as Yir'at Het), in particular chapters 1–3.[44] It is more difficult — perhaps impossible — to reconstruct the original language of the hypothetical treatise from which the extant texts derive, not least because there probably existed different versions of the original text — a common phenomenon in literature of this sort. Indeed, even if we were to find the original Derekh 'Eretz tractate, we would undoubtedly find that it too is made up of various traditions and literary units.

We have already referred to the composite nature of "The Two Ways," and now note that the manner in which it was composed is readily appar-

---

41. True, according to both the reconstructed text of 1QS 3.18-19 and the midrash attributed to Rabbi Aqiva, already Adam had to choose between the way of life and the way of death (see above, nn. 10, 11). The midrash to Genesis 3:24 also refers to the time of Adam, that is, to the earliest days of humanity, well before Sinai. But even if we assume the tension between *derekh 'eretz* and the Torah is secondary, there is little doubt that *derekh 'eretz* represents a natural morality as opposed to the revealed morality of Scripture.

42. See above, notes 26-28.

43. See above, note 28.

44. See M. B. Lerner, "External Tractates," in *The Literature of the Sages* (Assen, 1987), 1.379-389. The earliest material is in the opening chapters of tractate Derekh 'Eretz Zuta.

ent,[45] including the literary reworking of the independent text that was incorporated into "The Two Ways" (Didache 3.1-6).[46] We have also uncovered the literary link between "The Two Ways" treatise and the theological tractate in 1QS.[47] Finally, "The Two Ways" belongs — both in terms of substance and of style — to the *derekh 'eretz* genre, which, like the eponymous rabbinic tractates, is concerned with *derekh 'eretz* in its original sense. These are, then, two branches of the same tree. However, we must admit that already in ancient times Ur-*derekh 'eretz* and Ur-"The Two Ways" existed as separate compositions. We found only one literary link between *derekh 'eretz* and "The Two Ways," namely the unit found in Didache 3.1-6. We even have one verse that is common to the two texts.

Tractate Derekh 'Eretz	Didache 3.1-6
Distance yourself from all that leads to sin.	
Avoid the ugly and all that is like it.	Verse 1
Recoil from even a minor sin lest it lead you to a major sin.	Verses 2-6
Hasten to perform the slightest commandment, for it will	
lead you to a major one.	

We have argued that the *derekh 'eretz* tractates are deserving of this name, and that the term appears here in its original sense, which is the focus of the tractates. The term *derekh 'eretz* appears once in the text of the tractate, in a very interesting context:[48]

> Reflect before the word issues from your mouth. Consider your actions in accordance with good manners *(derekh 'eretz)*. Set a reward for every step you take. Submit to divine judgment and refrain from grumbling.

We cannot understand the phrase *derekh 'eretz* in the narrow sense it now carries without doing violence to the passage. An attentive reading of the earliest stratum of the tractate provides a framework in which to understand the meaning of the phrase. We have already stated that it refers to practical ethics. However, this literature provides a unique understanding of this morality —

---

45. See, for now, my discussion in "The Two Ways."

46. See above, pp. 242-243. The list of "ways of the Amorite" in Didache 3.4 has no parallel in the enumeration of sins in chapter 5. On the former, see G. Alon, "The Halakhah in the Didache," 297-302.

47. See above, pp. 233-237.

48. Derekh 'Eretz Zuta 3.1. My thanks to Shmuel Safrai, who called my attention to this important passage.

precisely the same orientation as "The Two Ways" treatise in the Didache.[49] There is, for example, a strong emphasis on the demand that man "be humble and affable toward all people,"[50] or, in the language of the Didache, "You shall not exalt yourself or let yourself be arrogant. You shall not attach yourself to those who are highly placed but shall associate with those who are just and humble."[51] Empathy and companionship, a willingness to compromise with all — all elements of a clear and coherent moral doctrine that characterized the humanistic Jewish circles from which it emerged. A detailed description of this moral worldview will allow us to identify and map out the Jewish circles which were open to this teaching and further developed it.[52]

The very nature of the Jewish sources from the Hellenistic and Roman period requires that we find ways to fill the lacunae in our knowledge regarding certain points. With regard to the original meaning of the phrase *derekh 'eretz* we approached the question from a number of different and perhaps surprising directions. After all, we have no clear definition of *derekh 'eretz* in the ancient sources — and this is the case with most of the key terms in rabbinic literature — though such a definition would help us move further back chronologically and shed light on the Second Temple Period. The sources adduced lead us to the conclusion that the phrase *derekh 'eretz* was selected to refer to the way that man must choose in the land *('aretz),* that is, in the terrestrial world.[53] And there are other indications that the phrase *derekh 'eretz* is rooted in the doctrine of the two ways, the way of life and the way of death. The dualism of this doctrine is already diluted in "The Two Ways" tractate in the Didache, as most of the discussion there is devoted to the way of life (chapters 1–4) and only little to the way of death (chapter 5). "The Two Ways" treatise, though composed in Greek, belongs to the Hebrew *derekh 'eretz* literature, which also deals with only the one way (even though there too we find a hint of dualism). One of the conclusions of this study is that the meaning of *derekh 'eretz* began to narrow as early as the second half of the first century

---

49. The connection between the tractate Derekh 'Eretz and the Didache was already noted by G. Klein, *Der älteste christliche Katechismus* (Berlin, 1907), 7, who argues that an early *derekh 'eretz* tractate was the source of the Didache.

50. Derekh 'Eretz Zuta 3.5.

51. Didache 3.9.

52. Shmuel Safrai argues that the *derekh 'eretz* literature originates in the Tannaitic group known as *Hasidim,* which later produced *Tanna de-bei Eliyahu.* See S. Safrai, "The Teachings of the Hasidim in Tannaitic Literature" (Hebrew), *Y. Amorai Memorial Volume* (Tel Aviv, 1973), 147; idem, "Hasidim and Men of Deeds," *Zion* 59 (1985), 149-151.

53. See also the reference to "their paths in the world" in 1QS 4.2, and 1QS 3.18-19, as well as the opening phrase of "The Two Ways": Viae duae sunt in saeculo. It must be admitted, however, that the term *'eretz* does not appear.

C.E., because (among other reasons) *derekh 'eretz* was already then being contrasted to the revealed Mosaic law. Though the mainstream of rabbinic literature ultimately won the day, the original sense of *derekh 'eretz* is preserved in *Tanna de-bei Eliyahu*. If we can free ourselves of our *idées fixes* regarding the sages, I am confident we will find texts that employ the original sense of *derekh 'eretz*, as well as instances where the meaning has been constrained, but not to the extent that we find today.

17. Martyrology in the Second Temple Period and Early Christianity

Martyrdom is, of course, an important concept throughout Jewish history, but Second Temple martyrology is particularly important for western religious history, most notably for Christianity, which grew out of Judaism. Second Temple martyrology influenced Christianity in two primary ways: in shaping the narrative of the death of Jesus, perhaps the defining element of the religion as a whole, and in the later Christian martyr traditions.

Second Temple martyrological tales are preserved in various sources, including but not limited to the literature of the Sages. As we will see, there are times that rabbinic sources provide only meager information while other Second Temple texts are quite rich. The sources in question first appear in the Hasmonean period, which was — in view of the decrees of Antiochus — a time of suffering and martyrdom. The best-known tale, which appears in 2 Maccabees, is that of the mother (named Hannah in later Jewish traditions) and her seven sons. The story tells of the seven sons consoling each other and their mother, saying, "The Lord God is watching over us and in truth has compassion on us, as Moses declared in his song 'And he will have compassion on his servants' (Deut 32:36)" (2 Macc 7.6). Later, the seventh son states: "I . . . give up body and life . . . appealing to God . . . through me and my brothers to bring to an end the wrath of the Almighty that has justly fallen on our whole nation" (2 Macc 7.37-38). Already there, then, we find the idea of the martyr's death ending God's wrath, as the seventh son states: "If our living Lord is angry for a little while, to rebuke and discipline us, he will again be reconciled with his own servants" (7.33). Clearly, then, the verse "And he will have compassion on his servants" was interpreted as a reference to martyr-

248

dom in the Hasmonean period. God will have compassion on his servants because of the death of the holy ones, that is, of those who chose to martyr themselves.

In the rabbinic sources, martyrdom is linked with another verse, namely "For he will avenge the blood of his children, and take vengeance on his adversaries; he will repay those who hate him, and cleanse the land for his people" (Deut 32:43). The Sifre Deuteronomy glosses this verse as follows: "Whence do we learn that when Israelites are slain by the nations of the world, it serves them as expiation in the world to come? From the verses, 'A psalm of Asaph: O God, the nations have come into your inheritance, they have defiled your holy temple . . . the flesh of your faithful to the wild animals of the earth, they have poured out their blood like water' (Psalm 79:1-3)." Interestingly, this verse from Psalms (and others) was linked already in Hasmonean times to martyrdom. When the high priest Alcimus executed a large number of Hasidim, 1 Maccabees (7.17) ties their death to Psalm 79, "The flesh of your faithful ones and their blood they poured out all around Jerusalem, and there was no one to bury them." The citation is not completely accurate, but it stands to reason that the Hasmoneans linked the verse cited by the Sifre to martyrdom.

The Sifre passage just cited is important because it contains the idea that the death of Jews at the hands of gentiles atones for Israel as a whole. This is, then, a variant on the idea of atonement through the death of holy ones, which became so crucial to medieval Jewish traditions and to the passion narrative — the death of the martyr atones for the sins of the nation. Another relevant source is the apocryphal "Testament of Moses," which received its current form in the early first century c.e., but, as Licht has argued convincingly, was composed in the early Hasmonean times, perhaps during the reign of Antiochus.[1] In chapter 9 of the "Testament of Moses," we learn of a mysterious figure, whose precise nature and identity have eluded scholars, one Taxo who hails from the tribe of Levi, who lived with his sons during a time of persecution (much like that of Antiochus). Taxo asks his sons:

> which nation or which province or which people, who have done many crimes against the Lord, have suffered such evils as have covered us? Now, therefore sons, heed me. If you investigate, you will surely know that never did our fathers nor their ancestors tempt God by transgressing his commandments. Yea, you will surely know that this is our strength. Here is what we shall do. We shall fast for a three-day period and on the fourth

---

1. J. Licht, "Taxo or the Apocalyptic Doctrine of Vengeance," *Journal of Jewish Studies* 12 (1961), 95-103.

day we shall go into a cave, which is in the open country. There let us die rather than transgress the commandments of the Lord, the God of our fathers. For if we do this, and do die, our blood will be avenged by the Lord. (Test. Moses 9.3-7)

We do not know what happened to Taxo and his sons — whether they entered into the cave after purifying themselves with a three-day fast, or were martyred by Israel's enemies. Either way, the tenth chapter of the "Testament of Moses" contains a hymn to the messianic age, which begins: "Then his kingdom will appear through his whole creation" (Test. Moses 10.1). The kingdom of heaven will be established on earth as a result of martyrdom, in this case, the martyrdom — or at least willingness for martyrdom — of Taxo and his sons. It should be noted that even the New Testament does not connect the death of Jesus and the kingdom of heaven so explicitly.

We turn now to the Dead Sea Scrolls, which were by scholarly consensus composed by the Essenes. Now, it is hard to imagine that the Essenes, as we know them from the writings of Josephus and other sources, could have esteemed martyrdom so highly. The Essenes believed in predestination and understood themselves to be God's elect, the Sons of Light. As such, they do not need to atone for their sins or for the sins of others (by death or otherwise). Still, the idea of suffering — and perhaps death too — as a positive religious category, was important to the Essenes. After all, we know how joyously they greeted their own death at the hands of the Romans, and how willing they were to martyr themselves. The apocryphal "Ascension of Isaiah" writes of Isaiah's martyrdom, and I have already argued elsewhere that it was composed in the same circles that produced the Qumran scrolls.[2] If so, the idea of a joyful and dignified death, of death that is transformed into a positive act, of a martyr's death, was apparently important to the Essenes. Though the Essene sources say little on this topic — at least as far as we have found up to this point — there is reference to the religious importance of suffering during times of persecution. One particularly interesting passage occurs in column 17 of the Hodayot, where we find "I have chosen my judgment, I have been pleased with my affliction" (line 10), "in the face of affliction you have upheld my spirit" (line 12), and "your rebuke has been changed into happiness and joy for me, my diseases into everlasting healing and unending [. . .], the scoffing of my rival into a crown of glory for me, and my weakness into everlasting strength" (lines 24-25).

2. D. Flusser, "The Apocryphal Book of *Ascensio Isaiae* and the Dead Sea Sect," *Israel Exploration Journal* 3 (1953), 30-47.

These statements reflect a deep desire to valorize religious suffering and persecution, to transform them into a positive value, a desideratum. We find a similar view in the sayings of Jesus (e.g., Matt 5:10-11, and see also Testament of Judah 25.4) and in Judaism more broadly, which knew much suffering. This may not be martyrdom in the strict sense, but it is similar.

Let us examine the last passage more closely: "the scoffing of my rival [has been changed] into a crown of glory for me." The phrase "crown of glory" refers here to a crown that is, figuratively, placed on the head of the suffering. That is, the act of suffering crowns the Essene like a diadem in the time of persecution. The Babylonian Talmud refers to life after death as "The righteous with crowns on their heads" (b. Berakhot 17a), though this in no way refers to martyrdom but rather to a diadem that crowns the righteous after their death. The same idea appears in Essene literature, namely, when 1QS speaks of the happiness that will be the lot of the righteous after their death, as they will be given "a crown of glory with majestic raiment in eternal light" (1QS 4.7-8). The righteous, then, will bear a diadem on their heads and be dressed in majestic garments (1QS here alludes to Psalm 8:5: "You have . . . crowned them with glory and honor"). The motif of "heavenly vestments" appears in other contemporary Jewish and Christian sources. Is the diadem merely a crown for the righteous, or is it akin to the halos that adorn the Christian saints? The halo or aureole has its origins in the ancient Near East, but it is quite likely that the motif passed through Jewish sources. After all, the Eighteen Benedictions recited on Saturday morning invoke Moses descending from Sinai "and you set a crown of glory on his head" — evidently an allusion to the light radiating from his face. It appears, then, that the saints' aureole is attested here, at least with regard to Moses. It stands to reason, then, that the "crown of glory" of the Essene saints — the aureole that will rest on the saints in the end of days — passed from the Jewish world to the Christian. True, Christian iconography tends to represent martyred saints as adorned with laurels, but that is a topic for another discussion.

We turn now to a number of passages from the New Testament, the most important of which is, "And when the chief shepherd appears, you will win the crown of glory that never fades away" (1 Pet 5:4). As with the two Dead Sea Scrolls passages, the "crown of glory" will adorn the heads of faithful Christians in the end of days. Similarly in Revelation 2:10: "Do not fear what you are about to suffer . . . be faithful until death, and I will give you the crown of life." This "crown of life" is undoubtedly the reward of the first Christian martyrs after their death.[3] The martyr's crown motif was no doubt influenced by the

3. See also 1 Thess 2:19 and 2 Tim 4:8.

laurels worn by athletes in antiquity (a theme that appears in 1 Corinthians 9:25). The "crown of glory" incorporates two motifs — suffering and martyrdom, on the one hand, and athletic victory, on the other. It is no surprise, then, that early Christian sources refer to martyrs also as "athletes."

For the Essenes, then, suffering and degradation in times of persecution is a badge of honor, and the phrase "crown of glory" appears in reference to the life the righteous experience after their earthly death, in a sense very similar to that of the New Testament. Since the New Testament ties the laurel or the aureole — the light of sanctity — with the willingness of the earliest Christians to die for their faith, it may be that the motif ultimately derives from Jewish sources.

Another Qumran text — which may play a key role in the evolution of later Christian martyrology — suggests that the martyred individual atones for the sins of the faithful. The text in question is the War Scroll, which discusses the imminent death of a number of Sons of Light in the eschatological battle: "the priests shall continue blowing the trumpets of the slain, in order that the battle against the Kittim is directed" (1QM 16.9). The death of these righteous warriors, then, serves as a test of sorts, an idea that is tied to martyrological motifs in both Jewish and Christian sources. In the War Scroll, the chief priest exhorts the community after it has suffered these losses in battle. The words of the priest are poorly preserved, but the extant fragments give us a clear idea of the force of his words: "The High Priest will approach and take up position in front of the line, and will strengthen their hearts" (1QM 16.13-14), and will speak of "those tested in the crucible" (1QM 17.1). The idea that suffering purifies appears elsewhere in the Dead Sea Scrolls, and is a core theological belief of the community. The idea of purification through suffering also appears in the New Testament, e.g., in 1 Peter: "In this you rejoice, even if now for a little while you have had to suffer various trials, so that the genuineness of your faith — being more precious than gold that, though perishable, is tested by fire — may be found to result in praise and glory and honor" (1:6-7). To be sure, this passage refers only to the suffering of the righteous, not their death, and the suffering in question is not even said to be the result of persecution. Nonetheless, the passage is important both for its reference to being tested by fire, like gold, and for the alluded-to idea that the righteous are accepted by God as a well-being offering *(shalem)*. Here lies the nexus between the notions of sacrifice and of the suffering and death of the righteous.

Returning to the War Scroll passage, we find the priest further exhorting the community: "And you, remember the trial of Nadab and Abihu, sons of Aaron; by judging them God showed his holiness to the eyes of all the people, and Eleazar and Ithamar he confirmed for the covenant of an everlasting priesthood" (1QM 17.3). The death of Aaron's two sons at the dedication of the tabernacle, before the eyes of the entire community, is linked to the death of the members of the community in the final, eschatological war — a war whose very purpose is to purify the sect's members for the end of days. According to Leviticus 10:1-6, Nadab and Abihu approached the Tent of Meeting bearing a foreign fire, and a fire came out from before God and consumed them: "Then Moses said to Aaron, 'This is what the Lord meant when he said, "Through those who are near me I will be sanctified, and before all the people I will be glorified."' And Aaron was silent" (Lev 10:3). In terms of the biblical narrative, Moses' statement is presented as a citation of words that do not appear anywhere else, a citation in poetic form. It may be, then, that the original description of the death of Nadab and Abihu was different from what appears in the Torah today. It is at least possible that the original account had the fire burning the sons of Aaron as a sacrifice of sorts, through which God was sanctified. The Sages come close to such an understanding on a number of occasions, representing the death of Aaron's sons as a form of sacrifice. The Sifra, discussing this passage, states: "Aaron stood wondering to himself, saying 'Woe is me that I have thus transgressed and that my sons have thus transgressed that you have thus rebuked me.' Moses came to him and consoled him, saying, 'Aaron, my brother, I was told at Sinai: I will sanctify the tabernacle through a man greater than me or you, and through them was the tabernacle sanctified.'" Another version of the same midrash is then cited: "Moses said: 'thus God said, "through those who are near me I will be sanctified"'. This statement was made to Moses at Sinai and they did not understand it until the event occurred. Since the event occurred, Moses said to him: 'Aaron, my brother, your sons died for the sanctity of God's name, as it is said, "I will meet the Israelites there, and it shall be sanctified by my glory" (Exod 29:43).' Since Aaron realized that his sons were known by God, he was silent and received reward for his silence."

It appears, then, that the Sages understood the death of Nadab and Abihu as a type of martyrology. Indeed, the midrash to the verse "through those who are near me I will be sanctified" states that Aaron's sons died "for the sanctity of God's name" — very possibly the source for קידוש השם, the Hebrew term for martyrdom. In any case, I see no reason not to interpret the War Scroll in accordance with the rabbinic understanding of the death of Nadab and Abihu, i.e., as a type of sacrifice that represents an act of martyrdom. If this interpretation is correct, the death of Nadab and Abihu alludes to human sacrifice and was later interpreted along martyrological lines. Another example of this phenomenon is the binding of Isaac, which was interpreted as early as the Church Fathers as prefiguring Christ's death on the cross.

There may also have been another type of martyrological narratives in Second Temple times, namely the recurring discussion (both within and without rabbinic literature) of the death of the prophets. It is not clear why exactly the death of the prophets became such a central motif in certain Second Temple circles — prophets who were killed by their own people, unlike, say, the kings who were killed by foreign powers. Matthew, for example, states: "Woe to you, scribes and Pharisees, hypocrites! For you build the tombs of the prophets and decorate the graves of the righteous, and you say, 'If we had lived in the days of our ancestors, we would not have taken part with them in shedding the blood of the prophets'" (Matt 23:29-30). As scholars have noted, this passage suggests it was customary in the time of Jesus to build graves and tombstones to righteous men from the past, a possible indication that Christian adoration of saints was ultimately a Jewish practice.[4] Among those venerated by the Jews were individuals who had died a martyr's death. We know of a site in Antioch dedicated to the mother and her seven children who died during the Hasmonean period. The site later came under Christian control, and they continued to venerate it and even canonized the Jews killed in the Antiochean persecutions. (The Catholic Church celebrates the "deeds of the holy Maccabees" on August 1st.)[5] Matthew 23 also suggests that the ancient persecutions and killings of the biblical prophets were a common topic, particularly that their death was at the hands of Jews. This is the central theme of a short work composed toward the end of the Second Temple or perhaps shortly after 70 and preserved in Greek, *The Lives of the Prophets*. The killing of the prophets is also mentioned in 1 Enoch 89.51-53, which emphasizes that of all the prophets sent by God only one, Elijah, survived. The same motif is reflected in Jesus' cry "Jerusalem, Jerusalem, the city that kills the prophets and stones those who are sent to it!" (Matt 23:37). The prophetic context of this statement is highlighted by what comes before it according to both Matthew and Luke: "I will send them prophets and apostles, some of whom they will kill and persecute, so that this generation may be charged with the blood of all the prophets shed since the foundation of the world, from the blood of Abel to the blood of Zechariah, who perished between the altar and the sanctuary" (Luke 11:49-51, and see Matt 23:34-36). The figure of Zechariah is here a composite of the biblical prophet and another Zechariah who was killed toward the end of the Second Temple period. Zech-

---

4. Th. Klauser, *Christlicher Märtyrerkult, heidnischer Heroenkult und spätjüdische Heiligenverehrung* (Cologne, 1960).

5. See Y. Gutman, "The Mother and her Seven Sons" (Hebrew), *Yochanan Lewy Festschrift* (Jerusalem, 1949), 36-37.

ariah appears quite often in rabbinic sources, and there are a number of studies devoted to this topic.[6] Interestingly, Jesus' statement in Luke appears to be a citation from a sapiential text, and there is in fact a close parallel in Jubilees: "And I shall send to them witnesses so that I might witness to them, but they will not hear. And they will even kill the witnesses, and they will persecute those who search out the Torah" (Jub 1.12). These texts are all referring to the biblical prophets, though there may be some allusions to post-prophetic Second Temple figures, or perhaps the more contemporary apocalyptic seers.

It is particularly interesting that so many texts refer to the death of Isaiah, including the "Ascension of Isaiah" discussed above. The Talmud too recounts Isaiah's death at the hands of Menasseh,[7] e.g. in b. Yebamot 49b. Why Isaiah? Apparently because Isaiah 53 was interpreted during the Second Temple Period as referring to the death of the prophet himself. Acts 8 speaks of an Ethiopian eunuch who reads Isaiah 53:7-8 and asks the Christian Philip, "'About whom, may I ask you, does the prophet say this, about himself or about someone else?' Then Philip began to speak, and starting with this scripture, he proclaimed to him the good news about Jesus" (Acts 8:34-35). The passage teaches us two things: that there were those who interpreted chapter 53 as referring to Isaiah, greatly increasing the fame of Isaiah's putative death, and that this is perhaps the earliest testimony to a Christian interpretation of this famous chapter as speaking of the death of Christ. Though it is generally understood as an Old Testament proof for the Christian beliefs, scholars have shown that Isaiah 53 was not interpreted thus by Jesus or Paul or John, but only by Luke in his Acts of the Apostles and in 1 Peter (2:22-24).

To summarize our findings thus far, beginning with the time of the Antiochean persecutions, we find a wide array of Jewish sources that deal with martyrdom, as well as suffering understood as a type of purification. The death of the righteous at the hands of the nations of the world serves as atonement for Israel, a motif already evident in 2 Maccabees, in the story of the mother and her seven sons. If the "Testament of Moses" was in fact written early in the Hasmonean period, as Licht surmises, it is an early witness to the idea that the atoning death has eschatological overtones, since the death of the righteous man and his sons hastens the ultimate salvation. Another motif, attested in the Essene War Scroll and rabbinic discussions of the

---

6. S. Blank, "The Death of Zechariah in Rabbinic Literature," *HUCA* 12-13 (1937-1938), 327; B. Marmelstein, "The Aggadah concerning the Blood of Zechariah" (Hebrew), *Shmuel Krauss Festschrift* (Jerusalem, 1937), 161. Neither Luke 11:51 nor Matthew 23:35 suggests knowledge of the later Zechariah's death, which occurred after the death of Jesus. Rather, they are based on 2 Chronicles 24:20-25.

7. See L. Ginzberg, *The Legends of the Jews* (Philadelphia, 1946), 4.279, 371, 374-375.

strange death of Nadab and Abihu, is that of the sacrifice — another Second Temple motif that would enjoy prominence in later Christian writings. Moreover, we saw how widespread the view was that transgressing Jews had killed the biblical prophets.

As for early Christianity itself, in 1 Peter we find: "For Christ also suffered for sins once for all, the righteous for the unrighteous, in order to bring you to God. He was put to death in the flesh, but made alive in the spirit" (1 Pet 3:18). This is a very archaic formulation of the notion of Jesus' death atoning for the sins of others; Jesus is called "the righteous," and his death at the hands of the wicked was intended to draw the faithful toward God. It is interesting that the New Testament itself does not emphasize the Romans' role in Jesus' death. The reason for this is clear — so as not to dissuade the gentile worlds from the new belief. It is true that Luke 18:32 (and parallels) states that Jesus will be handed over to the nations, but this is hardly the emphasis of the New Testament. Compare Romans 4:25, which describes Christ as being "handed over to death for our trespasses and . . . raised for our justification," a statement that, according to Bultmann, derives from the Jerusalem church.[8] It is clear that the phrase "handed over" is part of the primitive tradition, but Paul does not specify to whom he was handed over (though it was clearly to the Romans). The hypothetical statement of the early Jerusalem church, then, likely expressed the idea that Jesus was handed over to the gentiles for Israel's transgressions, and was resurrected to atone for Israel's sins — even though Paul (for obvious reasons) chooses not to say this explicitly. The motif of the death of the prophets is also picked up in the New Testament's representation of the death of Jesus, who is repeatedly identified as an eschatological prophet. According to Luke, Jesus goes to Jerusalem "because it is impossible for a prophet to be killed away from Jerusalem" (Luke 13:33). Whether this dictum was spoken by Jesus, it serves to emphasize that his death in Jerusalem was only the last of a long series of prophets' deaths in the city that slays its prophets.

Still and all, these are motifs that eventually became uniquely Christian, first and foremost in the Christian belief in the resurrection of Christ. Here the drama of the death of the righteous man ends favorably and serves as a justification of his death and as proof of his ability to overcome the sins of the believers who caused his death. Furthermore, Jesus and his disciples believed that Jesus himself was the messiah. From the outset, then, the motif of the death of the righteous at the hands of the nations was linked with messianic motifs. That is, the church had to believe from the very beginning that the

8. R. Bultmann, *Theologie des Neuen Testaments* (Tübingen, 1958), 49.

Messiah must come into the world only in order to die. This strengthened the belief in Jesus' atoning death, and the death of the savior for the sins of the believers became a core element of Christianity itself. But while Judaism has emphasized the atoning power of martyrdom, Christianity cannot allow its martyrs to have died for the sins of the collective. Rather, martyrdom for the sins of the faithful is appropriated by the death of Jesus. Christian martyrdom, as a result, was not about atonement for the community as such, but more about following in the footsteps of Jesus.

Be all that as it may, we have seen the key significance of early Jewish motifs in formative Christian martyrology, even as these elements were eventually transformed and became constitutive of Christianity. But within the Jewish context too, martyrology has maintained its central place even to this day, providing hope that the deaths of those who have sanctified God's name have not been in vain.

18. Jewish Messianism Reflected in the Early Church

Christianity was originally a Jewish messianic movement. Even when it separated from Judaism, changed its structure and became an independent religion, the Jewish messianic ideas within it continued their independent life within the church, sometimes with their original nature essentially unchanged. Early Christian sources are, thus, of utmost importance for the study of the variety of Jewish messianic beliefs in Second Temple times, just as familiarity with Jewish messianism is a *sine qua non* for a proper understanding of the early church. The present article will provide a general survey of the question, focusing on two main goals: to indicate the Jewish elements of Christian messianism, and to use the New Testament to demonstrate the variety of Jewish messianic beliefs. The study deals primarily with messianic figures, rather than the full spectrum of apocalyptic and eschatological beliefs.

Let us begin with Jesus himself, whose personality is reflected in the Synoptic Gospels. These Gospels were written in Greek and the early material in them reworked in different ways, making it difficult to reconstruct the original Hebrew traditions. Still, even if we had these traditions, they would not provide us with direct access to Jesus' self-consciousness, since they reflect, first and foremost, the understanding of Jesus' Jewish disciples, who remained faithful to their teacher after his death. Their faith in Jesus' messianic status underwent a deep crisis after his crucifixion, a crisis they overcame by means of their belief in his resurrection on the third day. Even if we ignore the later reworking in the Gospels and retrieve the earlier Hebrew sources, we are faced with an admixture of three elements: Jesus' own belief, the belief of his disciples prior to his death, and the belief of the disciples after the crucifixion and the ensuing crisis. My research in this field suggests that it is indeed possible to distinguish between the three, though for the present purposes the distinction is less important since we are not concerned with the personal beliefs of Jesus or his students, but rather with messianic motifs in early Christianity. We need only note that the belief in Jesus' atoning death is part and parcel of Jewish martyrology rather than messianism proper. Even in the New Testament Jesus' crucifixion does not serve as proof of his messianism: at most, the authors argue that the execution does not contradict the claim to Jesus' messianic status.

One of the core elements in Jesus' own belief system was his faith that the kingdom of heaven is manifesting itself and that he and his teachings play an important role in this process.[1] For Jesus, the phrase "kingdom of heaven" served as a buffer against the ideology of the zealots, and in this regard Jesus and the anti-Roman sages were in full agreement. The zealots (along with apocalyptic thinkers) believed that the kingdom of heaven would reveal itself in the end of days, and that God's reign would commence only after Israel had rid itself of the yoke of Rome. Against this view, there were those including Rabbi Yohanan ben Zakkai (and other sages) and Jesus, who believed that God already rules over the world and that the establishment of the kingdom of heaven on earth is not a future event following a revolt against Rome, but a present event that hinges on the Jewish people's moral virtue. If Israel would but accept the yoke of the kingdom of heaven in this sense, no foreign nation could vanquish it. Everything we know of Jesus' understanding of the kingdom of heaven accords with the view of those rabbinic sages — indeed, the phrase "kingdom of heaven" was coined by the sages.[2] As for the Dead Sea Scrolls, they contain extended discourses on the kingdoms of light and darkness, the latter to be destroyed in the end of days, but no mention of the kingdom of heaven in the sense used by the sages and Jesus.[3] The main difference

1. This is not the place to discuss the important question of Jesus' "time table" for the redemption process. On the role of the kingdom of heaven in Jesus' teachings, see D. Flusser, *Jesus* (Hamburg, 1968), 81-98. On the redemptive time table see my *Die rabbinischen Gleichnisse und der Gleichniserzähler Jesus* (Bern, 1981), 269-273. I hope to deal with this question more fully in the next volume of this work.

2. We first encounter the concept (though not the precise phrase) of the kingdom of heaven in "Testament of Moses" (beginning of chapter 10): "Then his kingdom will appear through his whole creation." Similar phrases are found, inter alia, in the targumim. The political sense of "kingdom of heaven" may have been an innovation of the zealots: either the kingdom of heaven or the kingdom of Rome! If this is, in fact, the case, the phrase was adopted by those opposed to the zealots as a counter measure. This suggestion must, however, remain hypothetical as none of the writings of the zealots are extant.

3. Matthew gives the impression that already John the Baptist knew the phrase "kingdom

between the rabbis and Jesus regarding this idea is the following: though the rabbis believed the kingdom of heaven would spread as more and more people accepted its yoke, they believed that God governs the world since time immemorial. Jesus, however, introduced an element of dynamism, according to which the manifestation of the kingdom of heaven in the social and political sphere is a dynamic process that began with the mission of John the Baptist. "From the days of John the Baptist until now[4] the kingdom of heaven has burst forth,[5] and those who break out take it by force" (Matt 11:12).[6] Jesus does not think that John the Baptist belongs to the era of the kingdom of heaven, for "among those born of women no one has arisen greater than John the Baptist;[7] yet the least in the kingdom of heaven is greater than he" (Matt 11:11). John, then, represents the termination of the earlier era, and from his arrival on the kingdom of heaven bursts forth.

Jesus expects a super-human judge, whom he calls "the Son of Man," to appear in the end of days, but this is a separate eschatological event, not causally related to the realization of the kingdom of heaven.[8] Jesus himself emphasizes that the Son of Man will appear suddenly, when no one expects it; according to the Synoptic Gospels, his arrival will be preceded by stunning

---

of heaven," and that Jesus received it from John, but this is particular to the Matthean text (3:2; 4:17), and one of several instances in which Matthew asserts a proximity between the dicta of Jesus and John. The other Gospels do not attribute this phrase to John, most probably rightly so. John the Baptist was aligned with the Essenes (see David Flusser, "John's Baptism and the Qumran Sect" [Hebrew], in *Judaism and the Origins of Christianity* [Jerusalem, 1982], 81-112). The kingdom of heaven theology does not fit with the Essene worldview, so it is unlikely that John the Baptist would have employed the phrase.

4. The words "until now" may be a Matthean addition.

5. For this translation, see the LXX to 2 Sam 13:28, and 2 Kings 5:23. For a linguistic analysis see A. Deissmann, *Neue Bibelstudien* (Marburg, 1897), 85-86. The correct interpretation was already recognized by E. Meyer, *Ursprung und Anfänge des Christentums* (Stuttgart, 1924), 1.86-87.

6. The entire passage (Matt 11:9-14) merits discussion. Jesus interprets Malachi 3:1 as referring to John the Baptist, saying: "and if you are willing to accept it, he is Elijah who is to come" (Matt 11:14), alluding to the connection between Malachi 3:1 and Micah 2:13, where Elijah is mentioned explicitly. It appears, then, that Matthew 11:12 is a midrash to Micah 2:13 (which is, in turn, quite similar to Malachi 3:1). Rabbi David Kimchi, in his commentary to this verse, states: "'The one who breaks out' refers to Elijah, and 'their king' to the shoot of David." Micah 2:13 is interpreted as a reference to Elijah also in Pesiktah Rabbati 35 (161a in the Friedmann edition). See Flusser, *Jesus*, 40, and A. Wiener, *The Prophet Elijah* (London, 1978), 65-66.

7. Here Jesus alludes to Deuteronomy 34:10: "Never since has there arisen a prophet in Israel like Moses." The phrase "born of woman" may be a reference to the midrash according to which the angels were upset that Moses, a mortal born of woman, received the Torah.

8. See P. Vielhauer, "Gottesreich und Menschensohn," *Aufsätze zum Neuen Testament* (Munich, 1965), 55-91.

cosmic events (Luke 21:25-27 and parallels). For Jesus, then, there cannot be a causal relationship between the kingdom of heaven and the eschatological appearance of the Son of Man.[9]

Let us begin with the figure of the Son of Man in the Jewish sources.[10] In the Bible there is a single occurrence of the epithet, in Daniel 7:13, a book that does not recognize a personal messianic figure, even though its author was surely familiar with this view. It is not surprising, then, that the book contains two symbols of the Messiah, but only in visions. The first in Nebuchadnezzar's dream, when the king sees the statue destroyed by a stone that Daniel interprets as "a kingdom that shall never be destroyed, nor shall this kingdom be left to another people. It shall crush all these kingdoms and bring them to an end, and it shall stand for ever" (Dan 2:44). So while in other

---

9. As we will see, the Son of Man is identified in many Jewish sources with the Messiah and this was almost certainly Jesus' view as well. All this makes Vielhauer's view ("Gottesreich und Menschensohn," 87), that rabbinic literature does not connect the kingdom of heaven and the advent of the Messiah, that much more interesting.

10. In the Gospels, Son of Man designates not only the eschatological judge, but also Jesus who lives or who is destined to die on the cross. The present study is concerned only with the eschatological sense. Outside of the Gospels, the phrase appears only four times: Revelation 1:13 and 14:14; Hebrews 2:6; and Acts 7:56, in Stephen's words prior to his death. We see, then, that the phrase does not play a meaningful role in the development of Christian doctrine outside of the immediate circle of Jesus' disciples and their followers. Reference to Jesus as the Son of Man is attested in the words of the Jewish-Christian historian Hegesippus, as cited in Eusebius (*Ecclesiastical History* 2.23.13) in the story of the death of James, the brother of Jesus. His words are similar to those of Stephen prior to his death (Acts 7:56) and to those of Jesus (Luke 22:69 and parallels). Jesus is also called Son of Man by Jerome (*Illustrious Men,* chapter 2), in a passage from the apocryphal *Gospel according to the Hebrews*. There too the Son of Man reference is tied to James, the hero of the Jewish-Christians. The reason the epithet "Son of Man" was marginalized so thoroughly in the early church, is that its original meaning was lost and it became incomprehensible. Moreover, it was understood literally: Jesus is the son of a human being. When the church began to emphasize the divinity of Christ, there emerged a tension between the "Son of Man" and the "Son of God." Already Ignatius of Antioch (died in 107 C.E.) writes in his epistle to the Ephesians of the belief in Jesus "who is, according to the flesh, from the family of David, the Son of Man and the Son of God" (20.2). This odd approach is reflected in the epistle attributed to Barnabas, which was composed in the early second century (12.10-11). There too we find a reference to Jesus' origin from the House of David, followed by the assertion that Jesus is not the Son of Man but the Son of God! Even though in the Jewish sources and in Jesus' dicta Son of Man refers to a superhuman entity, the term became suspect in the early church. On Son of Man in the Book of Daniel see K. Koch, *Das Buch Daniel* (Darmstadt, 1980), 216-234. On the קדישי עליונין, "the holy ones of the Most High" (Dan 7:18, 25), see pages 234-239, which discuss the view that they are angels. See also P. J. Kobelski, *Melchizedek and Melchiresa* (Washington, 1981), 130-137, who argues that Son of Man was not an eschatological term in Second Temple Judaism.

Jewish sources the stone appears as a messianic symbol, Daniel does not interpret it as an individual figure. The second vision is of the four beasts and their judgment, in chapter 7: "As I watched in the night visions, I saw one like a human being coming with the clouds of heaven. And he came to the Ancient One and was presented before him. To him was given dominion and glory and kingship, that all peoples, nations, and languages should serve him" (Dan 7:13-14). According to Daniel's interpretation, this refers to the heavenly judgment over the four kingdoms, while the Son of Man figure is "the holy ones of the Most High," i.e., Israel. As we shall see, this figure does not participate in the judgment, as it is a collective entity — the Jewish people — that will be granted kingship after the judgment.

As the above discussion indicates, the Son of Man figure likely preceded the Book of Daniel, as it appears there in a secondary role. Other Jewish sources affirm this hypothesis, for while they are often influenced by the Son of Man passages in Daniel, they nonetheless assume their readers' familiarity with the figure. What has not been properly appreciated is that in Daniel itself, the Son of Man is only a visionary symbol for Israel itself. 1 Enoch contains a Jewish composition that apparently dates to Herod's reign, in which the Son of Man plays an important role (chapters 37–61).[11] This text preserves the tradition that understands the Son of Man as an actual figure that will appear in the eschaton (though the work has apparently been influenced, indirectly, by Daniel, since it too juxtaposes the Son of Man and the Ancient of Days). The Son of Man is a sublime figure, towering above the angels and preceding the creation of the world, a hidden figure that will only appear in the end of days. During the eschatological drama, the Son of Man is charged with revealing God's secrets, and with sitting on the throne of God's glory and meting out justice in the eschatological judgment. The angels too will play a role in this process, at the end of which the righteous will receive their reward, while the wicked — including the wicked kings and rulers, will be eternally damned.

Roughly the same event is described in 4 Ezra, which was composed some thirty years after the destruction of the Second Temple. Chapter thirteen of that book describes a vision of a "figure of a man" (13.3) who flies with the clouds of heaven. Here the influence of Daniel on 4 Ezra is evident; however, it is worth noting that 4 Ezra refers to the *figure* of a man and not an actual Son

---

11. See the discussion in Vielhauer, "Gottesreich und Menschensohn," 80-87. There are no extant remains from this composition among the Qumran scrolls, a fact that has led some scholars to the conclusion that it is a later, Christian composition, even though it contains no Christological elements. See the statements made in my name, inter alia, by Jonas Greenfeld in his introduction to *3 Enoch*, ed. H. Odeberg (New York, 1973), xvi-xvii.

of Man. Like chapter 7 of Daniel, there is an incongruity between the 4 Ezra vision and its interpretation, which follows. On the one hand, 4 Ezra tends to interpret the vision allegorically (e.g., chapter 13). On the other, the interpretation does mention important apocalyptic details that have no counterpart in the vision. All this makes 4 Ezra's vision and subsequent interpretation very important in mapping out the apocalyptic traditions concerning the Son of Man that were known to 4 Ezra's author. The text emphasizes the bellicose nature of the Son of Man: He defeats a horde of enemies when "he sent forth from his mouth as it were a stream of fire, and from his lips a flaming breath, and from his tongue he shot forth a storm of sparks" (13.10), burning the attacking enemies. Only in the last two verses of the vision (13.10-11) is there a possible hint to the judgment that will follow the supernatural victory of the Son of Man.[12] The Son of Man, then, is associated primarily with the role of the משיח מלחמה, that war Messiah, that is, the anointed priest who strengthens the nation's spirit in times of war. The interpretation of the vision, in contrast, indicates that, as in Enoch,[13] this "man" was often watched over by God (4 Ezra 13.26). Moreover, in what follows there is explicit reference to his role as an eschatological judge (13.37-38), without the vagueness of the vision (13.13).[14]

In the Testament of Abraham (chapters 12–13),[15] we find another reference to the Son of Man as eschatological judge: a wondrous man-like figure, seating on a wondrous throne,[16] who judges the souls of all humans. The an-

---

12. The vision belongs to the same tradition as the Dream Visions of 1 Enoch (chapters 63–90), which begin with victory over the evil nations (90.19), followed by judgment (90.20 and following). There, however, it is God alone that sits in judgment. 4 Ezra 13, then, constitutes an independent apocalyptic tradition. The tradition concerning the burning of the enemies by the breath of the Messiah (4 Ezra 13.10-11) is alluded to in 2 Thessalonians (2:8), and see also Revelation 19:15. The entire group appears to be a later development of Isaiah 31:4 and 49:2 ("he made my mouth like a sharp sword"). See also Revelation 11:5!

13. At the end of the vision (13.12) are hints of the return of the ten lost tribes, a process set to begin after the defeat of the enemies, as noted in the interpretation of the vision (13.39-59). The 1 Enoch composition that mentions the Son of Man also juxtaposes these two events: the attack of enemies from the east that Jerusalem ultimately withstands (26.5-8), and the return of the ten tribes from the east (chapter 57).

14. According to the sages, the name of the Messiah was created during the creation of the world, a view shared by the early Christian view reflected in the Pauline epistles and in Revelation (1.1) — where God is understood to have created the world with the aid of Christ.

15. See M. Stone (ed.), *The Testament of Abraham* (New York, 1972). The first version is a Jewish composition that was later reworked by a Christian hand.

16. The Greek manuscripts of the Testament of Abraham state that he is "like the son of God," but this is a late corruption. Not only does Revelation state that he is "like the son of man" (1:13; 14:14), but later in the Testament of Abraham the judge is identified with Abel, the son of Adam. (But see Daniel 3:25: "but the fourth has the appearance of the son of God.")

gel at his right records the acts of righteousness performed by those who stand in judgment, while the angel on his left records their sins. The judge himself is none other than the son of Adam, referred to as "Abel," who was killed by the wicked Cain. He has been installed as judge because God wanted every man to be judged by a human being. This is fascinating description for understanding the term "Son of Man." Though the work is extant in Greek, the identification of the "Son of Man" with everyone suggests that the Aramaic בר אנש is in no way preferable to the Hebrew בן אדם (which latter appears to be the form that underlies the Testament of Abraham), particularly when we note that in 4 Ezra the figure is called אדם.

If Jesus spoke of this figure in Hebrew, he referred to it as בן אדם. This suggests that the superhuman eschatological judge of Daniel is, as argued above, secondary: a purely symbolic figure that was taken over by Daniel from other sources. The Testament of Abraham further suggests that this is not necessarily a messianic figure, since בן אדם is identified with Abel, the first "son of Adam (= son of man)." In 1 Enoch, the figure was probably referred to as בר אנש, assuming this work was composed in Aramaic, or, if in Hebrew (as is more likely), בן אדם. In one verse (71.14) the Son of Man is identified with Enoch, and twice (48.10 and 52.4) with the Messiah — though these are likely passing references.

Two significant points have emerged: that the image of the mighty eschatological judge is called אדם or בן אדם, and that it is identified with a wide array of figures — Enoch, Abel (literally בן אדם, the "son of Adam") — and not only the Messiah. It is likely, then, that the figure of the Son of Man grew out of an independent eschatological tradition, unrelated to the traditional belief in the Messiah. Note also that Daniel speaks of one "like the Son of Man," and the Testament of Abraham, Revelation (1:13), and the first mention in 4 Ezra all speak of one who is "similar to the Son of Man." It seems to me that 1 Enoch also indicates the biblical prooftext for this figure. Up to chapter 46, the figure in question is referred to as "the Chosen One." At the beginning of chapter 46, however, we find: "At that place, I saw the One to whom belongs the time before time. And his head was white like wool, and there was with him another individual, whose face was like that of a human being. His countenance was full of grace like that of one among the holy angels. And I asked the one — from among the angels — who was going with me, and who had revealed to me all the secrets regarding the One who was born of human beings . . ." (1 Enoch 46.1-2). The figure that up to now had been called "the Chosen One" now becomes "the Son of Man," and these verses may well hold the key to this shift. It is not difficult to demonstrate the influence of Daniel on the passage in question, specifically Daniel 7:9 and the reference to the "Ancient One . . . and the hair of his head like pure wool." And where Enoch describes the Son of Man as having "a countenance full of grace like that of one among the holy angels" (1 Enoch 46.1), Daniel describes an angel as follows: "Then someone appeared standing before me, having the appearance of a man, and I heard a human voice by the Ulai" (Dan 8:15-16), and elsewhere "then one in human form touched my lips" (Dan 10:16), and "again one in human form touched me and strengthened me" (Dan 10:18). It stands to reason, then, that Enoch's description of the angels is influenced by Daniel.

Can we now move on and discover the primary meaning of "Son of Man" (בר אנש or בן אדם or simply אדם)? In the Testament of Abraham, the Gospels, and 1 Enoch, the Son of Man sits in eschatological judgment. Indeed, in 1 Enoch[17] and Matthew (19:28; 25:31) the Son of Man sits on the throne of his glory, a detail that helps us to identify the biblical prooftext that gave rise to the Son of Man motif in connection with eschatological judgment. Ezekiel prophesies: "And above the dome over their heads there was something like a throne, in appearance like sapphire; and seated above the likeness of a throne was something that seemed like a human form" (Ezek 1:26). The language is very similar to that of 1 Enoch, who first introduces the Son of Man as an "individual, whose face was like that of a human being" (46.1). This, in any case, is the language of the extant Ethiopic text, though it is possible that the original Hebrew spoke of a figure "whose figure was like that of a human being."[18] The anthropomorphic description of God's glory in Ezekiel ("seemed like a human form") no doubt troubled later readers — after all, the prophet himself is ambivalent about this description! — and may have resolved the issue by associating the human image on "the likeness of a throne" with a vision of the superhuman eschatological judge. Ezekiel's hesitance may have influenced later writers dealing with the Son of Man: Daniel's "one like a human

---

17. In 1 Enoch the Son of Man sits on a throne (45.6; 51.3 — on the throne of the Lord!), or on a throne of glory (55.4; 62.5; 69.27, 29). 1 Enoch also states that the Lord will be seated on a throne of glory, and it is occasionally unclear (69.27) whether the seated figure is God or the Son of Man. On the "throne of glory" in Second Temple and rabbinic literature see H. Strack and P. Billerbeck, *Kommentar zum Neuen Testament* (Munich, 1922), 1.974-979. Jeremiah twice refers to God's throne of glory (14:21 and 17:12), the latter being more influential vis-à-vis the later development of the motif: "O glorious throne, exalted from the beginning, shrine of our sanctuary!" The Aramaic Targum interprets this difficult verse as stating that the divine presence resides on the throne of glory "in the highest heavens," exalted from the earliest time, facing the site of the temple. This suggests that God's throne of glory preceded the creation of the world.

18. This is a possible rendering because the Ethiopic text renders the two instances of "figure" with different terms. Knibb translates "whose face had the appearance of a man" (M. A. Knibb, *The Ethiopic Book of Enoch* [Oxford, 1978]).

being" (7:13), Enoch's "individual, whose face was like that of a human being"; Revelation's "one like the son of man" (14:14), and 4 Ezra's "something like the figure of a man" (13.2). Of course, once the figure has been introduced in these terms the writer is free to refer to it simply as אדם, "man," later. A similar dynamic is evident in 1 Enoch: the figure is first referred to as "the elect one" and then one "whose face was like that of a human being," and finally simply "Son of Man." The Gospels, however, do not reflect this shift as they consistently refer to the figure as "Son of Man." Our explanation of the (semantically equivalent) terms בר אנש ,בן אדם, and אדם as a particular interpretation of Ezekiel 1:26 obviates the widespread view that the Son of Man is rooted in the figure of a primordial man.

The Son of Man, then, is the judge of the eschaton, an independent figure originally not tied to the Messiah. If I am right that the nomenclature surrounding this figure is derived from a particular interpretation of a verse in Ezekiel, there was already a conception of this figure preceding this interpretation. I hope to show elsewhere that Jewish descriptions of the eschatological day of judgment were decisively influenced by Persian religious traditions. In the standard Jewish accounts, like their Persian counterparts, the judge who sits on a throne of judgment is none other than God. The Son of Man, however, sits on God's throne, a minor variant of the widespread view of the great day of judgment. Is this variant also of Persian origin? Not all the ancient Persian religious texts have survived, and those that have await thorough investigation. Still, from what is known, it is possible that the Son of Man was originally a Persian figure. One scholar has argued that the god who sits in eschatological judgment over the forces of good and evil is Mihr, that is, Mithra.[19] It may be that this figure was later "converted" to Judaism, and went on to play an important role in early Christianity.[20] Incidentally, another

19. See S. Shaked, "Mihr the Judge," *Jerusalem Studies in Arabic and Islam* (Jerusalem, 1980), 2.1-31. Already Grossman connected the Son of Man in Daniel to Mithra. See Koch, *Das Buch Daniel*, 232.

20. Though the Son of Man plays an important role (both as judge and as executor of punishment) in Jewish apocalyptic literature, the figure was never accepted in rabbinic sources, no doubt as a result of the danger of recognizing a supernatural entity alongside God during the eschatological judgment. There are traces of the Son of Man tradition in the Babylonian Talmud (Hagigah 14a; Sanhedrin 38b), where Rabbi Aqiva glosses Daniel 7:9 — "As I watched, thrones were set in place, and an Ancient One took his throne" — as "one for him and one for David," but this unfettered midrash is rejected out of hand for making the sacred profane. Another derashah follows immediately — the two thrones are for mercy and judgment, but this reading too is rejected. I suspect the first of these interpretations is not Rabbi Aqiva's. First, because Rabbi Aqiva identifies the Messiah with the very human figure of Bar Kosiba. More importantly, in the b. Sanhedrin passage, the two interpretations are embedded in a broader polemic against the *minim* —

piece of evidence for Daniel's Son of Man being a secondary figure that represents Israel and cannot serve as an eschatological judge comes from the narrative itself: the thrones are set and the court in session, but the judge is "the ancient of days." It is only after the trial that the Son of Man appears and receives dominion over the world and all its nations. Here the collective interpretation influenced the vision itself, as the Son of Man (in contradistinction from the other Jewish sources) cannot function as judge. He has become a symbol of earthly Israel.

It is possible that the Testament of Abraham — which identifies the Son of Man (בן אדם) with Abel — was composed at a later time, but all the same it appears that the prevalent view identified the Son of Man with the Messiah of the house of David. When Jesus is asked by the High Priest, "If you are the Messiah, tell us," he replies that "from now on the Son of Man will be seated at the right hand of the power of God" (Luke 22:67-69 and parallels). Here Jesus alludes to Psalm 110:1: "The Lord says to my lord, 'Sit at my right hand.'"[21] Jesus further alludes to this verse — in its messianic interpretation — in his somewhat obscure dictum: "How can they say that the Messiah is David's son? For David himself says . . . 'The Lord said to my Lord, "Sit at my right hand, until I make your enemies your footstool".' David thus calls him Lord; so how can he be his son?" (Luke 20:41-44). It seems to me that this saying is, inter alia, intended to demonstrate the priority of the Messiah of the house of David over David himself, for the latter addresses the former as "my Lord." The dictum may also be a polemic against the view that David himself will be the Messiah, a view current among the sages and against which the author of Acts also argues (2:29-36; 13:33-37).[22] There is also a striking parallel to the messianic meaning of "power" in the Dead Sea Scrolls. The author of the

---

perhaps Jewish-Christians who believed in the Son of Man — and the more wild interpretation may have been theirs. It should also be noted that in one of the Essene texts we find Melchizedek in the role traditionally associated with the Son of Man. See D. Flusser, "Melchizedek and the Son of Man," *Christian News from Israel* (Jerusalem, 1966), 23-29.

21. Mark adds here (14:62, and following him Matthew 26:64) a citation of Daniel 7:13. There is only one place where all three Synoptic Gospels attribute to Jesus a reference to Daniel 7:13: the apocalyptic vision at Luke 21:27 (and parallels). Even this may not be an authentic saying of Jesus. But even if we assume it is, it is remarkable that Jesus does not allude to the Son of Man, even though he was undoubtedly familiar with the Book of Daniel. Here, then, is another indication that the Son of Man figure does not have its origins in the Book of Daniel.

22. See L. Ginzberg, *The Legends of the Jews* (Philadelphia, 1946), 6.72, n. 128; G. F. Moore, *Judaism* (New York, 1971), 2.625-632; P. Volz, *Die Eschatologie der Jüdischen Gemeinde* (Tübingen, 1934), 207-207; M. Zobel, *Gottes Gesalbter* (Berlin, 1938), 90-91; and see also D. Flusser and S. Safrai, "The Apocryphal Psalms of David," in *Judaism of the Second Temple Period: Qumran and Apocalypticism*, 258-282.

Hodayot (11.5-18) presents an apocalyptic vision, presented in images and symbols, that includes the birth of a messianic figure. For our purposes, it does not matter whether this is a real Messiah or merely a symbol, as in Daniel. What matters is he is described as "a wonderful counselor with his strength" (11.10), an interesting interpretation of Isaiah, who states that the name of the Messiah will be "Wonderful Counselor, Mighty God" (9:6). In order to avoid associating the epithet "God" with a mortal figure, the Essene author transforms Isaiah's statement to "wonderful counselor *of* the mighty God." In other words, the Messiah was seated as counselor to power. Did this interpretation, along with Psalm 110:1, influence Jesus' statement that the Son of Man will sit at the right of power?

Jesus' assertion that the Messiah is greater than David (Luke 20:41-43 and parallels) is his only mention of the word "Messiah" that may be considered authentic,[23] and it is clear that the broader context forced Jesus to speak of the Messiah in this explicit manner. If Jesus' response to the High Priest's question is authentic (Luke 22:67-69), we find that he does not speak of the Messiah but of the Son of Man, though it is clear that he identifies the two. Why did Jesus speak so infrequently of the Messiah? The Hebrew משיח is biblical, but not in the meaning it now bears,[24] even though this sense is attested in the apocryphal writings (e.g., Psalms of Solomon 17.32: "their king shall be the Lord Messiah") and in the Qumran scrolls. The literature of the Sages contains references to משיח, though at times they prefer to speak of "the son of David" and the like. And it has not been sufficiently recognized that the word משיח is absent from the core Jewish liturgy.[25] There are, of course, ref-

---

23. Matthew 23:10 is certainly not original, and only in Matthew (24:5) does Jesus' denunciation of the false messiahs contain the word itself (Matthew is here [and in 24:23-24] influenced by Mark 13:21-22). Even if this is an authentic statement of Jesus, it refers only to false messiahs. On the other hand, we have seen that before Jesus was surrendered to the authorities he was asked by the High Priest if he was the Messiah, and that some taunted him on the cross, pronouncing him a failed Messiah (Luke 23:3, 5; Mk 15:32; but not in the Matthew parallel, 27:42). According to Matthew, Peter declares Jesus to be the Messiah (Matt 16:16).

24. The modern sense of משיח may be alluded to in Zechariah's discussion of the two olive trees (chapter 4), who are the two "anointed ones" (משיחים), one the anointed son of David, the other the anointed priest.

25. The only exception I know of is the prayer "May It Arise and Come" (יעלה ויבוא), which refers to "the memory of the Davidic messiah." According to Joseph Heinemann (personal communication), this prayer was originally composed as the Jerusalem benediction to the grace on Rosh ha-Shanah, which is itself a day of memory, and includes the prayer יזכר זכרוננו ("let our memory be remembered"). The date of its composition is unknown, though it spread throughout the Jewish liturgical traditions. Note, however, that in all four of the Genizah versions published by I. Elbogen ("Die Tefilla für die Festgabe," *MGWJ* 59 [1911], 433ff.) the word משיח is wanting. "May It Arise and Come" (יעלה ויבוא) is mentioned in Tractate Soferim 19.7

erences to the messianic figure, but he is referred to as "the offshoot of David." When the Hebrew משיח does occur, it is in reference to King David, as in the phrase "the kingship of the house of David, your Messiah," which occurs in the blessing for Jerusalem in the grace after meals, or the phrase "the kingship of the house of David, your righteous Messiah (משיח צדקך)," in the (Palestinian) Eighteen Benedictions,[26] and in the Eighteen Benedictions of the High Holy Days, which include the phrase "setting a lamp for the Son of Jesse, your Messiah." Liturgy is by its very nature conservative,[27] so it is not surprising that משיח in the sense of "a future messianic figure" does not appear, and is not widely attested in Second Temple literature. This may also be the reason that Jesus seems to have avoided using it.

Even though Christianity was originally a Jewish messianic cult, there are today reputable Christian scholars who argue that Jesus never saw himself as the Messiah. Is this a viable claim? Many of the arguments put forward in its support are mere curiosities, but there is one substantive issue — that the Synoptic Gospels, even after the editing of later generations, do not report Jesus as having identified himself with the Messiah or the Son of Man, speaking of the Messiah (once) and the Son of Man (often) in the third person.

(*Minor Tractates* 1.305). In the liturgy for the new month, 19.9 (*Minor Tractates* 1.307), we find another reference to the Messiah: "may the king Messiah (המלך המשיח) cause to spring forth in our days the happy time like the years when the temple was rebuilt." References to the Messiah in some versions of the *qaddish* are late additions, which were first developed in the liturgies of Spain, Rumania, and Yemen, and later received the present form: "May He cause His redemption to grow and bring near His messiah" (יצמח פורקניה ויקרב משיחיה) (see E. Fleischer, *Palestinian Liturgy and Liturgical Custom in the Genizah* [Jerusalem, 1988], 245). In Rav Saadia Gaon's prayer book (p. 35) we find only "May He cause His redemption to grow," with no mention of the Messiah! In current Ashkenazi liturgy, the "Our Father, Our King" (אבינו מלכנו) prayer exhorts God, "raise up the horn of your Messiah," but this is a late addition as it does not appear in the prayer book of Rabbi Solomon the Son of Samson of Worms (Jerusalem, 1972, pp. 229 and 236; I thank Shmuel Safrai for this reference). Indeed, the Messiah is mentioned in the commentary to the liturgy, indicating it was only later added into the body of the prayer. The poetic opening to the first benediction of the Shema for the Sabbath morning service refers to the messianic days and the world to come, but the date of its composition is unknown. The opening is not found in the liturgy of the Jews of Persia. There are also those whose grace includes the request that God "grant us the days of the Messiah and life in the world to come," but this language is not attested in all the traditions.

26. See Heinemann, *Prayer in the Tannaitic and Amoraic Period* (Hebrew) (Jerusalem, 1964), 48.

27. Note, for example, that ancient prayers do not contain the word שכינה ("divine presence"), only כבוד ("glory") and the like. The Aleynu contains the phrase שכינת עזו, but this refers to God's *might* residing in the highest heavens. The earliest attestation to שכינה in the context of the temple appears to be 2 Maccabees 14.35, where the Greek speaks of "a temple for Your habitation (שכינה) among us." See also Tobit 1.4 and Wisdom of Solomon 9.8.

While it is difficult to accept the argument that Jesus never saw himself as the Messiah (although it is based on the Gospels themselves), this much is certain: there were those who, already in his lifetime, saw Jesus as the Messiah. Otherwise we cannot explain why the Romans crucified him as "King of the Jews," as the trilingual inscription on the cross so clearly states. Moreover, the Gospels indicate that Jesus' own disciple, Peter, blessed him as Messiah, and Jesus' positive response is credible (Matt 16.17-19). One must also recognize the central role Jesus assigns himself in the manifestation of the Kingdom of Heaven, and his filial relationship with his heavenly father. Note also that Jesus speaks either of "your heavenly father" or of "my father"; only in the blessing he taught his disciples does he refer to "our heavenly father." In terms of the religious and psychological logic of Jesus' position, it is difficult for me to believe that he championed the view that a figure other than him — the Messiah or the Son of Man — will arrive at the end of days. It is, however, quite possible that Jesus understood himself to be the royal Messiah (he could not have been the priestly Messiah since he was not of Aaronite lineage), though the Gospels provide no evidence for this. It is interesting to note that there are a number of biblical verses that suggest the king or ruler is like the son of God, but Jesus' relationship with his heavenly father does not appear to be connected with a royal ideology. Jesus announced the advent of the Son of Man in the end of days, and understood this figure in the same way as his contemporaries, i.e., as an eschatological judge who will send the righteous to life eternal and the wicked to eternal punishment (Matt 25:31-46; Luke 17:22-37). Despite Jesus' close relationship with his heavenly father, it is no simple matter to assume that a mortal man will identify himself with the elevated figure of the Son of Man, a figure he refers to, as noted, only in the third person. I have tried to address this difficulty elsewhere.[28] Is there also an explanation for why Jesus never spoke of himself as the Messiah? From a religious perspective, it is almost impossible to assume that he would declare his messianic status before fulfilling the messianic expectations of the Jewish people. Even Bar Kosiba spoke of himself as a patriarch (נשיא), not a messianic king, since he had not yet realized the role intended for the messianic leader. For Bar Kosiba, as for Jesus, this is not an insuperable difficulty, so long as we assume that Jesus believed he was destined to be revealed as the Son of Man, but nonetheless spoke of this figure in the third person.[29] The present study is

28. See D. Flusser, "Two Notes on the Midrash on 2 Sam VII," *IEJ* 9 (1959), 104-109.

29. A fuller investigation would include the history of all Jewish messianic movements, with the aim of establishing the extent to which those who believed in their messianism spoke openly of their destiny. Shabbtai Zevi is a clear exception, though the premature announcement

not, however, concerned with the messianic consciousness of Jesus, and I merely sought to set forth the difficulties it entails.

When Jesus asked his disciples what people think of him, they answered that some see him as John the Baptist or Elijah redivivus,[30] or as קם *(qam)*, the prophet (Luke 9:18-19 and parallels).[31] Ultimately, these are three versions of a single answer, namely, that there were those who saw in Jesus the expected eschatological prophet. The wait for a prophet who would renew the now dormant prophetic office in Israel was based on a particular understanding of Deuteronomy 18:18: "I will raise up for them a prophet . . . from among their own people." This expectation is already attested in 1 Maccabees. During the dedication of the Temple, the Maccabees did not know what to do with the desecrated altar stones, so they "stored the stones in a convenient place on the temple hill until a prophet should come to tell them what to do with them" (1 Macc 4.46). A more explicit statement of this ideology is found in the appointment letter given to Simon, the son of Mattathias, who was appointed "their leader and high priest forever, until a trustworthy prophet should arise" (1 Macc 14.41). There were those who identified Jesus with Elijah, whose advent was a variation on the motif of the eschatological prophet, a view attested already in the Bible: "Lo, I will send you the prophet Elijah before the great and terrible day of the Lord comes" (Mal 4:5). Others believed that John the Baptist was none other than Elijah, and even Jesus said of him, "if you are willing to accept it, he is Elijah who is to come" (Matt 11:14). All three views of Jesus, then, are ultimately identical: Jesus is the eschatological prophet. After the apostles reported these views to Jesus, he asks them: "But who do you say that I am?" to which Peter answers: "The Messiah of God" (Luke 9:20). According to Matthew, Jesus responds: "Blessed are you, Simon son of Jonah! For flesh and blood has not revealed this to you, but my Father in heaven" (Matt 16:17). Jesus' answer to Peter ("flesh and blood has not revealed this to you") indicates that there some among the Jews of the time who saw Jesus as the eschatological prophet, but did not expect him to reveal himself as the Messiah. In such a situation it was no doubt difficult for Jesus to speak openly of his messianic ambitions — if he had any. Jesus undoubtedly saw himself as a prophet. Accord-

---

of his messiahship may be understood in light of the Christian precedent, with which the crypto-Jews among his followers were familiar.

30. Matthew (16:14) also lists Jeremiah, who some believed would return at the end of days. According to Matthew 14:1-2, Herod believed Jesus to be John the Baptist redivivus. Luke (9:7-9) reworks this tradition, and Mark follows in his footsteps; see my discussion in "Two Notes."

31. This is apparently the correct reconstruction of the third answer. It is based on Deuteronomy 18:18: "I will raise up (אקים) for them a prophet like you from among their own people."

ing to Luke 13:33-34, Jesus went to Jerusalem with the goal of dying there, for it is not fitting for a prophet to die anywhere but in "the city that kills prophets and stones those who are sent to it." Jesus, then, repeats the widespread motif of the murder of the prophets, which appears also in the writings of the sages.[32] Indeed, when Jesus was already in Jerusalem and knew he would be executed he told the parable of the vineyard (Luke 20:9-19 and parallels): The tenants to whom the vineyard has been entrusted beat the messengers of the owner and, when he sends to them his only son, they kill him. The vineyard is Israel, the wicked tenants the Sadducee establishment, and the murdered only son — Jesus himself. This parable links the motif of the murder of the prophets with the motif of the murdered son. Moreover, we find in the New Testament a vision of two prophets who are killed but will be reborn (Rev 11:3-12).

As noted, many of the Jews of the time believed that Jesus is the eschatological prophet, and we have already seen that 1 Maccabees (14.41) speaks of the eschatological prophet as "true prophet." This is precisely the language used to describe Jesus in the Jewish-Christian sect known as the Ebionites. The belief in an eschatological prophet is itself based on the recognition that prophecy has ceased and that only such a figure can restore it. This belief is found among the Qumran authors, and even the sages admitted the cessation of prophecy and hoped for the eschatological return of Elijah. Josephus agrees with the sages that prophecy has ceased (*CA* 1.40-41), though he does speak of false prophets who arose before the destruction of the temple.[33] Did all the Jews believe that prophecy was no longer viable? It appears not, as Jesus' statements — first and foremost the parable of the vineyard — cannot be understood without assuming a popular belief that the chain of prophecy continues to his day. Jesus saw himself as a prophet and there is nothing in his sayings to suggest that he understood this role in eschatological terms.

There is, however, an additional difficulty. Jesus says of John the Baptist that he is greater than a prophet, the fulfillment of Malachi 3:1: "See, I am sending my messenger to prepare the way before me" (Matt 11:9-10; Luke 7:26-27), and, moreover, that "all the prophets and the law prophesied until John came; and if you are willing to accept it, he is Elijah who is to come" (Matt 11:13-14). Jesus, then, accepts the popular identification of John the Baptist with Elijah, and it stands to reason that he believed John-Elijah was the last of the biblical prophets. I, for one, am convinced this was Jesus' original position.[34] Matthew

32. See Flusser, "Anti-Jewish Sentiment in the Gospel of Matthew," pp. 351-353 in the present volume.

33. On the blessing after the *haftarah* as a polemic statement against apocalyptic prophecies see Flusser, "Judaism in the Second Temple Period," pp. 6-43 in the present collection.

34. See Flusser, *Die rabbinischen Gleichnisse und der Gleichniserzähler Jesus*, 270-273.

and Mark preserve a conversation between Jesus and his disciples that is relevant to the topic at hand. After Jesus alludes to his messianic status, his disciples ask him, "Why, then, do the scribes say that Elijah must come first?" And Jesus responds: "'Elijah is indeed coming and will restore all things; but I tell you that Elijah has already come, and they did not recognize him, but they did to him whatever they pleased.'... Then the disciples understood that he was speaking to them about John the Baptist" (Matt 17:9-13; Mk 9:9-13).

It is doubtful that the conversation — especially some of the details we passed over — ever occurred. But its core insight may be legitimate, that is, that Jesus can be the Messiah if and only if Elijah has preceded him.[35] And while John the Baptist, who was of priestly lineage, never claimed he would be revealed as the priestly Messiah, those of his disciples who did not believe that Jesus was the Messiah saw John the Baptist as the priestly Messiah. Both Luke (3:15-16) and John (1:24-27) preserve polemic statements against this view. According to the Gospel of John, John the Baptist himself denies being the Messiah, and further denies that he is Elijah redivivus![36] The Gospels were clearly struggling with the question of Jesus' predecessor — has Elijah come or not? Jesus assured his students that he has, in the form of the executed John the Baptist. Irrespective of the historicity of the conversation between Jesus and his disciples, Matthew 11 does suggest that Jesus managed to incorporate John the Baptist-Elijah into his *Heilsgeschichte* in an interesting and original manner.

The Gospels, then, reflect the popular Jewish belief in an eschatological prophet, a belief predicated on the view that true prophecy had ceased and fueled by the hope for its future renewal. The same hope is also reflected in the "appointment letter" of 1 Maccabees, discussed above, when Israel and the priests appoint Simon "their leader and high priest forever, until a trustworthy prophet should arise" (1 Macc 14.41). That political arrangement was, then, only temporary, the final decision postponed until the arrival of a true prophet

35. A striking parallel to the exchange between Jesus and his disciples (whether real or imagined) is found in the fateful conversation between Shabbtai Zevi and Rabbi Nehemiah, the prophet, a conversation that eventually caused the downfall of the messianic claimant. Shabbtai Zevi was asked whether the Messiah son of Joseph had already come, since the advent and death of this Messiah is the *sine qua non* for the appearance of the Davidic Messiah: "Where is the Messiah son of Joseph?... Then Elijah will come and proclaim the final redemption, and the kingship of the Davidic Messiah will be revealed...." Shabbtai Zevi debated at length the legitimacy of his claim, arguing that his disciple who was killed in Poland was, in fact, the Messiah son of Joseph. But Rabbi Nehemiah was not convinced, and the result was a tragic turn in the history of the messianic movement. See G. Scholem, *Sabbatai Sevi: The Mystical Messiah 1626-1676* (Princeton, 1973), 658-668. According to other reliable sources, Rabbi Nehemiah claimed that he himself was the Messiah son of Joseph.

36. See also Justin Martyr, *Dialogue with Trypho*, 30.7.

who would provide it with heavenly sanction. The court of John Hyrcanus (Simon's son) sought to do away with the "conditional" status of the Hasmonean rule, as the propagandists of John, the high priest, announced that he united in his person the three chief offices — political leader, high priest, and prophet.[37] In this, John Hyrcanus's partisans sought to annul the temporary status of the Hasmonean rule (i.e., that it would stand only "until a trustworthy prophet should arise"), since their ruler wore all three crowns: the crown of kingship, the crown of priesthood, and the crown of prophecy.

This is not the place to chart the development of the three crowns doctrine, first in Jewish and then in Christian thought. What is significant is that it was originally a political doctrine that paralleled the three branch position in modern political thought with one significant difference: the three crowns contain an eschatological element (the renewal of the prophetic office) that was intended to prevent the establishment of a fixed and irreversible political arrangement, be it priestly-religious or secular. All Jewish political arrangements are strictly temporary, pending final prophetic sanction. Over time, the three crowns doctrine underwent different changes in two circles — that of the sages and that of the apocalyptic seers. Despite their differences, in both groups the political dimension of the three crowns doctrine largely disappeared. For the sages, post-biblical prophecy was perceived as a threat, in part due to the social and national radicalism and the disdain for *Realpolitik* found in apocalyptic messianism. All the same, the sages saw themselves as the rightful heirs to the prophets, and, as a result, reformulated the traditional crown formula, replacing the crown of prophecy with the crown of Torah: "Rabbi Shimon says, there are three crowns — the crown of Torah, the crown of priesthood, and the crown of kingship, and the crown of the good name is greater than all" (m. Avot 4.13).[38] Philo's *Life of Moses* preserves an echo of both versions (i.e., the "prophecy" version and the "Torah" version), when he describes Moses as a prophet, a king, a priest, and a legislator.

---

37. Josephus, *BJ* 1.67-69; *AJ* 19.299.

38. Rabbi Shimon understood that the three crowns function as adornments of sorts, and thus added the crown of the good name, even though it was originally different from the three original crowns. It is interesting that the expansion of Rabbi Shimon's dictum in the Fathers According to Rabbi Nathan (chapter 41 in version A, 48 in version B; page 130 in the Schechter edition) preserves an earlier version of the saying. Indeed, in version A the crown of the good name is not even mentioned! The Fathers According to Rabbi Nathan is closer to the saying of Rabbi Shimon in b. Yoma 72b, and see W. Bacher, *Die Aggada der Tannaiten* (Strasbourg, 1903), 2.80, n. 1. An echo of the original three crowns is preserved in Fathers According to Rabbi Nathan (version B, chapter 47; page 130 in the Schechter edition): "Three things Israel disdained and were taken from them: prophecy, the Davidic dynasty, and the temple."

In the apocalyptic circles, at least inasmuch as we encounter them in the Dead Sea Scrolls, the original three crowns formula was preserved, but its realization deferred to the eschatological future. The Qumran constitution is in effect "until the prophet comes, and the Messiahs of Aaron and Israel" (1QS 9.11).[39] Another allusion to the eschatological crowns is found in three short statements interwoven in Matthew 12: "I tell you, something greater than the temple is here . . . something greater than Jonah is here . . . something greater than Solomon is here" (Matt 12:6, 41, 42).[40] This statement refers to the temple, to Jonah the prophet, and to King Solomon, indicating that the messianic advent of Jesus will unify the three eschatological hopes — priest, prophet, and king — and surpass their earlier realization. This particular doctrine was developed by the Jewish-Christian community known as the Ebionites.[41] Though the channels of transmission are obscure, the same view made its way through Catholic theologians to Calvin, who systematized the view that Jesus fulfills three roles: priesthood, kingship, and prophecy.[42]

Jesus saw himself as a prophet who announced to Israel the advent of the Son of Man, whom he identified with the Messiah. We may assume that he believed he himself would be revealed as the Son of Man and the Messiah of Israel. Interestingly, Jesus' statements make no mention of the royal element of the Messiah. This is not to say that Jesus did not expect the downfall of the Roman empire once the kingdom of heaven is established. After all, the sages that opposed the zealots but upheld the kingdom of heaven, were convinced that once all Israel accepts the kingdom of heaven, no nation can rule over them. Still and all, there is no clear evidence that Jesus understood the Messiah as the political ruler in that way we find, e.g., in the Psalms of Solomon. Jesus be-

---

39. The collection of verses knows as 4Qtest is constructed in the same manner: it first speaks of the prophet, then the king, and finally the priest. The priests are sometimes referred to as "messiahs" in the Qumran scrolls, as when the War Scroll states "By the hand of your anointed ones, seers of decrees" (1QM 11.7-8), and the Damascus Document "by the hand of the anointed ones, the seers of the truth" (CD 2.12-13); cf. Y. Yadin, *The Scroll of the War of the Sons of Light,* translated by Batya and Chaim Rabin (Oxford: Oxford University Press, 1962), 310-311. So too we find the Qumran authors refer to Pharisees, who "spoke of rebellion against God's precepts (given) through the hand of Moses and also of the holy anointed ones" (CD 5.21–6.1). It appears the eschatological prophet is also called "messiah" in the Melchizedek Text, which states that "the messenger is the anointed of the spirit" (11QMelch 2.18). See my "Melchizedek and the Son of Man," 23, n. 1, and see below, n. 60.

40. Luke (11:31-32) omits the statement regarding the temple, and the order of the Jonah and Solomon statements is reversed.

41. See, e.g., H. J. Schoeps, *Das Judenchristentum* (Bern, 1964), 65-75.

42. This idea is already attested in Eusebius, *EH* 1.3.7-12. I assume that Eusebius depends here (as he states explicitly about other views) on the Ebionite Hegesippus.

lieved in the eschatological advent of the Son of Man who will sit in final judgment, but there is no reason to think that the judgment will be followed by the rule of the righteous. (The precise nature of the Son of Man's final judgment cannot be discussed here at length.) Christians, however, believed in the eschatological advent of Christ, a belief that likely emerged immediately after his crucifixion. Needless to say, the belief in his resurrection three days after the crucifixion facilitated the belief in the second coming. This faith is also to be understood in light of the fact that Jesus did not complete the expected messianic drama, since the world remained as it was even after his death. To reiterate, the roots of the church lie in Jewish messianism.

Of the Synoptic Gospels, only Luke (in his Gospel and in Acts) states that after Jesus rose from the dead, he ascended to heaven. Though Paul does not say so explicitly — his own view may have been somewhat different than Luke's — he accepts the basic view that Jesus resides with his father in heaven. Though not stated, this is also the view of the other works that make up the New Testament, including the Gospels. According to Paul, after his resurrection Jesus will hand the kingdom of heaven over to his father, to God (1 Cor 15:23-28).[43] Not surprisingly, the Christian emphasis on eschatology post-Golgotha led to a renewed emphasis on the royal component of Christian eschatology. Within the Gospels, we do not find an emphasis on the political, with the obvious exception of the apocalyptic Revelation, which prophesies the downfall of Rome. Revelation is also the only New Testament book to speak of a thousand-year messianic reign (Rev 20:1-7). The idea that the messianic era precedes the end of days crystallized within Judaism at about this time, namely, toward the end of the first century c.e. The idea of a thousand-year messianic reign is also Jewish that was taken over by the author of Revelation, himself a Jew by birth.

The expectation for the second coming was strong among the first Christians, particularly after the crucifixion — an expectation that is clearly reflected in the New Testament and other Christian texts composed in the late first and early second century. This is not surprising: the Christian faithful yearned for a speedy and successful conclusion to the messianic drama. The belief in Christ's advent parallels the Jewish messianic hopes, and it is clear that Christian thought on this topic, throughout history, was influenced by corresponding Jewish thought with regard to messianic biblical interpreta-

43. The Jewish sources are (understandably) reticent to identify the Messiah as God's son — only partially in response to Christian doctrine. See Volz, *Die Eschatologie der Jüdischen Gemeinde,* 174. This does not mean, of course, that this reticence was shared equally by all the Jewish groups that made up Second Temple Judaism. Volz's thesis appears, then, to be correct, though this cannot be discussed here.

tion and other matters. Jewish apocalyptic literature was particularly influential, and one could argue that, along with Revelation, it forged the Christian messianic movements even to this very day. What sets Christian messianism apart is the calculations of the eschaton and the belief that after the advent of the Messiah his kingdom will be established on earth. Since the days of Augustine, these believers are known as chiliasts, that is, people who believe in a thousand-year messianic kingdom (from the Greek word for "one thousand"). The belief in the imminent advent of Christ, and in his kingdom on earth, was viewed with suspicion by the church, in part because such views call into question the power and authority of the church itself. The institutional opposition to Christian messianic movements was more powerful and more principled than the Jewish aversion to Jewish messianic groups. This may be due to the fact that Christian messianism emphasized, almost from the start, the spiritual aspect of redemption, while Judaism kept the political, worldly dimension of messianic redemption at the forefront. An important messianic awakening occurred toward the year 100 c.e.[44] The same situation repeated toward the year 200: in Syria a bishop united the Christians on a journey into the desert where Jesus was to appear, while in distant Pontus another bishop convinced the faithful that he had learned from his dreams that the final judgment of mankind was to occur within the year.[45] These are but a few examples of eschatological awakenings within the Christian world, events that occur throughout Christian history down to the present day. Messianic awakenings have often resulted in the emergence of messianic movements and even discrete sects. Recently, the establishment of the State of Israel and the Jewish conquest of Jerusalem during the Six-Day War has stirred messianic hopes in the hearts of many Christians.

The church's resistance to the expectation of Christ's imminent advent entailed a certain skepticism toward the book of Revelation as well.[46] There were many in late antiquity who did not consider Revelation part of the Christian canon. However, the resistance of the church and its theologians to Chris-

---

44. See G. Duby, *L'an Mil* (Paris, 1966). I have discovered an unknown text that reflects the fears awakened as the year 1000 drew near, namely, the original Latin text of the *Sibylla Tiburtina*. According to this work, the wicked eschatological ruler will be Emperor Otto III. See D. Flusser, "An Early Jewish-Christian Document in the Tiburtine Sibyl," *Paganisme, Judaïsme, Christianisme — Influences et Affrontements dans le monde antique: mélanges offerts à M. Simon,* ed. P. Benoit, M. Philonenko, and C. Vogel (Paris, 1978), 153-183.

45. See W. H. C. Frend, *Martyrdom and Persecution in the Early Church* (Oxford, 1960), 330, 333, and 347. The relevant sources are Hippolytus's commentary to Daniel 4:18-19 and Tertullian, *Adversus Marcionem* 3.24.

46. See W. Bousset, *Die Offenbarung Johannis* (1906; repr. Göttingen, 1966), 19-34.

tian messianism was not part of an attempt to call into question the final judgment or the advent of Christ. In the Latin west, the Church Fathers, including Augustine — famously an opposition figure to the notion that Christian messianism entails the establishment of the savior's kingdom on earth — continued to debate the precise form and development of the eschaton. Western Christianity, after all, is rooted in the Christianity of the second century, which was strongly messianic. Indeed, western Christianity never fully integrated the novel approaches of its brethren in the Greek east. Under the influence of Hellenistic philosophy, the spiritual structure of Christian faith underwent a radical transformation beginning in the third century. At that time, the focus shifted to questions regarding the Trinity and the relationship between Jesus' human and divine natures. Salvation came to be understood in internal terms, and even where the Greek fathers did discuss the cosmic dimension of redemption, the historical, *heilsgeschichtliche* dimension was generally marginalized. Political messianism would not reappear in force within the Byzantine church until the seventh century, following the difficult wars with Persia and the rise of Islam, the latter understood as an eschatological event. It was then that Byzantine apocalypses were composed, works that were to influence the eschatological literature of the Latin west.

Bracketing these inner-Christian historical developments, there is clearly a substantive difference between Jewish and Christian messianic expectation. I have already noted that Christian messianism places a lesser emphasis on the material aspects of redemption, tending rather toward spirituality. A second, related difference is the understanding of historical processes as regards both the community of believers and humanity as a whole.[47] True, Christianity adopted the Jewish notion of eschatological redemption, but Christ's atoning death on the cross and subsequent resurrection offer a second point of historical focus, one that figures more prominently in the consciousness of the Christian faithful than the end of days. We have already noted that the idea of Jesus' atoning death is rooted in the Jewish motif of the atoning force of martyrs' death. From the days of Paul, however, the atoning death of Christ became the "Archimedean point" of the new faith, the act of sacrifice — that occurred in the *past* — and holds the key to the salvation of the soul of the Christian believer. One of the most beloved verses in Christian circles is: "For God so loved the world that he gave his only Son, so that everyone who believes in him may not perish but may have eternal life" (John 3:16).

---

47. On the biblical understanding of Israel's historical evolution, see J. Licht's important study, "The Biblical Foundation Claim" (Hebrew), *Shenaton* 4 (1980), 98-128. A pity he did not discuss Second Temple and Rabbinic literature!

Man's future eternal life is dependent upon a meta-historical past event of cosmic importance. As John subsequently states: "Indeed, God did not send the Son into the world to condemn the world, but in order that the world might be saved through him. Those who believe in him are not condemned; but those who do not believe are condemned already, because they have not believed in the name of the only Son of God" (John 3:17-18). Clearly, Christian faith is now centered around a past event and not future redemption, which comes to be understood largely as the result of this earlier act.[48] The theology of Jesus' atoning death, then, does away with the exclusive status of the future redemption, i.e., of the second coming.

It is also worth noting that the religion of ancient Persia, like Judaism and Christianity, recognizes a final judgment and resurrection, along with a beliefs in the eternity of the soul and reward and punishment following death. Moreover, all three religions maintain a tension — consciously or not — between these two historical points. Unlike Judaism, Christianity places a strong emphasis on the release of the soul from the body, since sin resides in the flesh, and "whoever keeps my word will never taste death" (John 8:52, and see John 5:24).[49] Christianity links the atoning death of Jesus to the eschaton and to reward and punishment after death, but ultimately places the strongest emphasis on its link with the salvation of the believer's soul immediately after death. Belief in Christ and his atoning death is understood primarily in terms of individual salvation, and the eschatological advent is relegated to a secondary role. It seems to me that this is true even of Paul, who yearned for Christ's advent during his own lifetime. As far as I can tell, the Gospel of John consciously seeks to minimize the eschatological dimension of the second coming, while emphasizing the salvific importance of faith in Christ for the soul of the living believer. In this respect, the Gospel of John and Revelation stand at polar opposites, the latter expressing a messianic yearning that is channeled into the expectations and hopes that have given rise to Christian messianic movements over the centuries.

The various developments within Christian doctrine are also reflected in the various meanings and contexts of the term "messiah" — already in the New Testament. The Jewish translators of the Torah rendered the Hebrew משיח as *christos*, which appears in the New Testament in this sense, but also takes on new, Christian meanings that draw it away from the original He-

---

48. Needless to say, eternal life is not exclusively a matter of faith in Christ, but depends also on the moral behavior of the Christian during his lifetime.

49. The Essenes held a similar view. See Josephus (*BJ* 2.154-158) who couches their position in Platonic terms. It appears the Essenes (unlike the Christians and Pharisees) did not believe in resurrection.

brew.[50] This is true not only with regard to *christos* among Greek-speaking Christians (of Pagan or Jewish origin), but also for מָשִׁיחַ among Hebrew or Aramaic-speaking Christians of Jewish origin.[51] The New Testament nowhere suggests that Jesus' atoning death proves his messianic status (only an understandable need to show that the Messiah could die an unusual death), but all the same there has emerged a link between Jesus' death and his messianism. Ultimately, the terms מָשִׁיחַ and *christos* became so associated with Jesus, that even in the Pauline writings *christos* is simply a reference to (or even ersatz name for) Jesus,[52] while the followers of Jesus were called "Christians" (Acts 11:26).[53]

Our analysis has strayed from Jesus' self-understanding and his belief that he was a prophet and apparently the Messiah as well. We have already alluded to the fact that during late Second Temple times there circulated the belief in three messianic figures: the royal messiah, the priestly messiah, and the eschatological messiah anointed by the spirit: "the messenger is the anointed one of the spirit"

---

50. On this issue see F. Hahn, *Christologische Hoheitstitel* (Göttingen, 1964), 133-230. Hahn often adopts a too skeptical approach to his texts, after the fashion of Hebrew Bible scholars.

51. Aramaic-speaking Christians of Pagan origin did not employ the term *christos* but מָשִׁיחַ.

52. Even Josephus refers to Jesus as *christos*. In *JA* 20.200 he speaks of James, "the brother of Jesus who is called *christos*." Josephus was, of course, well aware that the Greek *christos* corresponds to מָשִׁיחַ, but his political caution prevented him from mentioning the messianic hopes of the Jews. Only once, when discussing the birth of Christianity, does he state that Jesus' disciples believed in the resurrection, and that "he is considered [by them] to be *christos*, of whom the prophets foretold miracles." Thus according to the more original text preserved in an Arabic translation discovered by S. Pines, *An Arabic Version of the Testimonium Flavianum* (Jerusalem, 1971), 16. Josephus here explains the term *christos* as nothing more than a reference to a wondrous figure mentioned by the prophets!

53. Tacitus (*Annals* 15.44) also refers to Jesus only as *christos*, while Suetonius speaks of "Chrestus" (*Life of Claudius* 25.4), and see the discussion of M. Stern, *Greek and Latin Authors on Jews and Judaism* (Jerusalem, 1980), 2.113-117. The name *christianos* appears three times in the New Testament: twice in Acts (11:26 and 26:28) and once in 1 Peter (4:16). In each of these passages, Sinaiticus reads "Chrestianos," a reading attested for Acts 11:26 in another manuscript as well and, as noted, in Suetonius (see Stern, *Greek and Latin Authors*, 2.92). In all these manuscripts, the reading was later "corrected." In all likelihood, Tacitus too read "Chrestus" though this was altered by the copyist himself. Chrestos was a fairly common name, thus explaining the error of those who thought Christianity was established by a man who bore that name and his adherents were named for him. The error is shared by Pagans and Christians of Pagan origin, as "Chrestianoi" is attested in NT manuscripts, striking evidence for how loosely Pagan Christians understood the connection between *christos* and Messiah. See the bibliography collected by W. Bauer, *A Greek-English Lexicon of the New Testament* (Chicago, 1979), 886-887, to which should be added the attestation of "Chrestos" in the Gnostic "Treatise on Resurrection" (43.36-37 and 48.18-19). My thanks to G. Stroumsa for calling this last source to my attention.

(11QMelch 2.18).[54] Already Matthew linked all three figures with the person of Jesus, suggesting the tripartite messianic belief played a role even in contemporary Christian thought. In the Qumran Scrolls, however, we generally find reference not to three but two messianic figures, "the messiahs of Aaron and Israel" — the priestly and royal messiahs, respectively. A dual messianism is also attested in Jubilees and the Testament of the Twelve Patriarchs.[55] It is an ancient view indeed, already found in Zechariah's reference to "the two anointed ones" (Zech 4:14). Even after the destruction of the Second Temple, it was widely believed that after its reconstruction Israel would be led by a political leader and a high priest. The coins minted by Bar Kosiba indicate that alongside "Shimon, Patriarch *(nasi)* of Israel" there stood "Elazar the Priest."[56] The midrashic corpus provides further evidence of the hope for the advent of a Messiah along with a righteous priest.[57] Jesus could not have seen himself as the priestly Messiah of the eschaton, since he was famously not a descendent of Aaron, but *qua* Davidic Messiah of the tribe of Judah. Still, the early Christian tendency to connect Jesus with all Jewish messianic motifs (before the Church severed its ties to Judaism) led to his association with the priesthood as well, as we find, e.g., in Hebrews, where Jesus is described as a heavenly high priest, albeit in a loose, typological sense, since Jesus was not a priest.[58] For Jesus to be represented as a priest in Hebrews, he had to undergo a transformation similar to that of the biblical Melchizedek, who was also not of Aaronite descent. According to Hebrews, Jesus is greater than the Temple priests: the latter offer sacrifices of flesh and blood, while Jesus offered himself. And while the Temple offerings are ongoing, Jesus' is the one, ultimate sacrifice. Since the Qumran Scrolls elevated the Messiah son of Aaron above the Davidic Messiah, there are scholars who argue that Hebrews was influenced — at least with regard to Jesus' priestly status — by the Essenes.[59]

54. See my "Melchizedek and the Son of Man," particularly the last note therein.

55. See my "Two Notes on the Midrash on 2 Sam VII," and J. Liver, "The Doctrine of the Two Messiahs in Sectarian Literature of the Second Commonwealth," *HTR* 52 (1959), 149-185.

56. See E. Schürer, *The History of the Jewish People*, 544-606.

57. See Avot According to Rabbi Nathan A, 34 (page 100 in the Schechter edition), as well as Midrash Psalms to Psalm 43 (page 267-268 in the Buber edition). Note also Rav Saadia Gaon's commentary to Daniel (Jerusalem, 1981), 148-149, which was translated into Hebrew and annotated by Rabbi Yosef David Qafih. Saadia's comments are most likely based on a midrash that touches on many of the motifs relevant to our analysis, though I have not been able to find this text elsewhere.

58. See Hahn, *Christologische Hoheitstitel*, 231-241. Jesus is characterized as a high priest in the first epistle of Clement of Rome to the Corinthians (36.1; 61.3; 64), which may have been influenced by Hebrews or the tradition preserved in it.

59. See Y. Yadin, "The Dead Sea Scrolls and the Epistle to the Hebrews," *Scripta Hierosolymitana* 4 (1958), 36-55.

This hypothesis was strengthened by the discovery of the "Melchisedek Midrash" from Qumran.[60]

We must devote a short discussion to another eschatological figure present in Christian thought, namely the Antichrist, the human incarnation of future evil prior to the advent of Christ, who will be vanquished by the savior.[61] The term "Antichrist" appears three times in 1 John (2:18, 22; 4:3) and once in 2 John (v. 7).[62] From these passages we find that the figure is tied to the imminent eschaton, but according to John even a person who questions Christian dogmas or denies the messianism of Jesus is called an antichrist. It is hard to ascertain, then, how John understood the figure of Jesus' satanic antagonist who will struggle with the returned savior. There are, however, two key passages in the New Testament that clarify the meaning of the Antichrist, though neither refers to him by name (2 Thess 2:1-12; Rev 12–14). There is no doubt that the figure and its attendant motifs are of Jewish origin, and the entire issue requires renewed investigation, especially in light of the Dead Sea Scrolls. It is further necessary to examine the influence of Persian eschatology on the concept of the Antichrist. As far as the Jewish origins are concerned, the Antichrist is evidently a personification of the Jewish belief that the forces of evil will burst forth in the end of days — only to be vanquished. One might, then, speak of the king of the north in Daniel 11 as an Antichrist figure, whose death in the Land of Israel is understood as an eschatological event.[63] (The king in question is none other than Antiochus IV, and the prophecy of his death was not truly fulfilled.) There are those who argue that "The Testament of Moses" was composed during the reign of Antiochus,[64] attributes to Moses prophecies concerning the persecutions of Antiochus (chapter 8) and further tells of a man from the tribe of Levi who lives in a cave with his seven sons and is willing to martyr himself for the sake of the kingdom of heaven (chapter 10).[65] It appears the author of "The Tes-

---

60. See M. De Jonge and A. S. van der Woude, "11Q Melchizedek and the New Testament," *NTS* 12 (1965), 301-326. The authors' view that the sectarian Melchizedek is none other than the archangel Michael is to be rejected out of hand. The Qumran texts also refer to Melchiresha, perhaps a reference to the Antichrist. See P. J. Kobelski, *Melchizedek and Melchiresa* (Washington, 1981).

61. See Wilhelm Bousset, *The Antichrist Legend: A Chapter in Christian and Jewish Folklore*, trans. A. H. Keane (London, 1896).

62. The term also appears in the Epistle of Polycarp 7.1.

63. On the end of Daniel 11 and its ramifications for the Qumran War Scroll see my "Apocalyptic Elements in the War Scroll," in *Judaism of the Second Temple Period: Qumran and Apocalypticism*, 140-158.

64. See J. Licht, "Taxo, or the Apocalyptic Doctrine of Vengeance," *JJS* 12 (1963), 95-103.

65. See the discussion in Flusser, "Martyrology in the Second Temple Period and Early Christianity," pp. 248-257 in the present volume.

tament of Moses," like the author of Daniel, lived during those days and saw Antiochus IV as the wicked eschatological king. A later writer interpolated into "The Testament of Moses" — just prior to the account of the decrees of Antiochus — a prophecy that deals with Jewish history up to the time of Herod. This second author, then, lived at the beginning of the Christian era and rightly recognized the eschatological role of the wicked king. His historical interpolation, then, transformed the real, political Antiochus to a meta-historical and fantastic figure of the eschaton. Clearly, then, there existed a full-fledged Jewish concept of the Antichrist at the turn of the eras.

If the later author of "The Testament of Moses" understood the description of Antiochus IV as the eschatological wicked king — a prophecy of the Antichrist — there is a Dead Sea Scrolls fragment that describes the Antichrist according to his classic markers.[66] It appears that this text too refers to a wicked eschatological king. This Aramaic Qumran fragment speaks of the global rule of an evil kingdom, an evil nation. They will "crush everything; a people will crush another people, and a province another province. Until the people of God arises and makes everyone rest from the sword. The sword will cease from the earth, and all the provinces will pay him homage. The great God is his strength; he will wage war for him" (4Q246 2.1-8).[67]

The evil ruler is said to be "great over the earth," and all will worship him and call him "son of god" and "son of the Most High" (4Q246 1.7–2.1). This last statement is reminiscent of 2 Thessalonians 2:3-4, which speaks of a time when "the lawless one is revealed, the one destined for destruction. He opposes and exalts himself above every so-called god or object of worship, so that he takes his seat in the temple of God, declaring himself to be God." The Christian tradition according to which the Antichrist will stand against Jesus but be vanquished is attested in 2 Thessalonians and in Revelation, as well as in a Jewish composition known as "Oracles of Hystaspes."[68] In this work, composed before the destruction of the Second Temple, the Antichrist is killed by the great king, who is the Messiah. The figure in question, who is never referred to as the Antichrist, will be a king who comes from Syria, the son of an evil demon, who will seize power, designate himself a god, and com-

---

66. See my "The Hubris of the Antichrist in a Fragment from Qumran," *Immanuel* 10 (1980), 31-37. The figure of the Antichrist may appear in other sectarian works under the name Melchiresha, the opponent of Melchizedek; see the discussion above, n. 60.

67. The phrase "people of God *('el)*" indicates that the author of the work was a member of the Qumran community or at least close to its religious and ideological world, as the form *'el* was adhered to in Qumran circles, while the tetragrammaton and *'elohim* were avoided.

68. See my "Hystaspes and John of Patmos," in *Judaism and the Origins of Christianity,* 390-453.

mand his subjects to worship him. As we just saw, in 2 Thessalonians the Antichrist sees himself as a god, while in the Qumran fragment he represents himself as the son of a god. Both statements are united in the "Oracles of Hystaspes," though ultimately they form a single claim, namely, that of the self-deification of the Antichrist.

I should note that I believe the "Oracles of Hystaspes" is one of the sources of Revelation. Moreover, a link can be demonstrated between the 2 Thessalonians passage that deals with the eschatological appearance of the Antichrist and Essene thought. 2 Thessalonians 2:6-7 states that the Antichrist will be revealed when his time comes "for the mystery of lawlessness is already at work." The Qumran War Scroll speaks of the "mysteries of enmity" (1QM 14.9), while the Hodayot speak of the "mysteries of sin" (1QH 12.36). A fragment of the Essene Book of Mysteries speaks twice of "mysteries of sin," the second of these in reference to the ultimate disappearance of evil in the eschaton: "And this will be for you the sign that this is going to happen. When all that is born of sin is locked up, evil will disappear before justice as darkness disappears before light. As smoke vanishes, and no longer exists, so will evil vanish forever.[69] And justice will be revealed like the sun which regulates the world. And all those who support the mysteries of sin will no longer exist. And knowledge will pervade the world, and there will never be folly there" (1Q27 [1QMysteries] 1.5-7).[70] The picture painted by the scrolls accords with the position of 2 Thessalonians regarding the action of the mystery of sin. Where the scroll asserts that "all those who support the mysteries of sin will no longer exist," 2 Thessalonians speaks of "those who are perishing, because they refused to love the truth and so be saved. For this reason God sends them a powerful delusion, leading them to believe what is false, so that all who have not believed the truth but took pleasure in unrighteousness will be condemned" (2 Thess 2:10-12). Even the dualistic terminology is similar to that of the Scrolls.

69. This passage has a fascinating parallel in the *qedushah* liturgy of Rosh ha-Shanah, which is a vestige of the earlier *malkhuyot* liturgy (see E. Fleischer, *Palestinian Liturgy and Liturgical Custom in the Genizah* [Jerusalem, 1988], 132). Here are the parallel passages:

When all that is born of sin is locked up. . . . As smoke vanishes, and no longer exists, so will evil vanish forever. . . . And all those who support the mysteries of sin will no longer exist. And knowledge will pervade the world. . . .	Then the righteous will see and rejoice, while the upright exult, and the virtuous sing joyously. And injustice shall shut its mouth. And all evil shall dissipate like smoke. For you shall pass the government of evil from the earth. And you alone will rule over all your creatures [. . .]

It appears that the Essene worldview had a literary influence on Jewish liturgy as such.

70. See also *Megillat ha-Hodayot*, ed. J. Licht (Jerusalem, 1957), 242.

The Qumran passage cited above states that "all that is born of sin" will be "locked up" in the end of days, so that evil can no longer burst into the world.[71] This expectation is to be compared with the Qumran hymn that has been referred to as "birth pangs of the Messiah" by its interpreters: "for through the breakers of death she gives birth to a male, and through the pangs of Sheol there emerges from the crucible of the pregnant woman a wonderful counselor with his strength, and the boy is freed from the break-ers" (1QH^a 11.9-10). The messianic figure is referred to here as "a wonderful counselor with his strength," following Isaiah 9:6 and the "Wonderful Coun-selor, Mighty God." The interpretive tradition reflected in the Hodayot could not abide the elevated title "mighty God" and so interpreted the verse as though it meant "wonderful counselor *of* the mighty God." This wonderful counselor will be seated alongside the power of the Lord. It appears the same interpretive tradition is reflected in Jesus' response when, captive, he is asked whether he is the Messiah. According to the Gospels, Jesus replies: "From now on you will see the Son of Man seated at the right hand of Power and coming on the clouds of heaven" (Matt 26:64; Luke 22:69).[72] In this statement, Jesus unites the messianic understanding of Isaiah 9:6, and "Sit at my right hand" from Psalm 110:1, a verse Jesus also cites in a passage that includes the term "Messiah" (Luke 20:41-44; Matt 22:41-44). This Psalms verse would take on an important messianic sense in the New Testament and among the Church Fa-thers. If so, the birth pangs of the Messiah hymn allow us to more fully under-stand the biblical background of the bound Jesus to his taunters.

Scholars have argued that the hymn in question is tied to Revelation 12, but we will not be able to discuss all the relevant apocalyptic links between these texts.[73] Revelation mentions a wondrous woman — "She was pregnant and was crying out in birth pangs, in the agony of giving birth" (Rev 12:2) — against whom arises the great dragon who symbolizes Satan: "Then the dragon

71. The Qumran community holds that "From the spring of light stem the generations of truth, and from the source of darkness the generations of deceit" (1QS 3.19).

72. The Luke reading is the more original. Mark, and Matthew in his footsteps, add to the dictum an allusion to Daniel 7:13. Luke's more original saying does mention the Son of Man, but no allusion to Daniel. Kobelski, *Melchizedek and Melchiresa*, 136, proposes that Jesus' response ("From now on you will see the Son of Man seated at the right hand of Power and coming on the clouds of heaven") is also influenced by Psalm 80:17, "But let your hand be upon the one at your right hand, the one whom you made strong for yourself."

73. See also the discussion of this text in J. Maier, *Die Texte vom Toten Meer* (Munich, 1960), 2.72-86. Maier cites (pp. 72-73) the various scholarly views regarding the messianic con-tent of the hymn and whether it refers to the actual birth of the Messiah. This question is not decisive for our discussion, since even if the reference to the Messiah is symbolic, it is nonethe-less significant since it is akin to the messianic and symbolic Son of Man figure in Daniel.

stood before the woman who was about to bear a child, so that he might devour her child as soon as it was born. And she gave birth to a son, a male child, who is to rule all the nations with a rod of iron" (Rev 12:4-5). The content of this passage, along with the parallels to Revelation itself, indicates that the boy in question is none other than the Messiah. Indeed, the passage alludes to Isaiah 66:7: "Before she was in labor she gave birth; before her pain came upon her she delivered a son." It is worth noting that the Targum to Isaiah also alludes to the Messiah, "and the kingdom will be revealed (יתגלי מלכה)."[74] The Hodayot too understands Isaiah 66:7 as hinting at the birth of the prophet: "through the breakers of death she gives birth to a male," the male in question being "a wonderful counselor with his strength" (1QH 11.9-10).

According to Revelation and the Qumran hymn, the birth of the Messiah is greeted by a counter response on the part of evil. Thus, the Hodayot describe the birth of the savior and, in contraposition, a cosmic eruption of evil that is also couched as birth pangs: "In the woman expectant with [the Messiah] rush all the contraction and the racking pain at their birth; terror (seizes) those expectant with them, and at his birth all the labor-pains come suddenly, in the 'crucible' of the pregnant woman. And she who is pregnant with a serpent is with a racking pang; and the breakers of the pit result in all deeds of terror" (1QHᵃ 11.10-12). The horrible process culminates at the end of the Qumran hymn: "and the gates of Sheol open for all the deeds of the serpent. And the doors of the pit close upon the one expectant with injustice, and everlasting bolts upon all the spirits of the serpent" (11.17-18). These passages provide important insights into the broader meaning of the rabbinic phrase חבלי משיח, "birth pangs of the Messiah," which refers to the calamities that precede the coming of the Messiah. In the Qumran hymn, the same image is used to describe the simultaneous birth of the Messiah and eruption of evil in the eschaton. Both the Hodayot and, indirectly, Revelation 12 help clarify the conceptual roots of the rabbinic "birth pangs of the Messiah," even allowing for the independent developments governed by the dualistic tendencies in Essene thought.[75] The occurrences of "birth pangs of the Messiah" in

74. On the future revelation of the Messiah see also 1 Enoch 52.15; 69.29; Luke 17:30; 4 Ezra 7.28; the Syriac Apocalypse of Baruch 29.3; 39.7; Numbers Rabbah 11.2; Pesiqta Rabbati 36; b. Sukkah 52a; the Targum to 1 Chronicles 3:24. Is this phrase related to the view that the kingdom of God will be revealed in the future time, a view already attested in the Testament of Moses (chapter 10)? See also Matthew 24:30: "then the sign of the Son of Man will appear in the heaven."

75. The early Christians were familiar with the phrase "birth pangs of the Messiah," as evidenced by Matthew (24:8) and Mark (13:8), who state that the eschatological wars are the beginning of the birth pangs. See also John 16:21. On Revelation 12 and 2 Thessalonians see R. D. Aus, "The Relevance of Isaiah 66:7 to Revelation 12 and 2 Thessalonians 1," *ZNW* 67 (1976), 253-268.

rabbinic literature do not define the content of the term, only who will be spared the pangs.[76] The phrase occurs in the Mekhilta of Rabbi Ishmael, where it is one of three calamities that those who observe the Sabbath will be spared: "If you will succeed in keeping the Sabbath you will escape three visitations: The day of God, the birth pangs of the Messiah, and the Great Judgment Day."[77] In other words, after the war of Gog and Magog, the Messiah will appear and defeat the wicked nations, and usher in the ultimate judgment,[78] this being the standard sequence of Jewish eschatology.[79] As noted, Revelation 12 and the Qumran hymn shed light on the background of the rabbinic phrase "birth pangs of the Messiah," though it is still difficult to establish its original content. In other words, "the birth pangs of the Messiah" uses the image of labor pains to cast the period just prior to the advent of the Messiah as particularly difficult, and perhaps hints at the eruption of evil prior to redemption. In any case, the messianic pangs belong to the same worldview that gave rise to the figure of the Antichrist.

We have devoted our study to the various messianic figures reflected in the New Testament and early Christianity. One of our goals was to show that the

---

76. See Volz, *Die Eschatologie der Jüdischen Gemeinde*, 42-43, and Bacher, *Die Aggada der Tannaiten*, 1.112, n. 1 and 2.510, n. 5. It appears the later dicta have Rabbi Eliezer ben Hyrcanus as their source. See the Mekhilta of Rabbi Ishmael (page 169-170 in the Horovitz-Rabin edition) and the Mekhilta of Rabbi Shimon Bar Yohai (page 113 in the Epstein-Melamed edition), where the sayings of Rabbi Eliezer and Rabbi Yehoshua were likely reversed, though it is possible that the attribution in the latter is the original.

77. Mekhilta of Rabbi Ishmael, Vayissah 4, Lauterbach 2.120. This appears to be the original order (and see the Mekhilta of Rabbi Shimon Bar Yohai; page 113 in the Epstein-Melamed edition). However, when the Mekhilta repeats the saying, it states: "The birth pangs of the Messiah, the day of Gog and Magog, and the Great Judgment Day" (Vayissa 5, Lauterbach 2.123). B. Shabbat 118a reads: "The birth pangs of the Messiah, the judgment of *Gehenom* and the war of Gog and Magog."

78. The Mekhilta of Rabbi Ishmael (page 113) refers to בית דין הגדול, "the great court house," which corresponds to the Aramaic בית דינא רבא in Targum Jonathan to 2 Samuel 23:7. The same phrase appears in t. Ohalot 18.18 (I owe this reference to S. Safrai). In Targum Jonathan to Numbers 16:12 the Sanhedrin is also called "the great court house" (בי דינא רבא). The Targum to Psalm 73:20 speaks of "the great day of judgment" (יום דינא רבא), as does the Targum to Job 2:1. The same phrase appears in an Aramaic prayer recorded in the book of the Elcesaites in Greek letters, with the letters written backwards as an esoteric technique. See A. F. J. Klijn and G. J. Reining, *Patristic Evidence for Jewish-Christian Sects* (Leiden, 1973), 158; Epiphanius, *Panarion* 19.4.1. (The Elcesaites were a Jewish-Christian sect that belonged to the Ebionites.) For a list of the apocryphal occurrences of "great court house" see Volz, *Die Eschatologie der Jüdischen Gemeinde*, 163. This footnote is intended as a supplement to Volz's list.

79. See above, n. 12.

roots of Christianity are planted in Judaism — though this should be obvious since Christianity was once a messianic Jewish sect. From the time of Jesus on, early Christianity preserves various and sundry Jewish messianic ideas, ideas that can be traced by contemporary scholars using the New Testament and early Christian literature. The conceptual diversity is apparent even when the survey is limited to Jewish messianic figures, and even though we did not discuss the different understandings of the redemptive process and its significance. Scholarly advances in the study of Rabbinic and apocryphal literature, along with the discovery of the Dead Sea Scrolls, pave the way for a richer understanding of ancient Jewish eschatology. So much so, in fact, that it is now necessary to examine the extant sources anew and reach novel and more firmly established conclusions. The present study has sought only to touch on a small fraction of the important questions facing scholarship, as it is the study of the New Testament that may open our eyes to those aspects of the ancient messianic belief discussed here.

Scholarship on ancient Jewish messianism has maintained a dichotomous view, with Jewish messianism understood as grounded and realistic, while Christian messianism is suffused with supernatural hopes. This dichotomy is buttressed by a single-mindedly political interpretation of Jewish messianism and a stilted sociological approach. Combined with the one-sided scholarship of the *Wissenschaft des Judentums*, the end result of these approaches is a simple and simplistic understanding of Jewish messianism. While it is true that the sages sought to restrain the popular messianic impetus, even in the Talmud the messianic views are not so uniform or "realistic" or political as is commonly believed. Rabbinic statements have, from the outset, contained traces of and allusions to the "sublime" views we encounter in a more developed and explicit form in other Second Temple corpora. Indeed, we can show (though this should be obvious) that the rabbis were familiar not only with the political Davidic Messiah, but with other messianic figures as well, as well as with the universal aspect of cosmic redemption. In sum we have sought to use the New Testament to expand our understanding of ancient Judaism and its spiritual worldview.[80]

---

80. Since completing this study I have received *The Messianic Idea in Judaism*, a collection of essays celebrating Gershom Scholem's eightieth birthday (Jerusalem, 1982). The relevant articles for the present discussion are I. Gruenwald, "From Decline to Ascent: Jewish Eschatology and Messianism," 18-36, as well as Scholem's concluding comments, 254-262.

19. Nadab and Abihu According to Philo and the Rabbis

Written with Shmuel Safrai

The story of the tragic death of Nadab and Abihu raises many questions, some already rooted in its ambivalent portrayal in the Bible. The greatness of Sages is evident in their willingness to grapple with the obscure narrative in Leviticus, rather than shy away from the abyss that underlies it. There were sages who sought to reach the roots of this enigmatic story, so it is no wonder so many midrashim have sprouted up around it.[1] The present study will not try to survey all these midrashim; rather, it focuses on those that present the brothers' act in a positive or affirming light. A secondary argument will be that Philo's abundant affection for Nadab and Abihu is anchored in the thought of the Palestinian sages.[2] Even though Philo is more lavish in his praise, his approach is fundamentally similar to the interpretive positions of the sages who viewed the tragic death of Aaron's sons sympathetically.

In Leviticus 10:1-3 we find: "Now Aaron's sons, Nadab and Abihu, each took his censer, put fire in it, and laid incense on it; and they offered foreign fire before the Lord, such as he had not commanded them. And fire came out from the presence of the Lord and consumed them, and they died before the

---

1. See A. Shinan, "The Sin of Nadab and Abihu in Rabbinic Aggadah," *Tarbiz* 48 (1979), 201-214. Note the fascinating statement of Rav Saadia Gaon in *Rabbenu Saadia Gaon's Commentaries to the Torah*, Qafih edition (Jerusalem, 1963), 90.

2. The passages in which Philo discusses the death of Nadab and Abihu are listed in Colson and Earp's translation in the Loeb Classical Library (London, 1962), 10.390-391. To Colson and Earp's list should be added the *Questions and Answers on Exodus* at Exodus 2:27, which is only extant in Armenian and was published in the Loeb series in the translation of R. Marcus as a supplement (London, 1953), 2.67-69.

Lord. Then Moses said to Aaron, 'This is what the Lord meant when he said, 'Through those who are near me I will show myself holy, and before all the people I will be glorified.' And Aaron was silent." Following the tragedy, the sons of Aaron's uncle "came forward and carried [Nadab and Abihu] by their tunics out of the camp" (Lev 10:5). It is not our goal to provide new insights into the meaning of the original biblical text, though it is clear that Moses' words to his brother reflect approval and affection for the dead children. Now, Philo praises Aaron's two sons and finds nothing wrong with their behavior. According to Philo, the names Nadab and Abihu allude to their spiritual connection to God and their ability to elevate themselves above mortal affairs: Nadab, from the same root as the biblical מתנדב, refers to one who fears God willingly and not as matter of compunction, while Abihu means that the Lord is his father — he accepts God's authority as that of a father, not a master (*On the Migration of Abraham*, 168-169). This interpretation, which is based on the Hebrew meaning of the names, is otherwise unattested, though other readers have similarly focused on the motif of the sons' willing and enthusiastic acceptance of God.

The assertion that Aaron's cousins approached Nadab and Abihu, who were then "carried by their tunics," is ambivalent in Hebrew: do the tunics in question belong to Nadab and Abihu, or to the carriers? The Sifra states: "The verse teaches, '[the fire . . .] consumed them,' *them* but not their clothes."[3] The same view is attested in t. Berakhot 4.17, where the verse is explained as follows: "Since one has mercy on the righteous during times of ire, how much the more so during times of mercy."[4] Philo, however, argues that the tunics in question belonged to the carriers, and this is the basis of his expansive reading. When Nadab and Abihu drew near to the Lord, they left their mortal life behind them and received eternal life. They stand naked before the vacuous vanities of the world, for those who carried them would not have had to use their own tunics had Aaron's sons not torn from themselves the bonds of passion and physical compulsion (*Allegorical Interpretation* 2.57-58). It is hard to believe that such an interpretation existed in early rabbinic literature. Nonetheless, the general thrust is not wholly foreign to later rabbinic interpretations — even to this very day.

Philo's key discussion — which has fascinating parallels in early mid-

3. Sifra Shemini (page 45c-d in the Weiss edition). But see Leviticus Rabbah 20.9 (page 463 in the Margaliot edition), where the death of Nadab and Abihu is explained, inter alia, as a result of their having no clothes or, according to Rabbi Levi, "they were lacking coats." See also Shinan, "The Sin of Nadab and Abihu," 209.

4. According to Bacher (*Die Agada der Tannaiten* [Strasbourg, 1892], 1.347, n. 3), this dictum should not be attributed to Rabbi Tarfon.

rashim — occurs in his *On Dreams* 2.67. Here he argues that Moses assumed that Nadab and Abihu would not be mourned (Lev 10:6) since (unlike Joseph) they were not devoured by a wild animal, but were consumed by the power of an eternal flame. This, indeed, was their motivation for cleaving to God — the desire to annul the carnal and so draw near to the divine, the very desire that caused them to tear off any element that blocked their path to God. It is striking that Philo interprets the foreign fire they brought before the Lord in positive terms: the fire in question was, in fact, their own desire to cleave to God. It is called "foreign" because it overcomes materiality and thus is foreign to the created world, though it is close to God. In the statement that the burning desire is itself near to God, Philo is interpreting God's assertion that "Through those who are near me I will show myself holy." They did not ascend the steps of the altar (an action expressly prohibited in the Torah), but ascended spiritually to the highest heavens, becoming a pleasing scent like that of the burnt offering.

I have chosen to paraphrase Philo's account, largely because his style, though enthusiastic, is obscure. This may be due not only to his mystical tendencies, but to the fact that his portrait is based in part on midrashic traditions that he knew only by oral transmission. The use of existing interpretive motifs presents a problem for later readers, since not all these are still extant, so it is difficult to know what Philo received from other sources and what originated with him. It is possible that some of the motifs that appear at first glance to be the product of Greek thought, are in fact Jewish. The interpretation of the foreign fire as foreign to the created world but near to God is, to be sure, extreme, but there is no need to turn to Greek thought to explain its origin. Despite the linguistic difficulties of Philo's account, it appears the foreign fire of Nadab and Abihu may be the very same fire that consumed them like a burnt offering (but the matter is uncertain and ultimately has no bearing on my argument).

Needless to say, most of the midrashim are concerned with the nature of the sin for which Nadab and Abihu were smitten, and the multitude of proposed answers reflects uncertainty on the part of the sages (as we see also with regard to Nadab and Abihu's uncle, Moses, whose sin prevented him from entering Canaan). Leading sages took part in this debate as early as the tannaitic times,[5] though the midrashim sympathetic to Aaron's sons — and like Philo in this respect — are generally anonymous. The sole exception is the long and complex discussion in Leviticus Rabbah 12.2 cited in the name of

5. See the opening of Sifra Aharei Mot, as well as Leviticus Rabbah (461 in the Margaliot edition).

Rabbi Shmuel bar Nahman, though it is clear that he is merely transmitting the tradition of others.[6] Four midrashic units that offer qualified praise of Nadab and Abihu's behavior are preserved in the Mekhilta de-Miluim, an addition to the Shemini pericope of the Sifra.[7] The textual issue is complicated further by the presence of an interpolation into this section, marked as §§17-28 by Weiss.[8] But the secondary status of Mekhilta de-Miluim, and the fact that the interpolation is not attested in several manuscripts,[9] do not mean it is a late text. In what follows, I refer to the four units with the letters A-D. A and B are part of the interpolation in Mekhilta de-Miluim, while C and D belong in the Mekhilta de-Miluim proper. It is worth noting that A and B parallel C and D in their content and their order: A and C (§§ 22 and 32, respectively, in Weiss) deal with Leviticus 10:2 ("fire came out from the presence of the Lord and consumed them" etc.), and contain guarded praise for the devotion of Nadab and Abihu; B and D (§§ 23 and 36, respectively, in Weiss) refer to Leviticus 10:3 ("Then Moses said to Aaron" etc.), portraying Aaron's sons as great figures. We begin with the latter pair:

> Aaron stood puzzled, saying, "Woe is me that I and my sons have sinned and come to this." Moses approached him and sought to encourage him, saying: "Aaron, my brother, I was told at Sinai that God will sanctify the tabernacle with a great man. I thought at the time that the tabernacle would be sanctified through you or me, but now we see that your sons were greater than either of us, for the tabernacle was sanctified through them." When Aaron heard this, he justified God's actions and fell silent. As it is written: "And Aaron was silent." (Weiss, §23)

And:

> Moses said to him, for it is written: "Through those who are near me I will show myself holy." This statement was made to Moses at Sinai, but he

---

6. See Leviticus Rabbah (256-258 in the Margaliot edition) and the parallels cited there, and in particular the interesting reading in b. Zebahim 115b. See also Bacher, *Aggadot ha-Amoraim*, 1.516, n. 2.

7. The readings follow Isaac Hirsch Weiss, *Sifra* (New York, 1947), 44-46. I have also consulted the facsimile edition of MS Assemani 66 published by E. Finkelstein as *Torat Kohanim* (New York, 1957).

8. See Shinan, "The Sin of Nadab and Abihu," 212, n. 65; M. D. Herr, *Encyclopaedia Judaica*, s.v. "Sifra," 24.15172-15179; H. L. Strack and G. Stemberger, *Introduction to Talmud and Midrash*, trans. Markus Bockmuehl (Philadelphia, 1992), 259-266, as well as Weiss's comments in his edition, 85d.

9. Including MS Assemani 66 (192, line 6 from the bottom).

did not understand it until the event occurred. Once it occurred, Moses said: "Aaron, my brother, your sons died solely for the sanctification of God's name. As it is written: 'I will meet the Israelites there, and I shall be sanctified by my glory' (Exod 29:43). Once Aaron realized that his sons were known by God, he fell silent and was rewarded for his silence. (Weiss, §36)[10]

It is evident that the unbridled praise heaped on the sons of Aaron is based on Leviticus 10:3: "Through those who are near me I will show myself holy, and before all the people I will be glorified." The Sifra (like Leviticus Rabbah and the parallel in b. Zevahim 115b) cites Exodus 29:43, whose conclusion ("I will meet the Israelites there, and I shall be *sanctified by my glory*") is interpreted as an allusion to "before all the people I will be glorified." The Talmud there states: "Do not read 'by my glory' (בכבודי) but rather 'by those whom I glorify' (במכובדי)." Nadab and Abihu, then, are great figures, more beloved of God than Moses or Aaron, men who were known to God and whose death sanctified the tabernacle. In other words, they martyred themselves "for the sanctification of the name of God" (Sifra Shemini §36; Leviticus Rabbah, page 257 in the Margaliot edition, and see the similar language in b. Zevahim 115b). We will return to the motif of martyrdom.

Now, Philo does not explicitly invoke the motif of martyrdom, but, like the midrashim passages, portrays Nadab and Abihu as great individuals, whose yearning for the divine brought them near to God. As noted, Philo sees

---

10. Here is the midrash preserved in Leviticus Rabbah (256-258 in the Margaliot edition): Rabbi Shmuel bar Nahman said: God said to Moses: "Moses, I am going to meet Israel and sanctify myself in this edifice, as it is written 'I will meet the Israelites there, and I shall be sanctified by my glory'" (Exod 29:43). This statement was made to Moses at Sinai but he did not understand it until the event occurred. When did that happen? On the eighth day, as it is written: "and when all the people saw it, they shouted and fell on their faces" (Lev 9:24). Moses said to God: "Eternal master, who is more beloved than I or my brother Aaron, through whom you would sanctify this edifice!" Once the two sons of Aaron entered to make their offering but were consumed, Moses said to Aaron: "Aaron, my brother, your sons died only for the sanctification of the name of God, as God said: 'Through those who are near me I will show myself holy' (Lev 10:3), and likewise it is written, 'I will meet the Israelites there, and I shall be sanctified by my glory'" (Exod 29:43). This is the statement Moses heard at Sinai but did not understand it until the event occurred. Once it occurred, Moses said to Aaron: "Aaron, my brother, I was told at Sinai that God was going to meet Israel and be sanctified in this edifice through a great man. I thought God was referring to me or to you, but now we find that your two sons are more beloved than we." Upon hearing this, and realizing his sons were known by God, Aaron fell silent and was rewarded for his silence, as it is written: "And Aaron was silent." This is clearly a composite midrash, which reflects the midrashic tradition in passages B and C. The same tradition is preserved in b. Zevahim 115b.

the bringing of foreign fire before the Lord as a symbol of their devotion. The same understanding is evident in the other midrashic pair (A and C). In Sifra Shemini §22 we read:

> When the sons of Aaron saw that all the offerings had been offered and all the ritual acts performed but God's presence had not descended onto Israel, Nadab said to Abihu: "Can you cook a meal without fire?" Immediately they took a foreign fire and entered the holy of holies, as it is written: "Now Aaron's sons, Nadab and Abihu, each took his censer, put fire in it, and laid incense on it; and they offered foreign fire before the Lord." God said to them: I will glorify you more than you glorified me! You brought to my presence a ritually impure fire, but I will consume you with pure fire.[11]

This midrash clearly praises the brothers for their righteous intentions and brave deed: God rewards their devotion by consuming them with pure fire, a view very similar to Philo's statement that the brothers were consumed by the force of the flame. It further appears the authors of the midrash may have resisted an explicit statement to the effect that the burning of Nadab and Abihu caused their odor to ascend to heaven as the pleasing scent of a burnt offering. Philo says this openly.

A similar view is attested in Sifra Shemini §32, which is preserved only in an abbreviated and corrupt form,[12] and is cited here in the corrected form:[13]

> "Now Aaron's sons, Nadab and Abihu, each took his censer" (Lev 10:1), they too in their joy, since they saw a new fire descend from the heavens, and its flames licked the burnt offering and the fats on the altar. They arose to add love to love, as it is written: "each took his censer" and "took" refers to joy, as it is written "On the first day you shall take . . . and you

11. See the passage from a Yemenite manuscript published by Z. M. Rabinowitz, *Ginze Midrash* (Tel Aviv, 1977), 57: "'Now Aaron's sons, Nadab and Abihu, each took his censer' (Lev 10:1). They said, Moses and Aaron entered the tabernacle to offer incense and a miracle occurred for their sake and a fire came down to consume all the offerings on the altar. We too are beloved enough for a miracle to occur for our sake." And see Rabinowitz's comments.

12. The Sifra text is published in Rabinowitz, *Ginze Midrash*, 50; the reading is as follows: "'Now Aaron's sons, Nadab and Abihu, each took his censer' (Lev 10:1), they too in their joy since they saw a new fire descend from the heavens, and its flames licked the altar, thus too they arose to add love to love, as it is written 'each took,' and 'took' refers to joy. . . ."

13. See Shinan, "The Sin of Nadab and Abihu," 212. I have relied on the Steinsalz edition of Midrash ha-Gadol to Leviticus ([Jerusalem, 1976], 219) rather than Shinan.

shall rejoice" (Lev 23:40). Here the text speaks of "taking" and there it refers to "taking." Just as that taking involves joy, so too this taking involves joy.

This midrash, which parallels the earlier interpretation, praises the deeds of Nadab and Abihu and in this is similar to Philo. Aaron's sons acted out of joy after seeing the new fire descend from the heavens, "and when all the people saw it, they shouted and fell on their faces" (Lev 9:24); they too rejoiced and wanted to add love to the existing love. The fire that descended from the heavens was a tangible expression of God's love, and they sought to add love to that love, and thus "each took his censer." The end result is recounted in the previous midrash: "God said to them: I will glorify you more than you glorified me! You brought to my presence a ritually impure fire, but I will consume you with pure fire."

It seems to me that, despite obvious differences, there is an undeniable similarity between these midrashim and Philo's approach to the story of Nadab and Abihu. So much so, in fact, that we must assume that Philo's account was indirectly influenced by midrashim such as these. This connection is instructive both in terms of Philo's biblical interpretation, and in terms of the sages', which are more sublime, more "mystical" (if I may use this term) than is usually assumed. As a result, our analysis has ramifications for our understanding of rabbinic midrash and, more generally, the rabbinic worldview.

In addition, the passage in question sheds new light on the concept of martyrology. To be sure, neither Philo nor the rabbinic midrashim portray a classic martyrdom, since Aaron's sons are not faced with the choice of veering from God's path. Their actions were rather motivated by their devotion to God, seeking to add love to the love, and bore witness to God in their joyous and voluntary death. For this, God glorified them more than they glorified him and they were consumed by a pure fire or, as Philo states, rose to the heavens as the pleasing odor of a burnt offering.

What is the relationship between the death of Nadab and Abihu and martyrdom as we understand the term today? The midrashim preserve a broader sense of the Hebrew *kiddush ha-shem*, which came to mean martyrdom in later Amoraic literature, but originally included devotion to God both in thought and in action. These cause the sanctification of the name of God. It is only in Amoraic literature that the phrase came to refer to withstanding a test during times of persecution.[14] The death of Nadab and Abihu does, in

14. See S. Safrai, "*Kiddush ha-Shem* in Tannaitic Thought" (Hebrew), *Itzhak Beer Memorial Volume* (Jerusalem, 1979-1981), 28-42.

fact, sanctify the tabernacle. They brought the fire before God as an act of joy, in order to add love to the existing love. The motif or religious death appears here without the persecution that normally attends martyrdom. They loved God "to the death," the most important justification for death for God's sake beginning with the thought of Rabbi Aqiva.[15] The idea of loving God "to the death" preceded that of martyrdom and would remain a key element in the Jewish understanding of dying for God for generations to come.

15. See Safrai, "*Kiddush ha-Shem* in Tannaitic Thought," and his discussion in *Immanuel* 8 (1978), 70.

20. Virgil the Wizard in an Ancient Jewish Narrative

Medieval Jewish literature was in no wise limited to questions of theology and philosophy. Like their gentile neighbors, medieval Jews enjoyed a good story, even one that had no religious meaning, and when they came upon such a story in Christian writings, they translated it to Hebrew. The medieval period witnessed a flowering of epic narratives — in poetry and prose alike — and Jewish writers took part in this enterprise as well. Needless to say, these works were understood in very different terms during the Middle Ages than we understand contemporary literature. Many modern works would be greeted with dismay and disgust in the "dark" ages. But without the naïve curiosity and the appreciation of fine plotting typical of medieval authors, masterpieces such as the *Decameron* and *Canterbury Tales* would never have been produced. One of the best-known medieval "novellas" (which does not suit the moral view of our times but presented no difficulty for the readers and even artists of the day) involves Virgil and his vengeance.

I have discovered a Hebrew manuscript of this story. Since the Hebrew text is masterful, a work of art in its own right, I have decided to publish it in its entirety. Hopefully, this publication will be a contribution to medieval Virgil studies, to the study of Jewish secular literature of the Middle Ages, and, hopefully, a pleasant literary experience for the reader.

The story is preserved in a large manuscript in the Bodleian Library in Oxford (2792 MS. Hebr. 11), the first part of which has already been published in an English translation.[1] The Virgil story appears in the second part of the

1. M. Gaster, *Chronicles of Jerahmeel* (London, 1899). Ktav Publishers has reprinted Gaster's work (New York, 1971) with a new introduction by Hayim Schwartzbaum.

manuscript, which has not been published. Though the manuscript is known as the "Chronicles of Yerahmiel (or: Jerahmeel),"[2] it is in fact a collection gathered by Rabbi Elazar ben Asher ha-Levi, of the Rhine region.[3] Since Rabbi Elazar lived in the second half of the fourteenth century, this will be the *terminus ad quem* of our story. For purposes of dating, however, it is important to determine whether the Virgil narrative is an original part of the Yerahmiel anthology, or included by Rabbi Elazar ben Asher. Clearly the author is Italian, since he has included the Italian word "bonomini" in his text.[4] But while Yerahmiel may have been Italian, he appears not to have been the author of the story, since his style — inasmuch as can be determined — is dissimilar to that of the author. Nor is Rabbi Elazar ben Asher the author, since he lived in the Rhine region and not Italy and, moreover, Rabbi Elazar's command of Hebrew is tenuous, while our author writes in a vivid and natural style. We conclude, then, that we are dealing with an anonymous Hebrew author who lived in Italy, whose work was either included in the "Chronicles of Yerahmiel" or added to it by Elazar ben Asher.

Elazar ben Asher tried to organize the material in his anthology chronologically. So much so, that he interrupted the *Sefer Josippon* manuscript in the "Chronicles of Yerahmiel" and inserted additional material that deals with the period described in *Josippon*. Thus, in the "Chronicles of Yerahmiel" there is a break in *Sefer Josippon* at 197a, which contains a short addendum concerning Titus's dispersion of the Jews that was already part of the *Josippon* tradition by the time it reached Elazar ben Asher (and is attested in other *Josippon* manuscripts). At this point, the text shifts to a discussion of Josephus and his writing, of Jesus and his family, and of other figures in the early Christian world (197a-b).[5] This passage, which is based on Christian sources

---

2. Named for Rabbi Yerahmiel ben Asher ha-Levi, a scholar and religious poet who apparently lived in Italy. The collection undoubtedly included *Sefer Josippon*, which was composed in 952, and parts of Rabbi Yerahmiel's sayings are cited in *Arugot ha-Bosem*, written by Abraham ben Azriel of Bohemia in 1234 (see Urbach's edition, 1.281; 2.107; 4.144). Yerahmiel put together his anthology some time between 952 and 1234, which means he lived in the eleventh or twelfth century. See A. Neubauer, "Jerahmeel ben Shlomo," *JQR* (o.s.) 9 (1898), 364-382 and 697-699. See also H. Albeck's comment to L. Zunz, *Ha-derashot be-Israel* (Jerusalem, 1947), 325; L. Zunz, *Literaturgeschichte* (Berlin, 1889), 485-486. On the *Josippon* see my Hebrew study on "The Author of *Sefer Josippon*," *Zion* 18 (1953), 109-126.

3. See J. Perles, "Die Berner Handschrift des Kleinen Aruch," *Jubelschrift zum 70. Geburtstage des Prof. Dr. H. Graetz* (Breslau, 1887), 19-23.

4. The influence of Italian is also evident in the question "how do you stand?" a calque of the Italian *"come state?"*

5. Both the addendum and the passage that follows were published in A. Neubauer, *Medieval Jewish Chronicles* (Oxford, 1887), 1.190-191.

(in Latin) and was apparently composed by Yerahmiel, is followed by a brief legend concerning the origins of the prayer *ve-hu rahum* ("he is indeed merciful"). The legend in question, which is attested in other sources,[6] describes the dispersion of the Jews by Titus. There follow two lines on the death of Titus, and then the story of Virgil the wizard, without any connection to Titus or his historical period. Following the passage in question there is a section (fourteen lines long) based on the Talmudic tradition regarding Hadrian's destruction of the city Beitar, in which Hadrian is erroneously identified as the heir of Titus. The last sentence states, "the rest of Hadrian's chronology is recounted in Lamentations Rabbati." Our story, then, is located within the chronological framework of the Yerahmiel Chronicles, and attributed to the days of Titus. We cannot determine whether it was already part of the Yerahmiel collection, or was added by Rabbi Elazar ben Asher. If the former is the case, the story originates in the eleventh or twelfth centuries, if the latter — most likely the thirteenth. Its provenance, as already noted, is Italian. Here is the story:

> There was in the days of the wicked Titus a very rich man who owned large houses and courtyards and gardens and towers. The man in question was one of the most prominent Romans and his family members were called *bonomini* in Latin. He had a very beautiful wife whose beauty was like that of the moon. On account of her beauty he built her a tower in his yard, and she did not leave it. Once there was a wedding ceremony and people marched through the streets dancing and playing timbrels and flutes. The dancing procession reached the tower in which the woman was located. Then a man, who was a wizard, saw the woman and desired her, and he sent his servant to the tower to see if she emerged from it at night, and the servant was always lying in wait for her. When he saw that she never emerged, he wondered: "What shall I do? If I go there myself it will end badly." He wrote her a note and sent it with a demon, informing her that he wanted to see her. In the morning, she went to the window as was her habit, and saw the letter before her and wondered: What is this letter? Whence did it arrive? What did she do? She called out to her maidservant and told her to summon a certain scribe, who resided

6. The story of the three Jewish sages appears in M. Herschler (ed.), *The Prayer Book of Rabbi Shelomo ben Shimshon of Worms* (Jerusalem, 1971), 127-128, and was earlier published by Neubauer (who found it in MS Oxford 1102) in "Settlements of the Jews in Southern Italy," *JQR* 4 (o.s.) (1892), 616. For a discussion of the story see L. Zunz, *Die gottesdienstlichen Vorträge* (Frankfurt, 1892), 388-389; H. J. Perles, in *Monatsschrift für Geschichte des Judentums* 106 (1876), 376.

in her court. She went and summoned him, and when he came the princess said to him secretly: When I awoke this morning I found this letter by my window. Tell me what it says! And he told her the content of the letter. She said: Write him in response that I am not interested, and curse him! After some time, her husband went off on a distant voyage and commanded her to remain in the house with her maidservant. The wizard heard that the husband had departed, and he sent her silver and gold and jewelry so that she would yield to him. She said to her maidservant: How foolish is this man for testing me! What did she do? She took the treasures and sent him a message, saying: I want you to come to me as I welcome you, only do not enter through the door, but only through the window. He did so, coming to her in the dead of night. But when he heard her response he was so overjoyed that he forgot his magic tools and books. So he looked out at the tower by night, but prior to his arrival she had gone to another of her husband's towers nearby, having ordered a large basket with three ropes wrapped around it, and when the wizard came, they said to him: get into the basket and we will draw you up. He entered and they drew him halfway up to tower. In the meantime she returned to her original tower, and they tied the ropes to the inner beams of the tower and neither raised him nor lowered him. The tower was tall and he was suspended in the air. He spent three days and three nights in the basket, without food or water, so that he grew hungry and thirsty and thought to throw himself from the basket. But when he would look down and see the height of the basket, he feared the fall would kill him. Nor could he ascend since the demons would not come to him, as they usually would, since he did not have his books and could not adjure them. He did not know what to do. He stood and wondered, and passersby would see him and wonder: who is that man, hanging from the tower? They were very perplexed. And young boys would pelt him with stones. On the third day, she looked out the window and said to him: Mister so and so, what do you wish and how are you doing [lit.: how do you stand]? For you knew when you sent me the silver and gold and jewelry that I am not a prostitute. Now you have lost your money without fulfilling your desire. All the while he was crying and pleading with her that, for the love of God, she lower him to the earth and not leave him in this shameful state. She said to him: This is proper punishment for men like you, who wish to commit adultery with the wives of their friends. And she left him for a fourth day. On the fourth day she took pity on him and ordered that he be lowered. They did so, but when the basket was at the height of a tall man, they dropped him suddenly from the basket onto the earth, his rib breaking from the force of the fall, as he landed on a rock. He shouted and a number of people gathered around him, for they heard his voice and they asked: What is with you? And he was afraid to tell them what had happened. So they led him to his home with a broken rib, and he ordered the doctors to heal him, and they did so.

When he had recuperated, he said to his servants: I will have my revenge on that woman. And he ordered them to bring him his magic books. What did he do? He used his magic to extinguish all the fires in Rome and the surrounding towns, so there was no fire to be found throughout Rome. When they tried to bring it from another location, be it with hot stones or with wood, after a third of the journey it would go out. Even great logs, like beams and tree trunks, would be extinguished. Thus many people died of hunger since without fires they could not heat their ovens to make bread.

All the residents of Rome gathered together to take counsel regarding how to find fire and what to do, each speaking his own view. Then the wizard answered, saying: If you want to give me money, promise you will not harm me but rather will do all that I tell you. If so, you will find fire. So they said: Well have you spoken. And they gave him much money. In the morning, behold the citizens of Rome came to him and said, Where is the fire you will give us? And he answered: Go to so-and-so woman — she has the fire and she will give it to you! So they went to her and he joined them, giving each and every one a wax candle. Grab her! he said, and they did so and seated her on a wooden tower and stripped her naked. Then the wizard approached her and placed the wax candle between her legs, and the candle lit spontaneously. And this is what all of them did, for no one was permitted to use a candle to light another candle, only directly from her vagina. And the woman was shamed, more greatly than anyone from the founding of the city to the present. After some time, the husband of this woman returned and was told what had happened to his wife, and he was furious. What did he do? He gathered all his clan and they came to her family, where they met the wizard and his clan, and they fought until none were left standing. All told forty thousand and thirty-five men of Rome died for the sake of that woman.

The story is a reworking of a well-known medieval tale about the wizard Virgil.[7] It appears the Hebrew author was unaware of the wizard's identi-

---

7. See D. Comparetti, *Virgilio nel Medio Evo* (Florence, 1946), 2.108-120, 151-153. See the texts at 180, 188-190, 200-207, 225, 232-236, 247-249, 260-261. Comparetti's book was translated into English by E. F. M. Benecke as *Virgil in the Middle Ages* (New York, 1959).

fication as Virgil, as both the wizard and the woman are anonymous. The word "bonomini" is clearly not the woman's family name, rather an indication that her family was of the nobility — our author does not know the equivalent Hebrew term. Since the author does not know the identity of the wizard, only that the event occurred in ancient Rome, it was easy for him to locate it during the reign of Titus.

The first part of the story, Virgil in the basket, is an independent narrative unit — the woman punishes the man wooing her by ridiculing him. The second part, the woman's punishment, is also an independent unit that merely alludes to the culpability of the woman. The two were joined because the woman's virtue and her sharp rejection of the wizard explain his cruel revenge. Since the stories were originally separate, it is not surprising that the wizard was not immediately recognized as the famous Virgil.[8] Interestingly, an eighteenth-century work written in modern Greek joins the two parts of our story but does not identify the wizard as Virgil but as Emperor Leo, "the philosopher."[9] The identification with Virgil is, nonetheless, clear enough, as there was a widespread medieval belief that Virgil was supernaturally gifted and had prophesied the coming of Christ and described hell in the *Aeneid*. Indeed, there developed a popular belief that he was a wizard, and since the hero of the second half of our story is a wizard, it may well have been Virgil himself.

We cannot ascertain the pre-history of our story. Some texts contain allusions to either the first or the second unit, but we cannot conclude that their authors did not know both parts. The first mention of the story is that of the troubadour Guiraut of Calanson, who alludes to "the fire that (Virgil) was able to extinguish." The story as a whole is attested in the thirteenth century, but we do not know if it was known earlier still.[10] As noted, Yerahmiel lived in the eleventh or twelfth century, and Rabbi Elazar ben Asher in the first half of the fourteenth, though we cannot determine whether our story was an original part of the anthology of the former or only appended by the latter. In any case, the Hebrew version of the Virgil story is no later than the thirteenth century and thus is one of the earliest witnesses to the tale — if not the earliest.

I have already indicated that the Hebrew author did not know the iden-

8. See Comparetti, *Virgilio nel Medio Evo*, 2.111-113.

9. See Comparetti, *Virgilio nel Medio Evo*, 2.112.

10. See Comparetti, *Virgilio nel Medio Evo*, 2.113. The image of Virgil in the basket is quite common in medieval art (see Comparetti, *Virgilio nel Medio Evo*, 2.114-115), though this does not mean the artists knew the second half of the story as well. Virgil's revenge is also depicted, but only at a later time.

tity of his protagonist. This suggests he had not read the story, but had heard it from his Christian-Italian neighbors. The latter may have forgotten the identity of the wizard, but it is more likely the Jewish author omitted it since he did not consider it meaningful and, indeed, may not have recognized the name. In any case, the story is recounted with great economy. The extant versions differ in a number of details, and it is clear there were other versions that have not survived, so there is no way to determine which details were invented by the Jewish author.[11] All the same, a comparative survey of the versions indicates the superiority of the Hebrew text, which already contains many of the hallmarks of the classic Italian short story. Only the slaughter at the end is unfortunate, and may have been invented by the author to conclude the story. The blow the wizard suffers in his fall from the basket fits poorly with the good taste of medieval writing, but the overall plotting is tight. The wizard first sees the woman during a wedding parade; the Roman woman cannot read and must summon a scribe to read the letter to her and write the response. The most important improvement the Hebrew author includes is his explanation of the wizard's inability to free himself from his predicament, namely, that he was so overjoyed that he forgot to take with him his magical instruments and books. Other versions of the story offer no explanation for the disparity between his helplessness in the first part of the tale and his great power in the second. In terms of text-history, the explanation is, of course, that the two were originally independent units, linked only by the presence of a wizard protagonist. The Hebrew author, however, noted the discrepancy and formulated a convincing explanation.

The goal of this study was not to offer a detailed analysis of the Hebrew version of the tale of Virgil the wizard, which would be easy enough. My goal was merely to present to the readers this brief tale and to identify its protagonist, thus enriching our knowledge of the history of Hebrew literature, and perhaps offering a modest contribution to the text history of the medieval tale. The Hebrew version is, after all, one of the earliest witnesses to the story (no later than the 13th century), and of Italian provenance — the land of Virgil himself.

It is a well-told tale, written moreover in fine Hebrew. Stylistically, the Hebrew is biblical, but the text is free from linguistic purism, and the influ-

---

11. For example, in both the Hebrew version and the *Weltchronik* of the German poet Jansen Enikel (circa 1280) the woman is married, the Romans are unable to cook or bake when the fires are extinguished, and the Romans tell Virgil that their women and children are dying as a result ("uns stirbet wif und kint"). In the Hebrew text, Virgil asks that the Romans not harm him prior to offering them help, and a similar statement appears in Enikel's version. In other details, however, the two texts differ.

ence of post-biblical Hebrew is clearly evident. The linguistic elements are combined in a way that allows for a consistent and vivid Hebrew style, not at all artificial. The story is of independent literary value, and its publication is, therefore, important to the history of Hebrew literature and to Hebrew literature itself. Modern Hebrew readers will undoubtedly enjoy it.

21. Januris — Janus

The Palestinian Talmud (Avodah Zarah 1.2, 39c) preserves a dictum attributed to Rabbi Yohanan that explains the origin of the name *Calendae Januariae:* "Egypt and Rome were at war with each other, until they said, 'How much longer will we die in war with one another? Let us decree that each kingdom will command its general to fall on his sword. If he obeys, that kingdom will govern first.' The Egyptian general refused, but the Roman was an old man named Januris and he had twelve sons. The authorities said to him: 'If you obey us we will make your sons generals and hyparchs and commanders.' He obeyed them. His sons shouted at him *'calends Januris.'* The next day they mourned him in a *melaina hemera.*"

This is clearly a pagan story. Januris is Ιανουίρις, the popular Greek form of the month Januarius. According to Rabbi Yohanan's story, this is the source of *Calendae Januariae,* and the twelve children are, of course, the twelve months of the year. Already Blaufuss recognized that *"melaina hemera"* (μέλαινα ἡμέρα) is the Roma *dies ater* ("black day") that begins on the second of January.[1]

We have here an etiological story that seeks to explain the name Januarius as well as the *Calendae Januariae,* and the origin of the "black day" that falls on January second. The condition posited by the Roman and Egyptian authorities, that the war be decided by the willingness of the general to sacrifice himself, is also tied to pagan beliefs. The story is similar to the Greek

---

1. H. Blaufuss, *Römische Feste und Feiertage nach den Traktaten über den fremden Dienst* (Nuremberg, 1909), 8.

legend regarding the death of Kodros, the king of Athens. In the battle between the Athenians and the Dorians the Delphic Oracle stated that the battle would be won by the side whose general is killed. Kodros disguised himself as a woodcutter or a shepherd and entered the enemy camp, instigated a fight and was killed. This fulfilled the prophecy and the Athenians were victorious.[2] We may assume that the Talmudic story originally involved a prophecy rather than an agreement between the two sides, with Januris fulfilling the prophecy and thus tilting the scales in favor of Rome. The Kodros tale also indicates that the Talmud's "political" story has a religious dimension: the motif of a general or king who sacrifices himself recalls ancient pagan practices, that is, human sacrifice.[3]

The Januris narrative is, inter alia, a legendary account of Rome's antiquity. Does Roman religion recognize the possibility of a general's self-sacrifice? Indeed, we find a number of cases in the early days of Rome that a general would offer himself and the army of his enemies to the gods of Hades. During this ceremony, the general would wear his festive clothing (his *toga praetexta*), cover his head, and stand on his weapons. He would then head into battle and actively seek out death, for if the gods were to take his life, they would also be bound to accept the second part of his vow and destroy the armies of the enemy. The Roman general's self-sacrifice is known as *devotio,* and is likely the source of the Januris legend.[4] Both the subject matter and the religious background of the tale are pagan, so it appears Rabbi Yohanan faithfully transmitted what he had heard from pagan sources.

Rabbi Yohanan's story is quite similar to an accepted Roman tradition that derives the name Januar from Janus, King of Latium, named for the Roman deity who bears the same name.[5] The shift from Janus to Januarius may be due to a "correction" on the part of an eastern scribe who was familiar with the personal name Januarius.

The story cited by Rabbi Yohanan sought to explain why King Janus, for whom the month Januarius is named, became a god. The answer: because he was willing to sacrifice himself in order to save his nation during wartime.[6] All this is verified by the parallel legend preserved in pseudo-

2. Velleius Paterculus 2.1. According to another version, the prophecy stated that Athens would lose if Kodros was not killed.

3. Pauly-Wissowa, *Realencyclopaedie* s.v. Menschen Opfer.

4. See Pauly-Wissowa, *Realencyclopaedie* s.v. Devotio.

5. On Janus, see Pauly-Wissowa, *Realencyclopaedie.*

6. Though Rome was not founded during the days of Janus, both versions of the legend assume its existence.

Bede's "On the Divisions of the Times" *(De Divisionibus Temporum).*[7] There (chapter 15) we find:

> Januarius is thus named for two reasons — for the idol and for the matter.[8] For the idol, that is, for the two-faced Janus, the king of Epirus, who came to the Romans as an exile after being expelled from his homeland, when a barbarian people were besieging Rome. Janus was a cunning man, and advised the Romans on how to free the city of the siege, namely, if they honored him as a god after his death. When they had promised him they would, he asked for eight sheets soaked in oil, wax, and water. He then asked them to wrap him in the sheets, set them ablaze, and give him two white-hot swords. He then climbed onto the ramparts and told the Romans that when he cried out as a god, they should open the gates of the city and attack their enemies — assured of victory. And it was thus. After his death, the Romans honored him as a god and constructed a large temple in his honor in Rome.[9]

There is no doubt that the Talmudic story and the one preserved in *De Divisionibus Temporum* are two versions of the same legend, according to which the month Januarius was named for a Roman general who sacrificed himself during wartime and thus saved his people. The Christian version confirms our assumption that the self-sacrifice was a form of Roman *devotio.* Livy, who describes the *devotio* in his eighth book, cites the words of the priest *(pontifex)* who cites Janus first (Livy, 8.9.6). The legend may, then, be tied to this incantation, i.e., an attempt to explain why it is Janus who is first mentioned.

We have already noted that Janus was identified as the first king of Latium, so the legend in question assumes that the gods were once humans

---

7. P.L. volume 90, 650-651. The language of the text suggests it was composed during the Merovingian dynasty.

8. The story goes on to connect the name Janus with *janua,* a gate.

9. Januarius autem duobus modis nomen accepit, hoc est ex idolo et re. Ex idolo hoc est ex Jano bifronte rege Epirotarum fugatus et proiectus de sua patria venit ad Romanos, apud eos exsul effectus. Contigit autem ut gens multa barbarorum Romam obsedisset. Erat autem Janus ille homo ingeniosus, qui dedit consilium Romanis quomodo potuissent urbem liberare ab illa obsidione; ita tamen, si post mortem suam illum adorarent quasi deum. Haec autem illis promittentibus, ille petebat octo linteamina oleo et cera et aqua intincta et uncta. Quod si cum factum esset, dixit, ut involuissent se de illis linteaminibus et igni incendissent, et duos gladios calefactos et ardentes sibi dari postulavit, et postea ascendit super murum, et dixit ad Romanos, ut cum ille levasset se super murum et clamasset quasi deus, illi totis portis apertis ruissent super hostes, et haberent victoriam. Et ita factum est. Quod post mortem suam Romani quasi deum adoraverunt et fecerunt ei templum magnum in Roma.

that were deified due to their special attributes. This view was used by Christians and Jews alike in their polemic against paganism, and these versions introduce us to one of the "scholarly" pagan legends, which circulated in pagan circles no later than the third century c.e., the days of Rabbi Yohanan.

22. Anti-Jewish "Blood Libels" in Light of Hellenistic Worldviews

I

The roots of medieval blood libels reach back into the Hellenistic period. As with any polemical narrative, we must examine the historical conditions that gave rise to such stories, and how their perpetrators thought such narratives would further their goals. After all, a person trying to defame a group does so by means that — given his knowledge of the Zeitgeist — he considers to be effective. Thus, we must examine the ethnographic and religious concepts of the period and their use in polemic literature more broadly. This will help us understand the genesis of the blood libel and its function as a piece of propaganda.

The early blood libel has been preserved in two sources. The more famous is Apion's attack (Josephus *Contra Apion* 2.89-91), and the second, less famous, is preserved in the Suda in the name of Damokritos: "(Damokritos says) that the Jews bow before the head of a donkey made of gold and that every seven years they capture a non-Jew and offer him as sacrifice, rending his flesh and thus killing him." The speaker in question, "Damokritos the historian," is not known from any sources outside the Suda, so we have only the citation in question to try to determine his floruit. The reference to sacrifice suggests that Damokritos composed his book "On the Jews" while the Second Temple still stood.[1] Inas-

---

1. Schwarz (Pauly-Wissowa: s.v. Damokritos) argues that Damokritos lived no earlier than the first century B.C.E. and no later than 70 C.E. Heinemann (ibid.: s.v. Antisemitismus) suggests Damokritos lived before Apion or shortly after him. Any attempt to determine Damokritos's time through the passage in question must deal with his use of the imperfect tense. If he is speaking of Jewish sacrifices that happened in ancient times, he should be located

much as we can use linguistic evidence to establish the time of our short citation, it would appear Damokritos's statement was not composed before the first century B.C.E., since it is written in Koine,[2] though none of this suffices to establish the date of Damokritos.[3]

For our purposes, Damokritos's statement is important only for its content, that is, in that it represents a new form of the blood libel, as scholars have failed to note the special nature of Damokritos's accusation. The reference to human sacrifice and the worship to a donkey's head, both of which are known from Josephus, led scholars to characterize Damokritos as a synopsis of *Contra Apion* or to suggest both Damokritos and Josephus draw on a common source. However, a close reading shows that Damokritos's narrative is substantively different from Apion's, particularly in his description of the sacrificial victim being rent limb from limb. This custom was part of the worship of Dionysius on the island of Tenedos, which worshipped Dionysus Anthroporrhaiestes, who "took pleasure in rending human bodies" (and thus his epithet).[4] It is also recounted that the inhabitants of Chios tore the limbs of a human being in honor of Dionysus Omadios,[5] and the same is said of the inhabitants of Lesbos.[6] Thus, Damokritos could have used the established model of Dionysian worship attested in a number of Greek islands in formulating his anti-Jewish accusations. Apion's blood-libel, on the other hand, is much broader and different in nature:

> This practice was repeated annually at a fixed season. They would kidnap a Greek foreigner, fatten him up for a year, and then convey him to a wood, where they slew him, sacrificed his body with their customary ritual, partook of his flesh, and, while immolating the Greek, swore an oath

after the destruction of the temple in 70 C.E. But the statement can also be interpreted as saying that Jews used to do this in the past and continue to do so in the present day. If so, the sentence was written before the destruction of the Second Temple. It is also possible that the past tense is a product of the textual history of this narrative. Ada Adler (Suidas 1.21) asserts that this passage made its way into the Suda from Hesychius Melisius, who wrote the Onomatologus, which includes biographies of illustrious men according to fixed literary conventions. The Suda used an epitome of the Onomatologus, on which see Pauly-Wissowa: s.v. Hesychius.

2. The use of ἀγρεύειν is particularly interesting. See *Iph. in Taur.* (1163), τὰ θύματ' ἠγρεύσασθε, and the similar usage in Aristophanes, Frg. 101, though there it takes the dative. See also Matt 5:24; Heb 11:4, and the appendix below for Diodorus. Διαξαίνω is a late word that is particularly common in Aelianus (e.g. Ael. N.A. 5.54: τοὺς μὲν τοῖς ὄνυξι διέξηνεν, τοὺς δὲ τοῖς ὀδοῦσι διεσπάσατο.

3. See Susemihl, *Griechische Litteraturgeschichte* 2.387 ("time unknown").

4. See Schwenn's discussion in Pauly-Wissowa, s.v.: Menschenopfer.

5. See Euelpis, cited in Porphyry, *De Abstinentia* 2.55.

6. Dosidas, cited in Clement of Alexandria 3.42.

of hostility to the Greeks. The remains of their victim were then thrown into a pit.[7]

The passage gives the impression that Apion has linked a series of horror stories without paying attention to their sequence or overall coherence. Already Bickermann demonstrated that the passage is made up of two discrete, independent sections, each attested elsewhere in the polemical literature of antiquity.[8] According to Bickermann, the first part — the sacrifice of the foreigner — is "an ethnographic tale about the sacrifice of the king of the Saturnalias," and the second part — the annual vow of hatred against the Greeks — is a "standard trope applied to plotters in Greek propaganda." Bickermann believes that the phrase "eiusque corpus sacrificare" (the sacrifice after the killing of the victim) links the two parts. The second part is not attested in Damokritos, and this absence is not the result of an omission but of the independence of the two parts. And while the first part is very similar in the tellings of Apion and Damokritos, both accuse the Jews of human sacrifice, they differ in some important details. According to Apion, the Jewish sacrifice follows the "king of the Saturnalias" model, a common practice in antiquity, in which the foreign victim would spend a period of luxurious living prior to his death. As noted, Damokritos's sacrifice is more in accord with that practiced in the cult of Dionysius. The two narratives also differ on the frequency of the sacrifice — Damokritos said it occurred once every seven years, while according to Apion it was an annual event. And whereas Damokritos identified the victim as a foreigner, Apion said he was specifically Greek.[9] These differences suggest that Damokritos's version is not dependent on Apion, and that we are dealing with two separate blood libels.[10]

---

7. Josephus, *Against Apion* 2.94-95. This section is only extant in a poor Latin translation: ". . . et hoc illos facere singulis annis quodam tempore constituto et comprehendere quidem Graecum peregrinum eumque annali tempore saginare et deductum ad quondam silvam occidere quidem eum hominem eiusque corpus sacrificare secundum suas sollemnitates et gustare ex eius visceribus et iusiurandum facere in immolatione Graeci, ut inimicitias contra Graecos haberent, et tunc in quondam foveam reliqua hominis pereuntia abicere."

8. Bickermann, "Ritualmord und Eselskult," *MGWJ*, 1927, p. 172.

9. See the discussion below.

10. Apion, however, may be dependent on Damokritos. It stands to reason that Apion embellished the human sacrifice trope (i.e. the first part) with the account of the Jews' anti-Greek vow (the second part). Note that Damokritos accused the Jews of the very same offenses (worship of the head of a donkey, sacrifice of a foreigner) that Apion includes in his account of Antiochus's visit to the temple. (See the comments in T. Reinach's edition of *Against Apion* [Paris, 1930]). It is possible that another author accused the Jews of the same two offenses — describing their human sacrifice only in general terms — and both Apion and Damokritos used this source, reworking it according to their respective cultural and historical assumptions.

II

An ancient author wishing to describe human sacrifice among the Jews could draw on a veritable treasure trove of narratives dealing with cultic killing — both from ethnographic texts describing barbarian customs, and from literary descriptions of horrific acts, mostly in Greek tragedy, the historiography that grew out of tragic literary sensibilities, and Hellenistic novels. All these genres typically describe religious or cultic killings as part of a single complex that includes all such acts, from human sacrifice to cultic cannibalism. Hellenistic authors did not distinguish between these very different types of killings, as is particularly evident from the literary admixture of rituals possessing very different character. Wishing to make a strong impression in his *Thyestes,* Seneca describes Atros wreaking vengeance on his brother Thyestes by having him eat the flesh of his sons, adding that he had earlier sacrificed the sons on the altar in his home — thus combining human sacrifice and anthropophagy.[11] This combination is found in a number of texts, including Wisdom of Solomon's description of the sins of the ancient Canaanites (who also practiced child sacrifice), including "their merciless slaughter of children and their sacrificial feasting on human flesh and blood" (Wisdom of Solomon 12.5-6). When Juvenal in Satire 15 describes a hate-driven cannibalistic murder in Egypt, he cites as parallels a description of anthropophagy in Homer and eating the dead during the siege of Saguntus, but also the sacrifice of a foreigner in Taurus. Josephus, similarly, describes a starving Jewish woman who must eat the flesh of her child, and unintentionally attributes to her the word θυσία ("sacrifice").[12] Hegesippus (the Christian chronicler who reworked Josephus) has Titus compare this cannibalistic act to the binding of Isaac and the sacrifice of the daughter of Jephthah, cursing the Jews: "What manner of nation sees in murder a religious act and the killing of family members a sacrifice?"[13] The blood libel also belongs to the narrative genre that mixes all manner of killing, placing them under the heading of cultic murder.

The literary trope of a cannibal covenantal-meal (standard in the description of plotters) attested in the second part of Apion, may be the result of this genre mixture of different cultic killings. That is, human sacrifice is offered in place of the standard animal offering that accompanies covenants and symbolizes the punishment for breaking the covenant. This, according to

---

11. Seneca, *Thyestes* 1057 and following.

12. The story begins in *BJ* 6.201, the word θυσία occurs at 6.211.

13. Hegesippus (ed. Ussani), 5.41: "Qualis ista gens, quae religioni tribuat hominis necem et sacrificium putet esse paricidium?" (p. 387).

Bickermann, is the reason the meat of the sacrifice is taboo, and cannot be eaten.[14] The ancient authors, then, polemically transformed the animal sacrifice into a human sacrifice, symbolizing the plotters' association against humanity itself. And since these plotters were accustomed to human sacrifice, the authors included descriptions of the plotters eating the flesh of their human victims, without sensing that this undercuts the notion of covenantal sacrifice. This motif, then, that Apion appends to his description of human sacrifice, is an attempt to vilify Judaism as an ongoing plot against humanity, a connection possible only within a conceptual framework that assigns all ritual killings to a single complex.[15]

III

We must ascertain why the authors in question linked human sacrifice and cannibalism. One of the reasons is that sacrifice often entails eating of the meat of the animal. This connection is made explicitly by Theophrastos, Aristotle's philosophical heir. In his book "On Piety," Theophrastos argues that animal sacrifice is not suited to true piety — only flora should be offered to the gods.[16] In support of this position, Theophrastos argues that the ancients were sustained by vegetable foods alone, and used these for sacrifice as well. But when human piety grew weak, and the earth's harvest was less bountiful, they were driven by hunger to cannibalism and — since they tended to sacrifice their food to the gods — to human sacrifice. It was only later that they substituted animal meat for human and, seeking to show that they valued their offerings, ate animal flesh.[17] Elsewhere, however, Theophrastos offers

14. Bickermann, "Ritualmord und Eselskult."

15. The development of the anti-Jewish blood libel:

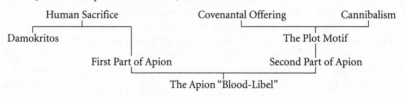

16. Fragments from Περὶ εὐσεβείας are preserved in Porphyry's Περὶ ἀποχῆς. The fragments were identified by Jakob Bernays, *Theophrastos' Schrift über Frömmigkeit* (Berlin, 1866). Quotations are from Porphyry's *On Abstinence from Killing Animals,* translated by Gillian Clark (Ithaca, 2000).

17. Bernays, §§86-87, p. 118. Passages such as these caused Porphyry to include fragments of Theophrastos in his book. However, the goal of the two philosophers is quite different and

the opposite argument, that identifies cannibalism as the result of human sacrifice: "Then there were the Bassarai long ago, who not only emulated the sacrifices of the Tauroi but, in the bacchic madness of their human sacrifices, added eating to them — just as we do now with animals, for having made an offering we use the rest for dinner."[18] Though the direction is reversed, both arguments understand cannibalism and human sacrifice as analogous to the relationship between human food and divine food, i.e., sacrifices.

Another factor in the emergence of the ritual killing paradigm involves the unique thought patterns of the ancients. Cultic killings belong to the religious realm, but were also the object of scientific investigation, particularly ethnography. To fully understand the connection between human sacrifice and cannibalism, we must examine the nature of ancient ethnography, a discipline that sought to understand man in light of his traits, ambitions, environment and history. At its core, ethnographic study is a form of humanism that seeks to understand all people by the same criteria, the better to understand their differences. This approach drives the ethnographer to link cross-cultural phenomena to the traits and characteristics of the individuals that manifest them. Modern ethnography, in contrast, studies the development of general processes and views man as subject to their internal causality. These processes are ordered taxonomically and only later does their cause become the object of investigation. In this, modern ethnography is similar to the physical sciences, and in particular to the taxonomical approach of classical botany. Each of these approaches, the ancient and the modern, has its advantages and disadvantages. The modern approach provides a precise and explicit analysis of the datum, but also tends to connect similar phenomena without exploring their origin,[19] and, at

---

arguably opposed: Theophrastos argued against animal sacrifice, while Porphyry favored vegetarianism, but with no apparent opposition to animal sacrifice, which was the custom of the day. Unlike Theophrastos, Porphyry distinguishes between the slaughter of the offering and its consumption: "These arguments have demonstrated that eating animals does not necessarily follow from sacrificing them" (see *On Abstinence* 2.58, Clark translation, page 78). Porphyry also distinguishes between human sacrifice and cannibalism: "History . . . has handed down the memory of how in ancient times they sacrificed people, but that does not mean that people should be eaten" (*On Abstinence* 2.53, Clark translation, page 76). The analogy he draws between human and animal suggests that he would allow human sacrifice but oppose cannibalism: "Now, it is obvious that human flesh is not also to be eaten because, through some necessity, a human being has been taken for sacrifice" (*On Abstinence* 2.56, Clark translation, page 77).

18. Bernays, p. 57, from Porphyry *On Abstinence* 2.8 (Clark translation, page 58).

19. Thus, e.g., Frazer identified the "King of the Saturnalia" type of sacrifice and tried to explain its origins, but offered a new explanation in each edition of *The Golden Bough*. It is hard to imagine this happening to an ancient ethnographer.

times, undermines the unity of the phenomena in question.[20] The main advantage of the modern approach is that it does not require the moral judgments so common among ancient ethnographers, as they threaten scholarly objectivity. All of which explains how the ancients connected human sacrifice with magical and cannibalistic killings — each a discrete category for modern scholarship. The common denominator is the moral judgment of these activities as crimes against humanity.

Cannibalism was viewed as an expression of cruelty and hatred.[21] Greek authors tell of the Jews of Cyrene, who rebelled against Rome during the reign of Trajan, "ate the flesh of their enemies, smeared themselves with their blood, threw them to wild beasts, and so forth."[22] Josephus writes of the fear of cannibalism as a motivating factor in wartime: "After this victory [over Jannaeus] Ptolemy overran other territories, and when evening fell, halted in some villages of Judaea, which he found full of women and infants; he thereupon commanded his soldiers to cut their throats and chop them up and then to fling the pieces into boiling cauldrons and to sacrifice them.[23] This order he gave that those who had escaped from the battle and had returned to their homes might get the notion that the enemy were eaters of human flesh, and so might be the more terrified by this sight" (*JA* 13.345-347).[24] The motivation for such a claim is evident: it marks the fierce hatred the plotters feel for their rulers, casting this hatred in a repugnant light.

As with all social phenomena, the ancients addressed human sacrifice in moral terms, for while they recognized that it was a religious phenomenon, they did not believe religion could be opposed to morality.[25] True religion, to

20. Bickermann, "Ritualmord und Eselskult," interprets the first part of Apion's polemic both in terms of a "King of the Saturnalia" offering and as a *devotio.*

21. Already in the *Iliad*, Zeus addresses Hera, saying: "If you could walk through the gates the through the towering ramparts and eat Priam and the children of Priam raw, and the other Trojans, then, then only might you glut at last your anger" (*Iliad* 4.34-36, Lattimore translation). And following Hector's death, his mother is supposedly willing to eat Achilles' liver (*Iliad* 24.212). See also Xenophon, *Anabasis* 4.8.14.

22. Tcherikover, *The Jews of Egypt in the Hellenistic-Roman Period* (Hebrew) (Jerusalem, 1945), 206.

23. Τὰ μέλη ἀπάρχεσθαι. In other words, they placed the limbs of the dead on the altars, as though they had been sacrificed. Here too cannibalism is linked to religiously sanctioned human sacrifice.

24. The legend that enemy soldiers eat babies has enjoyed wide currency over the ages. In World War II, German propaganda made the same claim about British soldiers in Italy.

25. True, the Epicureans saw religion as the cause of sin. Writing on the sacrifice of Iphigenia, Lucretius writes: "But 'tis that same religion oftener far hath bred the foul impieties of men" (*De Rerum Natura* 1.82-83, William Ellery Leonard translator), and concludes that

the contrary, is rooted in piety and instructs us to walk truly in the eyes of the gods, and thus to act morally. The immoral religious phenomena, then, are classified by the ancients as a corruption of true religion, as a *superstitio* that does not stem from piety but from fear (δεισιδαιμονία) — and no further analysis is necessary.[26] Thus, a Hellenistic Jewish author speaks of the Canaanite mysteries, which included human sacrifice and cannibalism, as works of sorcery and "unholy rites" (τελεταὶ ἀνόσιοι) (Wisdom of Solomon 12.4). Cicero states that the Gauls who sacrifice human beings are "distant from religion" (ab religione remoti),[27] as the sacrifice does not stem from religious conviction but from fear (aliquo metu adducti).[28]

These ritual killings are a crime or a prohibition, "nefas" in Latin. Juvenal wonders how it is that the Egyptians are prohibited (nefas) from eating the meat of sheep and goats, but permitted to eat human flesh.[29] In his naiveté, Juvenal identifies religious and moral prohibitions. Livy speaks of the criminal gatherings (nefarii coetus) of Bacchus worshippers in Italy, who were widely believed to offer human sacrifices, and asserts that they did not acknowledge any prohibition (nefas),[30] and even saw this as a superior religion.[31] He calls these assemblies "coniuratio impia," an impious plot,[32] and their religion "pravae religiones," depraved customs.[33] Cicero speaks of the Pythagoreans — who were rumored to sacrifice children for magical purposes — as practicing "inaudita ac nefaria sacra" (unheard of criminal rites).[34]

The distinction between true religion and superstition cannot be maintained without attributing to the former moral (alongside religious) values. Phrased in inner-religious terms, the distinction is only possible if the gods cease being purely demonic forces and are understood as the beings that rule the world according to principles of eternal justice. This moral conception en-

---

"Such are the crimes to which Religion leads" (*De Rerum Natura* 1.101). But the opposition between religion and morality is only apparent. Lucretius critiques religion from a moral perspective, but he does not distinguish between *religio* and *superstitio,* including all forms of religion in the latter category.

26. Only Posidonius tries to uncover the religious significance of human sacrifice among the Gauls, on which see the appendix.

27. Cicero, *Pro Font.* 10.21.

28. Cicero, *Pro Font.* 14.31.

29. Juvenal, *Sat.* 15.11.3.

30. Livy, 39.11.7.

31. Livy, 39.13.11: si qui minus patientes dedecoris sint et pigriores ad facinus, pro victimis immolari. Nihil nefas ducere, hanc summam inter eos religionem esse.

32. Livy, 39.16.3.

33. Livy, 15.3.

34. Cicero, *In Vatinium* 6.14.

tails a rejection of immoral religious views that carried over from the "age of innocence." Euripides has Iphigenia say: "Nay, I hold unworthy of credence the banquet given of Tantalus to the Gods — as though the Gods could savor a child's flesh! Even so, this folk, themselves man-murderers, charge on their Goddess their own sin. I believe that none of the Gods is vile."[35] Clearly, this position is the result of a shift that occurred between the days of "the ancient ignorance"[36] and classical Greek culture. This evolution finds its mythological expression in the just reign of Zeus, who defeated all the primordial gods. According to Plutarch, human sacrifice is to be rejected on the grounds that "such a lawless and barbarous sacrifice was not acceptable to any one of the superior beings above us, for it was not the fabled typhons and giants who governed the world, but the father of all gods and men."[37] Still and all, there remained traces of the old religion, but they were now considered curious anachronisms. Theophrastos writes: "From then until now, it is not only in Arcadia at the Lykaia and in Carthage for Kronos that everyone engages in public human sacrifice, but periodically, in remembrance of the custom, they stain altars with the blood of their own kind."[38] Similarly, Cicero is shocked that the Gauls maintain the practice of human sacrifice, "even to this very day" (usque ad hanc diem),[39] and Pliny expresses the same sentiment regarding the druids, who sacrifice "to our own era" (ad nostrum memoriam).[40]

The Greek displays the same critical approach to amoral elements in non-Greek religions as he does to the corresponding archaic elements of his own. He sees himself as spiritually superior to them, due to the purity of his religion, treating other religions as inferior. He compares the ancient shortcomings of his religion to those of other religions, examining religious phenomena through a purely moral prism, judging the more corrupt to be a reflection of the savage nature of their practitioners whose culture has not been purified by culture, i.e., of their barbarian nature. "Barbarian" is not only a geographic or ethnographic designation, but also a cultural one and thus, in a sense, religious. Cicero calls the sacrifice of children to the gods of the netherworld "immanes et barbari mores" (terrible barbarian customs),[41] much as he refers to the Gauls' sacrifices as "immanis ac barbara consuetudo" (a terri-

---

35. Euripides, *Iphigenia in Tauris*, 386-390 (Arthur S. Way, translator).

36. Following Dr. Preuss's term "Urdummheit." And see G. Murray, *Five Stages of Greek Religion* (London, 1935), 2.

37. Plutarch, *Pelop.*, 21.

38. Bernays, 86-87, from Porphyry, *On Abstinence* 2.27 (Clark translation, page 65).

39. Cicero, *Pro Fonteio* 14.31.

40. Pliny, *Natural History* 30.13.

41. Cicero, *Vat.* 6.14.

ble barbarian custom).[42] The barbarian is typically ignorant of theological matter and does not distinguish between good and evil. When Herodotus recounted the hoax perpetuated on the Athenians when a woman was proclaimed a goddess who desired the return of Peisistratos, he marveled that this could have occurred in Athens, as the Greek people have, since the earliest times, been wiser than the barbarians, keeping themselves distant from their ignorant ways.[43]

Human sacrifice is part of the "ignorance" and "errors" of the barbarians, which stem from a poor grasp of theology. Only cultural nations are suited for proper worship. Iphigenia and her brothers annul the human sacrifice to Artemis by transferring the cult of the goddess from barbarian lands to Athens for "it is not fitting that you dwell here, when so blessed a city may be yours."[44] The Greek and the Roman sees himself surrounded by barbarian nations whose cultic practices fill him with dread. Pliny compared the terrible Druid rituals in Britain to the religious customs of the Persians, and concluded by asserting that "So universal is the cult of magic throughout the world, although its nations disagree or are unknown to each other."[45] As a result, the Roman considered it his right, nay his duty, to introduce appropriate amendments to the barbarian religions. Pliny praised Tiberius's laws against the Druids, "this tribe of seers and medicine men," stating that "it is beyond calculation how great is the debt owed to the Romans, who swept away the monstrous rites, in which to kill a man was the highest religious duty and for him to be eaten a passport to health."[46]

The above discussion explains how and why the Greeks linked all the ritual practices they considered immoral — whether preserved in distant memories or practiced among the barbarians — and designated them all "barbara superstitio," with its attendant connotations of magic, human sacrifice and cannibalism. When Cicero wishes to inflame the masses against the Jews, he plays on their ignorance of Jewish custom and calls Judaism too a "barbara superstitio."[47] This opens Judaism to the whole range of accusations usually associated with barbarian religions. Indeed, in order to justify such an accusation it now becomes necessary to invent these very accusations: the anti-Jewish blood libel is an attempt to portray the "elevated" Jewish religion as, in fact, secretly barbaric.

42. Cicero, *Font.* 14.31.
43. Herodotus 1.60. See Murray, *Five Stages,* 39.
44. Euripides, *Iphigenia in Tauris* 773-776, 1084-1088.
45. Pliny, *Natural History* 30.13 (W. H. Jones, translator).
46. Pliny, *Natural History* 30.13.
47. Cicero, *Pro Flacco* 28.67.

IV

The accusation of ritual murder is the simplest and most convincing means of proving the barbarism of any given society, and thus it is employed by authors and rhetors to turn public opinion against nations and communities. As we have seen, Cicero discussed human sacrifice among the Gauls and the Pythagoreans, and in both cases his goal was the same: to disqualify the witnesses of the opposing counsel by disparaging the religion by which they vow.[48]

The author of Wisdom of Solomon engaged in a heated polemic against Gentiles living in Israel who claimed the land did not belong to the Jews and argued that the Jews had stolen it from the Canaanites.[49] In response, the Wisdom of Solomon, very much in the spirit of the Greeks, develops the biblical accounts of the Canaanites along gruesome lines. The question of land ownership was central in Mediterranean polemics more generally, as we see in, e.g., the story that Aeneas came to Italy on divine orders — a response to "the Greek fabrications that the Romans are the descendents of a gang of criminals."[50] The accusations leveled at the Canaanites sought to justify the conquest of the land and, moreover, to provide it with a religious justification. At times, these stories were accompanied by the discovery of the victims' bodies. This, in any case, occurred when the Roman police razed the temple of Ma-Bellona in the year 48, allegedly discovering many pots filled with human flesh. Also, when the Christians shut down the temples of Mirapis and Mithra in Alexandria, they were said to have found evidence of human sacrifice,[51] and Christians in Antioch discovered crates filled with human heads and mass graves.[52] Such discoveries were recorded — and on occasion perhaps invented — by ancient authors. It may be that the closing sentence of Apion's narrative, "[t]he remains of their victim were then thrown into a pit," derives from another anti-Jewish libel known to Apion that involved the "discovery" of the victims' bodies. If so, Apion omitted the story, preferring the "historical" and dramatic tale of Antiochus and his discoveries.

---

48. On the refutation of witnesses generally and on Cicero's *Pro Fonteio* — where he discusses the Gauls — see Y. Levy, "Cicero on the Jews" (Hebrew), *Zion* 7, 115-120.

49. See above, the discussion of the Wisdom of Solomon 12.5-6; Y. Levy, "Ein Rechtsstreit um den Boden Palästinas im Altertum," *MGJW* 77 (1933), 88 and 172.

50. See Y. Levy, "Tacitus on the Jews' Antiquity and Their Characteristics" (Hebrew), *Zion* 8, n. 119.

51. Bickermann, "Ritualmord und Eselskult," 186.

52. Theodoretos, *Hist. eccl.* 3.27. See also D. Chwolsohn, *Die Sabier und der Sabismus,* 2.150.

V

Polemic writings draw from tragedy (and the pathos-drenched historiography and novels that are its outgrowths) and ethnographic literature. The wide use of these genres for polemic purposes was facilitated by their general decline during the Hellenistic period, when "tragedy" no longer referred to a discussion of the problems facing man and the world and a search for appropriate solutions, as it had in the classical Greek period. Instead, tragedy became a litany of terrible sufferings or poetry that recounted ancient tales of criminal kings, thus eliciting sorrow from its audience.[53] Ritual murders also appeared to be part of the "tragic" repertoire. Juvenal recounted a case of cannibalism in Egypt, and then asserted that the deed in question was worse than any tragedy since none of the tragic plays attributed such an act to any nation.[54] Josephus too described Apion's anti-Jewish blood libel as a tale full of tragedy ("fabula omni tragoedia plenissima").[55]

Tragedy communicated the archaic Greek myths from its own, enlightened perspective, describing the brutal religious killings in a negative light.[56] Later writers took from the tragic corpus its rich literary motifs, but also its moral pathos, by which they sought to shock their audience. A tragic motif of this sort is found in Josephus's justification of the destruction of Jerusalem, a passage alluded to above: when a Jewish mother must eat her child in order to ward off starvation, Titus is enraged and decides to "bury the abomination of infant-cannibalism beneath the ruins of their country, and not leave upon the face of the earth, for the sun to behold, a city in which mothers were thus fed."[57] The story serves as a proemium of sorts to the story of the destruction

53. Here are the statements of the two encyclopedias that conclude late antiquity: "Tragoedi sunt qui antiqua gesta atque facinora sceleratorum regum luctuosa carmine spectante populo concidebant," Isidorus, *Eth.* 18; τραγῳδία δεινοπάθεια, Suidas.

54. Juvenal, *Sat.* 15.9-11. ". . . et cunctis graviora cothurnis nam scelus, a Pyrrha quamquam omnia syrmata volvas, nullus apud tragicos populus facit."

55. Josephus, *CA* 2.97.

56. A negative approach is evident already within the mythological stratum itself. See Schwenn (Pauly-Wissowa), s.v. Menschenopfer. Of the classical tragedies that deal with human sacrifice, only two, both by Euripides, are extant: *Iphigenia in Aulide* and *Iphigenia in Tauris*. Seneca's Latin tragedy, *Thyestes,* must be treated with great care, since Seneca reworked his classical sources in light of the pathos-drenched rhetoric and the philosophy of his day. All the same, the work does reflect a tendency to conflate criminal behavior as such with religious crime. Atraeus's anger is impious ("impia ira," 712) and leads to an immoral ("nefas") act that is without precedent (1047). Seneca rhetorically links religion and crime when he says of Atraeus: "Hactenus si stat nefas, pius est" (744).

57. Josephus, *BJ* 6.217.

of the temple and the city, "an *apologia* for the burning of the temple, which is now described."[58] In his oration, Titus employs the known motif of the sun turning in its course so as not to see how Atreus gives his brothers the flesh of his children.[59] As a result, the destruction of Jerusalem is represented as a religious commandment: Titus upholds the myth by siding with the forces doing battle against evil.

Similarly, it was Apion's tragedy-inspired understanding that led him to present the blood libel as a dramatic novella — a conversation between Antiochus IV who had just burst into the temple, and the Greek who was held there as a sacrificial victim. In the course of the conversation, the Greek reveals the horrible fate that awaits him (of which he has learned from the temple attendants) and begs the king for help. The entire narrative unfolds as a dialogue within a dialogue. The dramatic developments are also reminiscent of the literary norms of tragedy: Antiochus appears at the very last minute — *deus ex machina* — and saves the tragic hero, i.e., the Greek victim.

The ethnographic literature, with its moral taxonomy of national characteristics, also paved the way for the laudatory or derisive use of these characteristics. The ethnographic genre could be applied to any nation, since "from the outset, ethnographic authors established a detailed series of requisite topics for the representation of any foreign nation."[60] During the Hellenistic period, ethnographic writing grows increasingly formulaic both in the questions it poses and the answers it provides, with the descriptions of foreign customs becoming something of a cliché,[61] and rhetors draw on the entire ethnographic corpus to sway public opinion.[62] Anti-Semitic authors used these same topoi to "explain" Jewish traits, i.e., invoking convoluted explanations or outright fabrications to attribute to the Jews a barbaric nature. Apollonius Molon, for example, who was Cicero's teacher, said that the Jews are ἄθεοι, impious, and that they are misanthropic. Like all barbarians, they are brave and daring in the attack, but become cowards as the result of the

---

58. G. Alon, "The Burning of the Temple," in *Jews, Judaism and the Classical World*, trans. Israel Abrahams (Jerusalem, 1977), 252-68.

59. See Roscher, *Ausführliches Lexikon der griechischen und römischen Mythologie* (Leipzig, 1886), s.v. Atreus, 1.74.

60. Y. Levy, "Tacitus on the Jews," 9.

61. Levy, "Tacitus on the Jews," 10.

62. On the literary norms for national praise or censure, see Levy, "Cicero on the Jews." A comparison of the *loci communes* of the rhetors and the ethnographers reveals that the former drew from the work of the latter. Levy alludes to this dynamic, but only with regard to narratives of national antiquity ("Tacitus on the Jews," 9-18).

slightest setback.[63] The Jews, indeed, are the least talented of the barbarians for they are the only ones who have made no contribution to world culture.[64] Already the Exodus narrative suggested that the Jews were not fully autochthonous, a trait considered the "highest praise for nations."[65] But the Anti-Semites were still not satisfied and added that the Jews were *expelled* from Egypt on account of their leprosy. This tale is cited in Quintilian's *Institutions of Rhetoric* as a paradigmatic tale of opprobrium.[66] One of the outstanding characteristics of the barbarian nations is their intemperate sexual appetite,[67] and we find in Tacitus a description of the Jews as slaves to their sexual appetite.[68] Jews are considered a misanthropic nation, lacking basic human sentiment — like other barbarians.[69] The barbarians were also known for their sloth,[70] a trait anti-Semitic authors find in the Jewish Sabbath and *shemitah* (letting fields lie fallow) laws.

One of the areas that most appealed to Greek polemicists was religion, and especially Judaism which was unlike the pagan religions and basically an enigma. And, indeed, we find just about every slanderous statement possible aimed at Judaism. Cicero defines the religion of the Jews as "barbara superstitio";[71] Tacitus refers to the Jewish (and Egyptian) customs as "profani ritus";[72] and Apollonius Molon casts them as ἄθεοι.[73] All these statements seek to devalue Judaism and portray in a negative light everything known

---

63. This is the sense of Josephus's statement that Apollonius "accuses us of temerity and reckless madness" (*CA* 2.148). Josephus failed (or refused) to understand Apollonius's true intent. Ancient authors commonly attributed to barbarian nations a daring anchored in ignorance, (ἀπόνοια in Molon's account), and thus become cowards when circumstances force them to use their intellect. In the *Antiquities*, Josephus writes of the German tribes: "It is a national trait of theirs to act furiously to a degree such as is rarely if ever met with among other barbarians, for the Germans pause less for calculation of their consequences. They are also physically powerful and win great success in the first onset whenever they engage any whom they consider enemies" (*AJ* 19.120). Josephus's source is apparently Cluvius Rufus, on whom see E. Norden, *Germanische Urgeschichte in Tacitus' Germania* (Stuttgart, 1922), 157, n. 1. Yohanan Levy has called my attention to the fact that in the *Jewish War* too Josephus characterizes the Jews' bravery as a sign of their ignorance in matters of war — in contrast to the organized Roman forces.

64. Josephus, *CA* 2.148.

65. Levi, "Tacitus on the Jews," 20.

66. Quint. 3.7.21; See Levy, "Tacitus on the Jews," 19.

67. Levy, "Tacitus on the Jews," n. 46.

68. Tacitus, *Histories* 5.5.5.

69. Levy, "Tacitus on the Jews," n. 146.

70. Levi, "Tacitus on the Jews," n. 87.

71. *Pro Flacco* 28.67.

72. Tacitus, *Annals* 2.85.

73. Josephus, *CA* 2.148.

about the religion, thus paving the way for concrete accusations such as the blood-libel. Indeed, the blood-libels demonstrate the depravity of Judaism and the misanthropy of the Jews. That both these accusations are related to the key elements that distinguish Jews from other nations — their belief in a single God and their separation from their neighbors in order to maintain their laws — is only one element in the genesis of these accusations, not the reason.

It is perhaps understandable that anti-Semitic authors saw Judaism as a "barbara superstitio," and this may help explain the type of blood-libel found in Damokritos and in the first part of Apion's accusation, namely, that the Jews offer human sacrifice. However, we have to uncover another reason for the accusation — in the latter half of Apion's statement — that Judaism is a plot against humanity. We find that all the international religions that spread through the Roman Empire and competed against the dominant religion were accused of plotting against the existing order. Even in the days of the re-public, the Romans outlawed the cult of Bacchus in Italy, primarily for fear of the moral corruption of their citizens.[74] The cult was considered a public menace and its adherents labeled criminals.[75] The "conservatives" considered such religions a plot (coniuratio) against humanity. Livy attributes to the consul discussing the Bacchus cult in Italy the view that it is an irreverent plot (coniuratio impia) aimed at the critical interests of the republic (ad summam rem publicam spectat).[76] Mithraism too was depicted as a plot, as was Chris-tianity.[77] In the early days of the empire, Judaism became a world religion that attracted adherents among the gentiles. In this, it was similar to Mithra-ism and, later, Christianity — religions that could undermine the value system of ancient society, and thus potentially revolutionary. Here, then, lies the explanation for why "the Roman authors . . . who professed the national tra-dition, became anti-Jewish on account of the spread of Judaism within Ro-man society; fearing for the vitality of their ancestral laws, these authors exe-crated Judaism as a religion that teaches its adherents to deny the validity of Roman law."[78] The tension between Judaism and the Roman state came into view in the days of Caligula, when the Jews refused the explicit imperial order to place the emperor's statue in the Jerusalem temple, and it seemed the entire Jewish world — spread throughout the Roman empire — would rise up against this order. The echoes of this event can be discerned in the decision of

74. Levy, "Tacitus on the Jews," 64.
75. Levy, "Tacitus on the Jews," 65.
76. Livy, 39.16.3.
77. Levy, "Tacitus on the Jews," 66.
78. Levy, "Tacitus on the Jews," 61.

Claudius, Caligula's successor, who reinstated the rights the Jews of Alexandria lost in the days of Caligula, but warned them lest they establish ties with their brethren in neighboring lands — as though they were capable of inciting a world-wide rebellion.[79] The reaction to the spread of Judaism, on the one hand, and the Jewish opposition to the Rome-sanctioned emperor worship, on the other, gave rise to a new type of anti-Semitism that portrayed Judaism as an ongoing plot against the cultured nations. Apion lived during this period and took part in the great battle between the Jews and Greeks of Alexandria in the court of Gaius Caligula. It is likely, then, that he added to the standard accusation of human sacrifice another accusation, the second, which Josephus describes as "renovata coniuratio" — a renewed plot.[80]

It is clear that the second part does not refer to the time of Antiochus's reign, and there is no real reason to suppose that the first part is tied to Antiochus either. Apion, a contemporary of Caligula, knew that no foreigner would be allowed into the glorious temple in Jerusalem, so he found a scroll — its author being the only anti-Semite to enter the temple. This literary conceit allowed him to present his story as historically accurate and highly dramatic at the same time.[81] The notion that the Jews' hatred is directed against the Greeks may be due to the circumstances in Alexandria, the site and audience of Apion's composition.[82]

In summary, we see that neither Damokritos nor Apion invoked partic-

79. Levy, "Tacitus on the Jews," 72-73.

80. *CA* 2.99.

81. Josephus argues that the libelous account was written by Antiochus' scribes, who sought to justify their king's entrance into the temple (*CA* 2.90), and Bickermann ("Ritualmord und Eselskult," 172) accepts this position. I do not see any reason to abandon the views I have expressed here on account of Josephus, since Josephus himself says elsewhere that Apion fabricated the story (*CA* 2.110). The contradiction may be due to the fact that in the first instance he tried to undermine the story by describing the enormity of Antiochus' sin in bursting into the temple to rob it — describing the account as a criminal's attempt to cover over his crime — and so accepted uncritically Apion's vague attribution of the story as "fabulam . . . de Graecis." (Apion, as a rule, likes to present his sources as "reliable." Thus, e.g., he heard from the Egyptian elders that Moses was a resident of On, and that he learned from an Ithacan of the game Penelope's suitors played [Athanaeus 1, p. 16 F]). In the second statement, Josephus based himself on well-known information regarding the temple cult and, with no interest in Antiochus, accused Apion directly of fabrication.

82. Apion, then, transformed the notion that the Jews plot against the world, into a plot against the Greeks. The process is already evident in the "oath of allegiance" the Josephus cites in Apion's name elsewhere (*CA* 2.121-124), which may also be related to the blood-libel literature (see the discussion in Reinach's edition, *ad locum*). The oath is aimed at all gentiles, but especially the Greeks, namely "to bear no good will to any foreigner, and particularly to none of the Greeks."

ularly Jewish traits in their blood libels; to the contrary, they sought to attribute to the Jews the traits that were widely associated with barbarians, religious sects, and revolutionary ideologies. In this, the blood libels serve to impede social, judicial, and political equality, while neutralizing any influence the moral and ascetic Jewish way of life might have on the surrounding pagans.

Posidonius on Human Sacrifice among the Gauls

Aside from Theophrastos's comments, there is only one classical source that discusses the religious significance of human sacrifice. I am referring to Caesar's comments in *Gallic War* (6.16.2-3). A comparison of Caesar's statements and the parallel in Cicero's *Pro Fonteio* (31) suggests that Caesar is merely transmitting the teachings of an earlier writer:

Caesar	Cicero
. . . [the Gauls] either sacrifice human victims or vow to do so, employing the Druids as ministers of such sacrifices. They believe, in effect, that unless a man's life be paid for another man's life, the majesty of the immortal gods may not be appeased; and in public, as in private life, they observe an ordinance of sacrifices of the same kind.	. . . if ever [the Gauls] are struck by some fear as to deem it necessary to placate the gods, they defile the altars and temples of those gods with human victims, such that they cannot even practice religion without first violating that very religion with crime. . . . What, then, do you think, is the honor and the piety of those who even think that the immortal gods can best be appeased by human crime and bloodshed?

Cicero clearly did not copy from Caesar's book or even from his notes, since the *Pro Fonteio* was delivered ten years before Caesar's first campaign to Gaul. It appears, then, that Cicero is basing himself on an earlier author who wrote on the Gallic customs and whose influence is apparent in Caesar's work as well. Cicero's aim is purely rhetorical — to present the religion of the Gauls as a "superstitio" — and he transmits the Gauls' own theological justification in an incomplete and apocopated form. The original form is preserved in Caesar's text:[83] human sacrifice is a substitution that atones for the lives of the other men.

But who is the author from whom Cicero and Caesar draw? Contemporary scholarship on his ethnographic work on the Gauls suggests the author in question is Posidonius.[84] Here are the Greek texts that, according to Trüdinger, open Posidonius's discussion of Gallic human sacrifice:

Strabo (198.5)	Diodorus (5.31.3-4)
They used to strike a human being, whom they had devoted to death, in the back with a saber, and then divine from his death-struggle. But they would not sacrifice without the Druids.	. . . in such cases they devote to death a human being and plunge a dagger into him in the region above the diaphragm, and when the stricken victim has fallen they read the future from the manner of his fall and from the twitching of his limbs, as well as from the gushing of the blood, having learned to place confidence in an ancient and long-continued practice of observing such matters. And it is a custom of theirs that no one should perform the sacrifice without a philosopher.

The Posidonius passage in question (the source for Strabo and Diodorus) deals with human sacrifice as an oracular practice. But as Trüdinger notes, the last sentence in both passages indicates that Posidonius proceeded to discuss other types of human sacrifice. The subsequent discussion has been preserved by Strabo, and is evidently the source for Caesar as well:

Caesar	Diodorus	Strabo
. . . employing the Druids as ministers of such sacrifices. They believe, in effect, that unless a man's life be paid for another man's life, the majesty of	And it is a custom of theirs that no one should perform the sacrifice without a philosopher. For thank-offerings should be rendered to the	. . . they would not sacrifice without the Druids. We are told of still other human sacrifices; for example, they would shoot victims to death with

83. Incidentally, this proves that Caesar did not copy from Cicero's speech.

84. K. Trüdinger, *Studien zur Geschichte der griechisch-römischen Ethnographie* (Basel, 1918), 97.

Caesar	Diodorus	Strabo
the immortal gods may not be appeased; and in public, as in private life, they observe an ordinance of sacrifices of the same kind. Others use figures of immense size, whose limbs, woven out of twigs, they fill with living men and set on fire, and the men perish in a sheet of flame.	gods, they say, by the hands of men who are experienced in the nature of the divine, and who speak, as it were, the language of the gods, and it is also through the mediation of such men, they think, that blessings likewise should be sought.	arrows, or impale them in the temples or, having devised a colossus of straw and wood, throw into the colossus cattle and wild animals of all sorts and human beings and then make a burnt-offering of the whole thing.

The similarity between Caesar's first sentence and the language of Strabo and Diodorus clearly demonstrates that the three share a common source — Posidonius. Since the conclusion is also similar in Caesar and Strabo, it is evident that Caesar's middle sentence too ("that unless a man's life be paid . . ."), omitted in Strabo, is taken from Posidonius. Diodorus's statement "by the hands of men who are experienced . . ." also fits well with Posidonius's argument: the Druids are present during these sacrifices because they are "philosophers" who know the thoughts of the gods and provide instructions as to how best to seek the blessings of the gods.[85] It is likely that the theological justification of human sacrifice — an attempt to placate the eternal gods — came after this last statement. In summary, Posidonius's discussion of human sacrifice among the Gauls covers the following topics: (i) Human sacrifice for the sake of prophecy (Diodorus, Strabo). (ii) The presence of the Druids during these (and other) sacrifices (Diodorus, Strabo, Caesar). (iii) The reason for their presence. (iv) Human sacrifice justified as a form of atonement (Caesar and Cicero). (v) Other human sacrifices: the colossus (Strabo and Caesar).

85. In the beginning of the passage (Diod. 5.31.2) Posidonius refers to the Druids as "philosophers and theologians."

Author's Addendum

Not only pagans leveled blood libels against Christians, warring sects within the church adopted the pagan accusations and applied them to one another. The Catholic church famously leveled a blood libel against the Montanist sect of Asia Minor. Some of the Christians in Asia Minor, including the Montanists, celebrated Easter at the same time that the Jews celebrated Passover. This custom was rooted in the fact that, according to the gospels, the founder of Christianity was killed on Passover or Passover eve. Thus, many Christians celebrated the death of their savior on the day the Jews celebrated Passover, thus correlating their calendar to the New Testament account. The church saw this cooperation with the Jewish calendar as a grave danger, so determined the date of Easter such that it could not concur with Passover. The Montanists, however, ignored the directives of the Catholic church and continued to celebrate Easter during the Jewish Passover.

The Catholics considered the Montanists heretics, especially since the latter were opposed to those church institutions they considered corrupt. This dispute gave rise to the Catholic blood libel, according to which the Montanists placed the blood of a child into their wine during the Easter feast, apparently in order to transform the wine into actual blood. Why did the Catholics connect this anti-Montanist libel with Easter? Because it was at the first Easter meal that Jesus said of the bread "this is my flesh" and of the wine "this is my blood."

This terrible libel was a base lie, but it did possess its own internal logic: the Montanists are putatively drinking the blood of a child while Christ pointed to the wine and said "this is my blood." The libel against the Jews is also a base lie, but unlike the anti-Montanist claim, it is overall incomprehensible. We must assume, then, that the Church transferred its libel from the Montanists to the Jews who celebrated their Passover at the same time as the Montanists. Unfortunately, the anti-Jewish blood libels are attested only at a relatively late period, after the Montanists no longer existed.

23. "Have You Ever Seen a Lion Toiling as a Porter?"

One of the recurring questions in the study of ancient Judaism involves the extent to which Hellenism influenced the various streams within Judaism. Even with regard to the Jewish communities in the Greek-speaking diaspora, where the strong Hellenistic influence is evident, there is not complete agreement among scholars. Thus, for example, the extent to which Philo should be understood as a Greek or a Jewish thinker remains hotly debated. The question is more complicated with regard to the spiritual and intellectual world of the Jews living in Israel. There is no question that there was a Hellenistic influence, since Israel was part of the Hellenistic world. However, the Jewish groups in Israel, and especially the sages, possessed a fully formed spiritual world that was nourished by an internal tradition. As a result, some scholars have sought to deny any formative Greek influence on the world of the sages, suggesting the reception of a Greek motif has no bearing on the matter.[1] In a culture as independent as that of the Jews in ancient Palestine, the influence of a foreign culture — even a powerful one — must have been constant and usually subterranean. And if Greek culture did enrich the spiritual world of the sages, this did not indicate their surrender but rather an encounter of cultures. Indeed, the ongoing and constant encounter between Greek and Jewish wisdom paved the way for the reception of the few Greek motifs that entered Jewish thought. In what follows, we discuss a specific instance of this contact — brought to the forefront by the publication of a par-

1. See the discussion of S. Lieberman, "How Much Greek in Jewish Palestine," in Alexander Altmann (ed.), *Biblical and Other Studies* (Cambridge, MA, 1963).

ticular Greek text — without losing sight of the broader cultural and histori-cal question.

I begin by citing the words of Jesus in the Sermon on the Mount (Matt 6:25-34, parallel at Luke 12:22-32) as representative of the internal Jewish thought of the time:

> Therefore I tell you, do not worry about your life, what you will eat or what you will drink, or about your body, what you will wear. Is not life more than food, and the body more than clothing? Look at the ravens;[2] they neither sow nor reap nor gather into barns, and yet your heavenly Father feeds them. How much more you![3] And can any of you by worrying add a single hour to your span of life? And why do you worry about clothing? Consider the lilies of the field, how they grow; they neither toil nor spin, yet I tell you, even Solomon in all his glory was not clothed like one of these. But if God so clothes the grass of the field, which is alive today and tomorrow is thrown into the oven, will he not much more clothe you — you of little faith? Therefore do not worry, saying, "What will we eat?" or "What will we drink?" or "What will we wear?" For it is the nations of the world[4] who strive for all these things; and indeed your heavenly Father knows that you need all these things. Instead, strive for his kingdom, and these things will be given to you as well.[5] So do not worry about tomorrow, for tomorrow will bring worries of its own. Today's trouble is enough for today.[6]

It is clear that Jesus' teaching here is of a piece with an important stream within rabbinic thought.[7] Three times Jesus uses a קל וחומר (de minori ad maius) argument: one should not worry about food, drink and clothing since the soul is more important than the body and the body than clothing; if God

---

2. Thus Luke 12:24. Matthew has "birds of the air." Jesus apparently alludes to Psalm 147:9: "He gives to the animals their food, and to the young ravens when they cry." The change in Matthew is probably due to the fact that ravens were associated in Greek thought with the hanging tree; compare also Matt 6:26 and Luke 12:24.

3. Following Luke 12:28.

4. Following Luke 12:30. This appears to be the earliest attestation of the phrase "the na-tions of the world."

5. Following Luke 12:31.

6. Luke 12:32.

7. See Y. Baer, *Israel among the Nations* (Hebrew) (Jerusalem, 1955), 43-44, 124. Baer offers an interesting analysis of the passage in question, including a fascinating parallel from Philo (*Leg. Alleg.* 3.162 and following). However, anyone who views the Qumran texts as Essene will find it difficult to accept Baer's suggestion that the views of Jesus, the sages, and Philo are affili-ated with the Essene worldview. Baer is correct in asking where these views are to be situated within Second Temple Judaism, a question that requires further investigation.

sustains the ravens who do not sow or reap or gather into barns, how much more so human beings who do; and if God clothes the lilies of the field that neither toil nor spin, or the grass of the field that is alive one day and thrown into the oven the next, how much more so human beings.[8] Such concerns are typical of the gentiles, but you "do not worry about tomorrow, for tomorrow will bring worries of its own. Today's trouble is enough for today."

The position here attributed to Jesus enjoys a certain prominence in rabbinic thinking and is widely attested. Though there are rabbinic dicta that privilege labor and skilled work, there were those who argued that one should not worry about the future. It is in this spirit that Hillel the Elder cites Psalm 68:19: "Blessed be the Lord who daily bears us up" (in b. Betza 16a).[9] This was not a utopian view, but a true expression of religious conviction.[10] Indeed, there were some sages who adopted this approach as a practical matter. As Rabbi Eliezer said: "Anyone who has bread in his basket but says, 'What will I eat tomorrow,' behold, he is of little faith" (b. Sotah 48b). And Rabbi Elazar of Modiin said: "Whoever has what to eat today but says, 'What will I eat tomorrow?' — he is without faith." This is the view that underlies the teaching of Rabbi Shimon bar Yohai: "Behold, how can a man be sitting and studying when he does not know where his food and drink will come from, nor where he can get his clothes and coverings? Hence, only to those who have manna to eat is it given to study the Torah."[11] There is no question that one of the elements in Jesus' statement about those of little faith who worry about food, and clothing, and money, is an ancient midrash to Exodus 16:4: "Then the Lord said to Moses, 'I am going to rain bread from heaven for you, and *each day* the people shall go out and gather enough *for that day*. In that way I will test them, whether they will follow my instruction or not.'" The Israelites, then, were to gather the manna "for that day." If they gathered enough for the

---

8. It is worth comparing the frequent use of קל וחומר arguments in the synoptic gospels with similar modes of argument among the early sages. Of particular interest are the words of the *dorshei hamurot* in tractate Semahot 8.16 (Zlotnick edition, 24-25). Citations from this passage are scattered throughout rabbinic literature, and its conclusion is found in the Mekhilta of Rabbi Ishmael, Yitro 11 (page 245 in the Horovitz-Rabin edition). The teachings are similar to Jesus' homilies and it seems to me that one of the meanings of *dorshei hamurot* is "those that interpret *(dorshim)* on the basis of קל וחומר reasoning."

9. See Flusser, "Hillel the Elder and His Trust in God," pp. 207-209 in the present volume.

10. It is odd that some scholars characterize Jesus' sayings as utopian and thus incongruent with the active and positive orientation of Judaism, but ignore the very same views when expressed by the sages. It is not surprising to find many Christian scholars interpreting Jesus' dicta encouraging his audience not to worry about their daily needs in exclusively eschatological terms, as they are unfamiliar with the rabbinic parallels.

11. Mekhilta of Rabbi Ishmael, Veyssa 3, Lauterbach 2.104.

morrow, it spoiled and marked them as having little faith. Jesus went further than the sages, urging his followers not only not to worry about tomorrow, but not to pray for tomorrow's livelihood. Rather, they should pray: "give us this day our daily bread."[12]

Jesus' teachings, then, are representative of a robust and explicit Jewish worldview. Parallels may be drawn from the lives and teachings of Greek philosophers, first and foremost the cynics, who advocated a natural life, free from the worries of work and livelihood. However, this need not indicate Greek influence on the Jewish sages, as such views are found in various societies and religions. Moreover, Judaism could have fostered this view as part of an internal dynamic, with no clear external influence. The same is true of the gradual emergence of the rabbinic class during the Second Temple and post-70 Jewish world. The sages, e.g., debated what is more important — study of Torah or acts, ultimately deciding that study of Torah took precedence because it leads to action. Such debates are, to be sure, similar to those we find among the Greek philosophers concerning the relationship between the philosopher's thought and his role in the broader social context. It is hard to imagine that the Greek philosophers did not exert some influence on the sages, at the very least in terms of how the questions were formulated. We find in m. Avot 3.5: "Nehunia ben ha-Kanah states: 'Whoever accepts the yoke of Torah is released from the yoke of government and of proper conduct *(derekh 'eretz).*'" This statement is reminiscent of the view — quite prominent among Greek thinkers — that whoever devotes himself to the life of the mind is released from the obligations of practical and political life. However, it can be shown that the phrase *derekh 'eretz* has a broader sense and that the "yoke of Torah" was originally part of a "two yokes" worldview:[13] "Moses said before the Holy One blessed be He: 'You place two yokes upon your children, the yoke of Torah and the yoke of government.' He replied: 'Indeed, O favorite among peoples, all his holy ones were in your charge' (Deut 33:3)."[14] If the children of Israel accept the yoke of Torah, and are rewarded with the kingdom of heaven, then "all his holy ones are in your charge." But if they cast off the yoke of Torah, God burdens them with foreign dominion. It is this ideology, then, that gave rise to the phrase "yoke of government" that is used by Rabbi Nehunia ben ha-Kanah in

12. Matt 6:11. Luke (11:3) did not understand Jesus' stricture, and so cites the dictum as "give us each day our daily bread."

13. This question deserves a separate study.

14. This is the reading of the Sifre in *Magen Avot* by Rabbi Shimon bar Zemah Duran to Avot 3.5 (*editio princeps* [Livorno, 1762], 39a). The standard texts of the Sifre do not have this derashah, and the reading in Deuteronomy Rabbah, *Yalqut Shimoni,* and in *Tanhuma* includes additional elements.

his dictum — a dictum that exhibits a superficial similarity to the Greek view regarding the superiority of philosophy to the practical and the political.

It stands to reason that the interpretation of Exodus 16:4 underwent a similar transformation: in the past it referred to Israel as a whole, but already in the Jamnia period it came to be seen as a response to the challenges facing the sages, and more specifically to the debate between Rabbi Yehoshua and Rabbi Eliezer ben Hyrcanus.[15] Rabbi Eliezer says the interpretation of Torah was given only to those who eat of the Manna, that is, to someone who, in the midst of study, does not know where he will find food, drink, clothing, and shelter. Rabbi Yehoshua, on the other hand, states: "A man should study two *halakhot* in the morning and two *halakhot* in the evening and the whole day occupy himself with his trade."[16] It appears, though, that the earlier version of this dictum did not deal with the relationship between Torah study and livelihood, but with Jews detaching themselves from worldly cares. This earlier form is apparently how both Jesus and Philo knew it,[17] and it is not difficult to reconstruct: Instead of "the interpretation of Torah was given only to those who eat of the Manna," it was "the Torah was given only to those who eat of the Manna." Rabbi Shimon says: "So to Israel, who — on account of God's love for them — were given provisions daily, in order that they would propitiate and greet the divine presence every day."[18]

Scholars rightly cite Rabbi Shimon ben Elazar's famous saying — pre-

---

15. Rabbi Eliezer of Modiin merely transmits the dictum of Rabbi Eliezer ben Hyrcanus, as is evident from the parallels in b. Sotah 48b and Midrash ha-Gadol (pages 321-322 in the Margaliyot edition), and see also the Mekhilta of Rabbi Shimon bar Yohai (pages 106-107 in the Epstein-Melamed edition). The opposing views of Rabbi Eliezer and Rabbi Yehoshua are part of a broader dispute. "'*each day . . . for that day*': Rabbi Yehoshua says, [This teaches] that one should gather from one day for the next, and from one Sabbath eve to the next. Rabbi Eliezer says, [This teaches] that one should not gather from one day for the next" (following the Mekhilta of Rabbi Shimon bar Yohai, 106, and Midrash ha-Gadol, 321). Rabbi Eliezer interprets the biblical "*each day . . . for that day*" according to its plain meaning, while Rabbi Yehoshua incorporates the following verse into his interpretation: "On the sixth day, when they prepare what they bring in, it will be twice as much as they gather on other days" (Ex 16:5). This dispute explains the tannaitic passage preserved in b. Beitza 16a: "Throughout his life Shammai the Elder would eat in honor of Shabbat" in contrast to Hillel the Elder, who followed the verse "Blessed be the Lord who daily bears us up" (Ps 68:19). It is odd that Rabbi Eliezer, who generally followed the rulings of the school of Shammai, here sides with Hillel, while Rabbi Yehoshua, one of the disciples of Yohanan ben Zakkai, here rules with the Shammaites. See also the dictum attributed to Rabbi Eliezer in *The Fathers According to Rabbi Nathan* (version A, chapter 21, page 44 in the Schechter edition): "Israel were commanded to work, as it is written, 'Six days you shall labor and do all your work' (Ex 20:9)."

16. Mekhilta of Rabbi Ishmael, Vayissa 3, Lauterbach 2.103-104.

17. See above, n. 7.

18. Mekhilta of Rabbi Shimon bar Yohai to Exodus 16:4 (page 168 in the Nelson edition).

served in a number of sources in somewhat different forms[19] — as a parallel to Jesus' teachings.[20] The statement in question is: "Have you ever seen a lion (toiling as a) porter, a buck fruit-picker, a fox vendor, or a wolf cooper? How much the more so, if these were not formed in order to serve their creator but they find livelihood without toil, I, who was formed in order to serve my creator, is it not meet that my livelihood should be found without toil? Why then does my livelihood require that I toil? Say, therefore, that it is on account of my sins. Because my deeds are corrupt, I have lost my livelihood."[21]

Like Jesus' argument in Matthew 6, Rabbi Shimon ben Elazar presents a קל וחומר (de minori ad maius) comparison between the natural world and human concerns for livelihood. Unlike Jesus (and the derashah in the Mekhilta), however, Rabbi Shimon ben Elazar views working for one's livelihood in a positive light. Another relevant saying attributed to this sage is:[22] "Even Adam tasted nothing before he worked, as it is written, 'The Lord God took the man and put him in the Garden of Eden to till it and keep it. And the Lord God commanded the man, You may freely eat of every tree of the garden'

19. For a discussion see W. Bacher, *Die Agada der Tannaiten* (Strasburg, 1890), 426, n. 4. The sources in questions are: m. Qiddushin 4.14; t. Qiddushin 5.15; b. Qiddushin and p. Qiddushin, toward the end of the tractates. Y. N. Epstein notes that the dictum does not belong to the Mishnah itself, since the original mishnah tractate ended with the words "a man should not teach his son a craft that is practiced among women." Everything that follows is a late addition found in t. Qiddushin 5.14-17. See Epstein's *Introduction to the Text of the Mishnah* (Jerusalem, 1964), 977.

20. To my knowledge, the first to draw this comparison was Hugo Grotius in his commentary on the New Testament. On the dictum itself see E. E. Urbach, *The Sages*, trans. Israel Abrahams, 445-446.

21. In addition to the printed editions, I have consulted Mishnah MSS Parma and Kaufmann (MS Leiden is missing a large section), Tosefta MS Vienna, Babylonian Talmud MS Munich, and the Palestinian Talmud fragments published by Levi Ginzberg, ad loc. i. The survey of the sources leads me to the following conclusions: a. The standard reading of the Mishnah and of MS Erefurt of the Tosefta is abbreviated. Instead of the list of animals and their various crafts, we find, "Have you ever seen a beast or an animal (or: a beast or a bird) that practice a craft?" b. The reading of MS Vienna and the *editio princeps* of the Tosefta is an amalgam of the longer and the shorter versions. c. Within the witnesses to the standard reading, MS Parma and MS Kaufmann preface the passage with "He would say," referring not to Rabbi Shimon ben Eleazar, but to Rabbi Yehudah, who was cited previously. These manuscripts (along with MS Munich) state that the animals "were not formed in order to serve their creator," while the other witnesses read "were formed only to serve me" (that is, to serve man). The latter reading is better suited for the קל וחומר argument that follows, but it is difficult to determine which is the more original reading. It is, however, clear that "a wolf cooper" (זאב גודר גדרות) is to be preferred to a "wolf selling ceramic pots" (זאב מוכר קדרות) of the other witnesses.

22. Fathers According to Rabbi Nathan A, 11 (page 45 in the Schechter edition; page 60 in Judah Goldin, *The Fathers According to Rabbi Nathan*). The B version (chapter 21, page 45) attributes the same saying to Rabbi Eliezer.

(Gen 2:15-16)." In other words, Rabbi Shimon ben Elazar holds that work was always a condition for human livelihood, and not the result of the sin of the first human. Jesus holds that the difference between natural creatures and man is that the former do not labor for their livelihood but are cared for by God, and man errs in choosing to labor. Rabbi Shimon ben Elazar suggests that the animals were not created for the sake of serving God and are sustained without labor, while man who was created to serve God usually toils for livelihood. The reason for this discrepancy is sin: "Because my deeds are corrupt, I have lost my livelihood." Rabbi Shimon ben Elazar is not referring to the concern for livelihood as such, but rather the moral corruption that brings mankind into a state in which they need to labor and toil, unlike the animals. It may be that Rabbi Shimon ben Elazar believes that the category of sin is not applicable to the animal world, since only man and not animals possesses reason.

According to the Palestinian Talmud, Rabbi Shimon ben Elazar transmits this saying "in the name of Rabbi Meir," his master. It further appears he transmitted another interesting teaching of Rabbi Meir's, preserved in the Sifre Deuteronomy:[23]

> Rabbi Meir says: When Israel was meritorious, they gave witness against themselves. When they corrupted themselves, tribes of Judah and Benjamin witnessed against them. When the tribes of Judah and Benjamin too were corrupted, God called the prophets to witness against them. When they rebuffed the prophets, God called the heavens to witness against them. After they had corrupted the heavens, God called the earth to witness against them. After they had corrupted the earth, God called the highways to witness against them. After they corrupted the highways, God called the nations to witness against them. After they had been corrupted by the nations, God called the mountains to witness against them. After they corrupted the mountains, God called cattle to witness against them. After they corrupted the cattle, God called the birds to witness against them. After they had corrupted the cattle, the beasts, and the birds, God called the fishes to witness against them. After they had corrupted the fishes, God called the ant to witness against them, as it is said, "Go to the ant, O sluggard . . . which . . . provides her bread in the summer" (Prov 6:6-8). Rabbi Shimon ben Eleazar says: What a humiliation for this fellow to have to learn from the ant! Had he learned from her and acted accordingly, it would have been humiliating enough; but here he should have learned from her ways, but did not even learn!

23. Sifre Deuteronomy §306 (Hammer, 297-298). I have omitted the biblical prooftexts, save the last one that is adduced by Rabbi Shimon ben Elazar.

As with the saying under consideration, the Sifre Deuteronomy here discusses moral corruption. In response to Israel's moral deterioration, God calls forth a series of witnesses (but to no avail) and at the end of the witness list we find beasts, animals, birds, fish, and ants. However, the similarity lies not so much in the invocation of the animal world as in the spirit that animates the two passages. For our purposes the words of Rabbi Shimon ben Elazar are particularly significant. According to this sage, man on his own is so debased that he must learn from the ant. Worse still — he *fails* to learn from it. From this we can conclude that the very need to compare human beings, who were created in order to serve their maker, with inferior animals, who were created to serve man, is in and of itself a sorry state of affairs.[24]

Such comparisons were common among Greek thinkers of the day. In part, this was due to the Greek dedication to the study of the natural world, and the desire to reach conclusions regarding the highest animal, man. But when this field of study began to find an attentive audience among popular philosophers, especially the cynics and the stoics, it became clear that zoological motifs could be used to critique human society. Thus, the philosophers began to contrast the corrupt human world with the natural existence of animals. This motif was used by the Greek thinker Celsus, a contemporary of Rabbi Shimon ben Elazar; Celsus wrote an anti-Christian work (circa 180 c.e.), parts of which were preserved in the writings of Origen.[25] Celsus rejects the anthropocentrism of Jews and Christians alike. Though these groups contend that God created everything for the sake of man, Celsus adduces scholarship from the study of the animal world to the effect that the world was created more for their sake than for man's and, moreover, the animals are endowed with superior moral and social qualities. "We indeed by labor and suffering earn a scanty and toilsome subsistence, while all things are produced for them without their sowing and ploughing."[26] Celsus's argument is similar both to the statement attributed to Jesus that the ravens "neither sow nor reap nor gather into barns, and yet your heavenly Father feeds them" and to that of Rabbi Shimon ben Elazer about the animals who procure their livelihood without toil. Celsus goes on to argue that "if men appear to be superior to irrational animals on this account, that they have built cities, and make use of a

24. See also the statement of Rabbi Yohanan: "Were the Torah not given to us, we would have learned propriety from the cat, [laws governing] theft from the ant, and improper sexual relations from the dove" (b. Eruvin 100b). On this dictum and others like it, see Urbach, *The Sages*, 324.

25. The similarity between Celsus's discussion of the animal world and the dictum of Rabbi Shimon ben Elazar was noted by Urbach, *The Sages*, 884 n. 94.

26. *Contra Celsum* 4.76 (Schaff translation). The conclusion is a citation from *The Odyssey* 9.109, where it refers to the land of the Cyclops. See also Josephus, *JA* 1.54 on Cain and Abel.

political constitution, and forms of government, and sovereignties, this is to say nothing to the purpose, for ants and bees do the same. Bees, indeed, have a sovereign, who has followers and attendants; and there occur among them wars and victories, and slaughterings of the vanquished, and cities and suburbs, and a succession of labors, and judgments passed upon the idle and the wicked; for the drones are driven away and punished."[27] Though he does not cite Proverbs, Celsus like Rabbi Shimon ben Elazar praises the ants' preparation for the oncoming winter, and asserts that the ants are more frugal than humans, help one another with their loads when one tires;[28] and that storks are more deferent to their parents than humans, since they feed their parents as a sign of gratitude.[29] Again, Celsus cites all this material to counter the Jewish and Christian claim that the world was created for the sake of man.

The surprising similarity between Celsus's statement that "all things are produced for [animals] without their sowing and ploughing," and Jesus' assertion that ravens neither sow nor reap nor gather into barns, does not in and of itself indicate Greek influence on Jesus' homily. However, a different Greek text indicates that there was contact between Rabbi Shimon ben Elazar and Greek thought. I am referring to the nine epistles attributed to the famous Heraclitus.[30] The pre-Socratic philosopher lived circa 500 B.C.E., but the epistles were composed between the 1st century B.C.E. and 150 C.E. This, in any case, is the terminus ante quem of the papyrus that includes the seventh letter.[31] In this papyrus,[32] the letter continues beyond the point known from other witnesses, though the papyrus ends before the conclusion of the letter. It now appears that the standard text of the letters of pseudo-Heraclitus is missing at least half of the seventh epistle. It was this new development that brought me to reexamine the matter.

According to Bernays,[33] the nine epistles attributed to Heraclitus are not the work of a single author. In the fourth epistle, for example, he sees the insertions of a later Jewish or Christian author[34] who reworked the epistle

27. *Contra Celsum* 4.81.

28. *Contra Celsum* 4.83.

29. *Contra Celsum* 4.98.

30. Published by R. Hercher, in *Epistolographi Graeci* (1871), 275-288. And see the important study of these texts in Jacob Bernays, *Die Heraklitischen Briefe* (1869), which includes the Greek text, and a German translation and commentary.

31. This papyrus was published in *Museum Helveticum* 16 (1959), fasc. 2, pages 77-139. Preceding the pseudo-Heraclitus letter there is an interesting account of a conversation that took place between Alexander the Great and a Jewish sage named Dandamis.

32. Siglum: Pap. Genev. Inv. 271.

33. Bernays, *Briefe*, 110-112.

34. Bernays, *Briefe*, 26-35.

and, according to Bernays, composed the seventh epistle.[35] It appears Bernays is correct regarding the late additions to the fourth epistle, but his arguments regarding the other epistles remain controversial: the fact that a text is critical of pagan society or couches its criticism in terms of a more elevated religious sensibility, does not mean its author was Jewish or Christian. One of Bernays' main arguments for Jewish or Christian authorship of the seventh epistle is its statement against "eating living things" — which Bernays interprets as an allusion to the Noachide Laws, and hypothesizes that a more fully developed critique existed in the second half of the epistle. However, these words are altogether absent in the papyrus.[36] Be all that as it may, for our purposes it does not matter if the pseudo-Heraclitus epistles were reworked by Jewish or Christian authors, since they constitute a typical and fascinating example of the trend toward the popularization of Greek philosophy, especially Stoic and Cynic.

The epistles contain sharp social criticism, sometimes bordering on satire, that includes comparisons of corrupt human society and the animal world.[37] In the ninth epistle the author attacks the institution of slavery: "What do you think, you men? If God did not make dogs or sheep slaves, nor asses nor horses nor mules, did he then make men slaves? . . . How much superior are the wolves and lions to the Ephesians? They do not reduce one another to slavery, nor does one eagle buy another eagle, nor does one lion pour wine for another lion, nor does one dog castrate another dog."[38] The author adopts a pacifist view toward war and, in typical fashion, argues for the superiority of animals over humans in this regard: "Lions do not arm themselves against each other, nor do mares take up swords, nor could you see an eagle armed with a breastplate against another eagle."[39] Animals use their limbs as weapons, and a sword does not elicit enthusiasm from these mindless beasts, for they abide by the laws of nature whereas man does not. In the newly discov-

35. Bernays, *Briefe*, 72-79. Bernays argues (p. 109) that the ninth epistle was also composed by a Jew or a Christian, but not the same individual as the author of the seventh. I. Heinemann (*PW Supplementband* 5 [1931], 228-232) denies there is any Jewish or Christian influence in the epistles, arguing they are rather an internal, Hellenistic critique against paganism.

36. The missing phrase (τὰ ζῶντα κατεσθίετε τοὺς νόμους παραβαίνετε προνομίας νομοθετεῖτε) is the longest sentence that is found in the standard version but absent in the papyrus. If the scribe did not accidentally skip over these words, their absence in the papyrus would be evidence for Bernays' argument. However, if this is a Jewish or Christian interpolation, there is no reason to accept Bernays' assertion regarding the author of the epistle.

37. See the discussion in *Museum Helveticum*, 138-139.

38. The Epistles of Heraclitus, Epistle 9.4, in Abraham J. Malherbe, *The Cynic Epistles* (Atlanta, GA, 1977), 213.

39. Epistle 7.7 (Malherbe, 205).

ered section of epistle 7 we find a similar argument:[40] "Lions do not murder lions, wolves do not poison wolves, horses do not plot against horses, and elephants do not attack a city's fortifications in order to destroy them."[41] Human beings, on the other hand, commit terrible crimes against one another, something not found in the animal world: "Elephants are not greedy, nor do lions horde money, bulls do not prepare cakes and honeyed treats, nor do oxen dress in Miletian fabrics or have a national uniform. [Animals] do not come to the aid of other animals[42] nor do they make one another servants, as men do."[43]

Were we to juxtapose Rabbi Shimon ben Elazar's statement concerning the animal world to those of pseudo-Heraclitus, they would fit quite nicely together, as they are quite similar both in content and in form. Each of the five passages — Rabbi Shimon's and four from pseudo-Heraclitus — lists acts that animals do not perform but humans do, and in each case it is to the credit of the animals. The similarity is most evident in the seventh epistle, where we find: "Elephants are not greedy, nor do lions horde money, bulls do not prepare cakes and honeyed treats, nor do oxen dress in Miletian fabrics or have a national uniform,"[44] whereas Rabbi Shimon ben Elazar asks: "Have you ever seen a lion (toiling as a) porter, a buck fruit-picker, a fox vendor, or a wolf cooper?"[45] The papyrus was written circa 150 C.E., that is, some time before Rabbi Shimon ben Elazar, and, as we have seen, is an instance of popular philosophic literature, which regularly compared humans and animals. There is no reason to assume that Rabbi Shimon ben Elazar was familiar with this literature, though he may have heard homilies of this sort. The examples are, after all, colorful and often amusing, so the parables would have made an impression on their audience or readers. We may assume, then, that Rabbi Shimon ben Elazar recalled some such parable and fashioned the opening of his famous homily accordingly.

The assertion that man toils for livelihood while animals do not may also have its origins in Greek wisdom, though it could also have been drawn from Jewish sources, namely, from the traditions that the Torah was given only to the eaters of the Manna and that anyone who is concerned with the

40. In column 12, lines 36-50 of the papyrus there is another comparison between mankind and the animal world, but the text is corrupt and its meaning difficult to reconstruct.

41. Epistle 7.13 (this new section does not appear in the Malherbe edition).

42. This reading is uncertain.

43. Epistle 7.13.

44. Epistle 7.13.

45. This phrase is reminiscent of pseudo-Heraclitus's statement "nor could you see an eagle armed with a breastplate against another eagle" (epistle 7.7). The papyrus altered the language of the epistle.

food and clothing of the morrow is of little faith. As we saw, Jesus too espoused this view, comparing those of little faith with the ravens who neither sow nor reap nor gather into barns, and with the lilies that neither toil nor spin, but whose glory is greater than King Solomon's. To repeat, there is no need to assume Greek influence on Jesus' homily, as its parallels to Greek sayings are less evident than Rabbi Shimon ben Elazar's. In this sense, Jesus' use of the animal motifs suggests an internal Jewish evolution that paved the way for the sages' receptivity to the Greek material. It is, then, hard to argue that the Greek texts substantively altered the Jewish thinking of the day. I believe that Greek wisdom influenced the Jewish thought primarily in forcing the Jewish sages to confront the questions and challenges facing them, though they may also have drawn on Greek solutions to those questions.

As for Rabbi Shimon ben Elazar, his saying is the product of an authentic Jewish *Weltanschauung*. True, he appears to be heir to the view that one should not be concerned with what he will eat or wear, but this is not the conceptual core of his saying. As he states, "Even Adam tasted nothing before he worked." In other words, though he is anchored in a Jewish intellectual tradition, into which he has introduced a whiff of Greek, his ultimate goal is to explain why man must toil for livelihood and animals do not. His answer is deeply Jewish and involves a recognition of sinfulness: "Why then does my livelihood require that I toil? Say, therefore, that it is on account of my sins. Because my deeds are corrupt, I have lost my livelihood."[46]

46. In conclusion, a general comment. We have discussed the comparisons between animals and humans, which also find expression in animal fables such as those of Aesop. These fables were very influential among the sages, and Rabbi Meir, Rabbi Shimon ben Elazar's teacher, seems to have been particularly taken with them. Nonetheless I have argued that Rabbi Shimon ben Elazar's dictum was not influenced by Greek fables, but by Greek popular philosophy, which drew on the findings of Greek zoologists. Even in its most populist forms, comparisons between the human and the animal world had a theoretical basis. Later, in Jewish, Christian, and Muslim writing, these fables became vacuous clichés, at least until the advent of modern zoology. Even into the twentieth century there were those who, following Descartes, explained the responses of animals in mechanical terms. This changed as the result of scientific advancements, and today there are those who again use the animal world to examine human society. Konrad Lorenz, for example, has revived interest in a topic that much occupied Hellenistic thinkers, namely, war between animals (particularly in his *On Aggression*). This modern scholar cannot, of course, argue that animals do not attack their own species — a claim repeated among Hellenistic thinkers — but does conclude that in many cases the attack is turned into a ritual interaction, and he recommends this behavior to human beings. Clearly this approach is not drawn directly from animal behavior, but from the emphasis on ritual in the modern social sciences. Be all that as it may, Lorenz's book is an example of how contemporary scholars of animal behavior can reach surprising conclusions regarding humanity.

24. An Ancient Hebrew List of Second Temple High Priests

The list of high priests in question is extant in two versions: one is part of *Sha'arei Zion* by Rabbi Isaac Lattes,[1] a chronicle that ends at 1372 and, as scholars have noted, is almost wholly copied from *Seder ha-Kabbalah* by Menahem ha-Meiri. The second version is embedded in *Seder 'Olam*, which was published by Neubauer.[2] This is part of a larger composition usually referred to as the *Yerahmiel*,[3] which was collected by Rabbi Elazar ben Asher ha-Levi circa 1325, based largely on the works of Yerahmiel ben Shelomo, a poet and scholar apparently of Italian provenance, who lived after 953 but before 1234. *Seder 'Olam* was copied by Yerahmiel himself, since he mentions his own name explicitly.[4] *Seder 'Olam* is also extant in another manuscript (MS

---

1. This book (which is also known as *Toledot Yitzhak*) was published by S. Buber (Yaroslav, 1885), who worked with MS Oxford. The same manuscript is the basis for a recent edition by S. Z. Havelin, *Seder ha-Kabbalah le-Rabbenu Menahem ha-Meiri* (Jerusalem and Cleveland, 1992), 147-180. This work contains a list of the high priests who held office up to the Babylonian exile (159-160), and another list of the high priests who served after the return of the exiles (165).

2. A. Neubauer, *Mediaeval Jewish Chronicles* (Oxford, 1887 [repr. Jerusalem, 1967]), 1.163-175. This work also includes a short list of priests from the first temple (165), which may correspond to the list in *Sha'arei Tzion* (159-160).

3. For a discussion of the *Yerahmiel* see my "Virgil the Wizard in an Ancient Jewish Narrative," pp. 297-304 in the present volume. The list of high priests appears at 221b-222a in the Bodleian MS 2797, Heb. 11.

4. "And I, Yerahmiel, found in *Josippon* that Samuel composed the Book of Judges," *Chronicles*, 174. This confirms the hypothesis I proposed in Flusser, *Josippon*, 2.8, n. 18. See also my comment at 68, n. 198.

Paris, Hebr. 326), which dates from the second half of the twelfth century, but it does not contain the list of Second Temple priests.[5] Most likely, Yerahmiel copied it from another, unknown source. We see, then, that the list was not part of *Seder 'Olam,* and that Rabbi Isaac Lattes also added it to his source, namely, to *Seder ha-Kabbalah.* The list is, then, no later than the composition of the *Yerahmiel,* that is, the eleventh or twelfth century.

The opening of the two lists (which date back to the Hasmonean dynasty) is of no historical interest; moreover, the profound differences between the two versions make it impossible to reconstruct a common source.[6] As we will see, there is only a very slight chance that the transmission of these lists preserves historically valuable information, and it is likely that the later additions are of no value. This is clearly the case with Isaac Lattes' opening, and it remains unclear whether it is the middle links in the transmission process that are responsible for the obvious corruptions, or perhaps the last copyist. We do not know anything about the high priest Yativ of the Galilee or of the priest named Yissachar of the village Barka. The latter appears to have been inserted in the middle of the name "Yannai" and "Alisandron" (= Alexander).

---

5. On this manuscript, see D. Chavelsohn, "Sarid u-Falit," in *Qovetz 'al-Yad* 7 (1857), 3-5. See also the comments of Neubauer, *Chronicles,* 197-198.

6. The beginning of the list according to Lattes is (Havelin, 165): "These are the high priests who served in the Second Temple upon the return from Babylonia. First was Ezra, followed by Yehoshua ben Yehozedek, Yehoiakim, Elishuv, Yedua, Hanania; then Menasheh, his brother, assumed the priesthood, then Hunah the priest and his son, Shimon, his brother Yeshua, and Hanania, his son, followed by Shimon the priest and Yetuv the Galilean. Of the Hasmoneans, Matithia of the House of Hashmonai, followed by Jonathan his son, Shimon — second, Judah — third, Eliezer — fourth, Yonatan — fifth. After him served Yehudah ben Shimon, Hyrkanos, Yannai, Yissachar of the village Barka, Alisandron, Hyrkanos, Antigonos and Aritolos [this should read: Aristobulus], and Hyrkanos, his brother." Here is the opening of the list in the *Yerahmiel* (Neubauer, 166): "These are the high priests who served in the Second Temple. Yehoshua ben Yehozadeq served in the temple, and Yehoshua begat Yehoiakim and Yehoiakim begat Eliashiv, and this Eliashiv was the high priest during the days of Ezra and Nehemia, and Eliashiv begat Yehoiada, and Yehoiada begat Jonathan who was the high priest in Jerusalem during the reign of Alexander the Great of Macedonia. And Jonathan begat Yedua, and Yedua was high priest during all the days of Alexander of Macedonia, and Ezra counted up to Yedua in his book. And Menasheh, Yedua's brother, was high priest in the temple at Gerizim. And Yedua began Honio, and Honio [begat] Shimon the Righteous, and Shimon [begat] Honio who lived in the days of Antiochus. And after him came Yohanan, and Yohanan begat Matithia who had three sons — Yehudah and Yonatan and Shimon. And Yehudah the Maccabee came to be the high priest and anointed for war, and he was followed by his brother Yonatan, and he by his brother Shimon, and then came Yohanan, his son, and Yohanan begat Aristobulus and Alexander, who is also known as Yannai. The latter had two sons, Hyrkanos and Aristobulus, who disputed over the priesthood, until Hyrkanos took it for himself, and then came Antiochus [this should read: Antigonos]."

We must bear in mind that both Rabbi Isaac Lattes[7] and the author of *Seder 'Olam* (preserved in the *Yerahmiel*) knew *Sefer Josippon*,[8] and that Yerahmiel's priestly list agrees with that of Josippon with regard to the orthography of the names. Yerahmiel also characterizes Judah Maccabee as having been anointed for war, an idea he borrowed from *Josippon*,[9] or perhaps from the ancient translation of 1 Maccabees.[10] As a result, the opening parts of the Lattes and Yerahmiel lists are more dissimilar still.

Our primary focus involves the historical value of the two lists of Second Temple priests. What follows is the remainder of the lists, along with the ordinal number of the priests in question in as much as can be determined by two important studies.[11] It is probably no coincidence that the lists converge with Herodian priesthood.

Yerahmiel	Lattes
Ben Yohanan	Ben Yohanan
Ben Hananel	Ben Hananel
Ben Matitah	Ben Matitia
Eliashiv	Eliashiv
Yehosef (14, 20)	Yehosef
Hananiah	Aniniah
Yoezer (7)	Yoezer
Yishmael (11, 22)	Yosef, his son
Yehezkel	Yehezkel
Hanan (10, 24)	Anan
	(Yehoshua ben Gamla)
	(Toblos ben Hyrcanus)
	(Hananel ben Yohanan)
	Eliyoeni
	Shimon the Great
	Yosef his son

7. See Havelin, p. 164.

8. In addition to my comments above, n. 4, see Neubauer's discussion of Cyrus and his son (*Chronicle*, 166). It has been established that Yerahmiel copied *Sefer Josippon* in its entirety.

9. See Flusser, *Sefer Josippon,* chapter 16, §§61-63 (1.79-80), and the comments of Neubauer, *Chronicle*, 166, 168.

10. See Chavelsohn, "Sarid u-Falit," 8. This ancient translation was published by E. S. Hartum in his Hebrew edition of the Apocrypha (Tel Aviv, 1959), 79-88. The anointing of Judah Maccabee is mentioned on page 82.

11. E. Schürer, *The History of the Jewish People*, ed. G. Vermes, F. Millar, and M. Black (Edinburgh, 1979), 2.229-232; J. Jeremias, *Jerusalem in the Time of Jesus* (Philadelphia, 1989), 377-378.

Yerahmiel	Lattes
	Hananiah
	Yeshua
	Yishmael
	Sharia
Elazar (8, 12)	The Eight Sons of Kimhit[12]
Yonatan (15)	Yonatan
Theophilos (16)	Heophilos (should read: Theophilos)
	Hanamel
Matitiah (5, 18)	Matitia ben Pinhas
Pinhas (28)	
Ishmael (11, 22)	Ishmael
Ben Yonatan	Hanamel the Egyptian[13]
Elioeyni (19)	Ishmael
Yosef (20)	Shimon
Shimon the Great (4)	Yohanan
Yosef ben Hananiah (14?)	Yehezkel
Yeshua (3, 9, 26, 26)	Fabi
	Ishmael, his son
	Tabai
	Yehudah, his son
	Anani
	Eliezer, his son
	Fani son of Penuel, of Sadeh[14]

These are the eighty high priests who served in the Second Temple.

There is an evident connection between the two lists — even the rare form "Yehosef" appears in both. The list of names at the beginning is identical, and it is not until the eighth priest that the two diverge ("Yosef, his son" in Lattes, "Ishmael" in Yerahmiel). Also, names 12-16 in the Yerahmiel group appear in Lattes at 22-27 (with the addition of Hanamel), while Yerahmiel 18-22 corresponds to Lattes 14-18, but in reversed order. I do not think it is possible to establish which of these sources preserves the original order of these groups, since their shared source corrupted the chronological order

12. See p. Megillah 1, 12, 72b: "Kimhit had seven sons and all served as priests." See also Schürer, *History*, 2.230, n. 11. The word "eight" appears to be an error.

13. Mentioned in m. Parah 3.5. See Schürer, *History*, 2.229, n. 5.

14. In *Josippon* chapter 69, §15 (1.124 in the Flusser edition) the Lattes list continues as follows: "Elisha, Ishmael his son who was killed by the wicked Titus. These are the eighty high priests who served in the Second Temple."

and fabricated names of high priests that never existed. It generally appears the Yerahmiel list is the more accurate since it is of a generally higher quality than that of Lattes, but while one might be tempted to propose that Yerahmiel's list was the source of Lattes, it is unlikely that Yerahmiel's text reached Lattes. The more likely hypothesis is that the two derive from a common source.

A clue as to the identity of this common source is the shared assumption of the two lists that there were eighty high priests during the Second Temple period, a view attested elsewhere in classical Jewish sources.[15] It appears, then, that at some point a scribe composed a list of eighty priests. In order to reach such a large number he must have drawn on other sources, one of which was clearly an important historical work, a Hebrew work most likely, as the form of the names indicates they were not translated from a foreign language. This fanciful list, replete with obviously fabricated names, survives in the works of Rabbi Isaac Lattes and the *Yerahmiel*. In the course of transmission, the chronological order was disrupted, and, moreover, there is no way to identify common names such as Ishmael, Yosef, Hanan, and Yeshua — another difficulty in retrieving the historical kernel of the source. Still, we do have six positive identifications of high priests from the late Second Temple period: Pinhas was the last high priest to serve in the temple (67-70 C.E.);[16] Yoezer's unusual name helps identify him as the high priest who served in the year 4 B.C.E.; and Eliyoeni served in 44 C.E.[17] Eliyoeni may have been the son of Joseph Caiaphas who is mentioned in the New Testament,[18] and who may be the individual referred to as Yehosef in a recently discovered ossuary. It is also possible that the *Yerahmiel* lists this priest (now spelled Yosef) before Eliyoeni. According to the Gospel of John 18:13, Caiaphas was the son-in-law of the high priest Hanan (= Annas). Of his five sons who served as high priests, four appear in our list, in the correct order of their service: Hanan, followed by Elazar (16-17 C.E.), Yonatan (36-37 C.E.) and Theophilos (beginning at 37 C.E.) and Matitiah (before 42 C.E.).

We have analyzed the list of Second Temple high priests as preserved in two mediaeval sources, primarily to investigate the historical value of some of the names it includes. However, the list can also contribute to the study of the historical consciousness of medieval Jewry. It appears that at that time there emerged among the Jews — as among the nations of Europe — a strong intel-

15. See Sifre Numbers §131 (page 173 in the Horovitz-Rabin edition) and the sources cited there, to which add Midrash ha-Gadol to Numbers 25:13 (page 353 in the Rabinowitz edition).

16. See Schürer, *History*, 2.232, n. 22.

17. See Schürer, *History*, 2.231, n. 14.

18. See D. Flusser, "Caiaphas in the New Testament," *Atiqot* 21 (1992), 50.

lectual desire to study their ancient history. The paths by which information concerning these times reached them were many and varied, and the examination of these paths may enrich our understanding of both Jewish history and its reception.

25. Who Is the Ruler of Gennesar?

For the blessed memory of Ara Tchividjian
"who loved our people" (Luke 7:5)

The form Gennosar, which is common in today's Hebrew, is secondary, and the correct form is without question Gennesar (or Gannesar),[1] an error found even in sources whose content suggests they ought contain the original form. Thus we find in Genesis Rabbah: "And why is it called Gennosar? Our rabbis said *ganei sarim* (gardens of rulers)." But in the critical apparatus we find both Gannesar and Gennesar.[2] This is an interesting derashah inasmuch as it indicates its authors knew the meaning of the name Gennesar — there were gardens of rulers there.

As for the Greek form, both the New Testament and the translations of the Hebrew Bible tend toward the form Γεννησαρέτ, though here too the correct form is Γεννησάρ.[3] In addition to the other ancient sources, the correct form appears in the important New Testament manuscript MS D (Codex Bezae) at Matthew 14:34 and Mark 6:53, while Luke 5:1 contains the more common, secondary reading. If so, both the Hebrew and the Greek form are Genne-sar, which already Genesis Rabbah understood as: *ganei sarim*, gardens of rulers. The question, then, is who were the rulers who owned these gardens?

It is unlikely that the ruler referred to in the name Gennesar predated the Hasmonean period since, inter alia, there is no evidence for the title *sar* at

1. See Y. Tsafrir, L. Di Segni and J. Green (eds.), *Tabula Imperii Romani: Iudaea, Palaestina* (Jerusalem, 1994), 132; W. Kappler (ed.), *Maccabaeorum Liber I* (Göttingen, 1936).

2. See Genesis Rabbah 98.17 (page 1267 in the Theodor-Albeck edition).

3. See W. F. Arndt (ed.), *A Greek-English Lexicon of the New Testament* (Chicago, 1979), 156.

that time, but when it appears in Hasmonean literature, e.g. 1 Maccabees (see below), its meaning is assumed to be self-evident to its hearers. 1 Maccabees 14.27-49 contains a "Declaration of Independence" of sorts, composed in September of 140 B.C.E. for the sake of Simon the son of Mattathias. It opens with a reference to "Simon, high priest and *sar* . . . ," and later "the Jews and their priests have resolved that Simon should be their *sar* (ἡγούμενον) and high priest for ever, until a trustworthy prophet should arise" (1 Macc 14.41). The Greek word translated here as *sar* also appears in verse 42 of the Codex Sinaiticus.

There are other witnesses to *sar* as an epithet for Hasmonean rulers. Thus the Hebrew name for 1 Maccabees ספר בית שר בני־אל, "The Book of the House of the *sar* (Leader or Commander) of God's Children," i.e., a book chronicling the Hasmonean history up to the days of John Hyrcanus. It appears this Hebrew name was known into the fourth century C.E., though the phrase "leader of God's children" (שר בני אל) was interpreted as "those who reject God" (סרבני אל).[4] After the discovery of the War Scroll, the phrases "leader *(sar)* of the nation of God" and "house of the leader of the nation of God" are no longer unfamiliar. Still, the Hebrew name of 1 Maccabees is secondary, as the end of the book does not contain a single reference to God or to any of God's titles. In this 1 Maccabees is like the scroll of Esther.

Our discussion suggests that *sar* served as an epithet for the Hasmonean rulers before they became monarchs, that is, up to the time of Aristobulus. The leader of Gennesar, then, was either Simon or Yohanan, his son, and the name indicates that the site contained gardens belonging to one or both of these figures.[5]

---

4. See Schürer, *History*, 3.182-183. For the Hebrew סרבני אל see p. Ta'anit 4.8.68d, where it is used as a pejorative and related to the name Yehoyariv (opponent [*yariv*] of the Lord), the high priest who served at the destruction of the First Temple. See also *Seder 'Olam* §30 (page 147-148 in the Ratner edition).

5. See also M. Aviad, "The Hasmoneans in the Galilee" in *The Hasmonean History* (Hebrew) (Jerusalem, 1996), 251-260.

26. Anti-Jewish Sentiment
in the Gospel of Matthew

Already in antiquity there developed the view that the Gospel of Matthew was composed for a Jewish audience. I too accepted this view for many years. However, it has now become clear to me that the last editor of the Gospel of Matthew was a sly and highly skilled forger with an anti-Jewish bias.[1] I believe the forger was active after the gospel had been completed and was already in its Greek version, i.e., that he was the final editor.[2] We do not know if the forger in question spoke Hebrew or Aramaic, but he was probably Jewish. This much is clear: the Matthean forgeries are one of the most vitriolic sources of Christian Anti-Semitism. One of the goals of the present study is to demonstrate that the self-accusation of the Jews at Jesus' trial (Matt 27:24-25) was understood by this editor as a factual statement and in no way spurious.

The voice of the falsifying editor is particularly clear in the end of Jesus' speech against the Pharisees in Matthew 23:32-36, which has a parallel in Luke 11:49-51. As I have shown elsewhere,[3] the final editor introduced radical changes into the original version, which was closer to the reading preserved in Luke. At the time I did not notice another important change that is likely the result of the falsifying editor's intervention. I am referring to the mention of

1. I have devoted two articles to this topic: D. Flusser, "Two Anti-Jewish Montages in Matthew," in *Judaism and the Origins of Christianity* (Jerusalem, 1988), 552-560; and "Verus Israel," in the same collection, 561-574.

2. It is theoretically possible that the forgery occurred in the formative stages of the gospel, but my experience counsels against this explanation.

3. I have offered a detailed comparison of the two sources in "Anti-Jewish Montages," 552-554.

Zechariah the son of Barachiah who was killed by the zealots at the end of the Second Temple period, rather than Zechariah who died at the end of the First Temple period, as appears to be the case in Luke. Scholars have erroneously attributed this change to scribal error.[4] This, however, appears not to be the case. Rather we have here another change introduced by the last editor of the gospel, one aimed at casting guilt on the generation of the falsifier himself. If my proposal is correct, this is a very clever change indeed.

The final editor lived after the destruction of the Second Temple, as we can see from Matthew 22:7, a verse written by the falsifier. There is no similar statement in Luke or Mark, where Jesus' prophecy concerning the destruction of the temple is patterned after the destruction prophecies of the First Temple. Thus, as one scholar has argued, these may be authentic prophecies pronounced while the temple still stood.[5] There is no way to determine whether the Gospel of Matthew as a whole was composed post-70, but it is clear the falsifier lived after the destruction since the verse in question is clearly an interpolation. This is clear, inter alia, from the fact that in Matthew's parable of the great feast the master of the household is replaced with a king. It is often difficult to distinguish the work of the original editor from that of the late falsifier.

We can, however, assume that Mark is an important source for Matthew. True, Matthew contains some material that is earlier and more accurate than Mark, but usually not in places that have Markan parallels. The unfalsified material in Matthew is generally credible. As for Luke, we have already noted that there is no evidence that it was composed post-70. Luke's *Tendenz*, which is evident in Acts, which he authored, is to argue that the transition from Judaism to Christianity proceeded smoothly.[6] Luke, who was a friend of Paul's, had no way of knowing that Paul's epistles — and their very different position — would be preserved.

It is not clear to me that the widely-held assumption that Luke did not know Matthew is correct. It stands to reason that if there is agreement between Luke and Matthew in certain (even minor) details — at least where the tradition in question is attested in all three synoptic gospels — then we may assume that these details are original and belong to the pre-redactional stratum. The work of Lindsey and others has cast doubt on the existence of Q. I personally believe that there was such a source, and that it was Greek, but, in

4. See J. D. Dubois, "La mort de Zacharie: memoire juive et memoire chrétienne," *Revue des Études Augustiniennes* 40 (1994), 23-28; H. J. Schoeps, "Die Jüdischen Prophetenmorde," in *Aus frühchristlicher Zeit* (Tübingen, 1950), 126-144.

5. See C. H. Dodd, "The Fall of Jerusalem and the Abomination of Desolation," *Journal of Roman Studies* 37 (1947), 47-54.

6. This is particularly clear in Acts 28:28.

the wake of Lindsey and his colleagues, it is hard to isolate the sections that stem from it.

Matthew 23:34-36 demonstrates the difference in *Tendenz* between Matthew and Luke, and that the latter (11:49-51) is closer to the original. Matthew 23:34 is simply imaginary. It is interesting that Matthew adds the scribes and the sages. But the more important statement is this perverse statement: "I send you prophets, sages, and scribes, some of whom you will kill and crucify, and some you will flog in your synagogues and pursue from town to town." It is as though the last editor was blinded by hatred. Another deliberate change relative to Luke involves the shift to a second person plural accusation "you will kill," and in verse 35 the statement "so that upon you will come all the righteous blood shed on earth." These changes, along with the mention of Zechariah son of Barachiah from the late Second Temple period, are indicative of the goals of the falsifying editor: "Truly I tell you, all this will come upon this generation" (Matt 23:36) echoes the self-accusation the editor places in the mouth of "the people as a whole" who say "His blood will be on us and on our children!"

The above arguments indicate: (i) The replacement of the First Temple Zechariah with the Zechariah who lived after Jesus' death is intentional. Most likely the falsifier lived close to the time of the destruction; (ii) The self-execration of Jews in Matthew serves as an affirmation of an existing condition that holds in the time of the final editor. It is not, contrary to the common interpretation, aimed at the future, and the editor did not mean to imply that God is obligated to act in accordance with the curse.

In summary, Christian Anti-Semitism passed through two main conduits: the Pauline conception of grace in opposition to acts and all that entails. And the vulgar Anti-Semitism of the final, falsifying editor of Matthew, who lived after the destruction of the Second Temple.

Index of Names

Index of Subjects

Index of Sources

8.9	181

Hagigah
| 2.7 | 9, 101 |

Ketubot
| 7.6 | 16 |

Nedarim
| 3.4 | 80 |

Qiddushin
| 4.14 | 336 |

Sanhedrin
4.5	159
6.2	100, 104
6.3	103
6.5	103, 159

Avot
1.2	21
1.12	181
1.13	211
2.1	232-47
2.2	238
2.5	212
2.9	239-40
3.5	85, 238, 334
3.17	238
4.2	241
4.13	274
6.1	181
6.2	86
6.3	175
6.6	181
6.11	89

Tamid
| 5.1 | 167 |

Middot
| 1.6 | 145 |

Parah
| 3.5 | 346 |

TOSEFTA

Berakhot
2.21	212
3.5	27
3.25	51-52, 54
4.17	290
6.13	194

Pe'ah
| 4.18-19 | 18 |

Demai
| 2.2 | 9 |

Yoma
| 1.12 | 8 |
| 4.9 | 100 |

Yebamot
| 9.4 | 160 |

Ketubot
| 105a | 241 |

Sotah
| 7.11 | 199 |
| 14 | 83 |

Qiddushin
| 5.14-17 | 336 |
| 5.15 | 336 |

Baba Kama
| 7.5-6 | 82 |
| 9.29-30 | 160 |

Sanhedrin
7.4	160
9.5	100, 104
9.7	103, 159
13.5	27, 52

Ohalot
| 18.18 | 287 |

MIDRASHIM

Avot According to Rabbi Nathan

A
2	86, 197
11	336
16	52, 180
20	83
21	335
26	211
34	281
41	274

B
21	336
26	178, 180
32	86
47	274
48	274

Genesis Rabba
32	157
48.9	41
48.18	196
65.22	101
98.17	349
99.2	140-41

Genesis Rabbati
| 49.27 | 140 |

Exodus Rabba
| 19.5 | 195 |

Leviticus Rabba 103
1.5	213
7	237
12.2	291
20.9	290
26	102
26.7-9	101
34.3	214
35	237